Humanism and Scholasticism
in Late Medieval Germany

JAMES H. OVERFIELD

Humanism and Scholasticism
in Late Medieval Germany

PRINCETON UNIVERSITY PRESS
PRINCETON, NEW JERSEY

Copyright © 1984 by Princeton University Press
Published by Princeton University Press, Princeton, New Jersey 08540
In the United Kingdom: Princeton University Press, Guildford, Surrey

All Rights Reserved

Library of Congress Cataloging in Publication Data will be
found on the last printed page of this book
ISBN 0-691-07292-2

Publication of this book has been aided by a grant from the
Henry A. Laughlin Fund of Princeton University Press

This book has been composed in Linotron Bembo
Clothbound editions of Princeton University Press books
are printed on acid-free paper, and binding materials are
chosen for strength and durability
Printed in the United States of America by Princeton
University Press, Princeton, New Jersey

To my parents ~

CONTENTS

vii

Contents ~

INTRODUCTION

IN THE LECTURE ROOMS that lined the narrow, crowded streets of the "Latin quarter" of Paris, there evolved during the late twelfth and early thirteenth centuries an approach to learning that would dominate the intellectual world of northern Europe for the next three hundred years. This new method of thought, known to historians as scholasticism, held out the intoxicating possibility that, through reason and the powerful tool of Aristotelian logic, men could resolve the seeming contradictions between faith and reason, Christian truth and Greek science, and attain insights into the nature of the world, of man, and of God. In these same years, as the teaching masters of Paris gained a corporate identity as the University of Paris, they formally adopted this new intellectual program as the basis of learning and instruction. Subsequently, these Parisian methods became the model for dozens of universities founded in England, Spain, the Low Countries, and the Holy Roman Empire. As a result, scholasticism—with its veneration of Aristotle, cultivation of logic, and enthusiasm for disputation and debate—became synonymous with northern European academic life for the remainder of the medieval era.

Some two hundred years after the emergence of scholasticism, another intellectual movement, known as Renaissance humanism, began to evolve in the rich and populous cities of northern Italy. Unlike the scholastics, the disciples of this new cultural movement had scant interest in Aristotelian thought, theological speculation, and sophisticated logical concepts. Spurred by a new appreciation of the classics, these Italian thinkers—in particular Petrarch (1304-1374)—warmed to the

Ciceronian ideal of the *studia humanitatis,* an approach to learning that stressed literary and moral rather than philosophical training. Rhetoric and oratory, with the related disciplines of Latin grammar, poetry, history, and moral philosophy, provided the foundation of humanist thought and culture. For the humanists, not logical acuity or the attainment of philosophical and theological truth, but eloquence and an ability to appreciate the literary heritage of antiquity became the hallmarks of true education and culture.

These two intellectual currents, one the creation of the Middle Ages and the other of the Renaissance, began to exist side-by-side in Germany for the first time during the middle decades of the fifteenth century. By then scholasticism had played a role in Germany's intellectual life for better than two centuries. Since the 1200s, small numbers of Germans had pursued scholastic studies in foreign universities or their own cathedral and monastic schools. When the first German universities were established in the late fourteenth and fifteenth centuries, scholasticism, with its stress on dialectic, metaphysics, and speculative thought, dominated their curricula. By the 1450s, however, it was facing a challenge, albeit a weak one at first, from a handful of individuals who viewed the humanist educational program as a superior alternative to existing scholastic practices. During the next seven decades, humanism in Germany steadily gained adherents, until by the 1520s and 1530s, humanist reformers were able to achieve fundamental changes in the goals and methods of university studies. These changes broke the dominance of scholasticism and marked a watershed in Germany's intellectual history.

How did these changes come about? What was the nature of the relationship between humanism and scholasticism? To what extent can the intellectual history of pre-Reformation Germany be understood in terms of a "clash" between humanists and scholastics? Despite more than a century of monographs and interpretive studies, these and other related questions have never been adequately treated. In fact a survey of the literature leaves the reader with little more than a jumble of confused and contradictory hypotheses.

The notion that humanists and scholastics were implacable enemies locked in an unceasing struggle can be traced back to the writings of the humanists themselves. Their works were filled with doleful plaints about unlettered scholastics who mocked, scorned, or ignored their efforts and whose stubborn resistance was overcome only through heroic struggle. This interpretation found its way into many scholarly works when, in the nineteenth century, Germans began to study and write seriously about their past. Influenced by the Burckhardtian conception of the modernity of the Renaissance or perhaps by a commitment to liberalism or nationalism, most nineteenth-century historians depicted the humanists as heralds of the modern world, destined to free the German soul from medieval bondage and scholastic barbarism. An example of such writing was the popular biography of Ulrich von Hutten by David Friedrich Strauss (1808-1874), the controversial scholar who stunned the world in 1836 with his *Leben Jesu*. His study of von Hutten, which was republished many times after it first appeared in 1858, portrayed the colorful humanist as Germany's heroic liberator. He was a fighter "for light against darkness, for culture against barbarism, for freedom against despotism, for the fatherland against foreign oppressors."[1] In the same volume Johannes Reuchlin, the famed Hebrew scholar, was depicted as the individual who "led the human spirit from the oppressiveness of the declining Middle Ages to the freer air of the Renaissance."[2] Such treatments of humanism and scholasticism also typified most nineteenth-century university histories. A characteristic example is Friedrich W. Kampschulte's influential study of the University of Erfurt, which, like Strauss's biography of von Hutten, was published in 1858.[3] The author's theme was basically one of conflict between

[1] *Ulrich von Hutten* (Leipzig: 1871), vi.
[2] *Ibid.*, 239.
[3] *Die Universität Erfurt in ihrem Verhältnisse zu dem Humanismus und Reformation*, 2 vols. (Trier: 1858).

progressive humanists and backward scholastics; and when the humanists "triumphed" over their enemies in the wake of the Reuchlin affair, the author's jubilation is barely concealed.[4]

Of course not all writers accepted the interpretations of Strauss and Kampschulte. In 1885, for example, Friedrich Paulsen (1846-1908) published his widely read history of German pedagogy without portraying the humanists as heralds of enlightenment battling hordes of dull-witted scholastics.[5] But Paulsen was an exception, and most studies through the 1880s were similar in tone: the relationship between humanists and scholastics was described in terms of a "struggle" or "battle"; the treatment of the struggle was favorable to the humanists; and the final chapter of the tale was always the triumph of the humanists and the scattering of their barbarian opponents.[6] Rarely, a writer like Dietrich Reichling defended the scholastics and deplored what he called "the poisonous hate and infernal evil" of the humanists; but he too could only see humanist-scholastic relations in terms of conflict and opposition.[7]

Reactions against such interpretations began in the 1890s, and are best seen in the scholarly work of the Silesian historian, Gustav Bauch (1848-1924). Bauch was among the first to realize that to understand the nature of humanist-scholastic relations it was necessary to go beyond the humanists' empassioned rhetoric. Judgments could be reached only after

---

[4] Other older university histories that followed similar interpretive lines were Johann Friedrich Hautz, *Geschichte der Universität Heidelberg*, 2 vols. (Mannheim: 1862, 1864); Johann Kosegarten, *Geschichte der Universität Greifswald*, 2 vols. (Greifswald: 1856, 1857); Heinrich Schreiber, *Geschichte der Albert-Ludwigs-Universität zu Freiburg-im-Breisgau*, 3 vols. (Freiburg-im-Breisgau: 1868).

[5] *Geschichte des gelehrten Untterrichts auf den deutschen Schulen und Universitäten*, 2 vols. (Leipzig: 1855).

[6] Among the many additional works that could be cited, the following must suffice: Heinrich Kämmel, "Die Universität Köln in ihrem Kämpfe gegen den aufstrebenden Humanismus," *Jahrbücher für Philologie und Pädagogik*, 2 (1875), 401-17; Carl Krause, *Helius Eobanus Hessus* (Gotha: 1879).

[7] *Ortwin Gratius, sein Leben und Wirken* (Heiligenstadt: 1884).

examing the experience of humanists, both famous and obscure, within the institutional framework of the universities themselves. Mounting this investigation more or less singlehandedly, this extraordinary researcher produced studies on the reception of humanism at many universities, including Erfurt, Wittenberg, Ingolstadt, Leipzig, Cracow, Frankfurt an der Oder, and Vienna. His works were models of scholarly thoroughness but were so crammed with information that the author often lost sight of broader interpretive issues. When he did draw general conclusions, his viewpoint differed markedly from those of his scholarly predecessors.[8] Bauch found, to be sure, examples of friction between humanists and scholastics, but it was not the titanic struggle depicted by Strauss or Kampschulte; nor was the end of the story a clear-cut humanist victory. His theme was rather one of mutual compromise and conciliation. Scholastics gradually overcame their opposition to classical studies and conceded rhetoric and poetry a place in the university curriculum; for their part, humanists abandoned their "Italian superficialities" and dedicated themselves to reforming scholasticism rather than rooting it out entirely.

Bauch's tentative revisionism found fuller expression in the works of Gerhard Ritter, the eminent historian who in the 1910s and 1920s concentrated his scholarly efforts on the intellectual history of pre-Reformation Germany.[9] In his well-

---

[8] Bauch most clearly enunciated his views in the opening pages of his long article, "Wittenberg und die Scholastik," *Neues Archiv für Sächsische Geschichte und Altertumskunde*, 18 (1897), 285-339.

[9] "Die geschichtliche Bedeutung des deutschen Humanismus," *Historische Zeitschrift*, 127 (1923), 393-453; see also, his *Studien zur Spätscholastik*, 3 vols. (Heidelberg: 1922); in another article, "Zur Frage des Ursprungs des deutschen Humanismus," *Historische Zeitschrift*, 132 (1925), 413-46, Ritter attacked the notion suggested some two decades earlier by Heinrich Hermelink that German humanism grew out of the revival of Thomism or the *via antiqua* in the mid-1400s. Hermelink's ideas, which attracted a swarm of unsympathetic critics, were expressed in the following works: *Die religiösen Reformbestrebung des deutschen Humanismus* (Tübingen: 1897); *Die theologische Fakultät in Tübingen vor der Reformation, 1477-1534* (Tübingen: 1906); "Die Anfänge des Humanismus in Tübingen," *Württembergische Vierteljahrshefte für Landesgeschichte*, N.F., 15 (1906), 319-37.

known article, "The Historical Meaning of German Humanism," Ritter utterly rejected the notion that the Renaissance was a battleground between "enlightened humanists" and "obscure scholastics." He argued that clashes between humanists and scholastics were rare and that their bitterness had been exaggerated. Such conflicts, he maintained, did occur in Italy, where humanism grew outside the universities and was hostile to the teaching traditions represented there. In contrast, German humanism was centered in the universities and, according to Ritter, encountered little opposition and quick acceptance. Those rare conflicts which did occur never involved the clash of ideals or principles, but rather were matters of personal pique, competition for jobs, or rivalries over academic promotion. On the whole, Ritter argued, humanist-scholastic relations were marked by "peaceful coexistence."

Ritter, whose research focused on an institution—the University of Heidelberg—where humanism was especially insipid and unaggressive, may well have exaggerated the compatibility of humanists and scholastics in Germany as a whole. In any case, his revisionist ideas rarely found their way into subsequent writings on pre-Reformation intellectual history.[10] Widely read surveys continued to dwell on the fundamental divisions between humanists and scholastics and the inevitability of conflict between the two camps. To Willy Andreas, in his *Deutschland vor der Reformation*, and Joseph Lortz, in his *Die Reformation in Deutschland*, humanist-scholastic tensions were anything but petty.[11] They involved a

[10] Paul Oskar Kristeller, who studied at Heidelberg in the 1920s, later applied to his studies of Italian humanism many of Ritter's ideas. He has argued that there was no clash of principles between humanism and scholasticism, and that the Italian Renaissance was a time of "peaceful co-existence" between the two movements. See especially his essay, "Humanism and Scholasticism," in *Renaissance Thought* (New York: 1961), 92-119.

[11] Andreas' survey, first published in 1932, has since gone through several editions. Humanism is discussed in Chapter Eight, "Der deutsche Humanismus beim Anbruch der Reformation." Lortz's work, first published in Freiburg in 1948, has appeared in an English version: *The Reformation in Germany*, 2 vols., trans. Ronald Wells (London: 1968). See especially Volume 1, Chapter 4, "Intellectual Life in Germany Before the Reformation."

clash of basic religious and intellectual outlooks and contributed significantly to the onset of the Reformation. Similarly,
the American historian Myron Gilmore wrote in his popular
work, *The World of Humanism*, that "in no major country of
Europe did there develop so sharp a division between the
followers of the new learning and those who upheld the scholastic tradition."[12]

Authors of monographs, on the other hand, have tended
to be more cautious in their assessments. Heiko Oberman,
for example, has suggested in his work on Gabriel Biel, the
pre-Reformation nominalist theologian, that "humanism and
scholasticism were apparently more compatible than we have
long been inclined to believe."[13] And in his important article,
"The Clash of Humanists and Scholastics: An Approach to
Pre-Reformation Controversy,"[14] Charles G. Nauert, Jr., has
cautioned that "the idea of an irrepressible conflict [between
humanism and scholasticism] needs to be demonstrated, not
taken for granted."

Other authors have found Ritter's ideas of "peaceful coexistence" valid for early, but not later humanism. Hajo Holborn, in *Ulrich von Hutten and the German Reformation*, argued
that tensions surfaced only in the early sixteenth century,
when the humanists abandoned "fiction for dogma" and began to use their philological methods "for new interpretation
of Biblical passages." Finally, wrote Holborn, in the 1510s
the heresy hunting of the ecclesiastical court during the Reuchlin affair revealed once and for all the incompatibility of the
intellectual worlds of humanism and scholasticism."[15] A similar change has also been described by Erich Kleineidam in
his history of the University of Erfurt. In his account, in the
years around 1500, early humanism (*Frühhumanismus*), "which
had attempted to live in peaceful coexistence with scholasticism" gave way to high humanism (*Hochhumanismus*), "which

[12] (New York: 1952), 219.
[13] *The Harvest of Medieval Theology* (Cambridge, Mass.: 1961), 19.
[14] *The Sixteenth Century Journal*, 4 (1973), 1-18.
[15] (New York: 1966), 56, 57.

attacked scholasticism with every means and sought to destroy it.[16]

In response to this long-standing historiographical jumble, several scholars since the early 1970s have begun once again to address the problem of German humanism's relationship with scholasticism. In addition to his previously cited article, Charles G. Nauert, Jr., has produced a detailed and insightful study of the events leading to the expulsion of the Italian jurist, Peter of Ravenna, from the University of Cologne in 1507.[17] Terence Heath has examined the impact of humanist grammar instruction on the curricula of the universities of Freiburg-im-Breisgau, Ingolstadt, and Tübingen.[18] More recently, Guy F. Lytle III and Steven Ozment have written insightful articles that discuss humanist-scholastic relations in terms of general university history and the onset of the Reformation.[19]

The book that follows, however, adopts a path different from these recent studies. Its focus is broad rather than narrow; its goal is to produce a general synthesis rather than further elucidation of individual case studies. It proposes to explore the changing nature of the German humanists' critique of scholasticism from the mid-fifteenth to the early sixteenth century. It also intends to explore the scholastics' response to this critique. The latter task involves not only an examination of the reception of humanism at Germany's universities but also the analysis of several controversies which in some measure involved a clash between the principles of humanism and scholasticism.

[16] *Universitas Studii Erffordensis*, 2 vols. (Erfurt: 1964, 1969), II, 38.

[17] "Peter of Ravenna and the 'Obscure Men' of Cologne: A Case of Pre-Reformation Controversy," *Renaissance Studies in Honor of Hans Baron*, ed. Anthony Molho and John A. Tedeschi (De Kalb, Ill.: 1971), 609-40.

[18] "Logical Grammar, Grammatical Logic and Humanism in Three German Universities," *Studies in the Renaissance*, 18 (1971), 9-64.

[19] Steven Ozment, "Humanism, Scholasticism and the Intellectual Origins of the Reformation," in E. F. Church and T. George, eds., *Continuity and Discontinuity in Church History: essays presented to G. H. Williams* (Leiden: 1979), 133-49; Guy Fitch Lytle, "Universities as Religious Authorities in the Later Middle Ages and Reformation," in Guy Fitch Lytle, ed., *Reform and Authority in the Medieval and Reformation Church* (Washington, D.C.: 1981), 69-98.

I am well aware of the many difficulties involved in such a study. It does, after all, propose to deal with no less than thirteen universities and many dozens of humanists and scholastics, at least some of whom were prolific authors.[20] An especially frustrating problem is the loss or inaccessibility of many university records. As a result of damage in the Thirty Years' War and World War II, major documents relevant to the early history of the University of Mainz have been lost completely. Thus, despite its active academic life from 1477 onward, this institution will receive almost no attention in the following study. The early records of the Baltic universities of Rostock and Greifswald are also sparse, as they are for the University of Frankfurt an der Oder. For the remaining institutions we are better informed, although important documents have been lost in several instances. The records of the University of Cologne, for example, become increasingly meager for the years before the Reformation, and for the University of Heidelberg the important reform statutes of 1522 are no longer extant.

Despite such gaps, substantial material remains. The humanists and scholastics whose thoughts and actions provide the focus for this study lived at the dawn of the age of print, and most of their works are accessible as published books. Early humanist works that remained in manuscript have in many cases found modern editors. And scholarly editions of correspondence have been published for all major humanists. The early history of the German universities attracted extensive scholarly interest in the late nineteenth and early twentieth

---

[20] Several more or less subjective decisions had to be made about what comprised a "German university" and a "German humanist." Essentially the universities examined were those which existed in those parts of the Holy Roman Empire where the German language was dominant. Thus Vienna is considered a German university, but not Basel, Cracow, or Prague. The "German" humanists and scholastics are those who taught at or had significant impact on these universities. We will accede to Erasmus's wish that he be considered a "citizen of the world, common to all;" his attitudes toward scholasticism will not be discussed along with those of the other German humanists. Chapter Eight will, however, examine his role in the Reuchlin affair, in which his behavior reveals much about the meaning of that famous controversy.

centuries. The era produced dozens of invaluable institutional histories and published source collections. Since the 1960s interest in university history has revived. Important work has been published on the universities of Ingolstadt, Vienna, Erfurt, Wittenberg, Freiburg-im-Breisgau, and Tübingen. Finally, both the intellectual life of the pre-Reformation era and its academic setting have been discussed in countless monographs and journal articles.

I am deeply aware of my debt to the hundreds of scholars whose works have served as the foundation for the present volume. They have provided information and insights that have been indispensable. I hope that the book that follows will be as useful to other scholars, both present and future, who are interested in understanding those intellectual and academic changes that helped bring an end to the German Middle Ages.

I would also like to thank especially Professors Guy Fitch Lytle and Lewis Spitz, whose encouragement and prodding brought the book to completion and whose reading of an earlier version resulted in a better final product. The University of Vermont and the American Philosophical Society both provided financial support for released time from teaching and for the purchase of microfilms. The staff of the Bailey-Howe Library of the University of Vermont has been most helpful, especially Sandy Gavett of inter-library loan, whose resourcefulness has put many rare volumes and obscure articles on my desk. My greatest debt is to my family—my wife, Susan, and my children, Andrew, Janey, and Katie—who for many years have put up with the German humanists and their scholastic adversaries with enduring patience and constant good humor.

Burlington, Vermont
January 11, 1984

*Humanism and Scholasticism
in Late Medieval Germany*

Late Scholasticism and the German University Environment ~

THE GERMAN UNIVERSITY MOVEMENT

> Studies in France were squandered, and the sun of wisdom was eclipsed; knowledge retreated so it might shine on other people. Certainly now the unfair mouth of the babblers is closed who said there is no brilliance of truth among the Germans but only the blind raving of barbarity.[1]

WITH these proud and enthusiastic words written in 1394, the 70-year-old philosopher, logician, and theologian, Henry of Langenstein, proclaimed that Germany had entered a new and fateful stage in her educational and cultural development. Wisdom now shone on Germany because in the previous three decades, long after they had assumed a prominent role in France, Italy, England, Spain, and even Portugal, the first universities had successfully taken root in German-speaking

[1] From "Epistola Henrici de Hassia informativa super scismate," in Gustav Sommerfeldt, "Die Stellung Ruprechts II von der Pfalz zur deutschen Publizistik bis zum Jahre 1400," *Zeitschrift für die Geschichte des Oberrheins*, N.F., 22 (1907), 310, 311.

lands. By 1400 universities had been established at Vienna, Erfurt, Cologne, and Heidelberg, and together they enrolled approximately 740 new students each year. New foundations rapidly followed in the fifteenth century, so that by the time of the Reformation Germany boasted of no less than thirteen thriving universities, more than any other area of Europe.

Before the foundation of Germany's first universities, educational opportunities had not of course been completely lacking. Major cities had cathedral schools where instruction was offered in elementary grammar, logic, computation, and occasionally more sophisticated philosophical subjects. In fact, schools at Trier, Erfurt, Vienna, and Cologne were large institutions that at times enrolled over one thousand students.[2] In addition, religious orders, especially the Dominicans and Franciscans, sponsored numerous monastic or friary schools at which lectures on theology and Aristotelian philosophy were offered for the edification of the brothers. But the expense and inconvenience of foreign travel meant that few Germans received university training. The University of Bologna, for example, whose famed faculty of law attracted a large and cosmopolitan group of students, rarely enrolled more than a dozen Germans per year before the fifteenth century. And at the University of Paris, of the four organized nations, the English-German Nation was smallest even though it included students from the British Isles, Scandinavia, and all of Europe east of the Rhine and north of the Alps.[3] Not surprisingly Germans played a peripheral role in the history of medieval scholasticism. The great Dominican Albertus Magnus (c. 1200-1280), a brilliant thinker himself and the teacher of Thomas Aquinas, stands out as the single exception. Others such as Thomas of Erfurt (c. 1280-c. 1330), Albert of Saxony

[2] Georg Kaufmann, *Geschichte der deutschen Universitäten*, I (Stuttgart: 1888), 159.
[3] Wilhelm Lucke, "Deutsche Studenten in Bologna," *Das Gymnasium*, 53 (1942), 43-61; Astrik R. Gabriel, "The English-German Nation at the University of Paris from 1425-1494," *Garlandia* (Notre Dame, Ind.: 1969), 167-200; G. C. Boyce, *The English-German Nation in the University of Paris during the Middle Ages* (Bruges: 1927).

(d. 1390), Marsilius of Inghen (c. 1340-1394), and Henry of Langenstein (1325-1398) achieved modest prominence in their own day and are occasionally mentioned in modern surveys of medieval thought.[4] But aside from these few, the Germans who traveled across the Alps or over the Rhine to learn and sometimes teach at foreign universities are nothing more than names listed on matriculation rolls or mentioned in faculty records.

The retarded development of universities in Germany is best explained by the chaotic political conditions and relative economic stagnation that plagued all levels of German society from the late eleventh to the middle of the fourteenth century. Significantly, internal disintegration and foreign intervention peaked between 1250 and 1350, the very years when universities proliferated in the rest of western Europe. Even a cursory survey of medieval university foundations reveals the close connection between politics and higher learning. Only the oldest and most venerable European universities—Bologna, Paris, Oxford, and Montpellier—grew spontaneously out of pre-existing schools with no governmental initiative. Several more—most notably Cambridge and a few Italian universities—were the result of migrations from established institutions. But the majority of medieval universities were political creations: some governmental authority—emperor, king, prince, city council, or high ecclesiastic—provided the inspiration, organizational effort, and financial support needed for their establishment.[5] But with their energies and resources sapped by war and internal strife, medieval Germany's polit-

---

[4] It is symptomatic of these Germans' scholarly reputations that Thomas of Erfurt's *Grammatica speculativa*, an influential grammar text, was until recently ascribed to Duns Scotus. See the introduction to *Grammatica Speculativa of Thomas of Erfurt*, ed. and trans. G. L. Bursill-Hall (London: 1977).

[5] On the founding of the medieval universities, the following works are fundamental: Hastings Rashdall, *The Universities of Europe in the Middle Ages*, II, part 1 (Oxford: 1895). The revised edition of Powicke and Emden (Oxford: 1936) has much added bibliographical material. All citations that follow refer to the 1936 edition; also Heinrich Denifle, *Die Entstehung der Universitäten des Mittelalters bis 1400* (Berlin: 1885); A. B. Cobban, *The Medieval Universities: Their Development and Organization* (London: 1975).

ical and religious leaders lacked the interest and means to support institutions of higher learning.

Germany's time of troubles slowly abated in the 1300s, and, as the political atmosphere calmed, the first universities appeared. Significantly, the ruler most responsible for stabilizing the Holy Roman Empire's political situation also provided the inspiration for the establishment of its first university. He was Charles IV of Bohemia, Holy Roman Emperor from 1355 to 1378 and the founder of the University of Prague in 1348. Charles was the first emperor in better than a century and a half who saw himself as a territorial prince and who avoided using the imperial crown as a lever to increase his power into Italy or Germany. By recognizing princely electoral rights in the Golden Bull and by settling long-standing feuds with his bitter rivals, the Hapsburgs and Wittelsbachs, he was able effectively to devote his energies to his hereditary holdings in Bohemia. He was a learned man who had lived and studied in Paris, and he was convinced that a university in Bohemia would strengthen his rule and enhance his prestige. Thus in 1348 he gained the necessary charter from the Avignon Pope Clement VI to found a *studium generale* in Prague with all the rights and privileges of other European universities. Lectures began in April 1348. The success of the new institution was immediate, as students from east and central Europe previously deterred by the cost and difficulty of traveling to France or Italy streamed to Prague.

Two new university foundations soon followed, but neither equaled the immediate and dazzling success of Prague. The University of Vienna, founded in 1365 by Charles's rival, Archduke Rudolph IV of Austria, faced seemingly insurmountable obstacles from the start. Rudolph died in Milan only a few days after receiving the papal charter and thus never had an opportunity to arrange adequate financial support for the new institutions. Vigorous support by Rudolph's successors might have brightened the university's prospects, but instead, a succession conflict between his brothers, Albert and Leopold, created an atmosphere of uncertainty that lasted more than a decade. By the 1370s Rudolph's creation was a university in name only, with the faculty of arts alone managing to carry on a feeble existence.[6] Conditions at the University of Erfurt, founded in 1379 under the patronage of the Erfurt municipal government, were also unpromising. Important faculty posts were not filled, and student enrollments were below expectations.[7] Hardly begun, the German university movement in 1380 seemed about to wither and die.

But the next thirty years showed a remarkable reversal.[8] Erfurt and Vienna both revived, and four new universities were successfully established. An important reason for this turnabout was the near-total departure of German scholars from the University of Paris in the early 1380s as a result of conflicts growing out of the Great Schism. Most German rulers were unsympathetic to the Avignon claimant, Clement VII, and German masters at Paris were among his most vociferous critics. As a result, supporters of the Italian Urban VI soon found their situation intolerable. Under pressure from Clement and the French king, Charles VI, benefices for German masters and scholars were withdrawn; and in 1381 on order from Clement the Parisian chancellor decreed that no degrees would be awarded to any Urbanists. German scholars had no choice but to abandon the University of Paris.

These Parisian scholars formed the nucleus of the new and revitalized German universities of the 1380s and 1390s. In Vienna Duke Albert III attracted to his moribund institution the well-known theologian, Henry of Langenstein, one of Clement's most outspoken Parisian opponents. Langenstein's

---

[6] Joseph von Aschbach, *Geschichte der Wiener Universität*, I (Vienna: 1865), 16, 17.

[7] Erich Kleineidam, *Universitas Studii Erffordensis*, I (Leipzig: 1964), 30-34.

[8] A general description of the founding of the German universities can be found in Kaufmann, *Geschichte der deutschen Universitäten*, I, 1-45; more recent scholarship is reflected in the useful anthology edited by Peter Baumgart and Notker Hammerstein, *Beiträge zu Problemen deutscher Universitätsgründungen der frühen Zeit* (Nendeln, Liechtenstein: 1978); especially useful is Ernst Schubert, "Motive und Probleme deutscher Universitätsgründungen des 15. Jahrhunderts," 13-74.

presence at Vienna drew new masters and students, and in 1384 Albert issued a new charter of privilege, which began the true life of the university. Exiles from Paris also breathed life into the University of Erfurt. Regular lectures and examinations began in the mid 1380s, and in 1389 the institution received a new bull of foundation from Urban VI. The disintegration of the University of Paris also stimulated the establishment of two new universities in the 1380s. In 1385 Ruprecht II of the Palatinate, aided by Marsilius of Inghen, a prominent logician and former rector of the University of Paris, established the University of Heidelberg, and in 1388 the city of Cologne received a charter from Pope Urban VI to establish the University of Cologne.

In 1409, twenty-eight years after German scholars departed Paris, another migration, this time from Prague, gave further impetus to the German university movement.[9] Conflict between Germans and Slavic Czechs and Bohemians had plagued Charles IV's university from its beginning. The Slavs resented the Germans' numerical and political dominance, especially their monopoly of lucrative lectureships and university offices. Brawls between German and Slavic students were commonplace. Tensions reached a flash point in the early fifteenth century when bitter philosophical and theological disagreements further antagonized the two nationalities. John Hus, whose ideas had been strongly influenced by the writings of John Wycliffe, had by 1400 become the heroic spokesman for Czech nationalism both in the university and Prague itself. Thus when in 1403 and 1408 the German-dominated university council declared it illegal to teach certain Wycliffite doctrines, the Czechs and Bohemians appealed to the Bohemian King Wenceslas to alter the council's voting procedures in order to break the German monopoly. In January 1409, Wen-

---

[9] Howard Kaminski, "The University of Prague in the Hussite Revolution: The Role of the Masters," in *Universities in Politics: Case Studies from the Late Middle Ages and Early Modern Period*, ed. John W. Baldwin and Richard A. Goldthwaite (Baltimore: 1972), 79-106.

ceslas complied, altering the statutes so that the Germans lost control of all major university councils. Then in May the king removed the German rector from office in favor of a Bohemian. At this point German masters and students, perhaps one thousand in all, abandoned Prague.

In direct response, two new German universities were founded. Only a few months after their Prague exodus, forty masters and four hundred students accepted the invitation of the Landgraves of Thuringia, Frederick and William, to establish a university at Leipzig. On September 9, 1409 Pope Alexander V issued the necessary charter, and lectures began in October. The founding of the University of Rostock also resulted from the Prague migration, for until 1409 numerous Baltic students had attended the Bohemian university. John III and Albert V, dukes of Mecklenburg, sought to fill the gap, and as a result of their cooperation with the Rostock city council, the University of Rostock began lectures in 1419.

After the establishment of Rostock, there was a thirty-year hiatus in university foundations. In the 1450s, however, the growing strength and competitiveness of the German princes resulted in the successful founding of three universities at Greifswald, Freiburg-im-Breisgau, and Ingolstadt. In the 1470s new universities were added at Mainz and Tübingen. By 1500 electoral Saxony and electoral Brandenburg were the only sizable principalities in Germany without universities. By 1502, however, Saxony had the University of Wittenberg, and by 1506 Brandenburg, the University of Frankfurt an der Oder.

Thus in the one hundred fifty years before the Reformation thirteen universities had been successfully founded in Germany. One, the University of Mainz, had been established by an archbishop, two, Cologne and Erfurt, by urban governments and the remainder by secular princes. Two universities founded by archbishops, Würzburg (1410) and Trier (1472), failed to survive more than a year or two. Proposed universities at Kulm (1366), Lüneburg (1471), and Regensburg (1487) received imperial and papal charters, but never went beyond the planning stage.[10] Despite these failures, the late Middle Ages was for Germany a time of impressive educational expansion. Belatedly, she now fully entered medieval Europe's scholastic era.

When it is said that a prince or city government "established" or "founded" a university, two things are implied. First, it meant that the sponsoring government took the initiative in ascertaining the necessary charters from emperor and pope. Second, and more important, it meant that the government arranged for the on-going financial support of the university once its academic life began. In this matter the fiscal arrangements of Germany's oldest universities set the pattern for the later foundations of the fifteenth and sixteenth centuries. The revival of the University of Vienna in the 1380s, for example, owed as much to the financial support of the Hapsburg Archduke Albert III as it did to the splintering of Paris. He provided, first of all, that 680 pounds from ducal customs revenues should annually be transferred to the university to fund professorships in law, medicine, and theology; on his death, the sum was raised to 800 pounds. The duke also established and endowed the *Collegium ducale*, an institution that provided stipends for twelve professors in the arts faculty and also established a dwelling for them and their students.[11] The Erfurt city council made a similar commitment in the 1380s. It assumed expenses for the construction of lecture halls for the faculties of arts and law and also established the *Collegium porta caeli*, which housed twelve students and twelve masters of arts. These twelve *Kollegiaten* were paid fifteen gulden per year and were granted a monopoly to sell Naumburger beer to the students. Then in the 1390s, in what soon became a common practice, the city

[10] On Kulm and Lüneburg, see Kaufmann, *Geschichte*, II, xv, xvi; on Regensburg, Alois Weissthanner, "Die Gesandtschaft Herzog Albrechts IV von Bayern an die Römische Kurie 1487—Stiftungsprivileg für eine Universität in Regensburg," *Archivalische Zeitschrift*, 47 (1951), 189-210.

[11] Paul Uiblein, "Die österreichischen Landesfürsten und die Wiener Universität," *Mitteilungen des Instituts für Österreichische Geschichtsforschung*, 74 (1964), 294, 295.

council successfully petitioned the pope to transfer to the university two canonicates each from the collegiate churches of St. Mary and St. Severin, the income from which was to be used to endow professorships in theology and canon law.[12] The city council of Cologne committed itself to pay the salaries of all professors of law, medicine, and theology and arranged for the transfer to the university of twelve canonicates, one from each of the twelve collegiate churches in the city.[13] At Heidelberg the Palatine elector was able to redirect to the university the income of thirteen canonicates from collegiate churches in the region; he also applied the income from tolls at Kaiserwerth and Bacharach to the support of professors in the three higher faculties.[14] Similar combinations of direct governmental subsidies and the utilization of income from church livings were utilized at the other nine pre-Reformation universities.[15]

It is true that at some universities private individuals were important benefactors. The bürgermeister of Greifswald, Hans von Rubenov, paid the cost of ascertaining papal privileges and made substantial contributions of cash and property in the early years of the University of Greifswald.[16] Amplonius Ratingh, a professor of medicine at Erfurt in the 1390s, pro-

[12] Georg Oergel, "Zur Erinnerung an die Universität Erfurt," "Urkunden zur Geschichte des *Collegium majus*," *Mitteilungen des Vereins für die Geschichte und Altertumskunde von Erfurt*, 16 (1894), 1-22, 111-42.

[13] Hermann Keussen, "Die Stadt Köln als Patronin ihrer Hochschule von deren Gründung bis zum Ausgänge des Mittelalters," *Westdeutsche Zeitschrift für Geschichte und Kunst*, 10 (1891), 65-104.

[14] Gerhard Ritter, *Die Heidelberger Universität* (Heidelberg: 1936), 130-53.

[15] See also Andreas Ludwig Veit, "Aus der Geschichte der Universität Mainz, 1477-1731," *Historisches Jahrbuch*, 40 (1920), 106-36; Hans Haussherr, "Die Finanzierung einer deutschen Universität: Wittenberg in den ersten Jahrzehnten seines Bestehens (1507-1547)," in *450 Jahre Martin-Luther Universität Halle-Wittenberg* (Leipzig: 1953), 315-54; Elizabeth Schnitzler, "Die Gründung der Universität Rostock," *Wissenschaftliche Zeitschrift der Universität Rostock*, 7 (1957-1958), 149-65; Fritz Ernst, *Die wirtschaftliche Ausstattung der Universität Tübingen in ihren ersten Jahrzehnten, 1477-1534* (Stuttgart: 1929); Georg Pfister, *Die finanziellen Verhältnisse der Universität Freiburg-im-Breisgau* (Freiburg: 1889).

[16] Kaufmann, *Geschichte*, II, 25-28.

vided the library for the university and established funds for eight collegiate professorships.[17] It is also true that princely subsidies sometimes came late or were withheld completely in times of fiscal exigency. In two extreme instances the University of Erfurt was forced in 1492 and 1506 to loan sums of 400 and 600 gulden to her bankrupt "patron," the Erfurt city government. The "loans" proved to be gifts since neither was repaid.[18] The Erfurt situation was exceptional, of course, and in general one can only be impressed by the willingness of thirteen German governments to lavish considerable amounts of time and money on their universities. Without such governmental support, the revolutionary expansion of German higher education in the late Middle Ages is unthinkable.

FACULTIES AND ADMINISTRATION

The most significant feature of the German universities was their "completeness." That is, they included each of the four faculties that existed at the University of Paris—arts, law, medicine, and theology. This was in contrast to most universities in Italy, provincial France, and parts of Spain, where legal studies were preeminent, and training in the arts and theology was reduced to an insignificant or even nonexistent role.[19] Since the late thirteenth century popes had denied theological faculties to newly created universities in order to preserve the theological monopoly of the University of Paris. Emperor Charles IV, however, gained papal approval for a theology faculty at Prague, in no small measure because Pope Clement VI had been his tutor while the young prince had resided in Paris.[20] But traditional policy was revived when Clement denied a theology faculty to the University of Vienna

[17] *Ibid.*, 36, 37.
[18] Kleineidam, *Universitas Studii Erffordensis*, I, 82, 83, 106.
[19] Rashdall, *The Universities of Europe in the Middle Ages*, 2nd ed., II, 59, 209, 210.
[20] *Ibid.*, II, 214.

in 1365. This was reversed in 1384, however, when the Italian Pope Urban VI granted a theology faculty to Vienna as a favor for the support he had received from Archduke Albert III. Succeeding popes followed this precedent when they issued charters to German universities.

The organization and administrative structure of the oldest German universities all reflect the Parisian background of the men who wrote their statutes. Albert of Saxony, who was largely responsible for the 1365 statutes of the University of Vienna, had had a long and active academic career at Paris and twice, in 1353 and 1362, had served as rector. Henry of Langenstein, who rewrote Vienna's statutes in the 1380s when the university established its theology faculty, had studied and taught at Paris for forty years. Marsilius of Inghen, the noted logician who wrote the statutes for Heidelberg, and the founders of Cologne and Erfurt had similar Parisian backgrounds. The organization of these older institutions served as models for later university foundations, and hence a general uniformity in academic structures and practice developed throughout German-speaking lands.

In the administration and formulation of policy, for example, the universities were all granted broad powers of self-government despite the significant financial commitments made by their princely patrons. The statutes of Vienna, Heidelberg, and Freiburg, in fact, specifically banned princely interference with the constitution and daily workings of the universities.[21] Others required that only major statute revisions had to receive princely approval.[22] But since the universities tended to be conservative institutions in which "major" statute revisions were rare, such provisions failed to promote frequent princely intervention. Even when governments reserved the right of

---

[21] Rudolf Kink, *Geschichte der kaiserlichen Universität zu Wien*, II (Vienna: 1854), 72; Eduard Winkelmann, *Urkundenbuch der Universität Heidelberg* (Heidelberg: 1886), 5; Heinrich Schreiber, *Urkundenbuch der Stadt Freiburg*, II (Freiburg: 1829), 449.

[22] Rudolf Roth, ed., *Urkunden zur Geschichte der Universität Tübingen* (Tübingen: 1877), 66.

appointment to endowed lectureships, they normally accepted the recommendations of the university faculty.

Thus, before the immediate pre-Reformation period, governments interfered in university affairs only at the request of the institutions themselves or else when conflicts affecting the university proved insoluble and disruptive. Town-gown relationships, for example, were a continual source of friction and often invited governmental intervention. Students and masters tended to view town merchants, landlords, and officials as greedy exploiters quick to inflate food prices, dilute wine, raise rents, and ignore university privileges. Burghers on the other hand tended to view academics as privileged parasites exempt from town taxes and justice who disturbed the peace and ruined sleep with their alcoholically inspired singing and brawling. Conflicts were common, for the perceptions of each side were essentially accurate. A sign of what the future held was the series of petitions received in the 1380s by Archduke Albert III of Austria. In them municipal and university officials denounced one another and demanded redress of numerous grievances. Fighting between students and young townsmen (in which city officials testily noted the use of swords by students) became endemic in 1385, and in 1386 the archduke intervened to declare "eternal peace" between the two sides. Thereupon the brawls immediately resumed.[23] Other princes in other university towns strove mightily to calm town-gown relationships, but the frequency of their efforts suggests they were no more successful than Albert III. Governments were also forced occasionally to intervene in disputes resulting from the famous *Wegestreit*—the conflict between the *via moderna* and *via antiqua*, which raged at most, but not all, German universities after the middle of the fifteenth century. Competition between the factions for deanships, salaried lectureships, positions as examiners, and seats on various university committees was intense. Rigged elections, public slanders, and unfair student recruitment led to frequent government appeals for "eternal peace" and the de-

[23] Uiblein, "Die österreichischen Landesfürsten," 390, 391.

sign of various schemes to achieve parity between the two *viae*.[24] But these perennially intractable problems were exceptions, and in other areas the universities of Germany controlled their own affairs. This began to change only in the three decades before the Reformation and was closely tied to the rise of humanism.[25]

Within the universities, the most important governing body was the gathering of masters described in university records as the *plena congregacio, generale consilium, generalis congregacio, consilium,* or sometimes simply as *universitas.* University statutes accorded this assembly broad powers and jurisdiction. It approved statute changes, in some instances elected the rector, and everywhere provided a forum in which university-wide issues such as finance, academic appointments, student deportment, building construction, and protection of university privileges could be discussed. In some instances the masters' assembly took specific action according to formal voting procedures; in others it met only to advise the rector or give him a sense of faculty opinion before he himself made a decision. Membership in the assembly at first was typically accorded to all individuals who were actively teaching and who held the Master of Arts or else a doctorate in law, theology, or medicine. Beginning students in the arts course and Bachelors of Arts were excluded, but students in the three higher faculties, if they held the Masters of Arts and were actively teaching, were accorded membership. As a result of such arrangements, the numerous Masters of Arts had the power to dominate proceedings; thus formal votes were normally taken by faculty rather than by head.[26]

During the second half of the fifteenth century, the general

---

[24] A more detailed discussion of the *Wegestreit* is given later in this chapter.

[25] The second volume of Kaufmann's *Geschichte* is still the best general survey of the German universities' constitutional development; two excellent monographs have recently appeared: Arno Seifert, *Statuten-und Verfassungsgeschichte der Universität Ingolstadt (1472-1586)* (Berlin: 1971); Waldemar Teufel, *Universitas studii Tuwingensis: die Tübinger Universitätsfassung in vorreformationischer Zeit* (Tübingen: 1977).

[26] Erfurt voted by head; Leipzig accorded one vote to each of the four nations. Kaufmann, *Geschichte*, II, 163.

assembly of all masters declined in importance. Due to the large numbers of individuals involved (close to one hundred at Vienna, Erfurt, Cologne, and Leipzig) deliberations were lengthy, resolution of conflicts was arduous, and meetings were difficult to arrange on short notice. Hence rectors at several universities came to rely more frequently on smaller representative bodies for consultation and aid in enforcing decisions. At Vienna, for example, the *consistorium*, comprising the four faculty deans and the heads (*procuratores*) of the four nations, steadily gained importance in the 1400s. According to the statutes of 1385, the role of the *consistorium* was to meet with the rector to discuss the agenda later to be considered by the whole university senate. But during the fifteenth century it gradually assumed more decision-making powers until by the 1480s it was generally accepted that any decision by the *consistorium* was binding on the whole university.[27] Shifts away from the primacy of the *plena congregacio* also took place at Leipzig, Erfurt, Heidelberg, and Cologne. At Leipzig the small council included representatives of both faculties and nations, while at Heidelberg, Cologne, and Erfurt, where no nations existed, only faculties were represented.[28] The original statutes of several institutions founded after the middle of the fifteenth century also provided for a restricted council. At Tübingen, for example, the senate, with the power to choose the rector, consisted of the doctors of the upper faculties and five representatives of the arts faculty, one of whom was the dean.[29] Thus, despite some exceptions such as Ingolstadt, where no "small council" existed until 1522, the German universities had by 1500 lost much of their early "democratic" character and instead were now controlled

[27] Kink, *Geschichte*, II, 84; Kaufmann, *Geschichte*, II, 164.
[28] Kaufmann, *Geschichte*, II, 164; Seifert, *Statuten-und Verfassungsgeschichte*, 179-88. At Heidelberg the small council originally consisted of all doctors in the upper faculties and three representatives of the arts faculty; in 1453 arts faculty representation was raised to five. See Winkelmann, *Urkundenbuch*, I, 53ff.; 161; Ritter, *Die Heidelberger Universität*, 121.
[29] Roth, *Urkunden*, 42.

by a small core of established doctors, largely drawn from the three upper faculties.

The chief administrative officer of the university and its official spokesman was the rector.[30] Unlike the practice of the University of Paris, where only arts faculty members could fill this office, in Germany any teaching doctor or master who was not a member of a religious order could be chosen. Election methods varied. At Freiburg, Tübingen, Wittenberg, and Vienna rectors were chosen directly by the senate, while at other universities the choice was left to smaller numbers of electors chosen by vote or by lot from the faculty as a whole.[31] The rectorate, held only for one semester, was prestigious but burdensome.[32] The rector led all university processions and had the right to wear the distinctive rector's gown and hat. He also received one-third of all income from matriculation fees and from fines levied on students or faculty. But his executive and administrative responsibilities were extensive. He presided over the senate, maintained matriculation records, and served as the university's official spokesman in dealings with representatives from the Church, city councils, and princely governments. Most importantly he judged and punished members of the university community who were accused of common crimes or acts counter to university statutes. Thus, despite the aid of assistants such as the vice rector and bedel, the rectorate was a time-consuming office that involved large numbers of difficult and potentially controversial decisions. It was awareness of the office's burdens that led most universities to adopt a policy that mandated extensive fines for anyone who was elected to the rectorate but refused to serve.

[30] For a general discussion of the rector's office see Kaufmann, *Geschichte*, II, 167-86.

[31] For example, at Erfurt all masters and scholars who had matriculated were called together to choose one representative from each faculty; these four chose an electoral committee of five or seven, from which three or four electors were finally chosen to elect the rector; see Johann C. H. Weissenborn, ed., *Acten der Erfurter Universität*, II (Halle: 1884), 3.

[32] Only at Cologne did the rector (and deans) hold office for a whole year.

In many ways the governance of the four faculties mirrored the practices of the university as a whole. Each faculty was administered by an elected executive officer, the dean, and a council made up of some or all of the faculty's teaching masters. Also like the university as a whole, each faculty maintained its own seal and matriculation book, controlled property, disciplined students and faculty members, and settled internal disputes. A faculty could also adopt changes in its statutes, although these typically had to be approved by the university senate.[33] But the most important responsibility of the four faculties was in the academic sphere: each faculty chose its own lecturers, scheduled lecture hours, planned disputations, and administered examinations.

Administration of the three higher faculties of law, theology, and medicine was straightforward. Since only holders of the doctorate could become deans or serve on faculty councils, few individuals were involved.[34] Even the larger universities had no more than six to eight doctors of law and four to six doctors of theology.[35] Many German universities completely lacked full-time medical professors, with instruction carried on by local practicing physicians, if at all. Thus where a formal faculty council existed, all doctors were members, and the deanship was rotated.

The situation was far different in the faculty of arts, where active teaching masters were comparatively abundant. Some of these were young men in their early twenties who had just received their master's degree and were completing their *biennium*, two years of required teaching, before leaving academic

[33] See for example the statement from the 1389 statutes of Vienna: "Quod si aliquociens facultati nostre placuerit novum statutum condere aut vetus tollere . . . quod illud iterum de novo sit confirmandum aut infirmandum per alme universitatis hujus Wiennensis pie matris nostrae consilium et decretum." Kink, *Geschichte*, II, 174.

[34] This meant that Bachelors and Licentiates of Theology were, in terms of university government, considered members of the arts faculty even if they offered theological lectures.

[35] Winifred Kausch, *Die Geschichte der theologischen Fakultät Ingolstadt* (Berlin: 1977), notes that Ingolstadt's faculty consisted of but one Doctor of Theology, George Zingel, for its first three decades.

life. Others were students in theology, medicine, or law who were supporting themselves by continuing to teach in the arts faculty; some may have actually completed their requirements and were delaying their doctorate until a suitable endowed position became available. Finally, a few masters who had abandoned or never begun advanced studies saw themselves as more or less permanent teachers of the arts.[36]

Members of the arts faculty also faced radically different economic prospects than their colleagues in the upper faculties.[37] Governmental subsidies and canonicates transferred to the university were used mainly to support professors in law and theology and hence were unavailable to professors of the arts. A handful of *artistae* who were also students in theology could be supported through endowments in colleges, but the number of such positions was small, and openings might not come up for years at a time. Thus most arts faculty members depended on student fees for their support. Some offered private lessons in a *bursa* or college on a subject of their choice; others provided *resumptiones* or *repetitiones*, summaries or reviews of required material; still others offered "extraordinary" lectures on subjects not necessarily required for degrees. Such endeavors were unreliable sources of income, particularly for the less gifted masters who failed to attract more than a few students. In contrast, "ordinary" lectures on texts required for degrees were much more lucrative and desirable; they were likely to draw a substantial number of fee-paying students and often carried with them stipends from university funds. Also profitable were positions as examiners, the officials who

[36] Arno Seifert, *Statuten-und Verfassungsgeschichte*, 154, exaggerates when he generalizes that arts course teaching was "keine Lebensstellung, sondern eine Station auf dem Wege zu den oberen Graden."

[37] The actual costs for students and the rewards for faculty members have never been thoroughly researched for the late medieval universities. See, however, Gaines Post, "Masters' Salaries and Student-Fees in the Medieval Universities," *Speculum*, 7 (1932), 181-98; J. M. Fletcher, "Wealth and Poverty in the Medieval German Universities," in *Europe in the Late Middle Ages*, ed. J. R. Hale, J.R.L. Highfield and B. Smalley (London: 1965), 410-26, esp. 413-23.

presided at examinations for bachelor's and master's degree candidates and who collected fees from those who successfully completed them.

These economic realities explain why for teachers in the arts course, the membership and deliberations of their faculty council were matters of such vital importance. In addition to giving counsel to the dean and interpreting the statutes, this body made decisions that affected the economic well-being of every faculty member. Most importantly, at the start of each semester the council chose both the individuals who would lecture on required subjects and those who would serve as examiners. Selection methods varied from university to university and often involved elements of vote, lot, and rotation.[38] In any case, only council members were qualified for selection.

Such practices explain why debates and disputes within the arts faculty often took particularly bitter and personal twists. They also explain why, toward the end of the fifteenth century, the academic prospects of young masters of the arts were becoming progressively bleaker. For the evolution of governance within the faculty of arts mirrored that of the university as a whole: democratic procedures of the early German universities gave way to practices that were increasingly restrictive and oligarchical.[39]

The increasing dominance of the faculty of arts by senior masters is best illustrated by events at the University of Leipzig. The original statutes of 1409 provided for arts council membership after two years. But the requirement was pro-

[38] Choosing by lot seems to have been the practice at Leipzig; see Friedrich Zarncke, *Die Statutenbücher der Universität Leipzig* (Leipzig: 1861), 13-15; at Ingolstadt some were chosen by majority vote of the council, others by lot; see Carl von Prantl, *Geschichte der Ludwig-Maximilians-Universität zu München* (Munich: 1872), I, 93.

[39] Seifert has written, "An den deutschen Universitäten begegnet schon im 15. Jahrhundert beinahe überall ein über die traditionellen Kriterien des Magisteriums und der Regenz hinaus verkleinertes Artistenkonzil, zu dem die Magister nicht mehr unterschiedlos Zugang besassen." *Statuten-und Verfassungsgeschichte*, 162, 163.

gressively raised to three years in 1420, to four years in 1436, six years in 1471, and finally to seven years in 1496. Other statute changes also had the effect of strengthening the senior masters at Leipzig. In 1443 it was decided that two-thirds of all required fees collected at degree-awarding ceremonies would be reserved for council members, and in the following year a statute change dictated that any voluntary gifts by new graduates to the faculty would be reserved exclusively for council members.[40] By the end of the century, similar trends were evident elsewhere. Although Vienna still required only two years of teaching, four years was the minimum at Ingolstadt, Freiburg, Erfurt, and Greifswald.[41] At several institutions rules had also been adopted that gave preponderance on the council to men who already held endowed positions in colleges. An Erfurt statute of 1439 required that of the twenty men on the council, fourteen were to be masters in the *collegium universitatis* or the *collegium portae caeli*. At Greifswald all ten masters who held positions in the colleges were automatically members of the twelve-man faculty council. *Collegiati* at Mainz also monopolized both the deanship and positions on the arts faculty council.[42]

Such practices caused real hardships for recent recipients of the Master of Arts who wished to remain in academic life. They were fated to spend a minimum of two years, but more typically four or even seven years, supporting themselves as best they could through private teaching and extraordinary lectures. Even when their requirements had been fulfilled there was no guarantee of an opening on the council. Realizing the obstacles they faced, many must have abandoned the university for other careers.

For those who remained, evidence from several universities

---

[40] Zarncke, *Die Statutenbücher*, 16-27, 305, 385.

[41] Kink, *Geschichte*, II, 183; Prantl, *Geschichte*, II, 88, 104, 154; Heinrich Schreiber, *Geschichte der Albert-Ludwigs-Universität zu Freiburg*, I, 42; Johann Kosegarten, *Geschichte der Universität Greifswald mit urkundlichen Beilagen* (Greifswald: 1857), II, 297.

[42] Weissenborn, *Acten*, 151-53; Kosegarten, *Geschichte*, II, 300; Kaufmann, *Geschichte*, II, 224.

reveals their understandable frustration. At the University of Leipzig in 1502 dozens of young masters submitted complaints to the university's patron, Duke George of Saxony, about their second-class status. Enlarging the council, weakening its power, limiting length of membership and other changes were proposed, all designed to break the powers of what was clearly a narrow oligarchy.[43] In 1469 Erfurt had witnessed a similar protest voiced by a certain master of arts, Paul Kyezingen; his proposal was to increase the size of the faculty council from twenty to thirty, thus creating ten new positions for younger masters. But the council acted quickly to suppress the proposal. Noting that "he had not blushed to set forth words of insult and injury," it suspended Kyezingen from all "scholastic activity." The suspension was lifted when "many masters petitioned on his behalf," but the proposed increase in the size of the council was rejected.[44]

An episode from the University of Freiburg-im-Breisgau in 1490 also reveals the problems faced at the end of the fifteenth century by masters whose junior status excluded them from lucrative lectureships.[45] In that year the arts faculty dean spoke to the university senate on their behalf. He alleged that there were many masters who "cannot obtain an income or sufficient exercises to pay for their own food and drink." He suggested a restriction on the number of required lectures allocated to individuals already receiving income from collegiate endowments. He further proposed that the university provide salaries for all lecturers, thereby negating the need for masters to rely on student fees. Neither suggestion was accepted by the university senate.

Thus, by the end of the fifteenth century the German universities were to a great extent controlled by a small elite consisting of professors in the upper faculties and the senior masters of the faculty of arts. They administered the univer-

---

[43] The complaints have been published in Emil Friedberg, *Die Universität Leipzig in Vergangenheit und Gegenwart* (Leipzig: 1898).

[44] Kleineidam, *Universitas*, II, 220.

[45] Fletcher, "Wealth and Poverty," 417-18.

sity, determined its academic policies, and monopolized the most prestigious lectureships. Young men and men with new ideas had difficulty finding a place for themselves in such an environment. This proved to be of no little significance in the late 1400s when traditional practices began to be challenged by individuals imbued with the ideals of Renaissance humanism.

STUDENTS, CURRICULUM, AND DEGREES

How many students attended the universities of late medieval Germany? Matriculation records allow us to make fairly reasonably accurate estimates.[46] They show that by a significant margin the University of Vienna had the highest number of annual matriculants in the seventy-year period from 1450 to 1520. In those years, despite drastic short-term decreases in enrollments caused by the Hungarian occupation of Vienna in the 1480s and the outbreak of plague in 1495, the university averaged 420 new matriculants a year. During the same period only three universities had annual enrollments in the three hundreds: Leipzig averaged 379, Erfurt, 330, and Cologne, 322. Other average annual enrollments were: Wittenberg, 248; Ingolstadt, 204; Frankfurt an der Oder, 198; Rostock, 165; Heidelberg, 126; Tübingen, 104; Freiburg-im-Breisgau, 76; Greifswald, 50.[47]

[46] Matriculation records have been preserved for all late medieval German universities except Mainz. They are only "fairly accurate" indicators because students often failed to register in order to avoid paying matriculation fees. A convenient summary of matriculation figures for the German universities is Franz Eulenburg, *Die Frequenz der deutschen Universitäten*, Sächsische Akademie der Wissenschaften, Philologisch-Historische Klasse, *Abhandlungen*, 24 (Leipzig: 1904).

[47] Figures for Wittenberg, Ingolstadt, Frankfurt, Tübingen, and Freiburg were computed from the year of their founding to 1520. Attempts to translate matriculation figures into the actual number of students attending a university at one time are largely guesswork. Eulenburg, *Die Frequenz* . . . , suggested that doubling the number of annual matriculations would give a rough estimate of all active students.

To characterize late medieval student populations is a highly speculative enterprise. Available evidence suggests, however, that during the fifteenth century a number of important changes took place. Matriculation records reveal, first of all, a marked decrease in the number of poor university students.[48] In the early fifteenth century fifteen to thirty percent of all matriculants at Vienna, Heidelberg, Cologne, Leipzig, and Rostock were identified as paupers, in other words, individuals considered too poor to pay the required matriculation fee. In fact between 1421 and 1425 no less than 40.8 percent of all Viennese matriculants were listed as paupers. By 1500, however, the number of paupers had sharply decreased. At Leipzig and Vienna, a gradual decline began in the 1460s, with the result that after 1500 paupers never exceeded five percent of all matriculants. At Heidelberg, Cologne, and Rostock the decrease was more sudden and drastic. In 1448 Heidelberg abolished the *privilegium paupertatis*, claiming that the previous statutes had been abused. Thereafter the designation "pauper" disappears from the Heidelberg *matricula* until well into the sixteenth century. Similar measures were adopted at Cologne in 1503 and apparently at Rostock around 1458.[49] Some institutions such as Freiburg and Ingolstadt continued to exempt substantial numbers of poor students at the end of the fifteenth century, but they were out of step with the other German universities.

At the other end of the socioeconomic scale, aristocratic

---

[48] The following is based on Overfield, "Nobles and Paupers at German Universities to 1600," *Societas—A Review of Social History*, 7 (1974), 175–210. For a general discussion, see Jacques Paquet, "L'universitaire 'pauvre' au moyen âge: problemes, documentation, questions de méthode," *Les Universités a la fin du moyen âge*, ed. Jacques Paquet and Jozef IJsewijn (Louvain: 1978), 399–425.

[49] Gustav Toepke, ed., *Die Matrikel der Universität Heidelberg*, I (Heidelberg: 1884), lii, liii; Hermann Keussen, ed., *Die Matrikel der Universität Köln*, I (Bonn: 1892), xxvi; at Rostock there is no record of any formal policy change affecting the status of paupers; after 1458, however, the number of matriculating paupers drops suddenly. See Adolf Hofmeister, *Die Matrikel der Universität Rostock*, I (Rostock: 1889).

university students were rarities in the pre-Reformation period. During the fifteenth century only one percent of all matriculating students were nobles, and most of these were churchmen who held canonicates in cathedral or collegiate chapters. A barely discernible increase is evident in the period from 1500 to 1520, but this is only a hint of the substantial rise in aristocratic enrollments that took place from the 1530s onward.

Matriculation records also show that, on the eve of the Reformation, university students were less likely to be ordained clerics than they had been one hundred years before.[50] Between 1386 and 1450, ordained clergy made up twelve percent of all matriculants at the six German universities that existed in those years. From 1451 to 1520, however, although average annual clerical enrollments increased in absolute terms by better than ten percent, they failed to keep pace with total matriculations, which tripled during the same time. As a result, clergymen constituted a smaller and smaller fraction of all matriculants. Within the clergy itself significant changes also took place in the ratio between regular and secular matriculants. From 1386 to 1400, only ten percent of all enrolling clergy were regulars. But the fifteenth century saw steady increases in matriculations of regular clergy and an equally steady decline for seculars. As a result, better than sixty percent of clerical matriculants from 1501 to 1520 were regulars.

Whatever their background, formidable expenses and inadequate preparation meant that only a handful of these students attained degrees. Throughout the pre-Reformation era only one in four matriculants attained even the lowest degree, the Bachelor of Arts. An even smaller number, one in twenty or twenty-five, achieved the Master of Arts.[51] Degrees in the

---

[50] On clerical enrollments, see Overfield, "Universities and the Clergy in Pre-Reformation Germany" in *Universities in Transition, 1300-1700*, ed. James Kittelson (Columbus, Ohio: 1984).

[51] Kaufmann, *Geschichte*, II, 305, cites figures for several representative universities.

three higher faculties were rarer still, with the awarding of a doctorate in theology or medicine, a once-in-a-decade event at some institutions. Only 1.6 percent of all Tübingen matriculants between 1477 and 1534 received a theology degree; only twenty-three theological degrees of any sort were awarded at Ingolstadt between 1486 and 1505; and at Leipzig only five doctorates of theology were awarded between 1472 and 1532. Even at Cologne, with its prestigious theological faculty, on average only one doctorate and three bachelor's degrees were annually granted in the late fifteenth century. Medical degrees were scarcest of all. Leipzig granted only thirty-nine medical degrees, including ten doctorates between 1409 and 1509; all but one were conferred before 1470.[52]

Thus despite their inferior position in university processions behind the doctors of theology, law and medicine, teachers of the arts were the cornerstone of the university. None of the three higher faculties came close to matching the size of the faculty of arts. A sense of its preponderance can be gathered from fifteenth-century Cologne matriculation records: four out of five enrolling students intended to pursue studies in the arts.[53] Naturally, teachers of the arts far outnumbered the *doctores* who made up the three higher faculties. Ratios at the German universities must not have been substantially different from those at the University of Paris in 1362, when there were 63 professors of law, theology and medicine compared to 449 professors of the arts.[54] Furthermore, the arts faculty's academic role was fundamental; for material covered in the arts course served as a steppingstone for work in the

---

[52] Werner Kuhn, *Die Studenten der Universität Tübingen zwischen 1477 und 1534* (Göppingen: 1971), 60-65; Kausch, *Die Geschichte*, 124, 125; Theodor Brieger, *Die theologischen Promotionen auf der Universität Leipzig, 1428-1539* (Leipzig: 1890); Gabriel M. Löhr, *Die theologischen Disputationen und Promotionen an der Universität Köln im ausgehenden 15. Jahrhundert* (Leipzig: 1926), 15, 16; Karl Sudhoff, *Die medizinische Fakultät zu Leipzig im ersten Jahrhundert der Universität* (Leipzig: 1909), 84.

[53] Cologne was the only university that noted the student's intended area of study in the matriculation book.

[54] Heinrich Denifle, ed., *Chartularium Universitatis Parisiensis*, III (Paris: 1894), 78-92.

higher disciplines.[55] This was especially true for theology, a discipline affected in every way by the methods, conceptions and basic vocabulary of the arts course.

The arts course of the German universities was modeled on practices that evolved at Parisian schools and the University of Paris from the mid-twelfth to mid-thirteenth century.[56] This Parisian curriculum was the product first of all of a new and intense interest in logic. Logic had been largely ignored by early medieval scholars despite its theoretical equality with the other two *trivium* subjects, grammar and rhetoric. But by 1200 indifference had given way to an intense preoccupation. Enormous energy came to be devoted to the subject; syllogism, disputation, careful definition of terms, and the orderly collection of arguments became intoxicating pursuits that pervaded every discipline and affected every intellectual endeavor. The revival of logic was well under way in the late twelfth and early thirteenth centuries when a second event of momentous intellectual significance took place: the recovery for western scholars of the complete corpus of Aristotle's works. It was a sign of the time's scholarly priorities that at first Aristotle's logical treatises received most avid attention. Aristotle's philosophical and scientific treatises were not neglected, however, and by the mid-thirteenth century, these works along with traditional logic texts had become the basis of the Parisian arts course.

The scholastic curriculum at Paris continued to evolve during the fourteenth century. In particular several new logical texts by medieval scholars were introduced that more deeply explored problems raised in Aristotle or else opened up completely new areas of logical investigation. At the same time the study and teaching of grammar experienced significant

[55] The notion that the Master of Arts was a prerequisite for advanced study in the higher faculties is a widely held misconception. Theology faculties generally required it, but not the faculties of law and medicine. See Seifert, *Statuten-und Verfassungsgeschichte*, 152.

[56] Louis John Paetow, *The Arts Course at Medieval Universities with Special Reference to Grammar and Rhetoric* (Champaign, Ill.: 1910) contains much useful material.

change as the discipline lost its ties to literature and became closely bound to logic and philosophy.

Texts and teaching methods of the Parisian arts faculty served as the model for all pre-Reformation German universities. As a result, their academic practices and requirements were remarkably uniform, even for late foundations such as Wittenberg and Frankfurt. Minor differences did exist.[57] A text such as Aristotle's *Physics* might be required at one university for the bachelor's degree while reserved for master's students at another. There was also some variety in the choice of texts for teaching introductory logic. Nonetheless, such insignificant differences should not obscure the essential uniformity of arts faculty instruction among Germany's late medieval universities.

The course of studies leading to the Bachelor of Arts lasted one and a half to two years and was designed to introduce beginning students, often no more than eleven or twelve years old, to the fundamental methods and vocabulary of scholastic discourse. Logic predominated. Requirements everywhere included the so-called "Old Logic," four ancient logical treatises known in western Europe throughout the Middle Ages. Included were Aristotle's *Categories*, which dealt with the problem of classifying the various types of predicates (substance, quantity, quality, relation, place, time, situation, state, action, passion) and his *De interpretatione*, which discussed forms of opposition or contradiction in pairs of statements. Also part of the *Vetus ars* were Porphyry's *Isagoge*, a third-century commentary on the *Categories*, and various short logical works of

---

[57] Curriculum requirements for some of the German universities can be found in the following works: Cologne: Franz Josef von Bianco, *Die alte Universität Köln* (Cologne: 1856), Anlage, 59-64; Greifswald: Kosegarten, *Geschichte*, I, 309-11; Erfurt: Weissenborn, *Acten*, II, 134-44; Freiburg-im-Breisgau: Schreiber, *Geschichte*, I, 45; Vienna: Alphons Lhotsky, *Die Wiener Artistenfakultät 1365-1497* (Vienna: 1965); Heidelberg: Winkelmann, *Urkundenbuch*, I, 31-44; Leipzig: Zarncke, *Die Statutenbücher*, 314, 397, 405; Ingolstadt: Prantl, *Geschichte der Ludwig-Maximilians-Universität*, II, 49-58; Wittenberg: Theodor Muther, ed., "Die ersten Statuten der Wittenberger Artistenfakultät," *Neue Mitteilungen aus dem Gebiet historisch-antiquarischer Forschungen*, 12 (1874), 176-208.

Boethius, which were largely derivative of Aristotle. Bachelor's degree students were also expected to study the material of the *New Logic*, four Aristotelian treatises which became available to western scholars only during the twelfth century: the *Prior Analytics*, which discussed the syllogism; the *Sophistical Refutations*, which dealt with fallacies of reasoning and argumentation; the *Topics*, which offered tactical hints for the conduct of competitive arguments; and the *Posterior Analytics*, which analyzed the special requirements of demonstration. At a few universities either the *Topics* or *Posterior Analytics* was reserved for master's degree students rather than bachelor's candidates.[58]

In addition to the Aristotelian logic of the *Ars vetus* and *Ars novus*, various manuals and compendia by medieval authors were included in the curricula of the German universities. Works of Albert of Saxony, probably his *Perutilis logica*, were required at Vienna and Freiburg.[59] At Heidelberg the statutes of 1452 mandated the study of the *Tractatus dialectices* of Marsilius of Inghen, the university's first rector, while the oldest statutes of Cologne required the compendium of the fourteenth-century Parisian logician Jean Buridan, simply entitled *Summula*.[60] At Leipzig, Erfurt, and several other universities, a text referred to as the *Logica Hesbri* was required.[61] This was undoubtedly a work by William of Heytesbury, an Oxford logician (d. 1380) best known for his treatise on insolubles, entitled *Regulae solvendi sophismata*. Of all the medieval manuals, by far the most important was the *Summulae logicales* by Peter of Spain, a thirteenth-century scholar and churchman who was chosen Pope John XXI in 1276, only to die a year

[58] At Erfurt the *Topics* was a requirement for the master's degree; see Weissenborn, *Acten*, II, 138; at Ingolstadt this was the case with the *Posterior analytics*; see Prantl, *Geschichte der Ludwig-Maximilians-Universität*, 57, 58.

[59] Lhotsky, *Die Wiener Artistenfakultät*, 88, 89; Schreiber, *Geschichte*, I, 45.

[60] Ritter, *Die Heidelberger Universität*, 167, note; von Bianco, *Die alte Universität*, Anlagen, 64.

[61] Weissenborn, *Acten*, II, 134; Rudolf Helssig, "Die wissenschaftlichen Vorbedingungen für Baccalaureat in Artibus und Magisterium," *Beiträge zur Geschichte Leipziger Universität*, II (Leipzig: 1907), 57.

later when the roof of his study collapsed and crushed him while he sat at his desk.

For two hundred fifty years after Peter wrote the *Summulae logicales*, the work was unquestionably the most studied, glossed, taught, and commented upon of all scholastic writings. It was required at universities throughout northern Europe, copied repeatedly in manuscript and went through at least 160 printed editions before the Reformation.[62] Tens of thousands of boys throughout the late Middle Ages were introduced to the intellectual rigors of medieval logic when they read the famous assertion in the first line of the *Summulae* that "Dialectic is the art of arts and the science of sciences, possessing the way to the principles of all curriculum subjects."[63]

Logical compendia such as the *Summulae* gained such widespread popularity throughout the Middle Ages largely because of their pedagogical usefulness. They typically contained, first of all, a summary of the major Aristotelian logical principles. In the first part of Peter of Spain's *Summulae*, for example, Aristotle's doctrines concerning propositions, predictables, categories, syllogisms, topics, and fallacies were summarized and discussed. Such a format was also followed in the works of Peter's many imitators. One strongly supposes, in fact, that for most students "Aristotelian logic" was learned less from original texts than from the summary of some medieval compiler and commentator. Second, and more importantly, the medieval logical *summulae* provided discussions of several logical problems not touched upon in Aristotle. In these areas medieval logicians showed their greatest inventiveness, making what are now recognized by modern logicians as important contributions to the development of the discipline.

Among the most striking innovations were their discus-

---

[62] See Joseph Mullally, ed. and trans., *The Summulae Logicales of Peter of Spain* (South Bend, Ind.: 1945), 133-58; a more recent scholarly edition is L. M. de Rijk, ed. and trans. *Tractatus, Called Afterwards Summulae Logicales* (Assen: 1972); see also I. M. Bochenski, ed., *Petri Hispani Summulae Logicales* (Turin: 1947).

[63] de Rijk, ed., *Tractatus*, 1, sets forth the various versions of this opening statement.

sions of the theory of consequence or *consequentia*.[64] These speculations involved establishing rules of valid inference in hypothetical propositions of conditional form. Specifically, they involved a proposition with an "if . . . then" structure or the connection of two propositions by means of the signs *ergo* (consequently) or *igitur* (therefore). A valid formal consequence (*consequentia bona de forma*) was such not because of the meaning of the terms in it but rather because of its conformity to a general logical-grammatical rule. In other words, conditional sentences that are "logically true" on syntactical grounds are valid despite possible changes in the terms in the sentences. Authors of treatises on *consequentiae* included sets of rules on valid consequence that varied from the simple ("From truth, falsehood can never result" or "If the consequent is false, then so is the antecedent") to the complex ("The contradictory opposite of a disjunctive proposition is a copulative proposition made up of the contradictory prepositions of the parts of the disjunctive proposition").[65]

Great interest was also shown in the semantical puzzles or paradoxes known as *insolubilia* or "insolubles."[66] Peter of Spain briefly discussed these problems, and later logicians such as Buridan and Albert of Saxony wrote whole treatises on the subject. *Insolubilia* were all variations on the so-called "liar's paradox," first discussed by the Megarian logicians after the death of Aristotle: "A man says he is lying. Is what he says true or false?" Medieval logicians developed variants of great subtlety and complexity, such as "Socrates says, 'What Plato says is false,' and Plato says, 'What Socrates says is true.'

[64] For discussion of medieval speculation on *consequentiae* see Ernest A. Moody, *Truth and Consequence in Mediaeval Logic* (Westport, Conn.: 1953), esp. 64-110; William and Martha Kneale, *The Development of Logic* (Oxford: 1962), 274-97; Anton Dumitriu, *History of Logic*, II, trans. Duliu Zamfirescu, Dinu Giurcaneanu, and Doina Doneaud (Tunbridge Wells, Eng.: 1975), 151-61. Other general surveys of medieval logic are Carl von Prantl, *Geschichte der Logik im Abendlande*, IV (Leipzig: 1870) and Philotheus Boehner, *Medieval Logic* (Chicago: 1972).

[65] Quotes are from Occam's *Summa totius logicae* cited in Dumitriu, *History of Logic*, II, 156, 157.

[66] Kneale, *Development*, 227-29; Dumitriu, *History of Logic*, 162-72.

Neither says anything else. Is what Socrates says true or false?" Or "Suppose this sentence is in Socrates' mind: 'Socrates is deceived,' and none else; is Socrates when thinking this sentence truly deceived?"[67] A few logicians conceded that such insolubles were just that—insoluble; but most experts insisted that their apparent absurdity could be explained away by revealing the logical flaw or flaws in their construction. Paul of Venice, writing in the early 1400s, summarized medieval thinking on the subject when he listed fifteen solutions to the "liar's paradox" and its variations.[68]

It was partly interest in "solving" insolubles that inspired the most important innovation in medieval logic, namely the discussion of a series of problems summarized by the phrase *proprietates terminorum*, or properties of terms.[69] Interest in these problems was based on the realization, never made clear in Aristotle, that much fuzziness in thinking resulted from inattention to the shifts in meaning that terms undergo when used in different relationships as subjects or predicates in propositions. Discussion of this issue began in the late twelfth century, and by the thirteenth century a fully developed theory of the properties of terms had been developed by logicians such as William of Shyreswood, Lambert of Auxerre, and, most importantly, Peter of Spain. In fact the seventh and concluding section of Peter's *Summulae logicales*, known as the *Parva logicalia*, was exclusively devoted to this subject. Its major sections—supposition (*suppositio*), relative terms (*relata*), extension (*ampliatio*), appellation (*appellatio*), restriction (*restrictio*), and distribution (*distributio*)—all dealt with properties of what were known as categemoratic terms, nouns and verbs with definite meanings and which are the essential build-

---

[67] Cited in Dumitriu, *History of Logic*, 163.

[68] Prantl, *Geschichte der Logik*, IV, 138, 139.

[69] Kneale, *Development*, 246-73; Dumitriu, *History of Logic*, 124-50; other important discussions are Philotheus Boehner, "A Medieval Theory of Supposition," *Franciscan Studies*, 18 (1958), 240-89; L. M. de Rijk, *Logica Modernorum*, II: *The Origin and Development of the Theory of Supposition* (Assen: 1967); Jan Pinborg, *Logik und Semantik im Mittelalter. Ein Überblick* (Stuttgart: 1972).

ing blocks of propositions. A separate treatise by Peter, *Tractatus syncategorematum*, dealt with the properties of what were called syncategemoratic particles—prepositions, conjunctions, indefinite adjectives, and so forth—which have no precise independent meaning but receive a definite sense only when used with other terms in a sentence.

The *Parva logicalia*, and indeed all treatises on the properties of terms, began with a treatment of supposition, the capacity of a categorematic language sign or term to be taken or "supposed" for something when combined with other terms in a proposition. Basic to this discussion was the twofold distinction between material supposition and personal supposition. Material supposition involved the use of a word to denote itself as a word, for example, in the propositions, *homo est nomen* or *homo est disyllabum*; personal or formal supposition was the use of a word to refer to its normal referents or to things it was meant to designate, for example, in the proposition *homo currit* or *homo est albus*. Some, but not all, logicians added a third general category, simple supposition, when a word was used to represent a concept or mental sign as in the sentence, *homo est species*.[70] Within the category of personal supposition authors made various other distinctions, such as those between common and concrete supposition, determined and confused supposition, real and logical, natural and accidental, and distributive and collective. To give one example of the kinds of distinctions made, in distributive supposition a term stands for each of its inferior terms; thus in the sentence, *sacramenta conferunt gratiam*, the term *sacramenta* connotes that each of the sacraments confers grace. But supposition is collective when a term stands for all its inferior terms taken together, for example *sacramenta* (all taken together) *sunt septem*.

Although medieval logicians devoted most of their intellectual energy to supposition theory, other aspects of the prop-

---

[70] "Simple supposition" was a subject of some controversy since it raised the issue of the nature of universals. See Moody, *Truth and Consequence*, 24, 25.

erties of terms were also investigated and discussed. *Ampliatio* meant the "extension" of a term to things past, present, future, possible, or imagined when it was used with certain verb tenses or with verbs such as "can be" or "is imagined to be." A verb of the past tense, for example, "ampliates" a term so it refers to something that is or was. This was used to justify such sophisms as "A Virgin was a mother"; in other words, "She who is or was a virgin was a mother."[71] *Restrictio*, on the other hand, limited the reference of the term by combining it with an adjective (so that in *homo albus, homo* refers only to white men), a verb (in *homo currit, homo* refers only to those who run) or a participle and verb (in *homo currens disputat, homo* refers only to running men who are disputing). *Appellatio* indicated the instance when a term denoted some actually existing object or person; for example in the sentence *Cicero est magnus orator, orator* specifically refers to Cicero in his capacity as orator. *Distributio* referred to the connotation of a term when used in connection with one of the universal modifiers such as *omnis, totus, nullus, qualiscumque, quantuscumque,* and the like. This aspect of the properties of terms was sometimes discussed in treatises on the syncategorematic particles; so too were problems concerning the use of terms with modifiers such as *uterque*, or in sentences with words such as *praeter* (except), *necessario* (necessarily), *nisi* (except) and other such prepositions, adverbs, and conjunctions.

These rigorous and complex logical doctrines provided the focus of studies for beginning university students throughout the scholastic era. Later this approach to logic became an object of scorn and derision for the humanists, who singled out Peter of Spain and the *proprietates terminorum* for particularly vociferous abuse.[72] Even for more objective modern

[71] This example is cited in E. J. Ashworth, *Language and Logic in the Post-Medieval Period* (Dordrecht, Holland: 1974), 90.

[72] Walter J. Ong has written, "When the humanists, particularly those of northern Europe, descend to particulars in their recriminations against scholastics, there is no name they cite with such regularity and cold fury as that of Peter of Spain. He represents the point from which there is no return." *Ramus, Method and the Decay of Dialogue* (Cambridge, Mass.: 1958), 57.

scholars, the tendency has been to respect the technical brilliance of the medieval logicians while wondering if in the end the great exertion of intellectual energy was worth the effort. What drove the scholastic logicians to the "subtleties" and "fine distinctions" that seemed so bizarre and repugnant to the humanists was their ambition to achieve scientific certainty in logical discourse. Such a goal is difficult in any case, but was especially challenging for the medieval logicians, who were using a natural language, Latin, rather than some form of symbolic or artificial language, as is the case among logicians today. For Latin, like all natural languages, contained a wealth of grammatical, syntactical and definitional ambiguities that frustrated the logical precision that the scholastics prized. They attempted to resolve these ambiguities through supposition theory and other concepts relating to the "properties of terms." To their credit, the medieval logicians went far in achieving their goal of certitude and exactness. But they did so only by creating a logic of such daunting complexity that it ultimately had little applicability to most forms of philosophical and theological discourse.

In comparison to logic, grammar received little attention at the universities of medieval Germany.[73] It was assumed that all students on matriculation had already received sufficient Latin training to enable them to follow lectures and read basic texts. For these students the universities required only one or at most two further grammar courses for the Bachelor of Arts degree. At Vienna, Ingolstadt, and Heidelberg even this minimal requirement could be waived if the student showed sufficient expertise.[74] In practice, however, many new students lacked the Latin skills necessary to participate fully in the university's academic life. For them the universities pro-

---

[73] On medieval grammar, see in addition to Paetow, *The Arts Course* . . . , J. J. Baebler, *Beiträge zur Geschichte der Lateinischen Grammatik im Mittelalter* (Halle: 1885) and the introduction of Dietrich Reichling, *Das Doctrinale des Alexander de Villa-Dei* (Berlin: 1893).

[74] Lhotsky, *Die Wiener Artistenfakultät* . . . , 236; Prantl, *Geschichte der Ludwig-Maximilians-Universität* . . . , II, 50; Winkelmann, *Urkundenbuch*, I, 34.

vided rudimentary grammar instruction, often in a special *bursa* or *pedagogium* reserved for beginning students.

Whether late medieval students learned their grammar in a local school or at a university, they studied a number of standard texts, taught according to similar methods. The two most popular texts were the *Institutionum grammaticarum libri XVIII* of Priscian, written around A.D. 500, and the *Doctrinale* of Alexander Villedieu, written in 1199. As originally written, Priscian's grammar showed a deep awareness of Rome's literary greatness. His approach was to expound systematically the rules of Latin grammar and to illustrate them through citations from the best Roman authors. By drawing students to the study and imitation of such authors, he hoped to preserve the purity of "classical" Latin in the face of deteriorating standards. Alexander, on the other hand, had little feeling for Rome's literary heritage and was writing for an audience whose native language was not Latin. Thus his grammar was briefer, largely lacking in classical citations, and written in hexameter verse to aid memorization. One also sees in Alexander a comparatively greater interest in the philosophical analysis of grammatical rules. Although other grammar texts, most notably the fourth-century *Ars grammatica* of Donatus, were occasionally mentioned in school and university records, Priscian and Alexander dominated the discipline. The historian of linguistics, Robert H. Robins, estimates one thousand extant medieval manuscripts of Priscian, while another scholar, Dietrich Reichling, writing in 1893, was able to list 279 printed editions of the *Doctrinale*, 163 of which appeared before 1500.[75]

By the late Middle Ages, however, few students studied the texts as they had been originally written by Priscian and Alexander. Instead students were almost universally offered medieval commentaries or *summulae*, which typically included only portions of the original versions. Furthermore, these commentaries reflected the tendency, hinted at in Alexander's

---

[75] Robert H. Robins, *Ancient and Medieval Grammatical Theory in Europe* (London: 1951), 63; Reichling, *Das Doctrinale*, XLIV.

Doctrinale, to loosen grammar's ties to literature and bind it even more tightly to philosophy and logic. This approach to grammar, which was to dominate the discipline until the early sixteenth century, was based on the conviction that it was insufficient for a grammarian simply to describe the various word classes, categories, and rules and, in Priscian's case, to illustrate them with examples from ancient authors. Instead, if grammar was to be a true science, it must provide a theoretical underpinning for grammatical constructs. Such a goal reflected the thirteenth century's enthusiasm for Greek philosophy and especially the concerns of contemporary logicians. By the thirteenth century logic had become an increasingly broad discipline that considered many issues that today are discussed as part of the philosophy of language: the nature of language signs, types of terms, the nature of propositions, and theories of meaning and reference. Thus there emerged in the course of the thirteenth century a group of grammarian-philosophers who systematically set forth a grammatical statement embodying the principles of Aristotelian philosophy and the medieval logic of language. Among the most prominent were Martin of Dacia, Boethius of Dacia, Siger de Courtrai, and Thomas of Erfurt. They are commonly referred to as speculative grammarians or *modistae*, after the title they gave to many of their works, *Summa modorum significandi* or *Treatise on the Modes of Signifying*.

The doctrines of the speculative grammarians are not amenable to brief summation. Even distinguished Robert H. Robins has conceded, "the theory of the speculative grammarians involves a good deal of new technical terminology, and in detail its exposition is a formidable task.[76] The basic convic-

---

[76] Robert H. Robins, *A Short History of Linguistics* (Bloomington, Ind.: 1967), 78; see also the discussion in G. L. Bursill-Hall, *Speculative Grammars of the Middle Ages. The Doctrine of Partes Orationis of the Modistae* (The Hague: 1971), 46–65; Martin Grabmann, "Die Entwicklung der mittelalterlichen Sprachlogik," *Philosophisches Jahrbuch der Görresgesellschaft*, 35 (1922), 122–35, 199–214; Jan Pinborg, *Die Entwicklung der Sprachtheorie im Mittelalter. Beiträge zur Geschichte der Philosophie und Theologie des Mittelalters*, 42, Heft 2 (Münster/Copenhagen: 1967); also by Pinborg, *Logik und Semantik im Mittelalter—Ein*

tion of the *modistae* was that the rules of grammar were not the result of customs, traditions or historical accidents which might cause them to differ over time or from one language to another. Instead grammatical rules were thought to be unchanging and eternal, equally applicable to all languages in all stages of development. This was so because they were founded on universal extra-linguistic premises, namely the nature of reality and the conceptualization of that reality by the human mind. Languages might differ in vocabularly but not in their basic structure. As one anonymous medieval grammarian stated it, "He that understands grammar in one language understands it in another, as far as are concerned the essential properties of grammar. The fact that he cannot speak or comprehend another language is due to the diversity of words and their different forms, but these are the accidental properties of grammar."[77]

Since it was philosophy's task to investigate reality and the workings of the mind, grammar came within its purview and became subject to the strict canons of logical analysis. Gerhard of Zütphen, the University of Cologne professor who wrote a lengthy and popular commentary on the *Doctrinale* published in 1488, wrote: "Who was the first inventor of grammar? The first inventor of positive grammar was a metaphysician and natural philosopher, because considering the diverse properties, nature and modes of being of things, he imposed on these things diverse names.[78]

The most influential and imitated modistic treatise was the *Grammatica speculativa* of Thomas of Erfurt, written between 1300 and 1310.[79] A brief summary provides a sense of the grammatical issues the *modistae* considered. In the first several

---

Überblick (Stuttgart: 1972) and his brief summary, "Speculative Grammar," in Norman Kretzman, Anthony Kenny, and Jan Pinborg, eds., *The Cambridge History of Later Medieval Philosophy* (Cambridge: 1982), 254-70.

[77] Cited in Robins, *Ancient and Medieval Grammatical Theory*, 79.

[78] Cited in Reichling, ed., *Das Doctrinale*, XI.

[79] Modern editions are *De Modis Significandi sive Grammatica speculativa*, ed. M. Fernandez Garcia (Florence: 1902) and *Grammatica Speculativa of Thomas of Erfurt*, ed. and trans. G. L. Bursill-Hall (London: 1977).

chapters, Thomas outlined his theory of grammatical usage. He described how the various properties of being (*modi essendi*) are apprehended by the mind (*modi intelligendi*), which then imposes on vocal sounds (*voces*) modes of signifying (*modi significandi*) through which these sounds become words and parts of speech capable of expressing complex mental concepts. The *modi significandi* provide the key to his grammatical theory: every part of speech differs from the others because it represents reality through a particular "mode" or point of view. An adverb, for example, simply defined by Priscian as "an indeclinable part of speech by which meaning is added to a verb," is defined by Thomas as "the mode of signifying by means of the mode of adjacency by means of the mode of being, signifying it simply and determining it in absolute terms."[80] A verb, to Priscian a "part of speech with tense and mood, without case inflection signifying action or being acted upon," is according to Thomas, "the mode of signifying the thing by means of the mode of being and separation from its substance."[81] The treatise then analyzed each of the parts of speech in terms of its "essential" and "accidental" modes; in the case of the noun these are type, gender, number, form, person, and case. It concluded with a brief section on syntax, to Thomas, "nothing more than applying the *modi significandi* to construction, congruity, and completion, by showing which modes of signifying are the principles of which constructions, their congruity, and their completion."[82]

Later grammarians added little to the doctrines of Thomas and other thirteenth-century *modistae*. But the speculative approach continued to dominate the fourteenth- and fifteenth-century commentaries on the *Doctrinale* and Priscian's *Institutes*. Gerhard of Zütphen's *Glossa notabilis* on the *Doctrinale*, published in 1488 and reprinted sixty times through the 1520s,

[80] Robins, *Ancient and Medieval*, 66; *Grammatica speculativa*, ed. Bursill-Hall, 247.

[81] Robins, *Ancient and Medieval*, 65; *Grammatica speculativa*, ed. Bursill-Hall, 208-209.

[82] *Grammatica speculativa*, ed. Bursill-Hall, 273.

39

is a prime example of this logico-philosophical approach.[83] Literary citations are lacking altogether; examples of word use and sentence form resemble the simple phrases used by Thomas and other *modistae: Homo albus currit bene, Socrates legit bene,* or *Ego sum.* Its over-four hundred pages are crammed with arguments and speculations on logical and philosophical subjects seemingly misplaced in a work whose apparent purpose was the teaching of Latin grammar. But then teaching grammar was not the author's primary goal. Instead he meant to provide an introduction to the basic definitions, concepts and ways of argument that the beginning student could apply to his study of logic and Aristotelian philosophy.

While grammar's purposes were redirected to meet the needs of a philosophically oriented educational program, the third element of the *trivium,* rhetoric, was virtually abandoned. The statutes of Freiburg, Heidelberg, and Cologne contained no rhetoric requirement whatsoever.[84] At Vienna and Ingolstadt students seeking their bachelor's degree were required to have heard one lecture series on an unspecified book of rhetoric.[85] The Greifswald and Erfurt statutes were exceptional in that they specifically mentioned the *Laborintus,* a thirteenth-century versified work by Eberhard the German that dealt with versification and style.[86] One can surmise that elsewhere the *Laborintus* or some similar medieval work was utilized. In the 1390s for example, a Viennese master lectured on the *Poetria nova* of Geoffrey of Vinsauf, a thirteenth-century Englishman; this treatise dealt with various aspects of composition, including memory and delivery. In the early 1400s the Viennese

---

[83] See the discussion in Reichling, *Das Doctrinale,* LXIV, LXV; and Terrence Heath, "Logical Grammar, Grammatical Logic and Humanism at Three German Universities," *Studies in the Renaissance,* 17 (1971), 9-65, esp. 10-15.

[84] Schreiber, *Geschichte,* I, 45; Winkelmann, *Urkundenbuch,* 34; von Bianco, *Die alte Universität,* Anlage 64.

[85] Lhotsky, *Die Wiener Artistenfakultät,* 236; Prantl, *Geschichte der Ludwig-Maximilians-Universität,* I, 57, 58.

[86] Kosegarten, *Geschichte,* I, 309; Weissenborn, *Acten,* II, 134; Ebehard the German should not be confused with Eberhard of Bethune, the author of the grammar manual, *Grecismus.* See James J. Murphy, *Rhetoric in the Middle Ages* (Berkeley: 1974), 180-82, for a brief summary of the *Laborintus.*

library also contained several other medieval rhetorical works: *De equivocis et synonymis poeticis*, ascribed to the thirteenth-century Frenchman John of Garland, and two anonymous treatises, the *Summaria primaria*, on verse making, and the *Tractaus de arte sermocinandi*, on ceremonial speech making. But nowhere were rhetorical studies taken seriously. At Vienna rhetoric was classed with grammar as a subject the student could avoid if he had studied it before coming to the university.[87] Elsewhere the rhetoric "requirement" seems not to have been strictly enforced. When in 1420 an Erfurt scholar composed a list of the twenty-two books he had studied in preparation for his bachelor's examination, he listed seventeen texts on logic but none on rhetoric.[88]

In addition to initiating the student in linguistical studies, especially logic, the other major goal of the arts course was to introduce the remaining works of Aristotle. At most German universities this began with bachelor's candidates, who were required to have studied the *Physics*. Erfurt statutes also required *De anima*, but this was an exception. For the most part Aristotle's non-logical works were reserved for students preparing for their master's degree. In addition to the *Physics* and *De anima*, they included the *De generatione et corruptione*, *De caelo et mundo*, *De metorica*, the *Politics*, *Economics*, *Ethics*, *Metaphysics*, and the group of minor treatises known as the *Parva naturalia* (the books of *De sensu et sensato*, *De somno et vigilia*, *De memoria et reminiscentia*, *De longitudine et brevitate vitae*). Of all the Aristotelian texts, only *De animalibus* was not regularly mentioned in statutes or lecture lists.

Of these works, the *Physics* seems to have been the most intensively studied. At Erfurt only lectures on this text and the *Ethics* were to last eight months.[89] In contrast, six months were to be accorded to the *Politics* and *Metaphysics*, four months

[87] Lhotsky, *Die Wiener Artistenfakultät*, 73-75.

[88] "Texts Required for A.B. Degree at Erfurt, 1420," in Lynn Thorndike, ed., *University Records and Life in the Middle Ages* (New York: 1944), 296, 297.

[89] Weissenborn, *Acten*, II, 134.

to *De generatione et corruptione* and *De caelo et mundo*, two months to the *Parva naturalia* and one to the *Economics*. The interest in the *Physics* also is confirmed by an arts faculty document from Vienna in 1391 that listed the teaching preferences of seventeen masters for the fall semester: nine requested to lecture on logical texts, four on the *Physics*, two on the *Parva naturalia*, but only one each for the *Ethics* and *Metaphysics*.[90] The reluctance of the Viennese masters to tackle the *Ethics* and *Metaphysics* seems to have been common in the late medieval German universities. Heidelberg records show that throughout the fifteenth century the university had difficulty finding lecturers for these two subjects.[91] And at Leipzig the number of months spent by masters degree recipients on the *Ethics* and *Metaphysics* regularly fell short of the time suggested in university statutes.[92] Several scholars have suggested that arts masters avoided these two important Aristotelian texts because there was little they could say about them without becoming embroiled in potentially controversial theological issues.[93] Economics might also have played a role, however: certainly student fees would be lower in courses required only for the relatively small numbers of masters students.

The last general area of requirements encompassed the traditional *quadrivium* subjects—arithmetic, geometry, astronomy, and music. The first six books of Euclid's *Geometry* were universally required for the geometry course, often in conjunction with the *Perspectiva communis* of the Englishman John of Peacham. And the *De sphaera* of another Englishman, John of Holywood, was a frequently required text for astronomy. Specific texts were rarely mentioned for arithmetic or music.

Of all "requirements," the *quadrivium* subjects received least

[90] Kink, *Geschichte*, I, Part 2, 10-12.
[91] Gerhard Ritter, *Studien zur Spätscholastik* (Heidelberg: 1922), II, 97.
[92] Helssig, "Die wissenschaftlichen Vorbedingungen . . . ," 58-62.
[93] See the discussion in Ong, *Ramus, Method and the Decay of Dialogue*, 135-49.

attention and emphasis. The failure of so many university statutes even to name texts for these disciplines is in itself a sign of indifference. Other evidence is more explicit. Two additions to the Ingolstadt statutes in the 1470s exempted all masters candidates from geometry, arithmetic, astronomy, and music along with the "more advanced" books of the *Topics* and exercises on the *Ethics*.[94] And at Erfurt, with the exception of Euclid's *Geometry*, which was to be studied six months, the mandated length of time for the other *quadrivium* subjects was but one month.[95] At Leipzig, the astronomical and mathematical lectures had been virtually abandoned by the late fifteenth century. Governmental reformers appointed by Duke George of Saxony in 1496 complained that mathematics was rarely taught and urged the university to institute courses on "the more useful mathematics books, Euclid, *Perspectiva communis* and the like."[96] These "rarely taught" texts had been formally required at Leipzig since the university's foundation in 1406.

In reviewing the arts course of the late medieval German universities, it is difficult to exaggerate the preeminence of logic. Its importance can be measured not only in terms of its preponderant role in the curriculum but also in terms of its pervasive influence on teaching and learning in other subject areas. As Peter of Spain had stated at the beginning of his seminal treatise, logic was indeed "the art of arts and the science of sciences, possessing the way to the principles of all curriculum subjects." Properly understood and applied, logic was utilized to resolve apparent contradictions and ambiguities in fields as diverse as grammar, ethics, and physics. More importantly, finely honed logical skills were necessary to defend one's philosophical positions against potential and actual intellectual opponents. Nowhere was this more important than in university disputations, where two or more bachelors or masters formally and publicly debated controversial phil-

---

[94] Prantl, *Geschichte der Ludwig-Maximilians-Universität*, II, 50, 75.
[95] Weissenborn, *Acten*, II, 134.
[96] Zarncke, *Die Statutenbücher*, 16-27.

osophical or scientific questions. For a participant in these scholarly combats there was no greater triumph than to humble an opponent by revealing the semantic and syllogistic flaws in his chain of argument. Nor could there have been a more gruesome academic nightmare than the prospect of standing tongue-tied and confused before a clever disputant who had just laid bare to a gathered crowd of masters and students one's inferior logical skills. To be a "scholastic" was first and foremost to be a logician. Theology might be the "queen of the sciences," but even she was lorded over by logic, the "empress" of all things knowable.[97]

The rare student who sought advanced theological training faced, like students of the arts, a curriculum that was modeled on Parisian practices and varied little from university to university.[98] After having received his Master of Arts, he spent his first five or six years as a simple *auditor*, attending disputations and hearing lectures on the only two required theological texts, the Bible and the *Sentences* of Peter Lombard. Lombard's work, the standard theological treatise throughout the Middle Ages, dated from around 1150 and was a compilation of opinions from a wide variety of authorities on four general areas: God as Unity and Trinity; Creation and Sin; Redemption; the Sacraments and Human Beatitude. Having completed his years as an auditor, the student became eligible for the Bachelor of Theology degree. No formal test or public disputation was required. Instead the student was recommended by a master or dean to a gathering of the faculty, which then decided if the degree should be conferred.

The new Bachelor of Theology was known as a *Cursor* or *Biblicus*, for in addition to attending the lectures of the doctors, he was required to lecture regularly on the Bible for two years to beginning students. The books were assigned by the faculty

[97] Logic was accorded the title *"benevola imperatrix"* by the philosopher and theologian Jodocus Trutvetter, one of Luther's teachers at Erfurt. See his *Breviarium Dialecticum* (Erfurt: 1500), B i a.

[98] On Parisian theological studies, see Rashdall, *The Universities of Europe*, I, 471-96.

and theoretically were rotated so that none could be repeated before all others had been read. This provision, however, was routinely ignored; at Ingolstadt, for example, the Psalms and the four gospels received almost continuous attention while other books were neglected year after year.[99] The goal of the lectures was simply to acquaint beginning students with the Bible. Thus long excursions into metaphysics or dogma were discouraged. At Freiburg bachelors were warned to stick to the text and the "more notable glosses," while completely omitting "superfluous glosses concerning logic and physics.[100] At Erfurt the statutes allowed lecturers "if they wish to raise and solve literal doubts compendiously and briefly."[101] Thus these "cursory" lectures must have been brief indeed—little more than a reading of the text while listeners followed their own copies and made corrections. In fact George Eisenhart, an Ingolstadt bachelor, managed to cover the whole book of *Isaiah* in the remarkably short time of two and a half weeks in the fall of 1481.[102]

On completion of his biblical lectures, the student then devoted one year of intensive study to the *Sentences*. Then after having received faculty approval, he became a *sententiarius* and lectured on the *Sentences* for the next two years. These lectures had the same goal as those on the Bible—to introduce beginning students to Lombard's text. In two years all four books of Lombard had to be read; this meant that one distinction (a group of two to ten questions on a given topic) had to be covered in every lecture. This too left no time for extensive comment and interpretation, although statutes generally were less restrictive about avoiding "superfluous questions." Those of Cologne warned the bachelors to "read the text faithfully and not take it upon themselves to propound suspect doctrines," while those of Erfurt required them to

[99] Winifred Kausch, *Die Geschichte,* 74.

[100] J. König, ed., "Statuta facultatis Theologice Catholici studii Friburgensis," *Freiburger diözesan-archiv,* 21 (1890), 13.

[101] Weissenborn, *Acten,* II, 55.

[102] Kausch, *Die Geschichte,* 75.

read the text "word for word" and expound "only when the passage was difficult."[103]

Once the lectures on the *Sentences* were completed, two more years of study were required to prepare for the licentiate; the student was expected to attend lectures, participate in disputations, and perhaps deliver a number of sermons. An examination for the licentiate was required at Ingolstadt, Vienna, and Erfurt but none at Cologne, Leipzig, Tübingen, and Heidelberg.[104] Licentiates had for all intents and purposes completed their theological training. All that remained were several festive and largely ceremonial disputations. Once completed the licentiate became a Doctor of Theology and thereby reached the pinnacle of medieval academic achievement.

Late scholastic theology has attracted little scholarly interest and almost no admirers. To most medievalists the great age of scholastic theology ended with Occam's criticism of Aquinas and Scotus in the first half of the fourteenth century. Thereafter nothing original was accomplished. In the words of Etienne Gilson, "intellectual life was as intense as it had ever been, but it was degenerating into a mere commentary on what had been created before."[105] Students of the Renaissance and the Reformation, on the other hand, have tended to follow uncritically the humanists and reformers in their attacks on the theologians for neglecting the Bible and miring themselves in "superfluous questions" and "useless controversies." Heiko Oberman, the eminent historian of pre-Reformation thought, is an exception when he rejects the stereotype of decay and finds in the career of Gabriel Biel, "not the barren wastelands of sterile debates, but a richness of deep pastoral and searching theological concern."[106]

---

[103] von Bianco, *Die alte Universität*, Anlage, 39; Weissenborn, *Acten*, II, 56.

[104] Kaufmann, *Geschichte*, II, 278, 279.

[105] Etienne Gilson, *History of Christian Philosophy in the Middle Ages* (London: 1955), 533.

[106] Heiko Oberman, *The Harvest of Medieval Theology* (Cambridge, Mass.: 1963), 5. On the varied accomplishments of Parisian theologians, see the invaluable work, James Farge, *Biographical Register of Paris Doctors of Theology, 1500 to 1536* (Toronto: 1980).

Biel was not unique. One could point to any number of intelligent, competent, and committed theologians who were actively teaching in Germany in the late fifteenth and early sixteenth centuries. Conrad Summenhart, a colleague of Biel's at Tübingen, Conrad Wimpina at Leipzig and Frankfurt an der Oder, Johannes Eck at Ingolstadt, Jacob Trutvetter at Erfurt, and Jacob von Hochstraten at Cologne all were prolific authors and formidable intellectuals who produced theological works, teaching manuals, and commentaries on a diversity of contemporary issues, among them usury, capital punishment, and witchcraft. Certainly their careers all belie Luther's complaint in the *Address to the Christian Nobility* that "Our worthy theologians have ceased from worrying and working."[107]

It also is clear, however, that many criticisms of late scholastic theology were justified. Biblical studies, for example, received comparatively little emphasis. As noted, the biblical lectures of the bachelors were brief and superficial. Although no German university permitted bachelors to bypass them (as had been the case at Paris since 1387),[108] they could be presented while *in absentia* from the university itself. Bachelors at Ingolstadt routinely fulfilled their requirements by lecturing on the Scriptures at monasteries or parish churches where they were serving as curates.[109] Doctors of Theology had a choice whether to lecture on the Bible or the *Sentences*. Books and manuscripts from the pre-Reformation period show a clear preference for the *Sentences*. So, too, do extant lecture schedules. A document from Frankfurt an der Oder, which listed the topics for theological lectures in the early sixteenth century, reveals the imbalance between Lombard and the Bible. Six lectures dealt specifically with subjects related to the *Sentences*. Each of the four books received separate treatment; in addition Gerhard Funck lectured on Scotus's commentary on Book I, and George Volprecht lectured on Bonaventure's

---

[107] Martin Luther, *Selections*, ed. John Dillenberger (New York: 1961), 473.
[108] Denifle, ed., *Chartularium Universitatis Parisiensis*, III, 441, 442. Denifle comments, "Lectura bibliae in oblivionem venit" (II, 704, note 24).
[109] Kausch, *Die Geschichte*, 76, 77.

commentary on Book II. The final three lectures were based on Aquinas's writings on the subjects of good and evil, the trinity, and the power of God.[110] Of the nine lectures none was devoted to the Scriptures.

When doctors did turn to the Scriptures, their lectures often turned out to be wide-ranging discussions of all kinds of questions, many of which had no obvious relevance to the text. We know, for example, that Henry of Langenstein, the leading theologian at the University of Vienna in its early years, utilized his biblical lectures as a starting point for lengthy expositions on astronomy and cosmology. As a result, in thirteen years of teaching he managed to complete only three or four chapters of *Genesis*.[111] At the end of the fifteenth century at Ingolstadt, George Zingel took four years to lecture on *Ecclesiastes* and seventeen years to complete his lectures on *Hebrews*.[112] The most extreme example was related by Aeneas Sylvius, the Italian humanist and future pope who resided at Vienna during the 1450s. He claimed to have known a Viennese theologian, Thomas of Hasselbach, who had lectured on *Isaiah* for twenty-two years and still had not completed the first chapter.[113]

Extensive commentary was not the only reason for the tortoise-like pace of the theological doctors. Infrequency of lectures was a more important cause. The provision at several German universities that at least one doctoral lecture be presented every day must have been one of the most widely flaunted statutes. Doctors of theology, as men of high standing and prestige, often absented themselves from the university for months or even years at a time to conduct business connected with their religious order, the administration of the Church, or a princely government. They also received salaries

---

[110] Gustav Bauch, ed., *Acten und Urkunden der Universität Frankfurt a. O.*, VI (Breslau: 1906), 34.

[111] Ritter, *Die Heidelberger Universität*, 214.

[112] Kausch, *Die Geschichte*, 56.

[113] Aeneas Sylvius Piccolomini, *Ausgewählte Texte*, ed. Bertha Widmer (Basel: 1960), 279.

or held benefices, income which was assured no matter how much (or little) they taught. At Paris affairs had reached a point where a 1452 statute required that doctors lecture at least once every two or three weeks.[114] By the early 1500s, however, most lectured only once a year![115] German sources contain references to nothing so extreme, but nonetheless lackadasical teaching by salaried doctors was a universally recognized problem. Reformers at Ingolstadt demanded in 1497 that delinquent doctors lose a percentage of their salary, and ten years later the Bavarian government passed a series of edicts intended to insure that all doctors lectured "with diligence."[116] The clearest evidence of negligence among doctors of theology comes from the University of Leipzig in the early 1500s. Students bitterly complained to the government of Ducal Saxony about the paucity of theological lectures and the long absences of the doctors of theology. Theology, said one, grew at Leipzig "like grass in winter," while another claimed that lectures were so few he would need "the years of Methusela" to complete his degree requirements.[117]

THE *Wegestreit*

No account of late medieval German academic life would be complete without mention of the famous *Wegestreit*—the divisive conflict between the proponents of the *via moderna* and *via antiqua*, which touched every German university in the second half of the fifteenth century.[118] The roots of this con-

---

[114] Charles Thurot, *De l'organization de l'enseignement dans l'université de Paris au moyen-âge* (Paris: 1850), 159.

[115] Rashdall, *The Universities of Europe*, I, 473.

[116] Arno Seifert, ed., *Die Universität Ingolstadt im 15. und 16. Jahrhundert. Texte und Regesten* (Berlin: 1973), 41, 42, 61, 62.

[117] Wilhelm Bruchmüller, *Beiträge zur Geschichte der Universität Leipzig und Wittenberg* (Leipzig: 1898), 6; see also the discussion in Chapter VI.

[118] On the conflict of the *viae* in Germany, the following works are most useful: Gerhard Ritter, *Studien zur Spätscholastik*, Part II, "*Via antiqua* und *via moderna* auf den deutschen Universitäten des XV Jahrhunderts"; Franz Ehrle, *Der Sentenzenkommentar Peters von Candia* in *Franzikanische Studien*, Beiheft

troversy can be traced back to the fourteenth century, when most prominent scholastics rejected the philosophical and theological doctrines of the great thirteenth-century masters— Albertus Magnus, Aquinas, Bonaventure, and Scotus. William of Occam was by far the most important of these critics; after his death in 1350, his ideas gained a wide following at Oxford, Paris, and the other universities of northern Europe. Among his leading followers were John Buridan (d. 1366?), Adam Wodham (d. 1349), Albert of Saxony (d. 1390), Gregory of Rimini (d. 1348), Henry of Langenstein (d. 1398), Pierre d'Ailly (d. 1420), and William of Heytesbury (d. 1380). During the 1400s Occam's disciples came to be known as the upholders of the *via moderna*; those who followed Aquinas and Albertus Magnus were identified as proponents of the *via antiqua*.[119] So designated, the two groups were intellectual and academic rivals for the rest of the scholastic age.

Much about the conflict remains mysterious to the historian. Why, for example, did it become so acrimonious at an institution like Ingolstadt while at Leipzig it caused only the slightest flurry? More basically, what real differences divided the two *viae*? How did one's affiliation to one faction or the other affect the way he taught or approached a problem of philosophy or theology?

Certainly there remains a good deal of validity to the traditional view that disagreement over the question of universals was at the root of the controversy. Disciples of the *via moderna* followed Occam in rejecting the position of Aquinas and other thirteenth-century realists that universals had any existence

---

9 (Münster: 1925); Friedrich Benary, *Zur Geschichte der Stadt und Universität Erfurt am Ausgang des Mittelalter*, Part III, *"Via antiqua und via moderna auf den deutschen Hochschulen mit besonderer Berücksichtigung der Universität Erfurt"* (Gotha: 1919), 1-72; Astrik L. Gabriel, *"Via antiqua and via moderna* and the Migration of Paris Students and Masters to the German Universities in the Fifteenth Century," in *Antiqui und Moderni. Traditionsbewusstein und Fortschrittsbewusstein im späten Mittelalter*, ed. Albert Zimmermann (Berlin: 1974), 439-83.

[119] Neal Ward Gilbert has recently traced the origins of these two terms: "Ockham, Wyclif and the *Via Moderna*," in *Antiqui und Moderni*, ed. Zimmerman, 86-125.

outside the mind; universals, they argued, were mere names, and reality was to be found in particulars or individual entities rather than common natures. That contemporaries viewed positions on universals as a basic difference between the two groups is strongly confirmed by their practice of frequently referring to the two *viae* as the *via realium* and the *via nominalium*.

But aside from this basic philosophical disagreement, other differences also separated the two groups. Gerhard Ritter has convincingly argued that the *moderni* were more likely to lecture and teach according to the so-called *modus quaestiones*. In this approach, relatively little attention was paid to the Aristotelian text; instead the lecturer raised a number of "questions" from the text, expounded the views of other authorities and then solved the problem through logical analysis. The *antiqui*, on the other hand, preferred the *modus expositionis*, in which the lecturer adhered more closely to the text, reading it, commenting upon it, and only at the end briefly answering a few questions of his own choosing. Evidence to support Ritter's position can be found in a speech delivered by Stephan Hoest, vice chancellor of the University of Heidelberg, to graduates in the *via antiqua* in 1468. One of his major points was that close adherence to the text was the great strength of the *antiqui*. He argued that students learned more effectively when the meaning of a text was not obliterated by the complex questions raised by the *moderni*. Their "verbose questions and commentaries," he argued, might appear subtle, but actually dealt with "superficial things more pedantic than ingenious." As a result, their students "wore out their minds" on empty words and "became babblers rather than learned men." The *antiqui*, on the other hand, "treat in the text matters that are useful and relevant, avoiding what is superfluous and profitless."[120]

Other scholars, most notably Carl von Prantl, have argued

[120] Stephan Hoest, "Licencia pro via antiqua" in *Reden und Briefe*, ed. Frank Baron (Munich: 1971), 152-54.

that the dispute was rooted in contrasting approaches to logic.[121] The *moderni*, he suggested, enthusiastically continued to embrace the methods and insights of the thirteenth- and fourteenth-century logicians who developed techniques related to "insolubles," the theory of consequence, and especially the properties of terms. Thus the *moderni* tended to believe that theological and philosophical discourse could be reduced to problems about the meaning and reference of terms and the truth conditions of sentences. The *antiqui*, he argued, rejected terminist logic because it prompted consideration of too many "superfluous questions." They called for a return to what they considered to be a purer Aristotelian logic pruned of thirteenth- and fourteenth-century accretions. Prantl argued further that such a logic provided a bridge to the "real" disciplines of metaphysics, ethics, and physics, subjects the nominalists generally ignored. According to Prantl, the proponents of the *via antiqua* were known as "realists" not so much because of their position on universals, but because they cultivated the *scientiae reales* in contrast to the purely linguistical studies (*scientiae sermonicales*) of the *via moderna*.

Although Prantl exaggerated the differences between the *viae* concerning their relative emphasis on the so-called "real disciplines,"[122] he seems to have built a strong case concerning the importance of logical disagreements. At the University of Paris in 1474, for example, the *moderni*, in response to Louis XI's ban on nominalist teaching, claimed that their major strength was the stress they placed on the "*proprietates terminorum, obligationes,* and *insolubilia*"; unlike the *realistae*, they viewed these "as indispensable aids in the determination of truth and valid argument."[123] Furthermore, in Parisian and German student slang the *moderni* were often referred to as *terministae*, suggesting their preoccupation with logical stud-

[121] Prantl, *Geschichte der Logik*, IV, 184-94, esp. 193.

[122] The flaws of this argument are pointed out in Ritter, *Studien zur Spätscholastik*, II, 88-94.

[123] Ehrle, *Der Sentenzenkommentar*, 324.

ies, especially the properties of terms.[124] An interesting series of documents from late fifteenth-century Ingolstadt also confirms the importance of logical differences between the *viae*. One document is a defense of the *antiqui* (an embattled minority at Ingolstadt) that asserted their superiority because of their closer reliance on Aristotle. Their opponents, so they claimed, rejected Aristotle or twisted his meaning, especially in logic, where they have a "mode of discourse entirely contrary to Aristotle and the doctrine of the realists." The author continued, "The realists and nominalists or *moderni* most disagree concerning the treatise of suppositions, restrictions, ampliations and appellations . . . the nominalists in fact set forth different divisions and especially suppositions, which the realists do not approve, but reject as superfluous; and without making use of them they still deal with logic and solve all things."[125] Another Ingolstadt realist document from the period made a similar point. It stated that the logic of the *moderni* "based on Marsilius and Buridan is thoroughly in disagreement with the principles of Thomas and Scotus." And, it continued, because "logic is the way to all other sciences," there could be little agreement in other areas. For "a small error in the beginning becomes a great one in the end."[126]

Thus it would seem that the scholarly debate about the nature of the *Wegestreit* resembles the fable of the six blind men of Industan who, having each touched a different part of an elephant, disputed "long and loud" whether the beast was like a wall, spear, snake, tree, fan or rope. Like the characters in the tale, historians have tended to seize on one issue as the "essence" of the controversy, and gloss over other sources of disagreement. To participants in the *Wegestreit*, their antagonism was rooted in several different disagreements about theological and philosophical issues, preferences in logic and pedagogical methods. As the actual history of the controversy reveals, it also involved many non-intellectual issues;

[124] Gilbert, "Ockham, Wyclif and the *via moderna*," 95.
[125] Ehrle, *Der Sentenzenkommentar*, 335.
[126] *Ibid.*, 328.

53

much of the *Wegestreit* can be understood as a struggle for power and preferment within the universities.

All the older German universities were originally dominated by nominalism, reflecting both the intellectual climate of late fourteenth-century Paris and the Occamism of men like Marsilius of Inghen and Henry of Langenstein who shaped the oldest German institutions. Even the University of Cologne, which later became Germany's leading bastion of realism, required in her original statutes the study of the famous Parisian nominalist, Jean Buridan.[127] But in 1415, in a move that reflected the strong Dominican influence at the university, the faculty proscribed "recently introduced Parisian methods" and demanded that "lecturing, teaching and expounding the works of the philosopher" should be based on Thomas and Albert the Great.[128] In 1425, however, five German electoral princes, Conrad of Mainz, Dietrich of Cologne, Otto of Trier, Duke Frederick of Saxony, and Louis of the Palatinate, appealed to the university to abandon Aquinas and Albertus Magnus and institute a course of studies based on "Buridan, Marsilius and the like."[129] As their appeal explicitly stated, the electors feared that realism might foster the spread of Hussite and Wycliffist heresies. The masters of the university rejected the princely appeal and composed a defense of their position. They stated that both *viae* could be taught at Cologne, denied that the *via antiqua* was "more difficult" than the *via moderna*, and dismissed the notion that there was any connection between Thomism and the errors of Wycliffe and Hus. Thus the electoral appeal had no results, and Cologne, along with Louvain and Paris,[130] remained bastions of the *via*

---

[127] Bianco, *Die alte Universität,* Anlagen, VII, 64.

[128] Hermann Keussen, *Die alte Universität Köln* (Cologne: 1934), 296, note 6.

[129] The appeal of the princes and the university's response are printed in Ehrle, *Der Sentenzenkommentar,* 282-84; incomplete versions in Prantl, *Geschichte der Logik,* IV, 148, 149.

[130] Thomists and Albertists apparently were able to suppress nominalist teaching at Paris for two or three decades after 1405. See Gabriel, "*Via antiqua* and *via moderna,* 446-50; thereafter the two *viae* battled to a standoff well into

antiqua throughout the fifteenth century. And graduates of these three institutions were primarily responsible for the movement to break the nominalist monopoly in Germany in the second half of the fifteenth century.

The battle was first joined at the University of Heidelberg, a strongly nominalist institution that had condemned realism in 1417 and had rejected a proposal in 1444 to introduce teaching according to the *via antiqua*.[131] In the 1440s, however, realists from Paris and Cologne who had matriculated at Heidelberg began to agitate for change, and in 1452 tensions once again broke into the open.[132] In April, in a stormy faculty meeting, three *antiqui* attacked their nominalist rivals, denounced Heidelberg's teaching methods, and demanded that the statutes be rewritten so that the *via antiqua* would dominate. Their speeches (described in university records as "scandalous" and "insolent") temporarily backfired. The faculty resolved that all masters had to swear to teach according to the methods of "Marsilius and other moderns"; it also suspended the three offending speakers from teaching for half a year. But these efforts of the Heidelberg *moderni* to maintain their monopoly soon became irrelevant as a result of the statute reforms mandated in May 1452 by Elector Frederick I, the university's patron. He decreed that both *viae* be taught at Heidelberg and that "vituperative remarks" from all parties end. The nominalists fought the new measure, but the elector was convinced that the representation of both ways would enhance the university's prestige and hence attract students. The dispute ended later in the year when the elector threatened to expel anyone who opposed his reforms.

Conflicts between the two factions spread to other institutions in the later 1400s, as proponents of the revived *via*

---

the sixteenth century; in 1427 the University of Louvain arts faculty banned the teaching of Buridan, Marsilius, Occam, and their followers. See Ehrle, *Der Sentenzenkommentar*, 159.

   [131] Winkelmann, *Urkundenbuch*, I, 106; Gabriel, "*Via antiqua* and *via moderna*," 459, note 102.

   [132] The following is based on Ritter, *Studien zur Spätscholastik*, 56-57.

antiqua, often with princely support, attempted to assure a niche for themselves in Germany. The resulting controversies often became disruptive, and universities adopted a variety of expedients to maintain stability. The statutes of Ingolstadt, for example, established what amounted to two separate arts faculties: each *via* had its own dean, requirements, and roster of lectures.[133] In the 1470s, statutes were introduced that required both *via antiqua* and *via moderna* be taught at Tübingen and Mainz.[134] In neither case was the faculty of arts formally divided; but the deanship had to alternate between the two *viae*, and each had its own *bursa* where its students lived and studied. Tübingen was unique in that the statutes stipulated that both *viae* also be represented in the faculty of theology.[135] In the 1480s representatives of the *via antiqua* at Greifswald and Freiburg-im-Breisgau also achieved statute revisions that required that their *via* be taught; each followed the Tübingen model, with alternating deans and separate living quarters and lectures for students in each *via*.[136] The *antiqui* also made substantial inroads at the University of Vienna at the end of the fifteenth century; in 1499, for example, it was proposed that a *bursa realistarum* be constructed for those who wished to study according to the *via antiqua*.[137] At Leipzig realism was represented within the faculty, but apparently no effort was made to alternate deanships or to establish formally separate lectures.[138] The strength of revived realism is most evident at the two institutions founded in the early 1500s, Wittenberg

[133] Prantl, *Geschichte der Ludwig-Maximilians-Universität*, I, 52-64.

[134] Roth, *Urkunden*, 327-30; Fritz Hermann, "Die Mainzer Bursen 'zum Algesheimer' und 'zum Schenkenberg' und ihre Statuten," *Beiträge für Hessische Geschichte und Altertumskunde*, N.F., 4 (1907), 94-124.

[135] For a list of the representatives of each *via* at Tübingen from 1477 to 1535 see Heiko Oberman, *Werden und Wertung der Reformation* (Tübingen: 1979), 38.

[136] Kosegarten, *Geschichte*, I, 132; Schreiber, *Geschichte*, I, 60.

[137] Gustav Bauch, *Die Reception des Humanismus in Wien* (Breslau: 1903), 97.

[138] Conrad Wimpina, the leading theologian at Leipzig, was a Scotist; see Josef Negwer, *Konrad Wimpina. Ein katholischer Theologe aus der Reformationszeit* (Breslau: 1909).

and Frankfurt an der Oder, where originally only Scotism and Thomism were taught. Frederick the Wise was interested in having nominalism represented at his university, however. Thus in 1507 Jodocus Trutvetter was lured from Erfurt, still a strong bastion of nominalism, to represent the *via moderna* in the faculty of theology. He returned to Erfurt in 1510, but a year later, his place was assumed by one of his former students. His name was Martin Luther.[139]

One might hypothesize that the "battle of the *viae*" was a sign of continuing strength and vitality within scholasticism. Could it not have meant that after years of nominalist domination the competition and rivalries among the various factions would bring about a fruitful reexamination of old issues and perhaps stimulate new lines of inquiry? It is safe to conclude that such revitalization did not occur. Rarely did the writers of the time attempt to examine systematically the comparative strengths and weaknesses of each side. And when they did, the "defense" of their *via* amounted to a recital of old slogans and extravagant boasting about their superior skills in disputation (typically, hostile acts by their opponents came after they had been publicly humiliated in debate). In fact the nonspecific nature of the controversy and the obvious eclecticism of many late scholastics explain why historians have had so much difficulty in giving clear shape to the *Wegestreit*.

In the daily life of the universities themselves, the conflict of the *viae* usually involved mundane matters far removed from the world of *universalia* and *suppositio communis*. It first of all meant competition for students, particularly in the arts course. In institutions where both *viae* were represented, more students naturally meant greater income from lecture, examination, and graduation fees. Thus one would surmise that

---

[139] See Gustav Bauch, ed., *Acten*; the lecture plan of 1512 demanded that logic be read "according to the opinions of Scotus and Thomas"; the theological authorities cited were Scotus, Thomas, and Bonaventure; on Wittenberg see Gustav Bauch, "Wittenberg und die Scholastik," *Neues Archiv für Sächsische Geschichte und Altertumskunde*, 18 (1897), 285-339 and Maria Grossmann, *Humanism in Wittenberg* (Nieuwkoop: 1975), 68, 69.

Heidelberg *moderni* lived more comfortably than *antiqui*, for between 1454 and 1500, of the 702 promoted students, 435 were in the *via moderna* and 276 were in the *via antiqua*.[140] Strenuous efforts were thus made to attract newly matriculated students. At Tübingen the competition became so fierce that in 1505 a statute tightly restricted recruitment propaganda and stated that no further efforts could be directed at students once they had made a decision.[141] The *Wegestreit* at Ingolstadt, on the other hand, seems largely to have been a matter of university politics, competition for preferment, and a strong measure of paranoia when the opponent was in power.[142] The arts faculty originally had been split into two distinct parts, with each *via* having its own dean, council, treasury, lecture schedule, and degrees. But in 1475 a leader of the *via antiqua* complained to the rector that the modernists, because of their numerical superiority in the university council had passed a number of narrowly selfish edicts. A short time later fifty proponents of the *via moderna* addressed Duke Louis of Bavaria, accusing the university's vice chancellor, a realist, of sowing discord, unfairly choosing examiners, and in general having the reputation of a thief. Louis now tried a new approach. In 1478 he ordered the unification of the *viae* into one faculty under one dean. But the *antiqui* found themselves hopelessly outnumbered, and in 1479 they broke off again, inviting all students wanting "sound teaching" to study with them. The realist "rebellion" ended only in 1481 when Duke George (1479-1503) threatened fines and the loss of all income for any masters not complying with the 1478 statutes. Thereafter the realists remained a small, vocal, and in their own view persecuted minority within the faculty. University documents from the late fifteenth century occasionally record their laments. One master complained he had few realist col-

---

[140] Toepke, ed., *Die Matrikel der Universität Heidelberg*, I, xii.

[141] Roth, *Urkunden*, 346.

[142] Documents relevant to the Ingolstadt *Wegestreit* can be found in Prantl, *Geschichte der Ludwig-Maximilians-Universität*, II, 72-90 (documents 9-11, 13-15); see also Ehrle, *Der Sentenzenkommentar*, 326-41.

leagues since most had been forced to leave because of "wars, strife and persecutions";[143] another in 1497 claimed he had "suffered more than a Jew" for eighteen years.[144] Conflict ended only in 1518-1519 when the names *"moderni, antiqui, realistae, nominales"* were abolished; all members of the faculty were now to be known as *artistae.*[145]

The *Wegestreit* became most absurd when students "defended" their *viae* through violence. Such was the case at Heidelberg in the 1450s when the realist Jodocus Calw required princely protection from modernist students who had invaded his classroom several times and disrupted his lectures.[146] And in 1497 realists complained to the university senate that nominalist students had stormed through their *bursa* shouting: "We thirst realist blood! Our swords must devour at least three realists! I'll not leave this place until I have chopped off the limb of a realist!" They also complained they had been called "Jew-children" because their living quarters were in Heidelberg's old Jewish neighborhood. Nor was the cause of learning advanced in 1503 when some students in the *via moderna* defended the following theses:

A Thomist is more stupid than any man.
A Thomist is no different from a Chimaera.
A realist is no different from a Chimaera.[147]

At at least one institution the battle of the *viae* had by the early sixteenth century degenerated to the level of student buffoonery.

Whatever differences separated the *via antiqua* and *via moderna,* they should not cloud the broad areas of agreement between the two groups. The importance of logic, the unquestioned authority of Aristotle, the disdain for literature,

---

[143] Ehrle, *Der Sentenzenkommentar,* 328.
[144] Seifert, *Statuten-und Verfassungsgeschichte,* 47.
[145] Prantl, *Geschichte der Ludwig-Maximilians-Universität,* II, 156; Seifert, *Statuten-und Verfassungsgeschichte,* 92-96.
[146] Ritter, *Studien zur Spätscholastik,* II, 61.
[147] Johann Friedrich Hautz, *Geschichte der Universität Heidelberg* (Mannheim: 1862), I, 348, 349.

and a tendency to structure theological studies around Lombard's *Sentences* were shared characteristics. For each, the ultimate goals of a university education were identical. But in the 1450s new voices began to be heard at the German universities. They proclaimed that German education was one-sided and irrelevant. They called on their countrymen to embrace a program of culture and educational reform that the Italians had perfected in the previous century and a half. These men of course were representatives of German humanism, a movement that in the next seven decades transformed the goals and nature of German university education. By the 1520s the era of medieval scholasticism had ended in Germany. But until then, humanism and scholasticism existed side-by-side at universities throughout the empire. The nature of that relationship and the process by which humanist ideals gained precedence will be the subject of the pages that follow.

II

*H*umanists and Scholasticism
to 1500: The Reform of
the Trivium ~

ALTHOUGH the origins of German humanism can be traced
back at least as far as the early fifteenth century,[1] the movement was introduced to the German universities only in the
1450s. The records of the University of Vienna show that in
1451 Phillip Mautther lectured on the pseudo-Ciceronian *Rhetorica ad Herrenium* and that Paul Swicker of Bamberg lectured
on Terence. They further show that in the same decade three
others, George Peuerbach, Johann Mandl, and Johann Regiomantanus, lectured on several Roman authors, including
Virgil, Juvenal, Terence, and Lucan.[2] And although his name

[1] The origins of German humanism have been widely debated. The movement has been variously linked to the revival of the *via antiqua*: Heinrich
Hermelink, *Die religiösen Reformbestrebungen des deutschen Humanismus* (Tübingen: 1907); the *Devotio moderna*: Albert Hyma, *The Christian Renaissance*
(Grand Rapids, Mich.: 1924); the Prague court of Charles IV in the 1350s:
Konrad Burdach, "Zur Kenntniss altdeutschen Litteratur und Kunst," *Zen-
tralblatt für Bibliothekswesen*, 7 (1891), 145-76, 432-88. Recent scholarship has
emphasized the importance of contacts with Italian humanism, especially at
the Church councils of Constance and Basel. See Lewis Spitz, "The Course
of German Humanism," *Itinerarium Italicum—The Profile of the Italian Renaissance in the Mirror of its European Transformations*, ed. Heiko Oberman and
Thomas A. Brady, Jr. (Leiden: 1975), 371-435, esp. 390-401.
[2] On the activity of these early Viennese humanists, see Joseph Ritter von
Aschbach, *Geschichte der Wiener Universität*, I (Vienna: 1877), 353; Karl Grossmann, "Die Frühzeit des Humanismus in Wien bis zu Celtis Berufung,"
Jahrbuch für Landeskunde von Niederösterreich, N.F. 22 (1929), 227; Alphons

appears in no university document, it is known that in 1452 and 1453 an Italian, William of Savona lectured on oratory and the *ars dictaminis*.[3] The 1450s also saw the first humanist lectures at the University of Heidelberg. Johann Wildenhertz lectured on rhetoric early in the decade, and in 1456 Peter Luder began a five-year career at the university by commenting on the satires of Horace and the histories of Valerius Maximus.[4]

Within the ranks of these pioneers were represented the three types of men who in the next several decades advanced the cause of humanism at the German universities. William of Savona, for example, was the first of several Italian humanists who taught in Germany in the second half of the fifteenth century. Petrus Antonius Finariensis held forth briefly at Basel and Heidelberg in the mid-1460s,[5] and another countryman, Jacobus Publicius Rufus did the same at Erfurt and Leipzig between 1467 and 1469.[6] In 1487 Cinthus de Burgo Sancti Sepulchri lectured on rhetoric at Vienna, and in the 1490s, Giralamo Balbi, a more prominent figure, also taught at the University of Vienna.[7]

More influential were the German humanists whose careers followed the model of Peter Luder. A self-styled poet who traveled from university to university to teach and proclaim

Lhotsky, *Die Wiener Artistenfakultät 1365-1497* (Vienna: 1905), 127; John Thomas Dunne, "Between the Renaissance and Reformation: Humanism at the University of Vienna," Diss., University of Southern California, 1974, 62-111.

[3] Grossmann, "Die Frühzeit," 230. William of Savona was undoubtedly the "certain Genoese monk" mentioned in a letter of Aeneas Sylvius in 1453; see Eneas Sylvius Piccolomini, *Briefwechsel*, 2 vols., ed. Rudolph Wolken (Vienna: 1909), II, 321.

[4] On the activity of Wildenhertz see Ritter, *Die Heidelberger Universität* (Heidelberg: 1936), 452-55; see below note 8, for material on Luder.

[5] Gerhard Ritter, "Petrus Antonius Finariensis, der Nachfolger Perter Luders in Heidelberg," *Archiv für Kulturgeschichte*, 26 (1936), 89-104.

[6] Gustav Bauch, *Die Universität Erfurt im Zeitalter des Frühhumanismus* (Breslau: 1904), 58, 59; Bauch, *Geschichte des Leipziger Frühhumanismus* (Leipzig: 1899), 4, 5.

[7] On Cinthus, see Grossmann, "Die Frühzeit," 303; on Balbi, see Bauch, *Die Reception des Humanismus in Wien* (Breslau: 1903), 46-49; and the discussion of his Viennese experiences in Chapter III below.

the value of the *studia humanitatis*, Luder was the first of those individuals known to historians as "wandering poets." He, for example, taught not only at Heidelberg but also at Erfurt, Leipzig, Basel, and Vienna.[8] Another itinerant poet was Samuel Karoch of Lichtenberg, a rather pathetic figure whose few letters are filled with anguished complaints about ill health and poverty. Nonetheless he remained on the university circuit for at least fifteen years, teaching in the 1470s and 1480s at Leipzig, Erfurt, Vienna, Cologne, Heidelberg, and perhaps Rostock and Greifswald.[9] By far the most prominent and best known of the "wandering poets" was Conrad Celtis, the German "arch-humanist," who studied at Cologne and taught at Rostock, Leipzig, Erfurt, Ingolstadt, and Vienna.[10]

But in final analysis neither the second-rate Italian humanists nor the enthusiastic and dedicated "wandering poets" carried the main burden of introducing humanism to the German universities. More numerous and significant were men like Mautther, Swicker, Peuerbach, Mandl, and Regiomontanus at Vienna and Wildenhertz at Heidelberg. None was truly a "humanist" in the sense of a man whose career was devoted entirely to the study and teaching of the *studia humanitatis.* Peuerbach and Regiomontanus were both astronomers, while Wildenhertz, Swicker and Mandl were all jurists. But all had developed an enthusiasm for the literary and rhetorical ideals of humanism—an enthusiasm they sought to impart to their

---

[8] On Luder: Wilhelm Wattenbach, "Peter Luder," *Zeitschrift für die Geschichte des Oberrheins,* 22 (1869), 33-127; "Peter Luders Lobrede auf Pfalzgraf Friedrich den Siegreichen," *Zeitschrift für die Geschichte des Oberrheins,* 23 (1871), 21-38; "Nachträgliches über Peter Luder," *Zeitschrift für die Geschichte des Oberrheins,* 28 (1875), 95-99; Gerhard Ritter, "Aus dem Kreise der Hofpoeten Pfalzgraf Friedrichs I," *Zeitschrift für die Geschichte des Oberrheins,* N.F. 38 (1922), 109-23; Frank E. Baron, "The Beginnings of German Humanism: The Life and Work of the Wandering Humanist Peter Luder," Diss., University of California at Berkeley, 1967.

[9] Wilhelm Wattenbach, "Samuel Karoch von Lichtenberg, ein Heidelberger Humanist," *Zeitschrift für die Geschichte des Oberrheins,* 28 (1876), 38-51; Heinz Entner, *Frühhumanismus und Schultradition in Leben und Werk des Wanderpoeten Samuel Karoch von Lichtenberg* (Berlin: 1968).

[10] The literature on Celtis is extensive; see especially Lewis Spitz, *Conrad Celtis, the German Arch-Humanist* (Cambridge, Mass.: 1957).

63

students. Many individuals were cast in this mold during the second half of the fifteenth century. Their ranks included jurists, physicians, theologians, and some who combined princely service and university teaching. Most, however, seem to have been recent recipients of the master's degree who offered courses on humanist subjects to generate income to support their studies in medicine, theology, or law. Although hardly mentioned in official university records (and thus ignored by most historians), the work of these young and often anonymous teachers in great measure was responsible for transforming humanism from an academic novelty in 1450 into a powerful intellectual force by 1500.

The careers and personalities of these early humanists were marked by a diversity that makes generalizations difficult. In terms of their social background, they included no nobles, but otherwise represented the broad spectrum of German society from peasant to patrician. Their ranks contained men of deep piety such as the puritanical Alsatian Jacob Wimpfeling, and others such as Peter Luder and Conrad Celtis, whose lives were decidedly Rabelaisian. Some, such as the Viennese Bernard Perger, maintained close ties with princely courts, and others such as Dietrich Gresemund successfully collected numerous ecclesiastical benefices. More typical were men like the unfortunate Samuel Karoch, who experienced real poverty by choosing to remain in academic life.

Despite their varied background and experiences, the early humanists showed a remarkable uniformity in their ideas about educational reform. They agreed to a man that the academic practices that dominated German higher education were deficient. They were all, therefore, in some sense critics of scholasticism. Despite their occasionally impassioned rhetoric, however, their demands for change were temperate and limited. They offered no criticisms of scholastic theology and said little about philosophy. Their concerns were quite literally "trivial," in that they were limited to the traditional subjects of the *trivium*, especially grammar and rhetoric. Only later did it become apparent that the seemingly innocuous reforms they proffered had more profound implications, capable of eroding scholasticism's very foundation.

THE *Studia humanitatis*

Just as the popular history of Protestantism begins at that single moment on October 31, 1517, when Luther posted his Ninety-Five Theses in Wittenberg, so too can the story of the German humanists' critique of scholasticism be traced to a specific time and place: July 15, 1456, at the University of Heidelberg. On that afternoon Heidelberg students and masters gathered to hear a well-publicized oration by a man of some forty years who had spent the previous twenty years in Italy. He held no university degree and styled himself a "poet." The speech, which must have lasted little more than thirty minutes, seems to have had little impact on the audience. Modern critics have justifiably viewed it as crude, unoriginal, almost puerile. Nonetheless, the oration is of signal importance for the history of German humanism. For in it the speaker enunciated a program of education and culture that provided the movement's central theme for the next seventy years.

The speaker was Peter Luder, the first of those early humanists known as "wandering poets." He was also the first in a long line of Germans, who having glimpsed the brilliance of the Italian Renaissance, returned home determined to bring "culture" to their countrymen. Born around 1415, Luder had studied perfunctorily at the University of Heidelberg in 1430 and 1431. Then, having been "stirred to see distant mountains and rivers," he traveled to Italy, where with the exception of one side-trip to the Adriatic coast, he lived, studied, and worked for the next twenty years.[11] One would be interested in knowing how a young German who had enrolled at Heidelberg as

[11] The only source of information for Luder's travels in Italy is Luder himself, specifically the brief autobiographical section at the beginning of his July 1456 oration. See Wattenbach, "Peter Luder," 100-110, esp. 100-102.

a pauper managed such a prolonged foreign visit, but details are few. According to Luder himself he spent time in Rome, served as a notary in Venice, made the acquaintance of the noted humanist educator Guarino da Verona, and ended up studying medicine at Padua. There, it seems, he met and impressed a German law student from a noble family with influence at the court of the Palatine Elector Frederick I. This connection probably explains how it came about that in 1455 the prince offered Luder a small stipend to teach the humanities at the University of Heidelberg. Luder accepted and arrived in Heidelberg to embark on his new venture in the early summer of 1456.

In the notice he posted to announce his proposed courses, Luder explained his major goals.[12] He related how Frederick, "desiring to restore to his school the Latin language, now almost completely twisted and turned into barbarism, had determined that the *studia humanitatis*, that is, the books of the poets, orators and historians are to be publicly read." For this reason he announced he would lecture on the satires of Horace and the histories of Valerius Maximus. "Therefore," he concluded, "whoever wants to make himself more illustrious by offering work in Latin eloquence, by preparing books in the *studia humanitatis*, and by adopting the golden knowledge of this teaching, should not think meanly of hearing these studies."

Luder must have realized that everything about his planned lectures—their educational goals, subject-matter, and the authors themselves—would strike most of the university community as bizarre and out of place. Thus he further proposed to initiate his lectures by delivering an oration that would articulate their purposes more fully than the brief course announcement. The result was the speech, essentially a reworking of a previous oration by Guarino of Verona,[13] delivered on July 15, 1456.

[12] Printed in Wattenbach, "Peter Luder," 99, 100.
[13] For Luder's debt to Guarino, see Baron, "Life and Work," 56; for the text of the oration, see above, note 11.

Luder's oration contained no direct attacks on the established scholastic curriculum of the University of Heidelberg. In fact after the brief autobiographical section, Luder took care to praise the various scholastic disciplines: dialectic refuted lies and led to truth; physics explained the workings of all nature; ethics showed the "way of happiness"; theology, which revealed the excellence of God, was the most worthy of all. But for his listeners' own use, and for the glory of their country and university, he urged them also to pursue still other disciplines—history, oratory, and poetry.

He devoted the rest of his speech to the praise of these studies. He began with history—"that trusty mistress of truth and instruction." He conceded that philosophy was the truest "guide of living" and the ultimate repository of truth, but he added that it was often too difficult and subtle to inspire good behavior and noble actions. To learn it, a person had to submit himself to the "highest possible torments," so that "the mind shudders and shuts itself off." History had none of these drawbacks. By studying the actions of men in the past, a student painlessly learned the precepts of philosophy. Furthermore, philosophy only affected the "cold intellect," but history inspired the emotions, so that a person not only learned truth but also carried it out in his daily life. Quoting Cicero, Luder summarized his ideas about history: "it is the witness of the times, the light of truth, the way to memory, the teacher of life and the messenger of antiquity." In addition to its usefulness, argued Luder, the study of history was also pleasant. It takes us to distant continents, describes far-away mountains and rivers, and acquaints us with the customs of other peoples. For all these reasons he urged his listeners to study history, "so we may gain profit from it along with pleasure."

Luder went on to praise rhetoric. Like history it was especially useful as a teacher of truth and virtue. Orators, said Luder, "are accustomed to ardently extol virtue and harshly fulminate against vice." They also teach us "to praise good deeds and detest villainy." Through them is taught how to "incite and arouse our listeners to indignation, hatred, sadness, tears and on the other hand, to mercy, love, joy and laughter." Rhetoric, in a word, was God's special gift to man. He gave brutes only stomachs, but to man he gave speech "so that truth could be propagated and men could be inspired to virtue." Furthermore, just as man stands above the beasts, so an eloquent man stands above the rest of his fellows. Thus, Luder concluded, everyone "except those with weak minds should want to apply himself to the works of the orators."

Finally Luder urged his listeners to "imbibe thirstily" the words of poetry. Without poetry, he asserted, no one could learn to pronounce and write words correctly or compose an eloquent speech. It not only teaches words and syllables, but "all kinds of linguistical ornaments." He conceded that some men thought poetry unworthy because of its corrupting influence. But to Luder, the arguments of these "supposedly learned men" were "inane and filled with error." In many instances these critics had never even read any poetry themselves. Besides, even the Bible contained "immoral" stories: the disgrace of Sodom and Gomorrah, the incest of Lot, the love of David and Bathsheba, and others. Luder reminded his critics that "from thorns we collect roses, from mud, gold." He finally pointed out many great and learned men who had cultivated poetry: among the Greeks, Aristotle and Plato, among the Jews, Solomon and David, among Christians, Jerome, Augustine, and Lactantinus.

At the end of his speech, Luder summarized his ideas. Again quoting Cicero, he concluded that the *studia humanitatis* "inspire youth, give pleasure in old age, embellish prosperity, offer escape and solace in adversity and give enjoyment at home." Once more, he urged "the noble and studious young men" in his audience to "devote their work, their labor and their industry to the humane studies." All were invited, he added, to hear his lectures when they began.

A little more than two years later, on December 6, 1458, the academic community at the University of Vienna heard a similar explication and defense of the *studia humanitatis*; it too was presented by a German who had recently returned from Italy. This time the speaker was George Peuerbach, best known to historians as an astronomer, but also an important early disciple of humanism at Vienna.[14] A slightly younger man than Luder, Peuerbach had been born in 1421. Sometime between 1450 and 1453 he traveled to Italy, where among other things he was the houseguest in Rome of Nicholas of Cusa, the famous German cardinal, mystic, and philosopher. Like Luder, he also attended the University of Padua, a prestigious center for the study of Aristotelian science. On his return from Italy until his death in 1461 he served as court astronomer for Emperor Frederick III, wrote on astronomy and mathematics and lectured on the classics at the university.

Peuerbach's speech in praise of the *studia humanitatis* was made during a disputation held in 1458.[15] He responded to three questions—two on astronomy and one on a humanistic theme: "To what extent the poetical or rhetorical art includes similes and metaphors—to be accepted according to the use of the poets; to be rejected in that fables and myths belong to natural and moral philosophy, while oratory and poetry are only linguistic disciplines." Actually Peuerbach largely ignored the proposed question and instead delivered an oration that spelled out the nature and value of the *studia humanitatis*. In the first part he defined the *ars oratoria* and *poetica*. Quoting Quintilian, oratory was "the art of speaking and persuasion to bring about conviction in the hearer." The first true students of oratory were the Greeks, especially Gorgias, Aristotle, and Hermagoras; the art attained its fullest perfection, however, in the work of Cicero and Quintilian. There was no better sign of a man's learning, argued Peuerbach, than the eloquence of his speech. Like Luder he argued that the orator's greatest responsibility was to inspire his listeners to avoid vice and follow the path of virtue. Poetry was also

---

[14] On Peuerbach's contribution to humanism at Vienna, see Grossmann, "Die Frühzeit," 235-54.

[15] Peuerbach's oration is summarized in *ibid*, 245-47; text published in Hans Rupprich, ed., *Die Frühzeit des Humanismus und der Renaissance in Deutschland* (Leipzig: 1938), 197-210.

defined according to its moral purposes. It was that *prima philosophia* which from youth onward provides a "proper guide for living." Poets accomplished this by altering reality in such a way so virtue is praised and vice censured. Peuerbach then described the various types of poetry—epics, satires, lyrics, elegies—and cited the major Greek and Roman poets. He also echoed Luder's notion that the study of poets, orators, and historians was a necessity for anyone who wished to develop a sound Latin style and eloquent speech. There was no conflict, argued Peuerbach, between the study of ancient literature and Christianity. The Church fathers provided the best examples of men who combined eloquence and poetry, but so too did "the prince of the muses, formerly Aeneas, poet laureate, and now most holy Pius II." Only after completing his *encomium* to the *studia humanitatis* did Peuerbach briefly return to the original question. Not surprisingly he sided with the orators and poets.

The message of both speeches—that German schools and universities could produce truly educated men only after the introduction of the *studia humanitatis*—provided the central theme and major educational goal of early German humanism. Succeeding humanists took every opportunity to hammer it home. In formal orations (most notably Conrad Celtis's inaugural oration at Ingolstadt in 1492),[16] pedagogical treatises (such as Rudolph Agricola's *On a Plan for Studies*, written in 1484),[17] dialogues (such as Johannes Landsberger's *Dialogue for and against the Poetical Arts*, published in 1494)[18] and in dozens of manuals and treatises for classroom use, arguments defending the *studia humanitatis* were advanced with enthusiasm and, one must add, a great deal of redundancy.

---

[16] Latin text and English translation in Leo Forster, ed. and trans., *Selections from Conrad Celtis* (Cambridge, England: 1948), 36-65; another translation by Lewis Spitz may be found in Lewis Spitz, ed., *The Northern Renaissance* (Englewood Cliffs, N.J.: 1972), 15-27.

[17] The treatise was first published in *Rodolphi Agricolae Opuscula*, ed. Peter Gilles (Louvain: 1511). I have used the version printed by Johannes Rivius in *Libellus de ratione docendi* (Freiburg: 153?), 77-90.

[18] *Dialogus Recommendacionis Exprobriacionisque Poetices* (Leipzig: 1494).

RHETORIC

Of all the subjects the humanists recommended none was praised as warmly as rhetoric. An excellent example of this preference was Rudolph Agricola's *On a Plan of Studies*, originally written in 1484 as a letter to his friend, Jacobus Barbarinus. Like the orations of Luder and Peuerbach, the work reflected the author's ten years of study and teaching in Italy between 1469 and 1479. It was written while Agricola was residing in Heidelberg, at a time when he was devoting much thought to the problem of educational reform in northern Europe. He began by warning his correspondent that what professors now taught in the schools was not true learning. "They claim for themselves these babblings, these clatterings in inane noises which we now popularly call the arts; they wear away the day in their perplex obscurities and (if I may speak more truthfully) enigmas of disputations which for so many centuries have found no Oedipus who could solve them."[19] He recommended instead a program of study that included extensive reading in moral and natural philosophy but whose ultimate purpose was the attainment of eloquence. Well over half the treatise is devoted to this goal, for as Agricola pointed out, without good style all other knowledge was useless.

Demanding that something must be done to improve "that corrupt instruction in speaking we now receive in the schools," Agricola outlined a three-part plan for the acquisition of a sound speaking and writing style. First, one must read the best authors of antiquity. Agricola urged his disciple not to concentrate on content alone, but to observe carefully the force and structure of sentences, the choice of words, and the methods for explaining difficult themes. Second, eloquence demanded the cultivation of good memory. This was essential to diplomats, councillors, and princes who often had to deliver impromptu speeches. He felt Quintilian was the best guide

[19] Rivius, *Libellus*, 77.

in the development of this faculty. Finally, Agricola recommended long hours of practice in composition. He advised Barbarinus to learn clever and wise things to say on topics that arose in daily conversation, such as ignorance, life, teaching, bravery, and virtue. For example, when discussing virtue, everyone would think him learned if he could tell the story of Lucretia, who "preferred death rather than a life of sin." He also recommended that Barbarinus "sweat through" the dialectical topics, which offered the speaker a reservoir of things to say on a wide variety of subjects. Having mastered these three aspects of the rhetorician's art, he would resemble those "old masters of arts which the Greeks called sophists, who could discourse on any matter."[20]

Even for a humanist like Conrad Celtis, who had a genuine interest in both Aristotelian and Platonic philosophy, eloquence was viewed as man's most exalted goal. This preference is clearly shown in his famous inaugural oration at the University of Ingolstadt, delivered in the summer of 1492 as he was about to assume a professorship provided by Duke George the Rich of Bavaria. The speech had a single theme, rephrased and restated several times by Celtis to have maximum impact on his listeners. It was this: in culture and politics, Germany was corrupt and decayed, to foreigners the home of "drunkenness, barbarism, cruelty and whatever is bestial and foolish."[21] Celtis painted a picture of unrelieved gloom. The empire was surrounded by enemies; much of its territory was controlled by foreigners; Italian bankers were bleeding the country white; heresy flourished at its very center. Germans were devoted to "sleep and gluttony, spending on feasting, with dice and Venus, evils with which we are inflamed, thanks to our stupidity."[22] The solution, according to Celtis, was a new devotion to the liberal arts, which he

[20] *Ibid.*, 88.
[21] Conrad Celtis, "Oration delivered publicly at the University of Ingolstadt," in Spitz, *The Northern Renaissance*, 18.
[22] *Ibid.*, 25.

equated with the pursuit of wisdom and eloquence. He told his listeners he would consider his speech successful if he had:

> added, impressed, and as it were branded upon your spirits some stimulus to glory and virtue, so that you keep ever before your eyes that immortality which you must seek only from the fountain of philosophy and the study of eloquence. I cannot easily declare with what great labors and vigils you must linger and sweat over these two things . . . For they alone have prescribed for us the way to live well and happily and have set before us Nature . . . , as an example and mirror of life to be imitated.[23]

Although this passage and several others suggest that Celtis saw equal value in the attainment of wisdom and eloquence, the oration showed a decided preference for the latter. Philosophy was by no means denigrated. It was "a kind of seminary which teaches fully the knowledge of things human and divine and their jurisdiction."[24] But like Agricola, Celtis argued that all knowledge was useless unless cloaked in eloquence: "For what, by the immortal gods, does it profit us to know many things, to understand the beautiful and the sublime, if we are prevented from speaking of them with dignity, elegance and gravity, and if we are not able to transmit our thoughts to posterity, which is the unique ornament of human happiness?"[25] Like many humanists, he added that eloquence was the highest form of learning: "So it is by the faith of men: nothing shows a man to be learned and erudite unless it be the pen and tongue—the two things which eloquence governs."[26] For Celtis the power of an orator's persuasive speech was an object of awe and reverence, almost beyond understanding. He recounted how Greek and Roman orators gave public performances in which their "sublime

[23] *Ibid.*, 17.
[24] *Ibid.*, 20.
[25] *Ibid.*, 17.
[26] *Ibid.*

persuasion" inspired their listeners "to virtue, piety, modesty, fortitude and endurance of all things." He continued, "Therefore the allegory of the poets is not unseemly, according to which Orpheus is said to have tamed wild animals, moved stones, and led them where he wished; for it shows by metaphor the power of eloquence and the duty of the poet, who is able to move ferocious, monstrous and intractable spirits to gentleness, a right spirit, and love for the fatherland."[27]

Celtis concluded by outlining the proper sequence of studies for German youth. Young boys should first be introduced to poems and songs. They provide "a stimulant to industry" and allow young minds to "imbibe the gravity of words and meanings." The next step was the study of "weightier philosophers and orators." But the final goal was a man of literary skill rather than philosophical insight: "From these they can rise to their own inventions and to the sublimity of the poetic discipline and its figures, attaining to the praise of illustrious authors in writing histories and poems. They will then procure immortality for themselves and glory and praise for their fatherland."[28]

The early humanists' preoccupation with rhetoric and the development of a sound Latin style is shown not only in their speeches and writings but also in their teaching. This is clearly borne out by the notices they posted to announce their university courses. In an article published in 1915, Ludwig Bertalot edited a representative selection of thirty-eight such announcements from the 1450s through the 1470s, mainly from the universities of Heidelberg, Leipzig, Erfurt, and Ingolstadt.[29] Eleven of the proposed courses simply offered instruction in rhetoric or related subjects such as punctuation, letter writing, or metrification, without mentioning a specific author or text. The rest focused on the work or works of a single author; most popular was Terence, but also represented

[27] *Ibid.*, 26.

[28] *Ibid.*, 27.

[29] Ludwig Bertalot, "Humanistische Vorlesungsankündigungen in Deutschland im 15. Jahrhundert," *Zeitschrift für Erziehung und Unterricht*, 5 (1915), 1-24.

were Horace, Cicero, Ovid, Jerome, among the ancients, and Petrarch, Leonardo Bruni, Francesco Filelfo, and Augustinus Dati among recent authors. It becomes apparent in reading the announcements that these authors were to be studied less for the content of their works than as models of elegant Latin style. As previously noted, Peter Luder proclaimed in his announcement at Heidelberg in 1456 that he proposed to lecture on the letters of Horace so that "the Latin language could be restored." At Leipzig in 1462 he stated his intention to lecture on Terence, because "this comic poet to the greatest degree is preeminent among all others due to his rhetorical style and the uniqueness of his language."[30] He added that his course would enable his listeners to abandon "that kitchen Latin which offends the ears, and render themselves more illustrious with the elegance of their speech."[31] Similarly in 1470 at Leipzig, an anonymous humanist sought to attract students to his course on the letters of Petrarch by promising to make their speech "more learned, eloquent and polished with a more elegant variety of words."[32] "Admirable and elegant Latinity" was also the goal of the anonymous lecturer on Terence at Leipzig in 1472.[33] Even more practical results were offered by Samuel Karoch, when he announced his course on the Italian Humanist Augustinus Dati in the early 1470s, probably at Leipzig or Erfurt. He promised not only to cure his students' "stuttering in erroneous and rough kitchen-Latin" but also to help them "write letters to their parents or anyone else."[34]

GRAMMAR

The ambitions of the early humanists to instill in German youth a love of classical literature and the gift of eloquence

[30] *Ibid.*, 3.
[31] *Ibid.*, 6.
[32] *Ibid.*, 13.
[33] *Ibid.*
[34] *Ibid.*, 14.

met an immediate and imposing stumbling block: their students' training in Latin grammar made them hopelessly unprepared to appreciate their efforts. As outlined in the previous chapter, the teaching of grammar by the fifteenth century had lost any meaningful ties with literature and instead had become a subject of philosophical investigation. As a result of the doctrines of the speculative grammarians, grammar was viewed as an introduction to the techniques of linguistic analysis and the complex concepts of scholastic discourse. Such training was both useful and necessary for future logicians and philosophers but inspired no interest in the literary use of the Latin language.

Thus the humanists soon realized that if their countrymen were ever to approach the ideal of eloquence they so warmly espoused, the teaching of the second element of the *trivium*, grammar, would need drastic revision. Most importantly, the connection forged in the Middle Ages between logic and grammar would have to be severed, and the doctrines of the *modistae* suppressed. No other campaign on the part of the early German humanists was pursued with such unanimity and vigor as this effort to expunge the last vestiges of speculative grammar from the schools and universities of Germany.

The humanists' powerful aversion to the *modistae* was based on their conviction that the philosophical approach to grammar was a perverse distortion of the discipline. Grammar's true purpose was to teach the art of speaking and writing, not the elaboration of philosophical principles. This argument was forcefully made in the *Invective against the Modes of Signifying*, composed sometime in the 1480s by the Westphalian schoolmaster, Alexander Hegius (ca. 1433-1498).[35] He wrote, "No one is to be denied the name grammarian because he is

---

[35] It is not clear when this brief polemic was first written. However, it was included in the posthumous edition of his works published at Deventer by Jacobus Faber in 1503. I have used the only modern edition of the *Invectiva*: "*Invectiva in modos significandi*, Text, Introduction and Notes," ed., Josef IJsewijn, *Forum for Modern Language Studies*, 7 (1971), 299-319.

ignorant of the essential and accidental, material and formal, absolute and respective modes of signification of the parts of speech." Only the person "who knows how to speak and write Latin is worthy of the name grammarian." Without these skills, no one can lay claim to the title "no matter how much he knows about the modes of signification of words."[36]

Hegius went on to argue that language as actually spoken and written was simply not amenable to systematic philosophical analysis and categorization. Nothing in philosophy or logic, stated Hegius, could explain why a verb such as *amare* demanded the accusative case while another verb such as *meminisse* required the genitive. Nor could a philosopher offer any reasonable explanation why *habeo pecuniam* is correct, while *careo pecuniam* (because the verb demands the ablative) is incorrect. Thus rules of language could not be determined by a philosopher, but only by a grammarian who was thoroughly acquainted with the actual usage of the language. As Hegius put it, "If it would be agreed among grammarians that one could say *careo pecuniam* it would be correct to say *careo pecuniam*, and similarly, *pecunia caretur a me*. But because it is agreed among grammarians that *careo pecuniam* should not be said, it is not proper to do so."[37]

The humanists were also convinced that in a practical sense the speculative approach to grammar was disastrous: its students were doomed to a lifetime of crude and laughable Latin usage. This point was driven home by the Rhenish humanist Dietrich Gresemund the Younger (1475-1512) in his *Lucubraciunculae* or *Dialogue on the Seven Liberal Arts*, published in 1494.[38] Modistic grammar was denounced as "great madness and great stupidity" and characterized as "that old frightful and barbarous teaching." Those who studied it, even after

---

[36] Hegius, *Invectiva*, 306.

[37] *Ibid.*, 309.

[38] *Theoderici Gresemundi junioris Moguntini lucubraciuncule bonarum septem artium liberalium Apologiam eiusdemgue cum philosophia dialogum et orationem ad rerum publicarum rectores in se complectentes* (Mainz: 1494); the work is analyzed in Hans-Heinrich Fleischer, *Dietrich Gresemund der Jüngere. Ein Beitrag zur Geschichte des Humanismus im Mainz* (Wiesbaden: 1967), 48-69.

they earned their Master of Arts, were embarrassed to find themselves objects of scorn among the truly leaned: "They do not know how to speak Latin, compose poetry, draw up letters or relate histories, nor how to express themselves concerning the secrets of nature and morality, simply because they have given their lives to the *modi significandi*, the *quiditas* of nouns, confused universals and other frivolities of that kind."[39] Similar attacks on the speculative grammarians were common in the works of Paul Niavis, a prolific humanist grammarian who taught school in Halle and Chemnitz after receiving his Master of Arts degree from Leipzig in 1482.[40] In his *Latina ideomata*, published over twenty times in the fifteenth century alone, he remarked that "treatises on speculative grammar were among the few works which on reading made the student more stupid." One could study them for twenty years, he asserted, and still know nothing in Latin except the "Our Father" and a few verses from Alexander Villedieu's *Doctrinale*.[41]

To rectify these perceived deficiencies, humanists between 1480 and 1500 produced an imposing assortment of manuals, teaching aids, and treatises that discarded the speculative approach to grammar. The first such published manual was the work of Bernard Perger (144?-1502), the most important figure in the history of Viennese humanism from the death of Peuerbach in 1461 to the arrival of Conrad Celtis in 1497.[42] He received his Master of Arts degree from Vienna in 1464 and remained to lecture on Euclid during the mid-1460s. After traveling and studying in Italy, he returned to Vienna in the 1470s where he studied law, lectured on Virgil and Sallust, served as rector for the preparatory school at St. Stephan's Cathedral, and carried out several diplomatic missions for the

---

[39] Gresemund, *Lucubraciuncule*, a viii, ix.

[40] See Aloys Bömer, "Paul Niavis," *Neues Archiv für Sächsische Geschichte*, 11 (1892), 51-94. His *Latina ideomata* has been summarized in Bömer, ed., *Die lateinischen Schülergespräche der Humanisten* (Berlin: 1897), 19-55.

[41] Bömer, *Die lateinischen Schülergespräche*, 35, 36.

[42] J. Krones, "Bernard Perger," *Allgemeine Deutsche Biographie*, 25 (Leipzig: 1887), 374, 375.

emperor. In 1491 he received an imperial appointment to serve as superintendent of the University of Vienna. He began work on his manual for Latin instruction in the 1470s and had it published, so it seems, for the first time in Padua in 1482, perhaps on one of his diplomatic missions. Often referred to as the *Nova grammatica*, the work's full title was, *Introduction to the Art of Grammar; on eight parts of Speech, on Construction, on Writing Letters; transcribed by Master Perger from the Teachings of the most learned Grammarian, Nicholas Perotti*. As Perger freely admitted in his title, this unoriginal work was largely derived from the previously published and enormously popular *Rudimenta grammatices* of the Italian humanist, Nicholas Perotti (1430-1486).[43]

As Perger explained in the introduction, his classroom experience had taught him how grammar students were led "through long ambiguities and certain methods more subtle than useful."[44] From the very beginning, he complained, the study of grammar offered no respite from the obscure logical speculations of Alexander Villedieu and his commentators. To Perger this was especially harmful, for the sound grammarians of old, such as Priscian and Donatus, had faded into oblivion. As a remedy, explained Perger, he had compiled a small book on the basic grammatical rules, without considering "questions more suitable for a logician." He acknowledged his debt to Perotti and admitted that he himself had only removed some difficult passages from the Italian's text and added a few explanations appropriate for the German student. Finally Perger assured the reader that his book was worthy of intensive study: the student could reach the "peak of grammar" without weighing down his mind with "the unclear and doubtful explanations of Alexander's awkward verse."

As Perger promised in the introduction, he did indeed pro-

---

[43] For the numerous editions of Perotti's *Rudimenta* before 1500, see Ludwig Hain, *Repertorium Bibliographicum*, II, Part II (Stuttgart: 1838), 64-71.

[44] *Artes grammaticae*, A i. I have examined the Basel edition, printed by Nicolaus Lamparter in 1506.

duce a grammar manual far different from those then in use in Germany. In approximately one hundred twenty pages he presented in a straightforward, terse fashion, definitions of the parts of speech and rules for sentence structure and syntax. Philosophical discussions were avoided completely. Still drawing heavily on Perotti's work, the final section of the work described the forms and styles of letter-writing and offered many examples from the works of ancient authors and Perotti himself. As this section revealed, grammar's primary purpose to Perger was not to equip students with a vocabulary for the study of logic and philosophy, but rather to teach practical literary skills applicable to the students' daily lives.

Similar practical concerns dominated the numerous grammatical texts published by Paul Niavis, the humanist schoolmaster whose aversion to speculative grammar has already been noted.[45] His specialty was the colloquy—the short Latin dialogue that could be read by students to improve their diction or utilized by teachers to illustrate proper grammatical usage. His *Treasures of Eloquence* was designed for use at the University of Leipzig, where Niavis received his Master of Arts degree in 1482.[46] The two characters in the dialogue are Florian, who already had his bachelor's degree, and Arnolph, a new student destined for the clergy. They discuss a wide range of topics, including the history of local churches, courses at the university, religious processions, future careers, mountain climbing, and the benefits of early rising. His *Dialogue on Childhood* was directed toward a younger audience.[47] It contained a discussion between a pedagogue, Surgellus, and

---

[45] In addition to the works cited in note 40, see Aloys Bömer, "Ein vergessener Vorläufer der Dunkelmännerbriefe," *Neue Jahrbücher für das klassische Altertum, Geschichte und deutsche Litteratur und für Pädagogik,* 16 (1905), 280-87.

[46] This work was first published as one of several dialogues in *Latina Ydeomata Magistri Pauli Niavis . . .* (Leipzig: 1494).

[47] *Dialogus magistri Pauli Niavis parvulis scholaribus ad latinum idioma perutilissimus* (Basel: 1485); further editions listed in Bömer, *Die lateinischen Schülergespräche,* 20, 21.

his ineffectual pupil, Hortenatus, who is forever misplacing his clothes, losing books, complaining about school, and getting into fights. Scattered throughout each work were disparaging references to the methods of the speculative grammarians.[48]

Of all the grammar reformers of the late fifteenth century none was busier than the Alsatian churchman Jacob Wimpfeling (1450-1528).[49] The author or editor of almost one hundred volumes, he combined lengthy scholastic training with a late-developing commitment to certain humanist ideals. Wimpfeling received his Bachelor of Arts from the University of Freiburg-im-Breisgau in 1466, studied briefly at Erfurt, and completed his academic training at Heidelberg, where he became a Master of Arts in 1471 and a Bachelor of Theology in 1482. Until 1496, when he returned to lecture at Heidelberg, he served as cathedral preacher for the Bishop of Speyer. From 1501 until his retirement in 1515, he resided in Strassburg, where he supported himself with a small benefice and income from tutoring patrician children. His life reveals much about the intellectual priorities and limitations of early German humanism.

Wimpfeling's career as an editor and author began in the 1480s, when he published among other things a work on metrification, an edition of some works of Bonaventure, several Latin poems, and even a play "in the manner of Terence," entitled *Stylpho*. These early works introduced themes that became *leitmotifs* in his long list of later publications: a deep devotion to Catholic dogma, an abhorrence of clerical vice, and a prudish obsession with morality. His drama, *Stylpho*, performed at Heidelberg in 1480, catches the spirit of these

---

[48] See especially the exchange between Florian and Arnolph in the *Thesaurus eloquentiae*, in Bömer, *Die lateinische Schülergespräche*, 38, 39.

[49] On Wimpfeling, see Charles Schmidt, *Histoire littéraire de l'Alsace* (Paris: 1879), I, 1-188; II, 317-40; Joseph Knepper, *Jakob Wimpfeling. Sein Leben und seine Werke* (Freiburg-im-Breisgau: 1902); Lewis Spitz, "Jacob Wimpfeling: Sacerdotal Humanist," *Religious Renaissance of the German Humanists* (Cambridge, Mass.: 1963), 41-60; Hugo Holstein, "Zur Biographie Jakob Wimpfelings," *Zeitschrift für vergleichende Litteraturgeschichte*, N.F. 4 (1891), 227-52.

first ventures. Stylpho, a bright young student, is bent on becoming a priest. But he goes to Rome, lives as a prodigal, fails his examinations, and ends up as a swineherd.[50]

During the 1490s, when not defending the immaculate conception or thundering against the monastic orders, Wimpfeling turned his energy to educational reform and the upbringing of German youth. Symptomatic of this concern was his abandonment of his position at Speyer and his return to the University of Heidelberg in 1499. Before this move, he produced a number of classroom texts, the first of which was his *Elegantiarum medulla*—"The Kernel of Elegancies"—of 1493, a slim book on proper Latin style.[51] In the introductory letter, he expressed the fond humanist hope that Germans could learn to write Latin with the same skill as Italians. The book contained a few stylistic rules and a long list of "elegant Latin phrases" arranged in alphabetical order. Wimpfeling's source for the rules and almost all the phrases was Lorenzo Valla's *Elegancies of the Latin Language*.[52] Wimpfeling readily admitted his dependence, often citing the chapter and page where he had borrowed from the Italian humanist.[53] In 1495 Wimpfeling compiled a similar though longer work, the *Larger Elegancies*.[54] His books attained a modicum of popularity, each being republished a dozen times before 1520.[55]

Another work from the 1490's, his *Isidoneus Germanicus*,[56]

---

[50] In the climactic scene, the mayor of his city tells him, "Quantum . . . intelligere possum, aptior es, Stylpho, ut porcos quam homines pascas." See Hugo Holstein, ed., "Jacobus Wimphelingius *Stylpho*," *Lateinische Litteraturdenkmäler des XV. und XVI. Jahrhunderts*, 6 (1892), 13.

[51] *Jacobi Wimphelingi Slettstattensis Elegantiarum medulla: oratoria que precepta. In ordinem inventum, facilem, copiose, clare, breviterque reducta* (Speyer: 1493).

[52] Written in 1441, Valla's *Elegantiarum linguae latinae libri tres* was first published in 1471 in Rome; some three dozen editions appeared in Italy and the rest of Europe between 1471 and 1536; see John E. Sandys, *A History of Classical Scholarship*, II (Cambridge: 1908), 68, 69.

[53] *Elegantiarum medulla*, D v, D vi.

[54] *Elegantiae majores, Rhetorica eiusdem pueris utilissima* (Speyer?: 1495?).

[55] The editions are listed in Schmidt, *Histoire littéraire*, II, 319.

[56] *Isidoneus Germanicus* (Strassburg: 1498). I have used the German translation of Joseph Freundgen, *Jakob Wimpfelings pädagogische Schriften* (Paderborn: 1898), 81-179.

not only offers a clearer picture of Wimpfeling's mind but also summarizes three decades of attempted grammar reform on the part of the early German humanists. Published in 1497, the *Isidoneus* differed from books such as Perger's *Nova grammatica*, which were texts for students. This work was a guide for the teachers themselves. In the introduction, Wimpfeling began by affirming his convictions about the importance of education: "The true fundament of our religion, the condition of every honest life, the honor of every state, the prosperity of the republic, the knowledge of Holy Scripture and proper doctrines, the triumph over the passions all depend entirely on the direction they receive from the youngest age."[57] Of the various aspects of education, none was more important than training in Latin grammar. It enabled fruitful progress in other disciplines and made accessible the Scriptures and other religious writings. Without sound Latin, noted Wimpfeling, priests would bumble through the mass, and "laymen would have no protection against the spirits of Hell and the enticements of the flesh."[58]

He expressed the opinion that German boys were well-endowed with talents, but that they lacked teachers who knew proper methods of instruction. Teachers said and wrote many things, he continued, but students found only a "few good kernels in the midst of all the chaff." His answer to the problem was to adopt the approach used by the "clever Italians." Their methods, wrote Wimpfeling, were efficient and effective: "Thus the sons of the Italians soon attain the capability to hear lectures on Roman law, canon law, and Holy Scripture, and they enter easily into a lawyer's career at a time of their life when my pitiable countrymen still quibble among themselves about the vocative, figures of speech and apposition."[59] The author's effort to communicate Italian methods of Latin grammar instruction made up the bulk of the *Isidoneus*.

[57] Freundgen, *Wimpfelings pädagogische Schriften*, 82.
[58] *Ibid.*, 83.
[59] *Ibid.*, 113.

Several themes were stressed in the work. Much attention, for example, was given to the problem of perverting Latin by transferring to it German usage and pronunciation. Wimpfeling warned that certain teachers, notably Swabians, Hessians, Saxons, and those who lived around Mainz and Frankfurt, should not pronounce vowels too harshly, so that *"lego* is pronounced *laigo* or *leigo,"* or that *casa* is confused with *causa.* When foreigners hear such diction, he claimed, they laugh and ask, "Do these people really believe they have spoken Latin?"[60] In addition, Latinized German words such as *lansmannus* from *Landsmann* should be avoided like the plague.[61]

Another topic that was thoroughly explored in the *Isidoneus* was the selection of texts for classroom use. Not surprisingly, most of the grammatical works of the Middle Ages were condemned. Rejected were the commentary on Priscian by Peter Helias, the thirteenth-century French speculative grammarian; the *Florista,* a fourteenth-century poem on syntax by Ludolf von Luchow; and the *Catholicon,* another commentary on Priscian by a certain Johannes of Janua.[62] The grammars of Donatus, Priscian, and even Alexander Villedieu had some utility, but teachers should take care to avoid sections that were overly complex. This was particularly important with the *Doctrinale,* which contained "discussions of logical relationships that appear to be beyond the mind of the student and lead him into a dark labyrynth."[63] The safest path, said Wimpfeling, was to utilize one of the recent Italian grammars such as Nicholas Perotti's.[64]

As soon as the rudiments of grammar had been mastered, the attainment of true eloquence demanded that students proceed to the study of the Roman poets and orators. Wimpfeling spent several pages defending the usefulness of poetry and in doing so compiled a list of Church fathers, saints, and scho-

---

[60] *Ibid.,* 86.
[61] *Ibid.,* 118.
[62] *Ibid.,* 108, 109.
[63] *Ibid.,* 100.
[64] *Ibid.,* 113.

lastics (Aquinas and Gerson) who in his opinion had seen no conflict between poetry and Christianity. While defending poetry in general, he nonetheless found fault with individual poets. The works of Virgil, Lucan, and Horace (except the *Odes*) were acceptable. On the other hand, Juvenal (too lewd), Persius (too difficult), Ovid (too effeminate and obscene), and Martial (too corrupting) were all to be avoided, as were Tibullus, Propertius, Catullus, and Sappho (all too shameless). The comic poets, Terence and Plautus, were safe except for plays they wrote on love.[65] The orators were less dangerous. Cicero, Sallust, Valerius Maximus, Seneca (*sic*), St. Jerome, St. Ambrose, Petrarch, Bruni, and Francesco Filelfo all received his stamp of approval.[66] Safest of all were the Christian poets—old ones such as Prudentius and Sedulus, and modern ones such as Baptista Mantuanus.

Thus, even though Wimpfeling wrote in the *Isidoneus* that Latin was the "noblest of languages," and "that no other is more graceful, fluent or filled with such an abundance of wise and exalted thoughts,"[67] his commitment to ancient Latin literature was quite limited. There were few indications that Wimpfeling shared the Italian humanists' faith that knowledge of the classics was a prerequisite for man's full moral development. Significantly, in the *Adolescentia*, his guide for the proper moral training of Germany's youth, references to ancient authors were rare. His compilation of one hundred forty-eight alphabetically arranged proverbs from Seneca and one hundred seven passages from Ovid ("whose works cannot be entirely given over to boys and youths") were exceptions.[68] More common were citations from the Church fathers, Italian humanists such as Petrarch, scholastic theologians such as Gerson, and contemporaries such as Geyler von Keysersberg, Sebastian Brant, and Pico della Mirandola. Wimpfeling's deep

[65] *Ibid.*, 141, 142.
[66] *Ibid.*, 144, 145.
[67] *Ibid.*, 158.
[68] *Jakob Wimpfelings Adolescentia*, ed. Otto Herding (Munich: 1965), 296-313 (Ovid), 326-30 (Seneca).

piety and strict moral temperament caused him to see more dangers in pagan literature than most of his humanist contemporaries. But by perceiving the classics essentially as guides to Latin elegance and little more, Wimpfeling expressed an opinion which was by no means exceptional among the early humanists in German-speaking lands.

Logic

One year after his Heidelberg inaugural oration praising the *studia humanitatis*, Peter Luder decided to deliver another publicized speech to preface his lectures on Terence. Although the text of the speech, entitled "In Praise of Philosophy" has been lost, we still have the notice he posted to announce it. In it Luder depicted an inevitable clash between logic and the literary studies he espoused. He told "how prince dialectic, armed with black serpents," had established a dwelling for himself and had allowed his sisters, the other liberal arts, to be "expelled from the country and howl loudly." Then referring to himself, Luder said that rhetoric had recently returned to claim her rights, seeking "not part of the kingdom or a palace, but only a small field and a quiet corner of the house." Nevertheless, dialectic, "stretching his neck like a hissing snake . . ." sought to preserve his tyranny "by not receiving his bountiful sister and by driving her back across the Alps."[69]

Few German humanists in the next four decades voiced Luder's assertion that the study of logic and the *studia humanitatis* were incompatible. In fact, references to logic and its domination of the arts course were rare in early humanist writing. Those references which do exist are, to be sure, negative. Conrad Celtis, for example, in his ode, "To William Mommerloch, Citizen of Cologne and Philosopher," bemoaned the years he devoted to logic while a student at Co-

[69] Wattenbach, "Peter Luders Lobrede," 22.

logne. He recalled how "it was there with you that I learned to introduce misleading sophistries by tortuous syllogism, and all the other lumber of tortuous dialectic." He implied that because of the preeminence of logic "poetry was an object of derision," and the works of Virgil and Cicero "were regarded with that repugnance with which a Jew regards pork."[70] Other humanists expressed dismay about the endless controversies and arguments in which logicians took so much apparent delight. Such complaints were common in the works of Wimpfeling.[71] They also were evident in the previously mentioned *Dialogue on the Seven Liberal Arts* by Dietrich Gresemund the Younger. He wrote that nothing was more fruitless than the contentiousness of logicians "who spend their days shouting, wrangling, and shrieking." He commented that dialectic had degenerated into a contest in which "he is considered the most learned who can most fully stuff the ears of his listeners with his verbosity."

Nonetheless both Gresemund and Wimpfeling agreed that logic had utility. Gresemund saw logic as a necessary tool "to sharpen the mind" and an aid to "define, question and respond in debate and discern truth from falsehood."[72] Wimpfeling once commented on the "extraordinary pleasure" derived from logic[73] and even delivered a speech at Heidelberg in 1499 entitled *On Behalf of Harmony between Dialecticians and Orators*.[74] Although its main theme was the university's need to introduce regular lectures and exercises on the poets and or-

[70] "Ad Vilhelmum Mommerlochum civem coloniensem et philosophum." In Conrad Celtis, *Libri Odarum Quattuor*, ed., Felicitas Pindter (Leipzig: 1937), 88. English translation, Forster, *Selections from Conrad Celtis*, 23.

[71] See especially the introduction to *Adolescentia*, ed. Herding, 189.

[72] Gresemund, *Lucubraciuncule*.

[73] This comment was made in a 1477 oration to celebrate the attainment of the Master of Arts degree by a certain Ulrichus de Rotvilla. Printed in Gustav Knod, "Wimpfeling und die Universität Heidelberg," *Zeitschrift für die Geschichte des Oberrheins*, N.F., 1 (1886), 317-35.

[74] The title is *Pro concordia dialecticorum et oratorum . . . oratio habita ad gymnophistas Heydelbergenses*. It was published without place or date in 1499. Excerpts from the speech have been published in Josef Riegger, *Amoenitates Litterariae Friburgensis*, 2 (Ulm: 1775), 194-96.

ators, Wimpfeling took pains to stress the compatability of the *studia humanitatis* and the existing scholastic curriculum. Theologians and philosophers had nothing to fear, and the place of logic (still offering "extraordinary pleasure") need not be diminished.

Only one early German humanist sensed how fundamentally the rhetorical-philological interests of humanism clashed with the intellectual preoccupations of the late scholastic logicians. Not surprisingly he was Rudolph Agricola, the northern European of his generation who most fully internalized the spirit of the Italian Renaissance.[75] Many of his contemporaries believed that classical literature offered the surest path to Latin elegance. Agricola heartily agreed. But he also saw in the classics an invaluable source for moral regeneration. When he sent his translation of Isocrates' *Parenesis* to his brother, Johann, he summed up his attitude in one sentence: "May it then become not only an aid to your speech but truly also improve your soul."[76] Many of his contemporaries also believed that dialectical studies were over-emphasized and over-complex. Again Agricola agreed. But he did more than criticize; he composed a volume that claimed to do nothing less than reform the discipline itself.

Agricola's deep convictions about the need to effect fundamental reforms in the practice of dialectic were undoubtedly fostered during his stay in Italy between 1469 and 1479. Like many other northerners, he set out for Italy to study law, in his case at the University of Pavia. He had already received a thorough scholastic training at the prestigious northern universities of Erfurt, Cologne, and finally Louvain, where he received his Master of Arts in 1465. Although he had been introduced to humanism at Louvain, where a chair of rhetoric

---

[75] On Agricola, see William H. Woodward, *Studies in Education during the Renaissance* (Cambridge: 1906), 79-103; Lewis Spitz, "Rudolph Agricola—Father of Humanism," *Religious Renaissance of the German Humanists* (Cambridge, Mass.: 1964), 20-40; Friedrich von Bezold, *Rudolph Agricola* (Munich: 1884); Henricus van der Velden, *Rodolphus Agricola een Nederlansch humanist der vijftiende eeuw* (Leiden: 1911).

[76] Cited in Spitz, *Religious Renaissance*, 33.

had been established in 1443,[77] he was overwhelmed by the brilliance of Renaissance Italy. While in Pavia he wrote to a friend that in Italy were to be found "the holiest, greatest and most serious men of genius"; he would not praise things too much, he added, for fear his friend would not believe him.[78] Although he remained in Pavia until 1475, he soon abandoned the law. In 1475 he moved to Ferrara, where he became organist in the ducal chapel of the ruling d'Este family. He attended lectures at the university and made the acquaintance of Battista Guarino and Ludovico Carbone, the two men who had taken over the school of Guarino of Verona after that famous humanist's death. He came as close as any northern European to fulfilling the Renaissance ideal of the "universal man." In addition to his musical skill, he took up gymnastics, painting, and sculpture. He learned Greek, read widely in classical and humanist literature, composed a life of Petrarch and translated a number of Greek works into Latin. His virtuosity impressed even the Italians. He was asked to deliver several orations at both the University of Ferrara and the d'Este court, an honor indeed for a "barbarian northerner."

Agricola left Italy in 1479 and held a number of informal positions until 1484, when his friend Johann of Dalberg, bishop of Worms, convinced him to accept the patronage of Elector Philip of the Palatinate. Residing with the bishop, he was given the opportunity to pursue his own intellectual interests with few restrictions or obligations. He occasionally traveled to Heidelberg, where he lectured not only on rhetoric but also on physics, astronomy, Aristotle's *De animalibus*, and Pliny. These visits to Heidelberg troubled him. In letters to friends he criticized "the rude, stinking filth of the schools in our country,"[79] and complained that the Heidelberg students

---

[77] A. Polet, "Les origines et les débuts de l'humanisme à l'Université de Louvain," *Les études classiques*, 6 (1937), 28-39.

[78] Karl Hartfelder, "Unedierte Briefe von Rudolph Agricola," *Festschrift der Badischen Gymnasien* (Karlsruhe: 1886), 12.

[79] To Antonius Vrye, April 7, 1484, in *Rodolphi Agricolae Lucubrationes*, ed. Alard (Cologne: 1539), II, 177; see also P. S. Allen, "The Letters of Rudolph Agricola," *English Historical Review*, 21 (1906), 314.

and masters who heard his lectures had "to pay out all the time of day in their sophistries over the most petty and as it were superfluous questions."[80]

The work that in no small way helped end the "sophistries" of late scholasticism was begun while Agricola was in Italy and was completed after his return to Germany in 1479. It was entitled *Dialectical Invention in Three Books* (*De dialectica inventione libri tres*). No book by any German humanist had a greater impact on Europe's intellectual and pedagogical development.[81]

Dialectical Invention was a product of Agricola's disillusionment with the logic taught in the universities of northern Europe. As Agricola stated in his book, this "preposterous logic" was responsible for most of the intellectual deficiencies of his day. Most importantly, it failed to establish the methodological groundwork for other disciplines. "It is certain," wrote Agricola, "that this truly miserable and uneasy quibbling of speech which is taught not only is useless for learning the other arts, but is also prejudicial to many of them."[82] As a result, lawyers "stutter in their confused and involved disputing; the study of medicine has been reduced to physics; mathematics has disappeared." Worst of all, faulty logic had destroyed theology. Agricola complained that once metaphysics, logic, and physics had been removed from theological discourse, nothing was left. Theologians should be instructing the people in "religion, justice, and virtue"; instead "they strike the ears of the listeners with foolish noise."[83]

[80] *Rodolphi Agricolae Opuscula*, ed. Peter Gilles (Louvain: 1511), E iiii.

[81] There are many printed editions of the work; I have used *De inventione dialectica libri tres, cum scholiis Johannis Mattaei Phrissemii* (Paris: 1583). See also Lisa Jardine, "Lorenzo Valla and the Intellectual Origins of Humanist Dialectic," *Journal of the History of Philosophy*, 15 (1977), 143-64. Cesare Vasoli, "Dialettica e Rhetorica in Rodolpho Agricola," *Accademia toscanna di scienze e lettere la Columbaria, Attie Memmorie*, 22 (1957), 305-55; August Faust, "Die Dialektik Rodolph Agricolas," *Archiv für die Geshichte der Philosophie*, N.F., 34 (1922), 118-36; Walter J. Ong includes a lengthy discussion of the work in *Ramus, Method and the Decay of Dialogue* (Cambridge, Mass.: 1951), 92-130.

[82] *De inventione . . .* , Bk. II, Ch. I, 151.

[83] *Ibid.*, 150.

Agricola's *Dialectical Invention* has been called anti-Aristotelian, though with little justification. Agricola did criticize the "obscurities" of Aristotle's style and organization, but he never evinced the bitter anti-Aristotelianism of Valla's *Dialectical Disputations*. In fact, along with Cicero, Quintilian, and Boethius, Aristotle was one of Agricola's avowed sources.[84] In a real sense he saw his role as one of rectifying a perversion of Aristotle by medieval logicians. Aristotle had divided all human discourse into three areas—logic, dialectic, and rhetoric. Logic dealt with certainties and sought rigid scientific demonstration. Dialectic, however, dealt only with probabilities and probable conclusions. As Aristotle put it, dialectic was that branch of discourse "which reasons from opinions generally accepted." Rhetoric also dealt with probabilities, but differed from dialectic in its application, which was persuasion rather than demonstration. To put it another way, logic began with a question and moved from a strict argument to a strict conclusion; dialectic and rhetoric moved from a probable argument to a probable conclusion—the best that could be hoped for in most practical situations. Medieval logicians had abandoned these distinctions. Rhetoric was ignored, and dialectic, the art of probable discourse, was absorbed into logic. Dialectic and logic came to mean the same thing—the art of rigid scientific demonstration.[85]

Agricola tried to reform logic by again shifting the balance among Aristotle's three forms of discourse. He neglected the logic of rigid demonstration and expanded the field of dialectic to cover all human discourse in its rational and emotional elements. It became the "art of discussing with probability any proposed matter insofar as the nature of the subject is capable of creating conviction."[86] Its goal was to teach and convince the reader or listener. It therefore assumed many of the roles traditionally ascribed to rhetoric. Rhetoric no longer

---

[84] Ong, *Ramus, Method and Decay of Dialogue*, 98.
[85] *Ibid.*, 59-63; Wilbur S. Howell, *Logic and Rhetoric in England, 1500-1700* (Princeton, N.J.: 1956), 15, 16.
[86] *De inventione*, Bk. II, Ch. 3, 163.

dealt with finding and organizing arguments but only with final delivery, or "elocution."

Dialectic thus became less useful for the arts master bent on rigid demonstration. As stated by Walter J. Ong, "compared with the older dialectic or logic, Agricola's is 'humane' in a sense which makes it also amateur, graceful, and as logic scientifically irresponsible."[87] This was exactly what Agricola intended. He had concluded that the dialectic of the schools was impractical for everyone except professional logicians and philosophers. Outside the classroom or lecture hall, academic logic was worthless. Agricola expressed these convictions at the beginning of his work. His dialectic, he promised, would not only lay the groundwork for other disciplines, as medieval logicians had always claimed, but it would also be useful for people in their everyday lives. It was designed for those "who govern the commonwealth in council, for whom it is fitting to make conviction in the senate or to people on war, peace and other affairs of state, . . . also for those who have as a profession to accuse, defend, petition and deny before judges, and for those who may want to teach the people justice, religion and piety."[88] These things, he added, were rarely taught in schools and when they were it was done in an incomprehensible way.

Agricola had planned to treat dialectic in two separate books. The first, on invention, dealt with methods by which debatable propositions could be analyzed to determine what could be said for or against them. The second, never completed, was to deal with judgment—methods of arranging words into propositions, propositions into syllogisms, and syllogisms into whole arguments. The key to dialectical invention, as outlined in *Dialectical Invention*, was skill in the use of *loci*, usually translated "topics" or "common places." *Loci* were headings or key notions used to find out what was available in one's store of knowledge for discourse on any given subject. Lists

[87] Ong, *Ramus*, 100.
[88] *De inventione*, Bk. I, Ch. 1, 3.

of *loci* varied from author to author, but usually included definition, genus, species, wholes, parts, relatives, opposites, place, time, and so on, up to twenty-four in Agricola's case. These were the headings to run through when one had something to say on any given subject—while pleading a case in court, delivering a lecture, or debating a point in philosophy.

There is no need to summarize Agricola's definitions of the various *loci* and his rules for using them. It is, however, important to emphasize Agricola's revolutionary intent: to upset the medieval dialectical tradition by tying it to the precepts of classical rhetoric. Along with Aristotle, his major sources were the great rhetoricians, Cicero and Quintilian, and the influence of Valla is evident throughout. The very concept of "invention" had in fact traditionally been used by orators rather than logicians; Cicero, for example, named invention the first of five parts of rhetoric. "Topics" too had always been of interest mainly to orators; when mastered, they enabled a speaker to discourse fluently on any subject.

In the sixteenth century, Agricola's *Dialectical Invention* attained enormous popularity and vast influence. Between 1515 and 1589 it appeared in more than fifty editions.[89] In 1515 no less a figure than Henry VIII ordererd students of Cambridge University to read Agricola rather than "the frivolous questions and obscure losses of Scotus."[90] Most importantly, Peter Ramus and Philip Melanchthon, the two most important educational theorists of the sixteenth century, drew heavily on Agricola's theories of dialectic; through their influence Agricola's dialectic came to dominate the classrooms of Europe and in the seventeenth century even of the new world.

But among Agricola's contemporaries the work inspired little interest or enthusiasm. In the 1480s and 1490s, German humanists rushed into print hundreds of Latin grammars,

---

[89] Walter J. Ong, *Ramus and Talon Inventory* (Cambridge, Mass.: 1958), 534-58, lists fifty-three copies between 1515 and 1589; he admits his list is not exhaustive "and can doubtless be enlarged."

[90] E. J. Ashforth, *Language and Logic in the Post-Medieval Period* (Dordrecht, Holland: 1974), 14.

colloquies, and manuals for public speaking or letter writing. But *Dialectical Invention* remained in manuscript until 1515 when the first edition appeared in Paris. The early humanists' range of interests was too limited, and their place within the universities was too tenuous to expect anything but an indifferent response to Agricola's "new dialectic." As a result, in terms of logic, the first offspring of this "Father of German humanism" appeared only forty years after his death.

PHILOSOPHY AND THEOLOGY

The early humanists' criticisms of scholasticism rarely ranged outside the *trivium*. Disparagements of scholastic theology were virtually nonexistent. They seem limited to that one brief passage in Agricola's *Dialectical Invention* where the author referred to the deleterious effect of logic on theological discourse. Comments on philosophy were more common. But unlike the unanimity of the humanists on the virtues of the *studia humanitatis* and the importance of rhetoric, there was no single humanist position on philosophical issues. Nor can it be said that the reform of the universities' philosophical offerings was one of their priorities.

Among those humanists who did comment on philosophical issues, there was but one area of agreement: their antipathy for metaphysics. To the humanists, metaphysics too often degenerated into empty speculation and linguistic quibblings; or else it bred ceaseless controversy over issues that were at once insoluble and probably unimportant. The humanists' dismay over the wrangling involved in the *Wegestreit* is a case in point. As Wimpfeling sarcastically commented in the introduction to his *Adolescentia*, "As if the health of the soul and body, as if the growth of states and security of cities, as if the authority of the priesthood and the honor of the religious orders, as if the power of virtue and ruin of vise, as if the renown of peace and the banishment of war, the concord of princes, the defeat of Turks, the vindication of Christian blood, as if the end of human life and the very fabric of the whole world depended and rested on the question of universal concepts."[91]

What then was the most important aspect of philosophical inquiry? According to most Italian humanists, the answer was and had been "ethics." This response reflected the ties between moral philosophy and rhetoric that had been commonplace ever since the Greeks. As ancient and Renaissance authors never tired of stating, orators were "accustomed to praise virtue and castigate vice." Furthermore, poetry inspired men to praiseworthy deeds, and history offered countless examples of good and evil to be emulated or avoided.

Among the German humanists, the bond between rhetoric and morality was weaker. Although many mouthed words about the inspirational role of orators, most did so with little conviction. They saw the ancients as models for proper Latin style and little more. Others, such as Celtis, whose restless mind was attracted to a variety of philosophical issues, showed little interest in moral philosophy.[92] Agricola and Wimpfeling evinced a deeper commitment to moral reform. Both men agreed that ancient orators, historians, and poets offered moral inspiration. But for Wimpfeling, as seen, the ancients had to be carefully censored to prevent the pollution of youthful minds by the unsavory allurements of pagan authors. Christian writers were preferable. Even Agricola stressed that of all books the most valuable moral guide was the Bible, "which like no other book has for a long time been free of all error."[93]

Natural philosophy provided another focus of interest for a number of early German humanists. Agricola, for example, often stressed the importance of learning the "nature of things."

---

[91] Wimpfeling, *Adolescentia*, ed. Herding, 189.

[92] In regard to Celtis, Spitz has written, "Celtis made just a few gestures in the direction of developing a moral philosophy, but they remained merely gestures for the most part." *Religious Renaissance*, 88.

[93] "De ratione docendi," in *Opuscula*, 106.

In his *Plan of Studies* he wrote that a student should learn "the positions of lands, seas, mountains and rivers, the nature of the earth's peoples, their customs, borders, circumstances, and their rulers; also the qualities of trees and plants, treated by Theophrastus; and the functions, history and reproduction of all living things, treated by Aristotle."[94] Such enthusiasms were shared by Celtis, who more fully than any of his humanist contemporaries adopted Cicero's definition of philosophy as "the knowledge of all things divine and human and their causes." In the introductory letter he attached to his edition of Apuleius's *De mundo* in 1502, he exhorted his readers to "lovingly embrace this pristine and lucid consideration of the nature of things, and at last . . . to turn from old, empty trifles and slippery, foaming verbal controversies to solider, older and more praiseworthy disciplines."[95] Celtis had described these "more praiseworthy disciplines" in an ode written in 1492, entitled "What the Future Philosopher Ought to Know."[96] After learning Latin and putting away the "boorish sounds of your ancestral tongue," the young philosopher, Celtis urged, should explore the causes of all things in nature:

Find out the nature of the formless Chaos, where the elements stream forth in forms of beauty with discordant purposes, mixing the seeds of the world, which return in the end whence they came.

Find out with soaring mind the causes of individual things: investigate the blowing of the winds and the tides of the raging sea.

Find out why dark hollows of the earth produce sulphur and veins of fair metals and why hot springs restore the bodies of the sick.

[94] *Ibid.*, 80.
[95] The letter can be found in Hans Rupprich, ed., *Der Briefwechsel des Conrad Celtis* (Munich: 1934), 297.
[96] "Ad Sigismundum Fusilium Vratislaviensem De his quod futurus philosophus scire debeat." Latin text and English translation are in Forster, ed., *Selections from Conrad Celtis*, 28-33.

Find out why lightning cracks so loudly as it darts from the clouds, and study the storming of rain, slow falling snow and icy hail.

Learn to discourse on the planets which move in free orbits apart, and of the Sun's eclipse when the pale-faced Moon has put its chariot to flight.

Learn with wonder of shooting stars that escape from the vaulted sky, of the twin couch of the sun.

The knowledge of geography was also important:

Learn to tell the peoples scattered over the globe and their different languages and customs, and tell beneath what clime they occupy this earth that hovers in the air.

At the very end of his ode, Celtis added as an afterthought that the future philosopher should also know something of moral philosophy. He urged him to "climb nobly up the straight and noble path of virtue." But the study of ethics was obviously less appealing than the study of nature.

Celtis's impulse to probe the deepest mysteries of nature helped make him the only major German humanist before 1500 to develop an interest in neo-Platonism. He never systematically spelled out his beliefs, but one can find various neo-Platonic doctrines scattered throughout his works. In his dedication of the *Amores* to Emperor Maximilian I, Celtis spoke of the divine love that brought order and unity out of chaos and that imparted to man a spark of the divinity itself.[97] And in the introduction to his edition of Apuleius's *De mundo*, he discussed the shadowy world of divine things and the invisible forms beyond the world of everyday experience. Through contemplation and virtue, a few might attain the arcane and mysterious wisdom necessary to understand the higher order of the universe. Celtis wrote that "nothing more delightful and agreeable could happen to human minds in this

[97] For a brief summary of Celtis's dedication, see Spitz, *Religious Renaissance*, 92–93.

course of life than to have time for the contemplation of those things, whose knowledge calls souls out of their prisons and speeds them above into divine and ethereal movements and loves." Those who have achieved this higher wisdom experience "that highest felicity and blessedness promised by the divine oracle to all good men."[98]

If Celtis's interest in natural philosophy caused him to test the heady and rather uncharted waters of Florentine neo-Platonism, it also explains his admiration for two prominent scholastics, Albertus Magnus (1206-1280) and Thomas Aquinas (1225-1274). These two Dominicans had of course written extensively on Aristotelian science, and their works were taught at Cologne when Celtis studied there in 1480. In his ode. "To William Mommerloch," Celtis wrote that his only happy memory of Cologne was the study of the works of these two men: "There you and I handled sacred books of ancient wisdom, there I learnt what high lore Albertus Magnus and Thomas taught about the nature of the universe."[99] Of the two, Albertus, the German, was more attractive to Celtis, who composed two epigrams in his honor. In one of them, "On the Illusions of Albertus Magnus," an unnamed individual appears to Albertus in a dream and offers him high ecclesiastical honors and a great palace. Albertus is briefly interested, but then he realizes he is being deceived, and he rejects his tempter's offer. The meaning of the epigram is obscure, but it probably refers to Celtis's disapproval of the two years during which Albertus abandoned his scholarly career to serve as bishop of Regensburg.[100] The second epigram, "On the Fatherland and Teaching of Albertus Magnus," praised in a straightforward way Albertus's Swabian background and his achievements as a natural philosopher.[101] According to Celtis, Albertus had described the whole world and "revealed to all

---

[98] Celtis, *Briefwechsel*, 296.

[99] Forster, ed., *Selections from Conrad Celtis*, 23.

[100] "De praestigiis Alberti Magni," *Fünf Bücher Epigramme von Konrad Celtis*, Karl Hartfelder, ed. (Berlin, 1881), 32.

[101] "De patrice et doctrina Alberti Magni," *ibid.*, 41.

the stars of the wandering sky." He added that "whatever has the earth and sky, and what the air contains, that man showed us through his genius." The reader should "pay attention" to his teaching and "read his lucid writings."

Despite such pronouncements, it would nevertheless be a mistake to push Celtis into the philosopher's mold. The fact is he spent more time writing poetry than contemplating "ethereal movements and loves," more time organizing humanist sodalities than pursuing the "highest felicity" of philosophy. In his thirty-year teaching career, he offered only one course that can at all be construed as "philosophical." This was the series of lectures presented in 1501 at Vienna on the *De mundo* of Apuleius. Celtis was primarily a rhetorician and poet whose interest in philosophy was sincere, but dilettantish. As such, his thought and career were not markedly different from the "trivial" concerns of the other early German humanists.

Modern historians are apt to read back into the intellectual history of the late fifteenth century the inevitability of a clash between logic and rhetoric or between the *studia humanitatis* and the logic-soaked curriculum of the universities. Contemporary humanists viewed their world in less combative terms. As evidenced by the limited range of their anti-scholastic polemics, most believed that the *humaniora* could find a place in the German universities even if most of the traditional scholastic curriculum remained intact. Indeed, most of the intellectual activities and assumptions we identify today as "scholastic" elicited a response of "no comment" from the humanists.

Men were capable of living in both worlds. Wimpfeling, typically described as a "humanist with a thorough scholastic education," might just as accurately be known as a scholastic theologian who turned to humanism toward the middle of his life. Other examples abound. One thinks of Conrad Summenhart (d. 1502), the colleague of Gabriel Biel and the theological representative of the *via antiqua* at the University of Tübingen. Depicted by Lewis Spitz on one page as a "scholastic humanist" and several pages later as a "half-humanist scholastic," Summenhart frequently alluded to ancient authors in his works and was a sufficiently competent orator to deliver the eulogy at the funeral of Count Eberhard the Bearded.[102] One could also cite Conrad Wimpina, the Leipzig theologian, who in the 1490s published a treatise on letter writing, two lengthy poetical works, and an imposing compendium of logic.[103] One finally thinks of Stephan Hoest (1431-1472), a student of Peter Luder's, a licentiate of theology, and twice elected vice chancellor of the University of Heidelberg. As vice chancellor he was called upon to deliver orations at graduation ceremonies and on other festive occasions. Three such orations are worth noting: in one he praised the philosophical assumptions of the *via antiqua*; in another the logical perspecuity of the *via moderna*; in the third the value of the *studia humanitatis*.[104] His choice of topics reveals much about early German humanism and its relation with scholasticism.

[102] Spitz, *Religious Renaissance*, 17, 23. The eulogy was delivered in March 1496; later printed in *Oratio funebris . . . habita ad universitatem Tüwingensem in officio exequiarum: quod eodem universitas pro illustri principe domino Eberhardo primo duce in Wirtemberg et Deck* (Tübingen: Othmar: 1498).

[103] See Joseph Negwer, *Konrad Wimpina, ein katholischer Theologe aus der Reformationszeit* (Breslau: 1909).

[104] All three speeches with German translations have been published in Frank E. Baron ed. and trans., *Stephan Hoest, Reden und Briefe* (Munich: 1971), 118-41, 146-79.

The Response to Humanism,
1450-1500 ~

IN THE SUMMER of 1456, having been at the University of
Heidelberg for only one month, Peter Luder addressed a letter
to a Heidelberg academic, Johannes Wenck, in which he made
an assertion that would appear time and again in humanist
writings. He claimed that the Heidelberg scholastics were
adamantly opposed to his efforts. There was, he wrote, an
"ignoble crowd" at the university "who had never contem-
plated the books of the ancients," but who had the temerity
to greet his efforts with "loud laughter." He had also heard
the whispers of those who were trying to "slander the poets
and wound the divine study of letters with obscene words."[1]
In a similar vein some years later, he complained of his Heidelberg enemies and referred to them as "beasts who invidiously barked at me with mouths full of malicious insults."[2]

It was a rare humanist who did not echo Luder's comments.
Indeed much that the humanists wrote gives the impression
that their proposals for intellectual and educational reform
were met with relentless opposition by the upholders of traditional methods. Despite their ubiquity, such pronouncements are of course insufficient proof of an anti-humanist
scholastic conspiracy. The humanists were hardly unbiased

---

[1] Gerhard Ritter, "Aus dem Kreise der Hofpoeten Pfalzgraf Friedrichs I,"
Zeitschrift für die Geschichte des Oberrheins, N.F. 38 (1922), 117.

[2] Wilhelm Wattenbach, "Peter Luder," *Zeitschrift für die Geschichte des
Oberrheins*, 22 (1869), 120.

judges of their own plight and for any number of reasons might have been tempted to exaggerate the obstacles thrown in their path. The validity of their claims and the extent of scholastic obstructionism can be judged only after a careful examination of the humanists' experiences within the universities. This chapter will describe and analyze these experiences in the latter fifteenth century.

HUMANISM AT THE UNIVERSITIES TO 1500

The institution at which humanism progressed most rapidly in the fifteenth century was unquestionably the University of Vienna.[3] Introduced at midcentury, humanism flourished in the 1450s and 1470s, went into eclipse in the 1460s and 1480s and put its indelible stamp on the institution in the 1490s, largely as a result of pressure from the Hapsburg court. The early introduction of humanist lectures in the 1450s can be attributed to the influence of two Italians: the illustrious Aeneas Sylvius Piccolomini, who was a Hapsburg official in the 1440s[4] and the Franciscan William of Savona, who resided in nearby Klosterneuberg between 1448 and 1454.[5] Although Aeneas never taught at the university, he did have a number of formal

[3] There is extensive literature on the early history of the University of Vienna: Rudolf Kink, *Geschichte der kaiserlichen Universität zu Wien*, 2 vols. (Vienna: 1854)—the second volume contains a useful collection of sources; Joseph Ritter von Aschbach, *Geschichte der Wiener Universität*, 2 vols. (Vienna: 1865, 1877); Gustav Bauch, *Die Reception des Humanismus in Wien* (Breslau: 1903); Karl Grossmann, "Die Frühzeit des Humanismus in Wien bis zu Celtis Berufung," *Jahrbuch für Landeskunde von Niederösterreich*, N.F. 22 (1929), 150-325; Alphons Lhotsky, *Die Wiener Artistenfakultät, 1365-1497* (Vienna: 1965); Adalbert Horawitz, "Der Humanismus in Wien," *Historisches Taschenbuch*, 6 (1883), 137-200; John Thomas Dunne, "Between the Renaissance and Reformation: Humanism at the University of Vienna," Diss., University of Southern California, 1974.

[4] On Aeneas's presence in Vienna and his contribution to German humanism, see Georg Voigt, *Enea Silvo de' Piccolomini*, II (Berlin: 1862), 342-58.

[5] See J. Ruysschaert, "Lorenzo Guglielmo Traversagni de Savona," *Archivum Franciscanum Historicum*, 5 (1953), 195-210.

contacts with the institution; in 1445 he participated in two disputations in which he was invited to discourse on the charms of poetry and the connections between ancient literature and moral philosophy.[6] Savona, on the other hand, actually taught courses on rhetoric, drawing "large crowds" according to a letter by Aeneas written in 1453.[7] Each won disciples within the university, especially among academics who had studied in Italy. From this group came the five men, Phillip Mautther, Paul Swicker, George Peuerbach, Johann Mandl, and Johann Regiomantanus, who along with William of Savona, lectured on a wide range of classical texts between 1451 and 1461. Among their subjects were Virgil's *Aeneid*, the pseudo-Ciceronian *Rhetorica ad Herrenium*, Juvenal's *Satires*, Terence's *Adelphi*, Lucan's *Pharsalia*, and other works by Cicero and Horace.[8]

After 1461 evidence of humanist teaching disappears from university records for almost a decade. The death of Peuerbach, humanism's most eminent spokesman, in 1461 was one important cause. More damaging were the disasters that struck Vienna and its university in these years. During the Hapsburg civil war between Emperor Frederick III and his brother Adrian VI, Vienna was occupied by Adrian's forces, placed under an interdict by Pius II, and visited in turn by plague, famine, and inflation. Even after Adrian's death ended the feud in 1463, the university was slow to recover, in part due to enrollment competition from newly founded universities at Basel (1459), Freiburg-im-Breisgau (1457), and Ingolstadt

---

[6] In the first disputation he was asked to speak on two serious questions: "Whether prudence was identical with the science of morals taught in the books of *Ethics, Politics,* and *Economics,* and in canon and civil law," and "Why there are so few poets in the present day, although many consider them to be useful and necessary." He also responded to one purely humorous question: "Why cheap skins of dead animals and old cloths with wax were sold for such high prices in chancelleries." The questions and Aeneas's response can be found in Lhotsky, *Die Wiener Artistenfakultät,* 262-73.

[7] Eneas Sylvius Piccolomini, *Briefwechsel,* ed., Rudolf Wolkan (Vienna: 1909), II, 231.

[8] Aschbach, *Geschichte,* I, 353; Grossmann, "Die Frühzeit," 227; Lhotsky, *Die Wiener Artistenfakultät,* 127.

(1472) to the west and Pressburg (1465) to the east. With a return of stability in the 1470s however, humanist activity dramatically revived. From 1470 to 1472 Peter Luder taught at the university, thus making Vienna his last academic stop before his death in 1474. The well-traveled poet offered courses on letter writing and several Ciceronian texts.[9] His presence seems to have sparked new interest in humanism, for according to university records no less than nine Viennese academics lectured on ancient authors in the 1470s.[10] They were not professional humanists nor wandering poets like Luder, but rather professors in the arts faculty or else students of theology or law. Most prominent was Bernard Perger, the author/compiler of the *Nova grammatica* and the university's superintendent in the 1490s. Cicero and Virgil were the most popular authors, but Sallust, Horace, and Seneca also received attention.

The last two decades of the fifteenth century duplicated the pattern of the 1460s and 1470s: interest in humanism faded in the 1480s, but vigorously revived in the 1490s. The 1480s were once again years of political turmoil, marked by warfare between Emperor Frederick III and King Matthias Corvinus of Hungary. Vienna was besieged and then occupied by Hungarian forces between 1485 and 1490; in these years only one obscure Italian humanist, Cinthus de Burgo Sancti Sepulchri, appeared in university records. He lectured on rhetoric in 1487, but when his efforts to gain a stipend from the university or King Matthias failed, he quickly departed.[11]

When the Hungarian occupation was lifted in 1490, the university's condition was desperate. Students' fees had evaporated, faculty ranks had thinned, and financial assistance from the Hapsburgs had ended. Worse, the aged Emperor Frederick III was peeved because of the university's supposed cooperation with the Hungarians. As a result, in 1490 the institution

[9] Grossmann, "Die Frühzeit," 259, 260.
[10] Lhotsky, *Die Wiener Artistenfakultät*, 168, 169 lists the individuals and their subjects.
[11] Bauch, *Die Reception*, 98.

was forced to petition the emperor for a confirmation of privileges and renewed financial support. Both were granted in 1491, but only after the academic corporation agreed to accept the direction of a special superintendent, appointed by the emperor, who, though not a teaching member of any faculty, would become overseer of the university.[12] The emperor's choice was Bernard Perger, the dedicated disciple of humanism whose career had included at least six visits to Italy.

Perger's tenure as superintendent, which lasted until 1500, was of signal importance not only for the University of Vienna but for all pre-Reformation German universities. It represented the first effort of a German government to limit a university's independence and exert greater control over both administration and curriculum. In terms of governance this entailed efforts to streamline authority, end helter-skelter financial practices, and devise policies by which princely authority could be brought to bear more heavily on the universities. In terms of curriculum it entailed efforts to implement humanism and bring an end to many of the academic practices essential to late scholasticism.

Perger's pro-humanist policy took two directions. First, he sought to regularize teaching of the *studia humanitatis* by hiring a salaried humanist lecturer. Such a step, he felt, would not only enhance the prestige of humanism but also end the situation where rhetorical and poetical courses were offered haphazardly, according to the interest and inclination of individual masters. Thus in the 1490s Perger contracted three men to fill his newly created post. Hired in 1493 was the Italian Franciscan poet, C. Paulus Amaltheus; in 1494, another Italian, Giralamo Balbi, trained in both law and the *humaniora*; and in 1497, the German archhumanist, Conrad Celtis, who like the previous wandering poet, Peter Luder, made Vienna his last academic home. In addition, in 1493 and 1499, Perger and his supporters at court spearheaded two attempts to re-

---

[12] Relevant documents can be found in Kink, *Geschichte*, I, part 2, 114. The office of superintendent had existed previously, but the incumbent had had minor responsibilities such as monitoring the payment of student fees.

form Vienna's century-old scholastic curriculum. The proposed changes were restricted to the arts course and by no means reflected all the humanists' educational ideas. Nonetheless, the ambitions of the reformers and the pressures on the university were without precedent. The response of the Viennese academics to the new salaried humanists and the proposed reforms provides invaluable insight into the nature of the late fifteenth-century tensions between humanism and scholasticism and will be examined in detail at the end of this chapter.

At the opposite end of the spectrum from Vienna were the Baltic universities of Greifswald and Rostock,[13] where humanism had little discernible impact before 1500. With small enrollments,[14] and some two hundred miles from Leipzig, the nearest university town, the institutions had little appeal to the wandering poets. Hermann Buschius taught briefly at both institutions in the 1490s[15] and Conrad Celtis referred to a visit to Rostock in 1486.[16] Neither man stimulated any significant interest in humanism. Nor were conditions favorable for the development of humanist interests among existing faculty members. Italy was far away, and contacts of any kind—political, economic, and ecclesiastical—with the homeland of European humanism were few. Neither university was closely tied to a princely court where humanism was cultivated. The records of Rostock refer to only one regular faculty member who lectured on classical texts; he was Tillmann Heverlingh, a Master of Arts and student of theology who headed one of

[13] Recent scholarship has all but ignored these two universities. Only two general surveys, each over a century old, are available: Otto Krabbe, *Die Universität Rostock im fünfzehnten und sechzehnten Jahrhundert* (Rostock: 1854); Johann S. Kosegarten, *Geschichte der Universität Greifswald mit urkundlichen Beilagen* (Greifswald: 1857).

[14] Greifswald had the smallest average enrollment of any German university from 1451 to 1500. Only Freiburg and Heidelberg were smaller than Rostock. See Franz Eulenburg, *Die Frequenz der deutschen Universitäten* (Leipzig: 1904), 54ff.

[15] Kosegarten, *Geschichte*, 163; Hermann J. Liessem, *Hermann von dem Busche* (Nieuwkoop: 1965), 19. This is a reprint of the study originally printed in *Jahresberichte des Königlichen Kaiser Wilhelm-Gymnasiums in Cöln* (1884-1908).

[16] Celtis, *Briefwechsel*, 610.

the university's *bursae*. In the early 1490s, he offered courses on Juvenal and Virgil.[17]

Early humanism also made comparatively little progress at the Rhenish universities, Cologne and Heidelberg. This is surprising in the case of Heidelberg, where Peter Luder introduced humanist lectures in the 1450s, the same decade when humanism first took root at Vienna.[18] Moreover, Luder remained at Heidelberg for five years, between 1456 and 1461, longer than at any of the other universities at which he taught. It was also encouraging that Luder was subsidized by the Palatine Elector Frederick I, a sign that the prince and his councillors were interested in promoting humanism at the university. Actions by the arts faculty in the mid-1450s also suggest a tolerance if not an active interest in works relating to the *studia humanitatis*. In 1455 and 1456 it empowered its dean to spend fifty gulden for the purchase of numerous classical texts, including works by Cicero, Terence, Lucan, Quintilian, Valerius Maximus, Sallust, and Petrarch.[19] Even after Luder's departure for Erfurt in 1461, humanism's prospects seemed promising. As he did wherever he taught, Luder left behind disciples, including students of theology and law and several future court officials.[20] Most prominent among them was Stephan Hoest, who received his licentiate in theology in 1467 and remained at Heidelberg until his death in 1472.[21] He taught theology, served as court preacher, and carried on

[17] Krabbe, *Die Universität Rostock*, 261.

[18] On Heidelberg humanism, see Gerhard Ritter, *Die Heidelberger Universität* (Heidelberg: 1936) 450-90; Ludwig Geiger, "Der Humanismus an der Universität Heidelberg," *Die Nation*, 3, no. 46 (August 14, 1886), 677-80; Karl Hartfelder, "Heidelberg und der Humanismus," *Zeitschrift für allgemeine Geschichte*, 2 (1885), 177-95, 671-96.

[19] Wattenbach, "Peter Luder," 46. Many of the manuscripts were purchased from the estate of Ludwig von Ast, provost of the Worms cathedral, chancellor of the university, and an important adviser of Prince Frederick.

[20] Ritter lists the following Heidelberg academics who were attracted to Luder's teaching: Stephan Hoest, Jodocus Eichman, Johannes Wenck, all theology students; Johannes Wildenhertz, Petrus de Wimpina, and Johann Litifuguli, all jurists. "Aus dem Kreise der Hofpoeten Pfalzgraf Friedrichs I," 119, 120.

[21] On Hoest, see Frank E. Baron ed. and tr., *Stephan Hoest, Reden und Briefe* (Munich: 1971).

107

Luder's work in the *studia humanitatis*. During the 1460s he lectured on the comedies of Terence, the *Aeneid, Bucolics*, and *Georgics* of Virgil, the letters of Horace and several works by Cicero. One of his students was Jacob Wimpfeling, who later called Hoest as "eloquent as Cicero" and equal in learning to Albertus Magnus, Aquinas, and even Plato.[22]

Other signs were less favorable, however. Hoest's lectures, it seems, were poorly attended. In a poem dedicated to Hoest in the 1460s, Peter Luder praised his former student as the "apex of the poetical art" but expressed bewilderment that students did not flock to hear him. No one came, Luder surmised, because students "had no taste for the arts" and spent their time "in games and bufoonery."[23] Then in 1465 Elector Frederick I failed in his effort to replace Luder with another salaried humanist. The humanist in question was Petrus Antonius Finariensis, an Italian jurist who had previously taught poetry and law at the University of Basel.[24] He had successfully caught the eye of the Palatine elector with a poetical composition that lavishly praised the deeds and virtues of the prince. In 1465 he was invited to Heidelberg with the intent of holding a dual lectureship in law and the *studia humanitatis*. Frederick promised to provide Finariensis a stipend and petitioned the university to supplement it. But in the fall of 1465, the university senate rejected the prince's request, claiming that "the necessities of the university are too great, such that we ourselves are barely able to keep going."[25] As a result, the Italian's planned lectures on poetry and oratory never became a reality.

With the university's rebuff to Finariensis and the apparent unwillingness of the prince to press the issue, humanism regressed or at best stagnated at Heidelberg in the next several

[22] See citation in Charles Schmidt, *Histoire littéraire de l'Alsace*, I (Paris: 1879), 9.

[23] Wattenbach, "Peter Luder," 44, 45.

[24] Gerhard Ritter, "Petrus Antonius Finariensis, der Nachfolger Peter Luders in Heidelberg," *Archiv für Kulturgeschichte*, 26 (1936), 89-104.

[25] Eduard Winkelmann, *Urkundenbuch der Universität Heidelberg*, 2 vols. (Heidelberg: 1886), II, 49.

decades. It is probable that Samuel Karoch, the wandering poet, taught there in the late 1470s, but there is no concrete information about his stay.[26] Wimpfeling was also at Heidelberg in the 1470s as a professor of the arts and student of theology. At this stage in his career, however, his capabilities and interests in humanism were minimal.

In the early 1480s conditions again looked propitious for a possible revival of humanism at Heidelberg. The successor to Elector Frederick I, his nephew Philip, was known as a patron of humanists. Moreover, his chancellor, Johann of Dalberg, also bishop of Worms, was even more committed to humanist pursuits. Dalberg, for example, successfully lured the aging Rudolph Agricola to his court in 1484 and 1485.[27] Finally, in December 1484, the young poet Conrad Celtis matriculated at the university. He was a house guest of Dalberg and frequently conversed with Agricola. He soon left, however, and returned only ten years later when he was instrumental in founding the so-called Rhenish Sodality, a loosely organized group of men with a common interest in humanism.[28] None of this activity significantly touched the university, however. Agricola occasionally lectured there, and attendance was encouraging. But he deplored the traditionalism of the institution and complained to correspondents about the deficiencies of Germany's schools.[29] The Rhenish Sodality largely consisted of non-university men, the only exceptions being two theologians, Jodocus Gallus and Pallas Spangel. Until it broke up at the time of Dalberg's death in 1503, its impact on the university was minimal.

Thus when Wimpfeling returned to the university in 1499 after eighteen years as cathedral preacher in Speyer, his dismay over the institution's indifference to the *humaniora* is under-

---

[26] Heinz Entner, *Frühhumanismus und Schultradition in Leben und Werk des Wanderpoeten Samuel Karoch von Lichtenberg* (Berlin: 1968), 34.

[27] On Dalberg and his circle, see Ritter, *Die Heidelberger Universität*, 468-73.

[28] Lewis Spitz, *Conrad Celtis, the German Arch-Humanist* (Cambridge, Mass.: 1957), 46-52.

[29] *Rodolphi Agricolae Lucubrationes*, ed., Alard (Cologne: 1539), II, 177.

standable. In a speech delivered to the academic community on August 12, 1499, he castigated his colleagues for their utter neglect of poetry and oratory.[30] He pointed out that many other institutions, such as Basel, Freiburg, Tübingen, Ingolstadt, and Vienna, had already established regular salaried positions for professors of the *studia humanitatis*. Even most preparatory schools in Germany were offering students a chance to acquaint themselves with classical letters. Deplorably, when these students came to Heidelberg, the rectors of the *bursae* actually prohibited them from further study of the orators and poets. He warned that as long as this persisted, Heidelberg did not deserve to be called a true university.

At about the same time Wimpfeling delivered his speech at Heidelberg, another humanist, Rudolph of Langen,[31] was expressing similar misgivings about the University of Cologne. Langen had become a disciple of humanism while studying at the University of Erfurt in the 1460s. Since the 1470s he had been schoolmaster of the cathedral school in Münster, where he had introduced humanist methods of grammar instruction and the study of the classics. Since many of his students went on to attend the University of Cologne, Langen was disappointed that the institution offered so few opportunities for literary studies. In 1498, therefore, he addressed a letter to the university's patron, the Cologne city council, complaining about the neglect of the *studia humanitatis*.[32] Like Wimpfeling, he praised the classics and warned that unless literary studies were encouraged Cologne would lose its place among Germany's leading universities. Students, he predicted, would simply go elsewhere.

The University of Cologne had, in fact, experienced some humanist influence, although on a modest scale. The matric-

[30] Later published as *Oratio . . . ad gymnophistas Heidelbergenses*. See Ch. 2, note 74.

[31] Ludwig Geiger, "Rudolph von Langen," *Allgemeine Deutsche Biographie*, 17 (Leipzig: 1883), 659, 660.

[32] Hermann Keussen, "Regesten und Auszüge zur Geschichte der Universität Köln," *Mittheilungen aus dem Stadtarchiv von Köln*, 36, 37 (1918), 296.

ulation book includes the names of several individuals who came to the university with the intent of teaching humanist courses. In 1471 an early disciple of humanism, William Surigonus, who identified himself as "professor of the liberal arts,"[33] enrolled at the university. How long he remained and what he taught, if anything, are unknown. Even more mysterious is William Raymond Mithridates, who enrolled in 1484 and proclaimed himself "professor of the arts and sacred theology, acolite of the apostolic chair and interpretor of the Hebraic, Arabic, Chaldean, Greek, and Latin languages."[34] He remained in Cologne until the spring of 1485 where among other things he published a volume entitled "Seven Sayings of the Wisdom of the Greeks."[35] The 1490s saw the matriculation of three humanists. The first was Johannes Stammler de Augusta, who enrolled as *professor artis humanitatis* in 1491.[36] The second was Hermann Buschius, who enrolled in 1495; according to the matriculation book, he was "a man uncommonly learned in the *studia humanitatis*, who has been teaching various poetical subjects at our beloved university for almost a year."[37] Buschius remained (somewhat sporadically) in the vicinity of Cologne until 1500, during which time he offered private lessons to university students on a variety of humanist subjects. The late 1490s also saw the start of the teaching career of Andreas Kantor. Later named official *Stadtpoet* of Cologne, in the years around 1500 he worked to bring Latin instruction at the university up to humanist standards.[38] Thus, humanist penetration into Cologne was modest, but nonetheless sufficient to support the printing houses of Ulrich Zell, Conrad

[33] Hermann Keussen, *Die Matrikel der Universität Köln*, 2 vols. (Bonn: 1892–1919), I, 834.

[34] *Ibid.*, II, 158.

[35] On Mithridates, see J. IJsewijn, "Flavius Guillelmus Raymundus Mithridates," *Louvaniensia: Journal of Neo-Latin Studies*, 26 (1977), 236–38.

[36] Keussen, *Die Matrikel*, II, 302.

[37] *Ibid.*, II, 382.

[38] Hans Rupprich, *Humanismus und Renaissance in den deutschen Städten und an den Universitäten* (Leipzig: 1935), 26, 27.

Homberg, and Peter Quentel, all of which began to produce classical texts in the 1490s.[39]

Another group of universities where humanism followed a similar course in the late fifteenth century were the newer institutions founded at Freiburg-im-Breisgau (1457), Ingolstadt (1472), and Tübingen (1477). Most significantly, all three universities provided salaries for lecturers in the humanistic disciplines. This was in contrast to the practice at other German universities where the "poets" relied solely on student fees. Support from patron-princes and the willingness of new institutions to innovate explain the early inclusion of humanism at these universities. For Tübingen and especially Freiburg, one also suspects that rivalry with the nearby University of Basel (f. 1459) was also a decisive factor. Reflecting both the influence of Italian-educated *doctores* in the higher faculties and the impact of the great church council of the 1430s and 1440s the Swiss university voted in 1464 to establish a regular salary of twenty-five guldens for a professor of poetry and oratory. The first two men to hold the position are both familiar—Petrus Antonius Finariensis and Peter Luder.[40]

The University of Freiburg-im-Breisgau followed the lead of Basel in 1471. It established a salary of twenty-four guldens for a lecturer on poetry and rhetoric on the condition that he accept no added fees from his students.[41] Since twenty-four guldens were hardly enough to live on, it must have been assumed that the incumbent would have other sources of income. The first teacher of the *humaniora* was an obscure Swiss, Heinrich Gundelfinger of Constance; he held the position until 1481, when he resigned to devote full time to theology. He was followed by two others of equal obscurity, Johann Lun-

---

[39] On early Cologne printing, see Rudolf Juchoff, "Aufgang und Blütezeit des Kölner Buchdrucks," in *Fünf Jahrhunderte schwarze Kunst in Köln*, ed. Adam Weinart (Cologne: 1953), 9-26.

[40] Wilhelm Vischer, *Geschichte der Universität Basel von 1460 bis 1529* (Basel: 1860), 186-190; Edgar Bonjour, *Die Universität Basel* (Basel: 1960), 94-107; August Rüegg, *Die beiden Blütezeiten des Basler Humanismus* (Basel: 1960).

[41] Heinrich Schreiber, *Geschichte der Albert-Ludwigs-Universität zu Freiburg im Breisgau*, 3 vols. (Freiburg: 1868), I, 68-72.

son and Gabriel Münzthaler, neither of whom left any known literary remains. We do know that Münzthaler held a dual appointment in law and rhetoric but abandoned the latter in 1500. In that year he was succeeded by the more renowned Ulrich Zasius, destined to become one of the leading legists of the age.

At the University of Tübingen, its patron, Count Eberhard of Württemberg, followed the example of Basel and Freiburg in 1481. In that year he issued an order that determined the distribution of income about to be transferred to the university from five local churches. Provisions were made for three professors of law, two of medicine, and one "who would lecture in oratory." The professor of oratory was to receive thirty guldens, a meager sum in comparison to the one hundred ten guldens set aside for the highest paid legist. The decree added, however, "it should be recognized that if he is capable, the university should give him more."[42] Although there is a possibility that the ubiquitous Samuel Karoch held the position in the 1480s, in all likelihood it was filled at first on a part-time basis by professors whose expertise lay elsewhere. Only with the arrival of Heinrich Bebel in 1496 did the university have a true "humanist" to teach rhetoric and poetry.[43]

In 1476, four years after the University of Ingolstadt's foundation, Duke Louis of Bavaria also provided a stipend to support regular lectures on oratory. Samuel Karoch, that most traveled of the wandering poets, was perhaps hopeful of such a position when he matriculated in 1472.[44] If so, he was soon disappointed, for within a year he again took to the road. Instead, the first recipient of the stipend was a professor of medicine, Erhard Windsberger, who had acquired some interest and knowledge of ancient literature while studying at

---

[42] Rudolf Roth, ed., *Urkunden zur Geschichte der Universität Tübingen* (Tübingen: 1877), 71.

[43] Johannes Haller, *Die Anfänge der Universität Tübingen*, I (Stuttgart: 1927), 210, 211.

[44] Gustav Bauch, *Die Anfänge des Humanismus in Ingolstadt* (Munich: 1901), 8.

the University of Paris. In 1476 Windsberger petitioned the
duke for an increase in salary if he were to offer lectures on
the *studia humanitatis* in addition to medicine. The duke was
agreeable and soon directed the university to increase Windsberger's salary from sixty to one hundred guldens.[45] Although
Windsberger remained at the university until 1488, he abandoned his poetical lectures in 1484. He was succeeded in that
year by Johannes Riedner, who in the 1470s had studied law
at the University of Bologna and since then had taught rhetoric at several institutions, including Cracow and Erfurt.[46]
After some difficulties (Riedner's retirement was supposedly
imminent, but he kept postponing it), Conrad Celtis assumed
the position in 1492.[47] When his tumultuous Ingolstadt career
ended in 1497, he was followed by a former student, Jacob
Locher.

More so than Freiburg and Tübingen, the University of
Ingolstadt made a meaningful effort to fill its "chair" of rhetoric with individuals whose interest in the *studia humanitatis*
was more than an academic sideline. It was also among the
first universities officially to incorporate certain humanist features into its curriculum. In 1473 the arts faculty decided that
students should no longer be required to read the third part
of Alexander Villedieu's *Doctrinale*, the section largely devoted
to style and composition. In its place students were to study
the *Ars epistolandi* of the Italian humanist Augustinus Dati.[48]
This was hardly a major humanist triumph. It nevertheless
shows a willingness to disregard hallowed authorities and a
certain receptivity to new educational currents.

Not even Ingolstadt, however, can be said to have had a
strong pro-humanist element within the faculty. This becomes clear in the results of a four-day survey of faculty
opinion carried out in the fall of 1497.[49] The survey was spon-

[45] The duke's letter has been printed in Bauch, *Die Anfänge*, 14, 15.
[46] *Ibid.*, 27.
[47] Spitz, *Conrad Celtis*, 8, 9.
[48] Bauch, *Die Anfänge*, 86, 87.
[49] One must consult two sources to find the faculty responses in their

sored by government officials at the behest of Duke George of Bavaria, in the hope that the "university somewhat in decline, should again flourish."[50] Some thirty faculty members responded to questions that ranged over every aspect of the university, including the curriculum and performance of the four faculties. Although the survey resulted in no immediate changes, the responses of the faculty reveal much about their priorities and concerns: absenteeism among professors in the higher faculties; the ongoing feud between the two *viae*; methods of choosing examiners; dressing habits of students; market prices in the town; and for non-jurists, feeble lecturing in the faculty of law.

One seeks in vain, however, for any signs of widespread dissatisfaction with existing requirements and teaching methods. In fact the only suggestion for curriculum revision was offered by Johann Permeter von Adorf, the representative of the *via antiqua* on the faculty of theology. He proposed that "students should not spend so much time in the first and second part and in the *Parva logicalia*, rather they should learn in the logic of Peter of Spain and Aristotle."[51] The "first and second part" clearly refers to the beginning sections of Alexander Villedieu's *Doctrinale*; perhaps the theologian felt that having reached the university, students had no further need to study such an elementary text. His suggestion about logic seems puzzling at first glance. After all, the *Parva logicalia*, which he proposed to drop, was written by Peter of Spain, whom he recommended several words later as a suitable authority for the study of logic. It must be remembered, however, that the *Parva logicalia* was only that part of Peter of Spain's *Summulae* which dealt with supposition theory and

entirety. The responses of two theologians, Johann Permeter of Adorf and George Zingel were published in Carl von Prantl, *Geschichte der Ludwig-Maximilians-Universität zu München* (Munich: 1877), 132-35. Summaries of the responses of other professors have been published in Arno Seifert, *Die Universität Ingolstadt im 15. und 16. Jahrhundert: Texte und Regesten* (Berlin: 1973), 38-56.

[50] Seifert, *Die Universität*, 38.

[51] Prantl, *Geschichte der Ludwig-Maximilians-Universität*, II, 133.

the properties of terms. The remainder was a summary of Aristotle's logic. Thus it was only the "terminist" logic in Peter's treatises that Adorf proposed to discard. Although some writers have seen in Adorf's proposal signs of humanism, this was certainly not the case. Instead he was showing his loyalty to the *via antiqua*, whose followers were consistent critics of the *terministae* throughout the fifteenth century.

The universities of Leipzig and Erfurt present yet another pattern in terms of humanism's development. Although neither established stipends for full-time poets, humanism had become a major force at each institution by 1500. The teaching of classical literature was widespread, and the university community helped support active humanist presses within their respective cities. In 1496 Leipzig became one of the first German universities to enforce a requirement that all master's degree students study rhetoric. Unfortunately the loss of key university documents, especially the records of the two institutions' arts faculties, precludes a precise and detailed summary of humanism's growth. The following brief and general summary must suffice.[52]

The two universities' central location and comparatively high enrollments made them "musts" for the early wandering poets.[53] Peter Luder made Erfurt his first academic stop after leaving the University of Heidelberg. He arrived there in late 1460 and immediately delivered the same oration on the *studia humanitatis* that had initiated his career at Heidelberg five years earlier. He remained for two semesters, offering courses on Virgil, Ovid, and Terence. In 1461, he left Erfurt for Leipzig,

---

[52] The history of humanism at Erfurt is dealt with in several works: F. W. Kampschulte, *Die Universität Erfurt in ihrem Verhältnisse zu dem Humanismus und der Reformation*, 2 vols. (Trier: 1858, 1860); Gustav Bauch, *Die Universität Erfurt im Zeitalter des Frühhumanismus* (Breslau: 1904); Erich Kleineidam, *Universitas Studii Erffordensis*, 2 vols. (Leipzig: 1964, 1969); volume II contains material on humanism. On Leipzig, see Gustav Bauch, *Geschichte des Leipziger Frühhumanismus* (Leipzig: 1899) and Herbert Helbig, *Die Reformation der Universität Leipzig im 16. Jahrhundert* (Gütersloh: 1953).

[53] On the activities of the wandering poets, see Bauch, *Die Universität Erfurt*, 38–77, and *Geschichte des Leipziger Frühhumanismus*, 4–23.

where, after once again delivering his inaugural oration, he remained one semester. Samuel Karoch taught at Leipzig for two or three years in the 1460s and returned to central Germany in the early 1480s to teach at Erfurt. The Florentine poet, Jacobus Publicius Rufus, taught one semester at each institution in 1466 and 1467. Johannes Riedner lectured at Erfurt in the early 1480s, and in 1485-1486 Conrad Celtis taught at Erfurt, then Leipzig, with a brief trip north to Rostock squeezed in between.

More important than the wandering poets were the numerous academics at both universities who in the late fifteenth century offered private "unofficial" courses on letter writing, poetry, and classical authors. Announcements to publicize such courses are extant for Leipzig as early as the 1460s,[54] the same decade when they began at Erfurt. At Erfurt humanist courses became so widespread that in 1469 the arts faculty took steps to control them more closely.[55] It decreed, first of all, that all lectures, even those that dealt with non-required material, had to be held in the rooms of the main university building or the *collegium maius*. No longer could "extraordinary" lectures be held in *bursae*, private dwellings or rented rooms. It also set forth guidelines for the appropriate amount of time to be spent on the most popular ancient authors. One month of teaching was deemed sufficient for Cicero's *De senectute* and Virgil's *Bucolics*, but eight months were considered necessary for Virgil's *Aeneid*, Ovid's *Metamorphoses*, and the histories of Valerius Maximus. Other works by Cicero, Virgil, Terence, and Sallust were accorded two to six months. The reasons for these two steps are not readily apparent. Possibly the faculty was attempting to protect fee-paying students from irregular and shoddy teaching. Whatever the case, they provide strong evidence of humanism's early popularity at Erfurt.

[54] Ludwig Bertalot, "Humanistische Vorlesungsankündigungen in Deutschland im 15. Jahrhundert," *Zeitschrift für Erziehung und Unterricht*, 5 (1915), 1-24.
[55] Kleineidam, *Universitas*, II, 61, 62.

The Response to Humanism ~

The list of men who offered humanist courses at Leipzig and Erfurt is long but contains few prominent figures. Conrad Mutian, who taught at Erfurt for two years after he received his Master of Arts in 1492, is an exception. Some, such as Conrad Wimpina,[56] who taught poetry and letter writing at Leipzig in the 1490s, and Maternus Pistoris,[57] who in the same decade lectured on the *humaniora* at Erfurt, went on to become theologians in the early 1500s. Heinrich Boger[58] and Heinrich Aquilonipolensis (*née* Fischer),[59] who both lectured on classical literature at Erfurt in the 1470s, were prolific poets whose works, however, quickly fell into oblivion. Several taught briefly at one of the two universities and later became teachers or administrators of local schools. These included Tillmann Rasche,[60] who after receiving his Master of Arts in 1467 remained at Erfurt and lectured on the classics until becoming rector of the *Stadtschule* in Braunschweig in 1479; Paul Niavis,[61] the widely published grammar reformer who lectured at Leipzig in the 1480s and later taught in the schools of Halle and Chemnitz; and Andreas von Hundern,[62] professor of eloquence in Erfurt in the early 1490s and the editor of several compendia on rhetoric, who later taught school in several Silesian towns. Others, such as Johannes Unbehawer,[63] who taught at Erfurt in the 1470s and 1480s, largely lectured on traditional scholastic subjects but occasionally offered a course on rhetoric or letter writing. Many Erfurt and Leipzig humanists, especially in the 1490s, were active editors and publishers of the classical texts used in their courses. One thinks of Petrus Eolicus,[64] who in 1494 and 1495 produced in Leipzig

---

[56] Joseph Knepper, *Konrad Wimpina* (Leipzig: 1909), 13, 14.

[57] Bauch, *Die Universität Erfurt*, 220-25.

[58] Carl Krause, "Heinrich Boner," *Allgemeine Deutsche Biographie*, 3 (Leipzig: 1876), 39; Bauch, *Die Universität Erfurt*, 88-102.

[59] Bauch, *Die Universität Erfurt*, 172-89.

[60] *Ibid.*, 81.

[61] "Paul N. Niavis," *Allgemeine Deutsche Biographie*, 23 (Leipzig: 1886), 567, 568 (no author given).

[62] Bauch, *Die Universität Erfurt*, 117-20.

[63] *Ibid.*, 83.

[64] Bauch, *Geschichte des Leipziger Frühhumanismus*, 49.

118

editions of works by Persius, Lucan, Virgil, and Seneca, or Georgius Dottanius Meiningensis,[65] who while at Leipzig, edited in 1496 and 1497 Aristotle's *Rhetoric* and works by Seneca, Aeneas Sylvius, and Leonardo Bruni.

The widespread study of classical letters received official recognition at the University of Leipzig in 1496 when a course on rhetoric became mandatory for all master's degree candidates. This curricular change was but one small part of a "general reformation" of the university dictated by Duke George of Saxony, the university's patron, and Bishop Tilo von Merseburg, the university's chancellor.[66] University records provide no information about events leading to the reforms or about the men within the university and among the duke's councillors who were behind them. Apparently they were inspired by an apprehension that the university, despite continuing high enrollments, was stagnating. The preface to the edict stated that in the past Leipzig had produced large numbers of theologians, philosophers, astronomers, preachers, lawyers, and physicians, but that recently, "either through the injury of time or the idleness and torpor of individuals, the university had declined into a state of sluggishness." To halt this backslide, a long series of decrees followed, mostly involving matters of student discipline, adherence to university statutes, enforcement of dress codes, the quality and frequency of lectures, and the make-up of various university councils. Of the two edicts that dealt with curriculum, one concerned mathematics. Pointing out that books on mathematics were rarely taught, the edict directed the faculty of arts to institute courses "on the more useful mathematics books, Euclid, common perspective, and the like." The other proposal more directly showed the impact of humanism. It called for the discontinuation of lectures on the "logic of Hesbri" since it offered "no real result." "Hesbri" was the common spelling for the fourteenth-century English logician, William

---

[65] *Ibid.*, 52-54.
[66] The mandate has been published in Friedrich Zarncke, *Die Statutenbücher der Universität Leipzig* (Leipzig: 1861), 16-27.

Heytesbury, the author of a popular book on sophisms. In its place every student for the master's degree now had to hear lectures on Aristotle's *Rhetoric*.

Since Aristotle rarely appeared on the humanists' list of preferred rhetoricians, the choice of the Stagirite is puzzling. Nonetheless, the first faculty member chosen to deliver the rhetorical lectures, Georgius Dottanius Meiningensis, conscientiously followed the letter of the decree by publishing a copy of Aristotle's *Rhetoric* for use in the course.[67] Succeeding masters seem to have disregarded the prince's order and freely used other texts. Johannes Honorarius, for example, who offered the required course on rhetoric in 1498 and 1499, utilized a collection of letters by Leonardo Bruni and works by Horace and Ovid.[68]

In summary, although humanism's impact varied widely from institution to institution, by the 1490s it is hard to imagine any German university student who did not hear or at least hear of the new humanist courses on rhetoric, poetry, and classical literature. To this extent the dream of Peter Luder, expressed in 1456, that the *studia humanitatis* would find a place in Germany's universities had been fulfilled. It remains to be seen how the masters and students reacted to this new presence.

THE SCHOLASTIC RESPONSE

That humanism and humanists engendered some hostility is indisputable. Evidence of such opposition is apparent as early as the 1450s. Conrad Säldner, a theologian from the University of Vienna, attacked the new intellectual currents in two letters written in 1457 and 1458. Säldner at the time was a man in his fifties who had been connected with the university in the capacity of student, then Master of Arts and finally professor of theology since 1429. Undoubtedly he had heard

---

[67] Bauch, *Geschichte des Leipziger Frühhumanismus*, 52.
[68] *Ibid.*, 73-77.

the orations of Aeneas Sylvius and observed the coming of poetical and literary courses in the 1450s. In fact, in 1457 Säldner presided over the disputation in which Peuerbach presented his defense of the *studia humanitatis*. At about this time, he discussed these studies in an exchange of letters with Sigismund Gossembrot (1417-1493), an Augsburg patrician who had traveled in Italy and was leader of a small humanist circle in his native city. How he came to know Säldner is uncertain, but on April 24, 1457, he sent the theologian a letter in which he expressed his admiration for poetry and literary studies. His letter, no longer extant, apparently disturbed Säldner, for on September 19, 1457, he sent Gossembrot a response, "assailing the defenders of poetry and asserting that theology can be well-enough taught, adopted, and defended without poetry."[69]

Säldner's main reproach against the "poets" was their lack of true learning. They claimed, for example, to be elegant Latinists, and yet were ignorant of the basic rules of grammar. For Säldner grammar meant largely the speculative grammar of the *modistae*. In a probable reference to Aeneas Sylvius, he marveled "that there are not a few in the present with the name poet laureate who do not yet know grammar clearly and systematically in its four species, orthography, etymology, syntax, and accent, and have not intelligently studied metric versification."[70] And in another probable reference to Aeneas, he complained that the humanists did not dispute in the accepted manner. "These modern poets," he wrote, "who are not schooled in the several liberal arts, ignore the rules of speculative grammar and the *Doctrinale*, where may be found the true methods and art of speech; they also are ignorant of

---

[69] "Responsum invehens in poetrie defensores theologiamque defendens absque poetria sufficienter posse monstrari persuaderi ac defendi, per venerabilim dominum Maystrum Cunradum Saldner sacre theologie baccalareum formatum . . . ," printed along with other extant documents in Wilhelm Wattenbach, "Sigismund Gossembrot als Vorkämpfer der Humanisten und seine Gegner," *Zeitschrift für die Geschichte des Oberrheins*, 25 (1873), 36-68. The passage cited is on page 36.

[70] *Ibid.*, 38.

the rational sciences as logic." Instead, they are "inflated with great pride and bombast."[71]

Säldner also alleged that the study of poetry was wasteful and frivolous. Many men, he pointed out, had achieved fame without ever having read a scrap of poetry. Among the notables he named to support his argument were the prominent Parisian theologian, Jean Gerson, and a number of Viennese scholars, such as Henry of Langenstein, Henry of Oyta, and Nicholas of Dinckelsbühl. He then attacked Gossembrot's argument that poetry could offer inspiration to the theologian. In Säldner's opinion, natural and moral philosophy were the true basis of theology, not poetry. How could poetry be the handmaiden of theology, he asked, "when theology had been studied for so many years without the knowledge of poetry?" He added that poets were mere stylists who knew nothing of more serious matters.

Säldner stressed that he was not against all poets, only modern ones. Older Christian poets such as Lactantius, and even more acceptable Latin poets such as Virgil, were not one-sided men but were acquainted with the precepts of philosophy. He added, however, that even the reading of "acceptable poets" was dangerous. He feared that students would waste time on these pleasurable pursuits and neglect theology and moral philosophy—subjects "more suitable to the glory of God and His hope of reforming the Church militant." He concluded his letter by urging Gossembrot to abandon his humanist studies and devote his time to devotional literature and writings of Augustine, Ambrose, Jerome, and Bernard. These works, said Säldner, were much more suitable for the pious Christian layman.

Gossembrot replied to Säldner, but, except for a small, insignificant fragment, the letter has been lost. Säldner's largely repetitive second letter has been preserved, however. Again, he warned of spending too much time with poetry, and once more listed the great thinkers of the past who had never stud-

---

[71] *Ibid.*, 39.

ied it. He reiterated that he was not against poetry as such, only its modern practitioners. According to Säldner, these "new poets" cared nothing for true learning; they only sought glory and wealth through their literary pursuits and avoided more difficult and useful disciplines such as law, theology and medicine.

New in Säldner's second letter was his direct attack on the Italian humanists. Gossembrot had apparently mentioned several Italians as praiseworthy examples of modern humanism. Säldner was unimpressed. Guarino of Verona, for example, could not amount to much, since as far as he, Säldner, knew, no one in Austria, Bavaria, Hungary, or Bohemia had ever heard of him. "How can the honors of your Guarino resound all over the world, when most of the earth's provinces proclaim no knowledge of his glory?"[72] Nor had he ever heard of Lorenzo Valla. He recalled that Poggio Bracciolini had once written a book of some kind on rhetoric, but he added that he thought little of it. Gossembrot had also praised Bruni as a translator of Aristotle and other Greek authors. Säldner expressed doubt about the value of these efforts and warned his correspondent not to honor a compiler of such volumes more than God. He conceded that the study of these men might improve Latin style; more likely, however, one would end up like the person who studied poetry for thirty years and still did not know the name of Aeneas's wife.

Säldner's second letter also reveals that his reservations about humanism partly resulted from an aversion—not uncommon among fifteenth-century Germans—to anything Italian. He wrote that in recent memory the Italians had accomplished nothing in the "higher sciences and ethics." He could only grieve that "the Italians are occupied in studies of this kind of vanity, to me justifiably unknown, and are not occupied in exertions in those better and healthier teachers of morality and faith such as theology and moral philosophy."[73] In gen-

---

[72] *Ibid.*, 46, 47.
[73] *Ibid.*, 50.

eral, the Italians were "fickle and unstable men given to avarice, luxury, and pride." Taking a verse from Jeremiah VI:13, he prophesied dire results if men followed such guides: "For from the least of them even unto the greatest of them every one is given to covetousness; and from the prophet even unto the priest every one dealeth falsely." For all these reasons, he advised Gossembrot to devote his time to homilies, collections of sermons, and the Bible.

Thus to this scholastic theologian humanist studies were frivolous, morally dangerous, and inferior to the traditional disciplines of theology and philosophy. Pagan literature, already corrupting the degenerate Italians, had no place in Germany's universities. Did others share his views? Were efforts made to block and hinder humanism? To answer these questions it is necessary to examine the actual experiences of the humanists themselves.

One might well begin with Peter Luder's career at the University of Heidelberg, an institution filled, according to Luder, with "invidious beasts" who opposed his efforts. Actually in his five-year stay at Heidelberg, only two known episodes can be remotely construed as hostile. The first concerned the oration on the *studia humanitatis* that Luder delivered on his arrival at Heidelberg in 1456. Citing a statute of 1406 that allowed any faculty to "preview" speeches by new professors,[74] members of the faculty of arts demanded that Luder present them a copy of the speech for approval. Luder took umbrage and appealed to a friend on the law faculty, Johann Wildenhertz. Wildenhertz in turn composed a letter and sent it to the faculty of arts on July 14, 1456.[75] The lawyer related that Luder considered it demeaning to give them the manuscript of his speech since they knew "little or nothing of poetry." Luder, he continued, insisted that they hear the speech, and if they objected to anything he would submit it to a "neutral arbiter." Wildenhertz added that Luder harbored hatred

---

[74] Winkelmann, *Urkundenbuch der Universität Heidelberg*, 44.
[75] Printed in Wattenbach, "Peter Luder," 100.

and jealousy for no one and was a true friend of the arts. Moreover, the poet was perplexed why "cultivators of the arts" were trying to suppress his work rather than elevate it. He concluded, "In short, I can truly find nothing in him not worthy of a learned man. So do whatever you like. To me, however, it appears you have made known a concealed hate, or if I may speak the truth more clearly, the jealousy that secretly gnaws at you.[76]

Whether or not Luder submitted his speech for perusal is uncertain. Nor can one judge if Wildenhertz was correct in assuming that the faculty was motivated by "jealousy." One can only observe that the faculty was acting within its legal rights and that it is understandable if a few faculty members were anxious about what this "poet," recently returned from Italy, might say. One can also imagine that Luder was more than usually skittish on the eve of his German academic debut. In any case the speech was delivered on schedule on July 15, 1456. As far as can be determined, no "neutral arbiter" was needed to judge its contents.

The second concrete reference to an affront from the faculty came at the beginning of Luder's second year at Heidelberg. At that time Luder planned to deliver another oration to preface his new lectures on Terence. But he apparently had lost the room or hall where he had taught during the previous year. In the posted announcement of the speech, he claimed he had been "forced to flee" to the auditorium of the local Augustinian *studium*. What his "flight" signified is not certain. Luder clearly considered it both demeaning and an expression of opposition from the faculty. He went on in the announcement to decry the nefarious campaign of "prince dialectic" to drive the study of rhetoric from the university.[77]

What is one to make of Luder's assertions? It is tempting to dismiss them as mere paranoia. Luder's popularity seems to have declined during his second year. After his lectures on

---

[76] *Ibid.*

[77] Wattenbach, "Peter Luders Lobrede auf Pfalzgraf Friedrich den Siegreichen," *Zeitschrift für die Geschichte des Oberrheins*, 27 (1876), 22.

Terence he chose next to offer a course on Seneca. But this had to be abandoned due to a lack of students.[78] Perhaps his attacks on imagined enemies were efforts to cover his own sense of failure. On the other hand it is altogether possible that certain Heidelberg academics were criticizing or belittling his activities. Unfortunately, if they were, Luder never mentioned their names. He did however refer to a number of supporters within the university. Among them were three professors of the arts who were studying for theology degrees: Stephan Hoest, Joducus Eichman, and Johannes Wenck.[79] It is also worth noting that in five years, the demand to preview a speech and a forced move from a lecture hall hardly amounted to a major campaign of anti-humanist harassment.

Are there other concrete signs of opposition to humanism in the years before 1500? As already noted, the University of Heidelberg, claiming financial exigency, refused to contribute to the salary of Petrus Antonius Finariensis in 1456.[80] Some thirty years later, 1498, the same university resisted efforts of the Palatine elector to institute lectures on Greek. Dionysius Reuchlin, the brother of the famous Hebraist Johannes Reuchlin, was to have received the position, but the faculty of arts refused to cooperate. On August 1, it denied the elector's request to provide Reuchlin a lecture hall, stipulating that the new professor first participate in a disputation and give evidence that he had received his Master of Arts degree. On August 6, 1498, the elector urged the faculty to reconsider, but once again it refused.[81] The records of the University of Erfurt also contain references to obstruction of humanist endeavors. In 1458 an otherwise unknown figure, Frederick Gewerdo, petitioned the faculty of arts for permission to teach publicly the "oratorical arts." As the dean related, however,

[78] In the announcement for his lectures on Ovid's *Ars amatoria*, Luder claimed he had "terrified the minds of many" by lecturing on Seneca. Wattenbach, "Peter Luder," 44.

[79] For Hoest, see Wattenbach, "Peter Luder," 44, 62; in the same article, for Aichmann, 48, 68, 72; for Wenck, 50ff., 60.

[80] Winkelmann, *Urkundenbuch der Universität Heidelberg*, II, 49.

[81] *Ibid.*, II, 62, 63.

"it was decided he should not be permitted for certain un-mentioned reasons."[82] In 1476 a similar petition from a pro-fessor of medicine, Heinrich Geratwohl, was also rejected by the faculty of arts.[83]

Although one cannot be altogether certain, it is doubtful that the rejections of Gewerdo and Geratwohl resulted from anti-humanist sentiment. Many other wandering poets and Erfurt academics taught courses on the *studia humanitatis* in these years without encountering resistance. On the other hand the actions taken at Heidelberg seem more suspicious. When the elector sought financial assistance for Finariensis, he requested only ten florins, a small sum to pay if the uni-versity had wanted to see the continuation of formal humanist lectures. The demand that Reuchlin publicly dispute and give evidence of his master's degree also seems unreasonable. Peter Luder, for one, had taught five years at Heidelberg without his Master of Arts.

If the preceding episodes hint of scholastic opposition to humanism, examples of accommodation and outright support for the efforts of the poets can also be cited. Luder, for ex-ample, had nothing but praise for his enthusiastic reception at Erfurt in 1460. Shortly after his arrival he wrote to his Heidelberg friend, Matthias von Kemnat, that he had been met in Erfurt not "by the beasts which barking at me in Heidelberg were invidiously incited with malicious insults in their mouths, but by lovers of knowledge and illustrious men who rejoice and are glad that I have come to them as a Mercury sent from heaven."[84] He wrote further that they had received him into the university with honor and had given him a large hall for his lectures. He added that he had many listeners and promised to return to Heidelberg "with glory and the highest praise." A further sign of support for Luder was the enthu-siastic recommendation he received from the dean of the arts faculty, Heinrich Runen, when the poet left for Leipzig in

---

[82] Kleineidam, *Universitas*, II, 51.
[83] *Ibid.*, 52.
[84] Wattenbach, "Peter Luder," 120.

1461. Writing a friend on the Leipzig faculty, he called Luder a "pleasant, stable and learned man" and related how he had lectured on Ovid and Terence "before many *magistri* and other members of the university." He asked his friend to protect and defend him "against the bites and yelpings of those dogs who fear and envy in others those things in which they feel themselves deficient."[85]

Another example of positive support for humanism comes from the University of Vienna in the late 1460s and early 1470s. In 1467 the faculty of arts agreed to purchase a substantial number of humanist texts for the university library. On October 21 the faculty council met "to hear a proposition of the dean for a notable opportunity and advantage for the faculty." There was, the records state, a Veronese merchant in Vienna "offering for sale books concerning the humanities and the history of the whole world which are truly useful and would be to the perpetual glory of the faculty."[86] Then on November 17, the faculty agreed to spend one hundred ten guldens for Boccaccio's *Genealogy of the Gods*, Petrarch's letters, Guarino of Verona's commentary on Cicero's *Rhetoric,* Gasparino Barizza's *Introduction to Letter Writing*, Antonio Mancinello's *Introduction to the Reading of the Orators*, Valla's *Elegancies of the Latin Language* and Flavio Biondo's *Rome Restored*. In 1470 a somewhat smaller purchase, for forty-seven florins, was made of works by Pliny the Younger and Livy.[87] Then in 1474 the faculty bought a collection of Francesco Filelfo's letters and a number of new Italian humanist translations of Aristotle. When recording this purchase in the faculty minutes, the dean, Paul von Stockerau, expressed the hope that the new translations would be utilized in courses so "we might return a little from the dregs to the bright sources of the philosophers."[88]

[85] *Ibid.*, 121.
[86] Noted in Theodor Gottlieb, *Mittelalterliche Bibliothekskataloge Österreichs,* I (Vienna: 1915), 481.
[87] Lhotsky, *Die Wiener Artistenfakultät,* 167.
[88] Gottlieb, *Mittelalterliche Bibliothekskataloge,* I, 486.

Several other episodes suggest that much apparent opposition to humanism resulted less from the humanists' intellectual enthusiasms than from their occasionally outrageous behavior. There is no better example of this point than the checkered teaching career of Conrad Celtis. In 1486 he was forced to depart Leipzig in disgrace when the Bohemian humanist Bohuslaus von Hassenstein revealed that Celtis had plagiarized not only some of his poems but also verses by Gregorius Tyfernius, Virgil, and even Homer![89] Celtis's career at Ingolstadt was an almost unmitigated disaster. Having received a year-and-a-half appointment as salaried poet in early 1492, he taught diligently for several months, but then, after delivering his inaugural oration in the summer, absented himself for better than a year. Shortly after he left, he wrote to his jurist friend Sixtus Tucher that he could have "full hope" for his return and added, "I have no doubt you and my other friends will see to the continuation of my stipend."[90] Tucher wrote back that there was much grumbling about his absence.[91] Celtis retorted that he was gaining "immortal ornament, fame, advantage, and growth for our Germany and this school." He cursed his opponents and the "cleverness of servile men and barbarians, always opposed to things of virtue and sound teaching, things they do not know, do not wish to know, or what I would approve more, would not ever know."[92]

He returned to Ingolstadt in the spring of 1494, but by the end of the summer he embarked on another journey to Freiburg-im-Breisgau and Basel. His friends became convinced that such wanderings would exhaust the patience of university officials. Erasmus Australis, librarian at a Regensburg monastery, urgently warned him "to stop that wandering around and stay in one place and location." He added, "I hear that not a little talk may arise or rather has arisen, because you

[89] Spitz, *Conrad Celtis*, 8, 9.
[90] Celtis, *Briefwechsel*, 66.
[91] *Ibid.*, 72, 73.
[92] *Ibid.*, 73.

have hardly for six weeks concerned yourself with your main task of lecturing for which you after all were hired, and that it therefore could easily happen that you may be removed from your regular teaching post."[93] Celtis returned, only to leave again in the summer of 1495 when the plague struck the area. Other professors also departed, but, one imagines, they all returned when classes resumed in January, 1496. Not Celtis, however. He arrived a month late, carrying a letter from Prince Philip, the Palatine elector, which asked that the humanist's tardiness be excused because he had been tutoring his sons.[94]

Celtis closed out his unfortunate career at Ingolstadt in 1496 and 1497 in an atmosphere of ill-will and recrimination. He missed lectures, announcing in one instance that his class was canceled so that he could sample some new wine with a friend.[95] At other times he arrived in a state suggesting that the wine or perhaps some good Bavarian beer had already been amply sampled earlier in the day. His outraged students finally sent him a note damning his aberrant behavior. They claimed his "long and incessant scoldings" forced them "to make a reply in the name of truth." They wrote, "You accuse us of madness and charge that we are stupid barbarians, and you call wild beasts those whose fees support you. . . . This we might have born with better grace, but for the fact that you yourself abound in the faults of which you accuse us. For what of the fact that, while you carp about us, you yourself are so torpid from dissipation that in private conversation your drowsy head droops to your elbow like a figure eight." They insulted him further, saying that Celtis spoke neither "plain argument nor cultured speech nor elegant Latin expressions." Finally they warned of "more stringent measures" unless he changed his habits.[96] In return, Celtis showed his bad temper by pen-

---

[93] *Ibid.*, 137; English translation by Spitz, *Conrad Celtis*, 44.

[94] Spitz, *Conrad Celtis*, 52.

[95] *Ibid.*, 93.

[96] Celtis, *Briefwechsel*, 286, 287; English translation in Lynn Thorndyke, *University Records and Life in the Middle Ages* (New York: 1944), 366, 367.

ning a series of poems and epigrams that attacked the beet-eating Bavarians, his patron Duke George,[97] and some of his former friends in the faculties of medicine and law.[98]

Considering Celtis's behavior, it is not surprising that some professors at the university were not wildly enthusiastic about his presence. In 1494, for example, after he returned from his first protracted absence, he asked permission to use the arts faculty library. His request was granted, but only if he promised to abide "by the sense of the faculty's decrees." He was also told "to keep himself friendly toward the faculty, not belittling or slandering the other masters." If his behavior fell below expectations, library privileges would be revoked.[99]

Comments on Celtis's role at the university were invited in the survey of faculty opinion sponsored by the ducal government in 1497. This question elicited only a limited response, but the answers nonetheless shed some light on Celtis's reputation within the institution.[100] None of the nine Ingolstadters who commented objected to having a salaried poet on the faculty. But all were perturbed by his lack of diligence, particularly in view of his high salary of eighty florins. Peter Kraft, a Master of Arts and a student in law, observed, "In this regard Celtis has no fault other than he does not like to lecture and travels about a good deal." Magister Johann Stein's terse comment was, "If he lectured, he'd be fine." The most common recommendation was to dismiss Celtis and use his salary to hire two replacements. But Celtis escaped the ignominy of dismissal. While the faculty opinions were being collected in September, the poet was already preparing his departure for Vienna, where he was to become the salaried poet at the university.

When he arrived at the University of Vienna in the fall of

---

[97] Conrad Celtis, *Fünf Bücher Epigramme*, ed. Karl Hartfelder (Berlin: 1881), 44.

[98] Celtis, *Libri Odarum Quattuor*, ed. Felicitas Pindter (Leipzig: 1937), 109.

[99] Cited in Bauch, *Die Anfänge des Humanismus in Ingolstadt*, 59, 60.

[100] The comments on Celtis have been printed in Seifert, *Die Universität Ingolstadt im 15. und 16. Jahrhundert. Texte und Dokumente*, 52, 53.

1497, Celtis was beginning a career at an institution where humanism had been a major source of controversy for the previous seven years. As noted earlier, with the end of the Hungarian occupation, the university had agreed to accept the authority and direction of an imperial superintendent in return for continued financial support from the Hapsburgs. The first imperial appointee, Bernard Perger, immediately moved to enhance the role of humanism at the university. His efforts, which continued for nearly a decade, provide some of the most useful insights into the nature of humanist-scholastic relations in the years before 1500.

In his first speech to the university council, in 1491, Perger warned that he and the emperor considered many things in the university in need of change.[101] He also sponsored a series of open discussions at which members of the academic community could express their opinions. We have no record of what was said at these meetings, but they must have generated a good deal of emotion. They often lasted far into the night and finally became so heated that Perger, fearing a breakdown in student discipline, brought them to an end.[102]

Only in 1492 did specific proposals come forth. In October, the dean of the arts faculty, George Pettersdorfer, who had lectured on humanist subjects in the 1470s, announced in a faculty meeting that the government expected reforms in four areas.[103] First, the government claimed that scholars and bachelors were occupied in "vane things and useless sophisms" and ignored the "texts and other fundamentals." Second, lectures were not "regularly and usefully" given. Third, the faculty spent too much time on Occam and failed to teach "distinguished and approved doctors in the way of other universities such as Scotus (the 'subtle doctor'), Albertus Magnus, and others." Finally, students were not examined on texts but only on commentaries. The dean further announced that

---

[101] Grossmann, "Die Frühzeit," 300.
[102] Aschbach, *Geschichte der Wiener Universität*, II, 47, 48.
[103] Faculty records published in Kink, *Geschichte der kaiserlichen Universität* I, part I, 194; Lhotsky, *Die Wiener Artistenfakultät*, 178, 179.

the superintendent requested the formation of a committee to meet with him in the hope of finding remedies.

Thus as the first step in modifying the University of Vienna's curriculum, the 1492 proposals reflected humanist opinion only in a limited way. Certainly the demands that students and professors abandon "useless sophisms" and concentrate on original texts were frequently expressed in humanist polemics. But the proposals failed to touch on grammatical reform or the teaching of rhetoric, the two areas that most concerned the early humanists in general and Bernard Perger in particular. In fact the governmental demands seem less an expression of humanism than of the scholastic *via antiqua*. This can be seen in their attacks on "vane sophisms" and commentaries and more explicitly in their demand for the inclusion of lectures on Scotus and Albertus Magnus. In the second half of the fifteenth century the universities of Heidelberg, Ingolstadt, Tübingen, Freiburg-im-Breisgau and Erfurt attempted to bring parity between the two *viae*. Now it was being proposed that the staunchly nominalist University of Vienna do the same.

It is difficult to explain how and why support for the *via antiqua* suddenly burst upon the Viennese academic scene. There were no signs of a realist "revival" within the university until the October 1492 meeting. If the proposals were inspired by government officials, the question of their identity and motive remains. Whatever the case, the proposals do suggest that the humanists and *antiqui* shared some common ground, even if nothing more than a common aversion to nominalism.

Despite the limited nature of the reforms, humanist sympathizers at the university were pleased that at least curriculum reform was being discussed. A physician, Bartholomew Stäber, for example, wrote Celtis early in 1493 that "by the will of the emperor," the university was being cleansed "of its rough and thorny spines," and furthermore that the *studia humanitatis* would soon have a "special place among the arts."[104]

---

[104] Celtis, *Briefwechsel*, 96, 97.

Actually the arts faculty agreed to only one of the proposals; in June, 1493 it required that lectures and examinations on the *Posterior analytics*, the *Old Logic*, the *Physics*, and the *De anima* should be based more on texts than commentaries.[105]

Stäber had written in his letter that the "*studia humanitatis* would soon have a special place among the arts." He referred to Perger's intention of bringing to Vienna a special, salaried lecturer on the humanities, as had been done at Freiburg, Ingolstadt, and Tübingen. His first choice was C. Paulus Amaltheus, an Italian who had been in the emperor's entourage since the late 1480s. He seems to have enjoyed special imperial favor since 1489 when he composed a long flattering poem in honor of Frederick III. When hired in 1493, it was agreed he would receive a salary of fifty florins, with the understanding he would lecture twice a day.[106] But at the beginning of his appointment, in June 1493, he appeared before the faculty of arts and stated "it was impossible, inhuman, and disgraceful" that he should have to give two lectures in one day and actually was prepared to give only one lecture. The faculty, however, saw no reason to alter the original agreement and rejected the poet's request. Amaltheus then turned to Perger for support, and during the next few months faculty records include a long series of letters and personal appeals on his behalf from various government officials. Even Frederick III himself wrote a letter (or signed his name to one) supporting the humanist's cause. But the faculty refused to change its policy, and the frustrated Amaltheus ceased teaching. By September the faculty of arts stopped his salary altogether, with the dean noting that "he was a member of the Franciscan order, to whom it was not advantageous to lecture publicly on secular knowledge."

After Amaltheus left the university, some of Celtis's friends

---

[105] Lhotsky, *Die Wiener Artistenfakultät*, 179.

[106] Kink, *Geschichte der kaiserlichen Universität*, I, part I, 196; Bauch, *Die Reception*, 34, 35. Bauch has published the relevant faculty records concerning the career of Amaltheus.

attempted to obtain the Vienna lectureship for him. But Perger rejected their overtures and instead called on an Italian jurist, Giralamo Balbi (1464-1535), to fill the position. Balbi was a Venetian who at the University of Padua had achieved both a thorough humanistic education and a degree in Roman law. He taught these subjects at the University of Paris in the 1480s, but after a feud with William Tardif, the French humanist, he left France and traveled through much of Europe before arriving in Vienna in late 1493.[107] He was originally recruited to teach Roman law, but after displaying his poetic talents by composing laudatory verses in honor of Emperor Maximilian, he was offered the opportunity of also lecturing on the *studia humanitatis*. He was to receive an added fifty guldens, paid directly by the imperial government rather than the university. One lecture a day was all that was expected.

Amaltheus might have been satisfied with such an arrangement, but not Balbi. On July 4, 1494, he presented several new demands to the faculty of arts. Most important, he asked that the faculty make his lectures on poetry and rhetoric obligatory for all students, a step no German university had as yet taken. In addition Balbi asked permission to collect a lecture fee from his students, which again was without precedent for a professor receiving a regular salary. And as the record of the arts faculty put it, he sought "several other unnecessary things."[108] The faculty members temporized, alleging that it was first necessary to evaluate the quality of his lectures. But Balbi did not measure up to the faculty's standards, and his requests were denied. The report on Balbi's petition concluded by flatly stating, "How he lectured, anyone knows who heard him."[109]

But this first setback did not discourage Balbi. As Amal-

---

[107] P. S. Allen, "Hieronymus Balbus in Paris," *English Historical Review*, 17 (1902), 417-28; Augustin Renaudet, *Préréforme et Humanisme à Paris* (Paris: 1953), 121-24.

[108] Bauch, *Die Reception*, 45, 46.

[109] "Qualiter tamen legit, sciunt isti, qui audiverunt," *ibid.*, 46.

theus had done before him, he appealed for support from Hapsburg officials early in 1495. His demands were the same: that his courses be required and subject to student fees. But the regents, who held governmental responsibility in the absence of the emperor, chose not to pressure the faculty, and Balbi's requests were again denied. The dean of the faculty admitted in his summary of the proceedings that "this response pleased the faculty very much."[110] After this second rebuff, Balbi continued to lecture, but with diminished enthusiasm. By 1496 he abandoned his humanistic lectures and restricted himself to lectures on the law.

Celtis's friends again set to work to obtain the salaried lectureship for the German poet, whose career at Ingolstadt was rapidly disintegrating. In February 1497, Johannes Stabius wrote Celtis that he had many supporters at Vienna, but that Perger favored calling yet another Italian, Francesco Bonomo.[111] This time, however, Celtis's backers were successful. On March 7, 1497, Emperor Maximilian sent Celtis a letter offering him the position.

When Celtis arrived in Vienna in the fall of 1497 his days of wandering were over. For the final decade of his life the Danubian city would be the center of his activity. He began lecturing on the usual humanist fare—Cicero, Horace, grammar, and rhetoric—and perhaps some things not so usual; he edited a minor work of Nicholas of Cusa and the *De mundo* of Apuleius and may have lectured on both.[112] How was he received? When he first arrived, he had one minor dispute with the arts faculty over lecture hours. Some members of the faculty became exercised when Celtis chose three o'clock

[110] "In quam supplicationem in dorso concluso et responsio dominorum Regencium scripta erat; scilicet: Non artentur ad pastum scholares interim, quod habet stipendium pingwe a principe. Que responsio summe placuit facultati," *ibid.*, 52.

[111] Celtis, *Briefwechsel*, 251.

[112] The poems to announce his courses gave the subjects of Celtis's lectures but no hints of the dates; none of the poems mentions Cusa or Apuleius. Celtis, *Fünf Bücher Epigramme*, 102-104.

for his lectures, the same time when lectures on several required subjects were offered. Celtis at first refused to change and predictably appealed to the government. But he finally yielded, causing the dean to record, "thus was preserved the normal custom of the faculty."[113]

During Celtis's second full year at Vienna, superintendent Perger and the regents attempted another reform of teaching in the faculty of arts. Their proposals of 1492, moderate as they were, had gained only partial approval. Efforts were renewed in May 1499, when three regents, Johannes Fuchsman, Leonhard von Hanach, and Wolfgang Gwerlich, announced at a meeting of the faculty of arts that certain changes were "highly desirable." As the dean stated in his report: "they urged and desired for the higher fame and usefulness of the whole university that the scholars and bachelors of the faculty of arts might be instructed more habitually in the textual and original truths of some famed teachers and authors, not in those sophisms, now worn out for a long time, or similarly in those rather vulgar concepts, where almost nothing original is contained, but rather pale knowledge."[114] The regents also proposed "many other things," but the dean "resolved not to relate them in writing." He added, "So as not to appear to speak against his royal majesty," the faculty should agree to appoint a deputation to meet the regents and discuss reforms.

The two groups met during the early summer, and at a meeting of August 8, 1499, announced their proposals to the arts faculty. Most important, attendance at humanist lectures was to become mandatory for both Bachelor and Master of Arts degrees. The faculty records stated that the emperor had "most graciously ordered and instituted lectures in the *studia humanitatis*," and the faculty did not wish to appear disrespectful. Therefore each beginning student had to attend these

[113] Relevant sections of the arts faculty records are printed in E. Klüpfel, *De vita et scriptis Conradi Celtis Protucii* (Freiburg: 1827), I, 191.
[114] Relevant documents in Bauch, *Die Reception*, 95-98.

lectures for half a year, each bachelor, for a quarter of a year. Celtis was not mentioned, but the reference to the "order of the emperor" plainly suggests that his lectures were involved. A second proposal "for the growth of our students," would have required each bachelor's candidate to study Virgil's *Bucolics* and "a book on letter-writing," and each master's candidate to study Virgil's *Aeneid*. These additional requirements were to be taught "by one of our own masters" rather than a resident poet like Celtis.

Two of the proposed reforms dealt with elementary training in grammar and rhetoric. The use of the *Summula Jovis*, a thirteenth-century versified manual on composition, was to be discontinued and replaced by "a more useful book" on letter writing. The second proposal interdicted the use of the first two parts of Alexander Villedieu's *Doctrinale* and recommended instead the grammar of Nicholas Perotti. "Perotti's grammar" might very well have been Perger's *Nova grammatica*, a reworking of Perotti.

The final two proposals reflected the reformers' continued interest in ending the dominance of nominalism at the university. One demanded the formation of a committee to decrease the large number of authorities and commentaries used as texts in the faculty of arts. The committee was charged to collect "the scattered books" of the *via moderna*, "improve and correct them, bring them together into one book or course, and then let it be printed for the special use and benefit of the university." Until this was done, arts instruction was to be based on Thomas Bricot, a fifteenth-century Parisian nominalist who wrote a complete series of Aristotelian commentaries. Finally, masters were given freedom to lecture according to the *via antiqua*. If interest warranted, provision was made for the acquisition of a special house or *bursa* for students in that *via*.[115]

How were the reforms received? According to the records

[115] The inclusion of the *via antiqua* had become even more important for Perger since he had already recruited a realist for the theology faculty. He was yet another of Perger's Paduans, Dr. Johannes de Camerino. *Ibid.*, 98.

of the arts faculty all were "accepted and approved" at the very meeting at which they were introduced. Nonetheless none of the proposals seems to have been implemented. No realist *bursa* was acquired; no compendium of nominalist doctrine and no books by Bricot were published.[116] Perotti's grammar was almost certainly not put to immediate use. Statutes proposed ten years later again demanded that Perotti replace the first two parts of the *Doctrinale*.[117] The lectures on poetry and the *studia humanitatis* may or may not have been instituted. If they were, however, it is difficult to explain the speech given by the arts faculty dean in July 1501 asking "if there was a way of instructing our scholars in more useful teaching and humane letters, and not the other squalid, rough, unsuitable things, by which their most excellent minds are stained and oppressed."[118]

Did Celtis's courses become mandatory for all students? Unfortunately Celtis's own letters from the period have been lost completely. Significantly, however, the numerous extant letters *to* Celtis neither congratulated him nor commented in any way about his lectures becoming required. In fact the opposite was true. In the early months of 1500, soon after the government-sponsored reforms had been "approved" by the faculty of arts, three letters referred to conflict between Celtis and unnamed individuals within the university. In January a Rostock jurist, Christoph Kuppner, wrote that he had heard rumors of attacks on Celtis, but that the poet "in the presence of the regents so refuted the religious and certain antiquarians of the university, dialecticians, and Alexandrine philosophers, that you covered over the mouths of all those and their defamation against the poets."[119] On March 23 his Nuremberg friend, Sebald Schreyer, expressed sorrow that "that Stoic set

---

[116] Most printed editions of Bricot appeared at either Paris or Louvain; two of his logical commentaries were published at Basel, but in 1492. Wolfgang Panzer, *Annales Typographici*, X (Nuremberg: 1802), 195; Ludwig Hain, *Repertorium bibliographicum*, I (Stuttgart: 1826), 552, 553.

[117] Kink, *Geschichte*, II, 315-18, has printed the statutes.

[118] Bauch, *Die Reception*, 104.

[119] Celtis, *Briefwechsel*, 384.

is considerably set against you."[120] In mid-April, Hieronymus von Croaria wrote from Ingolstadt that he had heard of a conflict between Celtis and the faculty, with the regents and "all honorable and upright men" on the poet's side.[121] None of the letters is specific about the cause of Celtis's trouble; nor is there any useful information in university documents. But it is significant that these three letters, the only ones to mention friction during Celtis's ten years at Vienna, came in the wake of the reform attempt. It seems likely that the "conflict" meant an attempt, apparently successful, on the part of certain individuals to prevent the implementation of the proposed changes.

Who were these individuals, and how did they manage to obstruct changes even after they had been approved by the faculty of arts? It seems likely that the setback for the reformers resulted from a clause in the statutes of the university that stipulated that any major statute or curriculum change adopted by a faculty had to be approved by the university as a whole.[122] The "university as a whole" meant the faculty senate, originally consisting of all teaching masters, but by 1500 a small representative body consisting of the rector, four deans, and the procurators or heads of the four nations. One can only surmise that a coalition of individuals, for whatever reasons— distaste for literary studies, opposition to the *via antiqua*, a positive commitment to time-honored methods, or an aversion to government inteference—coalesced to block the measures.

That opposition to the reforms was closely related to issues of academic freedom and government interference in university affairs is clearly indicated by Perger's resignation in 1500, apparently under a barrage of criticism from faculty members.[123] His replacement as superintendent, Johannes Cuspi-

---

[120] *Ibid.*, 392.
[121] *Ibid.*, 397.
[122] Kink, *Geschichte*, II, 174.
[123] *Ibid.*, I, 195; Aschbach, *Geschichte*, I, 60.

anus, although personally committed to humanism, lacked Perger's aggressiveness.

~ ~ ~

IN RETROSPECT, it is not difficult to understand why humanism became a controversial issue at the University of Vienna in the 1490s. Perger's active interference in university affairs upset longstanding traditions of teaching and governance. The salaried humanists he hired had difficulty adjusting to the traditional practices of the university, and regularly appealed to court officials when their demands were not met. The Italian origins of Amaltheus and Balbi added to their problems of acceptance. As shown in Säldner's letter of the 1450s and in the short-lived academic careers of other Italian humanists in Germany, many Germans resented the smug sense of superiority exuded by the Italians. Balbi was a particularly obnoxious individual who had the poor taste to publish a volume of obscene poetry shortly after his arrival in Vienna. When his controversy with the arts faculty began, he loudly and publicly slandered his opponents. Finally, the Viennese masters were the first to confront the real possibility of substantive change in their academic practices and priorities. The 1499 reforms would have made the *studia humanitatis* an integral, *required* part of their curriculum. No longer would literary studies be peripheral to the university's activities; no longer would poetical and rhetorical courses be offered at the pleasure of interested professors. The arts faculty was ready to take such a step but not the university as a whole. One suspects the theologians, who justifiably saw the inevitability of change in their own discipline if arts teaching was altered, spearheaded the opposition.

The Viennese experience is also revealing about humanism's reception at other German universities. Elsewhere humanism was much less threatening. Its supporters were men of moderation, many of whom also had interests in traditional scholastic subjects. Their demands on the academic corporation were few. Most supported themselves through student fees, while those with salaries were paid directly by the university's princely patron. Outside the areas of grammar instruction and rhetoric, they made few concrete demands for change. Few German governments had begun to exercise a forceful hand in their universities' affairs. Under such circumstances humanism at most universities engendered little opposition and even occasional enthusiasm in the years before 1500.

IV

Humanists and Scholasticism after
1500: The Changing Critique ~

WHEN CONRAD CELTIS abandoned Ingolstadt for Vienna in
1497 his place was taken by a former student, a young man
of twenty-six, Jacob Locher. Until then Locher's career had
followed a path trodden by many humanist predecessors and
contemporaries. It included attendance at several German universities, a visit to Italy, the adoption of the sobriquet Philomusus, and a list of publications that reflected the tastes and
concerns of the early humanists. Among his books were manuals on grammar and rhetoric, an oration in honor of Emperor
Maximilian, and a defense of the *studia humanitatis*, entitled
*Oration Concerning the Study of the Humane Discipline and the
Praise of the Poets*.[1] In 1497, however, he published a work
different from anything thus far written by a German humanist. It was entitled *Theologica emphasis, or a Dialogue on
the Eminence of Four Doctors of the Church*. The work largely
comprised four laudatory poems in honor of the Church fathers, Gregory, Jerome, Ambrose, and Augustine. These were
preceded by a dialogue between Locher and Ulrich Zasius,
the well-known jurist. In it Locher took the bold step of
lashing out at the scholastic theologians of his day. These
boorish pedants were unversed in classical literature and ignorant of ancient languages. They "filled their days and nights

[1] (Freiburg [?]: 1496.) For his other publications, see Ludwig Hain, *Repertorium bibliographicum*, 4 vols. (Stuttgart: 1826-1838), II, 274.

143

in scholastic combats" and mired themselves in "the tortuous obligations of *elenchies*, the verbose disputes of the sophists . . . and the trickeries of the Stoic sect." In contrast to their "foolish noise,"[2] the Church fathers had "unleashed clear and gleaming missiles at the savage barbarians and the impudent enemies of the Catholic church."[3]

All but forgotten today, Locher's work was nonetheless a landmark in the development of humanist-scholastic polemics. It ushered in a twenty-five-year period in which the reforming ardor of the humanists was broadened to include both the philosophical offerings of the arts course and, more significantly, the goals and methods of scholastic theology. Older humanist themes were not abandoned during these years. Humanists continued to denounce the *modi significandi*, to publish handbooks on letter writing and grammar, and to deliver orations that catalogued the well-worn arguments in defense of poetry and the *studia humanitatis*. But the signs are unmistakable: after 1500 the humanist critique of scholasticism entered a new and fateful stage.

To illustrate these changes this chapter will examine the attitudes toward scholasticism of four leading humanists— Conrad Mutian, Willibald Pirckheimer, Heinrich Bebel, and Johannes Reuchlin. These are not random choices. They were among the most highly reputed German humanists whose scholarly and literary careers fell mainly after 1500. Furthermore, their writings provide a fair sampling of the new humanist criticisms of scholasticism. All four denounced the scholastics, but they did so for essentially dissimilar reasons.

BEBEL

Among the better-known humanists whose academic careers unfolded after 1500, the individual whose intellectual

---

[2] *Theologica emphasis sive Dialogus super eminentia quatuor doctorum ecclesiae* (Basel: 1497), a iiii.

[3] *Ibid.*, b iii.

priorities most closely mirrored those of the older generation was the professor of oratory and rhetoric at the University of Tübingen, Heinrich Bebel.[4] He knew little Greek and was untouched by the Florentine neo-Platonism that had begun to entice Celtis and others during the 1490s. Like Luder, Perger, and Wimpfeling, his ambition was to instruct and inspire his countrymen so they might express themselves in clearer and more elegant Latin. And like these predecessors, he angrily attacked the scholastic traditions of the German universities, arguing that retention of out-moded practices needlessly chained the Germans to their barbarian past. Understandably, many of his arguments had been stock-intrade among German humanists ever since Luder's inaugural oration at Heidelberg in 1456. Yet significant shifts in Bebel's writings set him apart from his humanist forebears. For like so many others of his generation, he sought to apply his knowledge and skills to the reform of religious life and scholastic theology.

Little is known about Bebel's development as a humanist. Born of a Swabian peasant family in 1472, he received his first schooling in the small village of Schelklingen. In 1492 he matriculated at the University of Cracow, where humanist courses were by then regularly offered. After receiving his Bachelor of Arts, he studied one year at the University of Basel, where he undoubtedly became acquainted with the salaried professor of oratory, Sebastian Brant, best known today as the author of the satirical poem, *Narrenschiff*. In 1496 he matriculated at the University of Tübingen. Whether he considered further serious study toward his Master of Arts is uncertain. In all likelihood, however, he was mainly attracted by the possibility of assuming the salaried chair of rhetoric

---

[4] Babel has failed to attract serious scholarly attention. See, however, Gustav Bebermeyer, *Tübinger Dichterhumanisten* (Tübingen: 1927), 1-47; Johannes Haller, "Heinrich Bebel als Dichter," *Zeitschrift für deutsches Altertum*, 66 (1929), 51-54; Adalbert Horawitz, "Analecten zur Geschichte des Humanismus in Schwaben," *Sitzungsberichte der kaiserlichen Akademie der Wissenschaften*, 86 (1877), 217-78, has printed several of Bebel's letters.

and poetry that had been established at Tübingen in 1481. Such suspicions are hardly dispelled when one learns that on arrival he wrote a series of verses that flattered several prominent Tübingen professors and Count Eberhard of Württemberg, the university's patron.[5] His blandishments proved effective, for in 1497 he became the salaried professor of poetry and rhetoric at the university. Four years later, on the recommendation of the Württemberg court, Emperor Maximilian awarded him the poet's laurel crown at Innsbruck. He remained at Tübingen until his death in 1517. In those years, despite limited poetical talents,[6] he proved to be a conscientious teacher and a widely published author.

Bebel's first publication during his Tübingen professoriate reveals his interest in applying his humanist skills to religion. Entitled *Book of Hymns recently Rendered into Verse* (1501), the book contained one hundred fifty-eight hymns from the medieval and patristic period and a brief exposition of "difficult terms" in the compositions.[7] Published along with the *Book of Hymns* was also Bebel's first printed attack on the deficiencies of arts course scholasticism—his "Apology and Defense of the Majesty of Poetry and Oratory." Bebel next published in 1507 *Art of Versifying and Composing Poems*, which described various kinds of poetry and outlined rules for poetical composition.[8] This was followed in 1508 by his *Commentary on the Writing of Letters*, which dealt not only with letter writing but also contained essays on other subjects.[9] For example, it included a "Commentary on the Abuse of the Latin Language" and brief compositions on the "art of speaking well"

---

[5] Bebermeyer, *Tübinger Dichterhumanisten*, 12.

[6] Heiko Oberman has recently judged, "But compared with the cultivated spirit of Conrad Celtis or even with such a traditional author as Jacob Wimpfeling, Bebel merits the title versifier rather than *poeta.*" *Masters of the Reformation*, trans. Dennis Martin (Cambridge, Eng.: 1981), 18.

[7] *Liber Hymnorum in metra noviter redactorum* (Tübingen: 1501).

[8] *Ars versificandi et carminum condendorum Henrici Bebelii. Quantitates syllabarum eiusdem. Racematio quedam: et recentiores atque exquisitiores observationes noviter collecte pro maiori carminis condendi & exornandi declaratione* (Strassburg: 1507).

[9] *Commentaria epistolarum conficiendarum* (Pforzheim: 1508)

and the etymology of Latin names. In 1513 he published another collection of orations and treatises that further illuminated his attitudes toward scholasticism; entitled *A Little Work on the Education of Boys*; it included, among others, "An Apology and Defense against Detractors," "An Oration on the Utility of Eloquence," and a "Little Work on which Authors should be Read for the Preparation of Eloquence."[10] In addition to these pedagogical treatises, he also collaborated with his colleague Johannes Heinrichmann in producing a popular Latin grammar (*Grammatical Principles*), delivered and published panegyrics to a host of notables, including Emperor Maximilian, and also edited a long collection of "witty tales" or *Facetiae*.[11]

The essential themes of Bebel's critique of scholasticism were spelled out in his "Apology and Defense of the Majesty of Poetry and Oratory," published with the *Book of Hymns* in 1501. Bebel began his "Apology" by praising the achievements of the Greeks and Romans, who had left behind a great fund of literature to nourish and instruct future generations. In his own day, Bebel complained, only the Italians had taken advantage of this heritage. Germans spent their time in barbarous exercises and were ignorant of the more honorable disciplines. He claimed that simple bakers and laborers of ancient Rome spoke more elegantly than even the most learned modern Germans. Not surprisingly, Bebel blamed these deficiencies on poor education, especially the retention of the "meager and twisted grammatical commentaries on Alexander Gallus."[12] Bebel's solution was equally predictable: increased study of the Greek and Roman poets and orators.

---

[10] *Opusculum . . . de institutione puerorum . . . Una cum apologia . . . poetices contra aemulos. Item. Opusculum qui auctores legendi sint ad comparationem eloquentiae . . . Oratio de utilitate eloquentiae. Apologia et Defensio Bebelii contra adversarios suos* (Strassburg: 1513).

[11] Bebel's *Facetiarum libri tres* is his only work to have attracted modern editors. See Karl Amrain, *Heinrich Bebels Facetien* (Leipzig: 1907) and Gustav Bebermeyer, *Heinrich Bebels Facetien: drei Bücher* (Leipzig: 1931).

[12] *Liber hymnorum*, iiii a.

Only studies such as these produced true learning and were, he added, particularly useful for priests and theologians.[13]

Bebel's later works were essentially elucidations of these few essential points. His most frequent theme was the importance of sound grammatical instruction and the dangers of deficient medieval grammar manuals. In his *Little Work on the Education of Boys* he cited Donatus as the most suitable text as long as it was studied "without any glosses and definitions, without a priori and a posteriori arguments and without modes of signification of terms, as certain barbarians are accustomed to deliver up."[14] He also approved the grammar by Nicholas Perotti and, not surprisingly, the grammar to which he himself had contributed, the *Grammatical Principles* of Heinrichmann.[15]

Bebel's comments on dialectic also have a familiar ring. Like most other humanists he conceded that moderate dialectical study was useful. But he often expressed the conventional criticism that students were forced to spend too much time on this one discipline. In his opinion, a mastery of the basic principles from Peter of Spain sufficed. He also warned students to avoid entanglement in nominalist-realist controversies. Since the *moderni* and *antiqui* sought to win over as many students as possible, they used all kinds of "subtle and sophistical arguments" to defend "the theories of holy Thomas, the formalities of Scotus, and the contentions of William of Occam." These same masters were happy when they made a convert even if their new follower proved "verbose, burdensome, and unreasonable."[16]

After they had mastered grammar, Bebel urged students to embark on the study of the great classical authors. In his treatise "Which authors should be read for the preparation of Eloquence," he endorsed the usual humanist favorites: for

[13] *Ibid.*, iiii c.
[14] *Opusculum*, A viii.
[15] Heinrichmann's grammar was first published by Anselm in Tübingen in 1511; Bebel's *Ars carminum condendorum* was included in most editions.
[16] *Opusculum*, A viii, A ix.

rhetoric, Cicero and Quintilian, and for poetry, Virgil and Horace. He also directed students to the writings of the Church fathers, all of whom he considered excellent stylistic models. Seneca and Boethius, however, because of their "crude and dry" style, should be given only to advanced students.[17] Mature students should also be encouraged to study Greek, "without which the Latin language never can satisfactorily be known."[18] Undoubtedly reflecting his own limited achievements in Greek, Bebel added that thoroughgoing instruction in the language was not necessary; an acquaintance with the grammatical rudiments and a "moderate knowledge" of Greek writings were sufficient.

More so than his tepid recommendation of Greek, Bebel's convictions about the relevance of humanism to Germany's religious life sets him apart from the pre-1500 humanists. These concerns are evident as early as 1501 in his "Apology and Defense of the Majesty of Poetry and Oratory." Here he argued that the *studia humanitatis* had special relevance for priests and theologians. Without eloquence a theologian could not properly defend truth or refute error; nor could a preacher "inspire contrition and joy or deter his listeners from sin and exhort them to virtue."[19] To counter the argument that poetry threatened piety and right-living, he compiled passages from Augustine, Jerome, and Basil that defended literary studies. He added that God himself must certainly approve poetry since he allowed so many beautiful hymns and psalms to be written in his praise. Bebel concluded by arguing that poetry was much more useful to the Church than "those sophistical and hateful disciplines that are now called the liberal arts." Dialectic and philosophy had always been seedbeds of heresy, but "poetry had never given support to any kind of heresy; instead it had always been the most agreeable attendant and servant of divine things."[20]

[17] *Ibid.*, A vii.
[18] *Ibid.*, A viiii.
[19] *Liber Hymnorum*, iiii c.
[20] *Ibid.*, iiii d.

Bebel's succeeding works both repeated and elaborated these thoughts. Thus in his *Little Work on the Education of Boys*, he argued that, because ancient literature taught "sound morality," it offered theologians and preachers countless examples to illustrate the rewards of virtue and the penalties of sin. Furthermore, knowledge of rhetoric and poetry was needed to understand both the biblical authors and the Church fathers. Bebel pointed out that many of these writers employed rhetorical and poetical devices in their work, and without an acquaintance with such contrivances the reader would lose important shades of meaning.[21]

But according to Bebel, ever the professor of oratory and poetry, the greatest reward the *studia humanitatis* offered the theologian was the acquisition of a truly elegant style. This was a common theme in many of Bebel's works, but a brief selection in the 1516 edition of his *Commentary on the Writing of Letters* best summarizes his ideas. Entitled "A Theological Dispute with a Friar," it recounted a dispute between Bebel and an Augustinian friar after one of the poet's lectures.[22] According to Bebel's account, his lecture had criticized theologians for neglecting sound Latin and for "corrupting a language which they use to appear learned." When his ideas were challenged by the Augustinian, Bebel immediately alluded to the example of the Church fathers, whose "style was golden" and whose "speech was serious, venerable, and full of majesty." Compared to these men, recent theologians were sad specimens indeed. Even the most learned—Albertus Magnus, Aquinas, Scotus, Occam, Egidius of Rome, Alexander Hales, Thomas Holcot, and Gregory of Rimini—were deficient because of their "rough, dry, meager, trampled and distorted way of writing." Such men, claimed Bebel, had valuable things to say but would forever remain unreadable because of their heathenish style. The "sole blame" for these

---

[21] Bebel also referred to recent papal support of the *studia humanitatis*; he listed Nicholas V, Pius II, Paul II, Sixtus IV and Alexander VI as patrons of the poets and orators. *Opusculum*, A iii.

[22] *Commentaria epistolarum conficiendarum*, CXLIII-CXLV.

flaws was the theologians' love of those "extraordinarily knotty and thorny teachings of the philosophers and dialecticians." The friar countered that philosophy was necessary so theologians could effectively fight heresy and defend dogma. Bebel responded with the argument made earlier in his career that philosophy more typically nurtured heresy than defended against it. And once again he raised the example of the Church fathers—"walls and pillars of the Church," who had effectively fought heresy without recourse to either philosophy or dialectic.

Bebel's attacks on scholastic theology lacked the wit and fervor of his more illustrious contemporaries. His writings reveal him as a moderate man, rather lacking in imagination, who was content to offer conventional and usually inoffensive arguments. During his twenty years at Tübingen he experienced no major conflicts with his "scholastic" colleagues and in fact often composed for them laudatory poems that were printed along with their works.[23] In one, the nominalist Gabriel Biel was said to be "girded with divine majesty" and to have expressed himself "wonderfully."[24] That such a man as Bebel wrote against the theologians at all is revealing evidence of the changing character of German humanism after 1500.

PIRCKHEIMER

One can hardly imagine two careers that differed more markedly than those of Heinrich Bebel and his slightly older con-

---

[23] Eight treatises by Tübingen theologians included introductory poems by Bebel; they were Gabriel Biel's *Epithoma expositionis Canonis Missae* (1499), *Sermones* (1499), *Collectiorum ex Occamo circa quatuor sententiarum* (1501) and *Expositio brevis Sacri Canonis* (1501); Conrad Summenhart's *Oratio funebris . . . pro principe Eberhardo* (1498), *Tractaculus exhortationis . . . supra decem defectibus virorum monasticorum* (1498) and *Quod deus homo fieri voluerit* (1498); and Wernherus Onsshusen's *Tractatus trium quaestionum*; all cited in Karl Steiff, *Der erste Buchdruck in Tübingen* (Nieuwkoop: 1963), reprint of 1881 edition, 49-75.

[24] Gabriel Biel, *Canonis missae Expositio*, ed. Heiko Oberman (Wiesbaden: 1967), IV, 185, 186.

temporary, Willibald Pirckheimer. While the life of the Swabian peasants' son was limited to the narrow world of the Tübingen lecture hall, the wealthy Pirckheimer traveled widely and was an influential man of affairs in his native Nuremberg. A master of Greek and the translator of some forty works, Pirckheimer was an intimate friend of Dürer, a correspondent of Erasmus, and the dinner host of Luther, Melanchthon, von Hutten, and other luminaries. Unlike Bebel's limited concern with "eloquence," Pirckheimer's intellectual interests were far-flung and immense. A sensitive poet, a lover of literature, and an energetic correspondent, Pirckheimer also was drawn to Greek philosophy, natural science, the occult, and, especially after the onset of the Reformation, theology. His attitudes toward scholasticism are well worth exploring.[25]

Pirckheimer was the only German humanist who never attended a northern European university. Born into a wealthy Nuremberg family, he received his early education from private tutors. His interest in humanism can be traced back to the influence of his father, Johann. The elder Pirckheimer bequeathed to his son an interest in antiquity that he himself had acquired while studying law in Italy in the 1460s. In 1488, at the age of eighteen, Willibald retraced his father's steps to Padua, where he too commenced the study of law. But like so many of his countrymen, he was soon seduced by the Italian achievement in literature and philosophy. He learned Greek and heard lectures on Plato and Aristotle. His father hoped that a transfer to the University of Pavia would rekindle an interest in the law. But in 1495, when Willibald returned to Germany after extensive travel throughout Italy, he packed

---

[25] On Pirckheimer, see Lewis Spitz, "Willibald Pirckheimer—Speculative Patrician," *Religious Renaissance*, 155-97; Friedrich Roth, *Willibald Pirckheimer, ein Lebensbild, Schriften des Vereins für Reformationsgeschichte*, 21 (Halle: 1887); Hans Rupprich, "Willibald Pirckheimer, Beiträge zu einer Wesenserfassung," *Schweizer Beiträge zur allgemeinen Geschichte*, 15 (1957), 54-110; above all, see the recent work, Niklas Holzberg, *Willibald Pirckheimer. Griechischer Humanismus in Deutschland* (Munich: 1981); it contains a lengthy and thorough bibliography; Pirckheimer's large correspondence has been collected in Pirckheimer, *Briefwechsel*, 2 vols., ed. Emil Reicke (Munich: 1940, 1956).

numerous books and manuscripts but no law degree. Soon marrying the daughter of another patrician Nuremberg family, he began an adult life that included scholarship, political activity and no little controversy. He died in 1530.

Pirckheimer achieved his prominence within German humanism through his mastery of Greek and his considerable skill as an editor and translator. In all he translated over forty works from Greek to Latin. The titles suggest the breadth of his learning. Among them were histories, plays, devotional pieces, scientific works, selections from the Greek Church fathers, and writings by Aristotle, Plato, and other philosophers. No other German humanist equaled the diversity of his thought or the soundness of his scholarship.

Nonetheless, much of Pirckheimer's anti-scholastic rhetoric, like Bebel's, was purely conventional. Throughout his correspondence, numerous passages could be cited that resemble the tone of two letters written in 1502. He called the schoolmen "worshipers of barbarian letters" who offered "young men straw, while spurning" more sumptuous nourishment." He added that they deserve the name *philopompi*, since they were "deficient in true philosophy and ignorant of all the liberal arts." He criticized their "idle talk, sophistical argumentations, and inane foolery." Finally he attacked their morals: "If you investigate the life and customs of these men, it is necessary to censure and detest them."[26] Elsewhere he made typical humanist criticisms of the scholastics' inept Latin. In 1513, in a letter of Johann Cochlaeus, for example, he lamented their monotonous language and "rough, uneven, style."[27]

Despite such statements, Pirckheimer was drawn to certain aspects of Germany's scholastic heritage. Within his literally voluminous library were Alexander Villedieu's *Doctrinale*, Lombard's *Sentences*, several volumes of Aquinas, and Aris-

---

[26] Pirckheimer, *Briefwechsel*, I, 172, 173; similar opinions with the exact wording were expressed to another correspondent shortly thereafter; see *Briefwechsel*, I, 178, 179.

[27] *Ibid.*, II, 246.

totle's complete works.[28] Such books did not simply gather dust. Even speculative theology was not beyond his range of interests. In 1496, for example, he composed a long letter to an unnamed correspondent about a problem stemming from the Genesis creation story: how could light have been created on the first day, if the stars and heavenly bodies were created only on the fourth?[29] In his discussion Pirckheimer cited not only Augustine and several Greek fathers but also Lombard's *Sentences*, Aquinas's *Summa*, and Aquinas's commentary on Lombard. Some years later, in the context of another discussion, he conceded that the study of Aquinas, Scotus, and other speculative writers of the Middle Ages had value for future theologians.[30]

Nor did Pirckheimer completely abandon Aristotle for Plato. He did at times attack Aristotelian logic. In a letter of 1513, he deplored how philosophy was being corrupted by the "unpleasantries of Aristotle" and the "impieties and blasphemies of Porphyry."[31] But Pirckheimer was a close student of Aristotle's writings on natural philosophy. After his return to Nuremberg, he urged his German friend in Italy, Anton Kress, to keep him informed of new translations of Aristotle.[32] When one of the Aristotelian works arrived with a page missing, he quickly wrote Kress in the hope of getting a new copy.[33] He knew his Aristotle well and frequently cited him when arguing disputed points.[34]

Pirckheimer conceded that some of the concerns and achievements of the scholastic philosophers and theologians were of lasting value. Nonetheless, he was an ardent critic of scholastics, and not solely because of their "inept and crude"

[28] Emile Offenbacher, "La Bibliothèque de Willibald Pirckheimer," *La Bibliofilia*, 40 (1938), 241-63.

[29] *Briefwechsel*, I, 199.

[30] See discussion later in section.

[31] Pirckheimer, *Briefwechsel*, II, 246.

[32] *Ibid.*, I, 180, 190.

[33] *Ibid.*, I, 164.

[34] See, for example, his letter from around 1507 when he employed Aristotle to defend astrology. *Ibid.*, I, 460-64.

style. Their greatest failure lay in the area of moral philosophy. It was this concern with ethics that gave unity to his seemingly aimless translating activity. As Lewis Spitz has written, "a survey of the scores of translations that he did and the interpretation placed upon them reveals that they were not only in the main ethical and religious in nature, but that many were specifically designed to enlarge available Christian literature."[35] With a few exceptions, most notably his impressive edition of Ptolemy's *Cosmography*, his translations were of writings somehow related to problems of daily living. Thus he concentrated on the works of Plutarch and Lucian and certain of Plato's non-speculative works such as *Achiochus, De justo,* and *Num virtus doceri possit.* Orators and Greek Church fathers attracted his interest because he believed they were adept at teaching the precepts of good behavior. He admired a rhetorician like Isocrates not only because of his eloquence but also because his writings contained "most suitable admonitions and the holiest precepts, agreeing very much with the Christian religion."[36] He translated many works by Gregory Nazanius, the fourth-century Greek patriarch, in the hope his words would inspire men responsible for teaching piety and virtue to the common believer.[37]

Pirckheimer's concern with ethics is clearly revealed in a letter to his sister Charitas that was published as an introduction to his translation of Plutarch's *De his, qui tarde a numine corripiuntur.*[38] In it Pirckheimer described what he meant by true philosophy. True philosophy taught virtue and offered consolation in times of trouble. It concerned those things "which securely and firmly lead men, wandering and drifting in this earthly sea, to the gate of the highest felicity and immortality; also with those things which can mend the wounds

[35] Spitz, *Religious Renaissance,* 165.
[36] Pirckheimer, *Briefwechsel,* I, 200.
[37] See the letters published in Pirckheimer, *Opera politica, historica, philologica,* ed. Melchior Goldast (Frankfurt: 1610), 231, 238-40.
[38] *De his qui tarde a Numine corripiuntur libellus* (Nuremberg: 1513).

suffered in human adversities and calamities."[39] He cited the Stoic precept that it was a gift of God that men lived, but a gift of philosophy that men lived well. He went on to assure his sister that if instructed in true philosophy, she could bear any injury or sorrow that fate might deal. Thus in this context, Pirckheimer's conception of philosophy had little in common with the speculative and metaphysical interests of the scholastics. As Pirckheimer put it, he had no use for "that sophistical and quibbling philosophy which is not able to lead to a good and blessed living."[40]

Pirckheimer's concern with ethics largely explains his disenchantment with scholastic theology. In 1513, when he wrote Johannes Cochlaeus about the theologians of his day, half the letter was given over to criticisms of the scholastics' moral shortcomings.[41] These men, he complained, "prided themselves on being imitators of Christ, our Lord and savior." But in their daily lives they showed none of Christ's gentleness, clemency, or patience. What a spectacle for laymen to see theologians eternally arguing among themselves and attacking opponents with hatred and malice! He concluded that these men were so ignorant and depraved that they could never help the laity lead good and pious lives.

Pirckheimer made his most thorough comment on scholastic theology in 1517, in the midst of the Reuchlin affair. In that year he composed a long letter about contemporary theologians, which he published as an introduction to his edition of Lucian's *Fisherman.*[42] He began the letter by criticizing the schoolmen for contentiousness and their rough treatment of Reuchlin. But Pirckheimer devoted most of it to a critique of the theologians' scholarship. In his opinion, overemphasis on logic was to blame for many of theology's shortcomings. He conceded, as most humanists did, that dialectic was useful if

[39] Pirckheimer, *Briefwechsel*, II, 232.
[40] *Ibid.*, II, 233.
[41] *Ibid.*, II, 245-48.
[42] *Luciani Piscator sue Reviviscentes* (Tübingen: 1517).

studied in moderation. But he further argued that theologians were so immersed in logic that all kinds of evils resulted: the Old Testament was neglected, the New Testament was belittled as the work of the unlearned, Jerome was condemned as a mere grammarian and Augustine was damned for his ignorance.[43] Pirckheimer claimed that if Augustine returned from the dead, he would find the disputes of modern theologians incomprehensible; for he knew nothing of *"instantiae, relationes, ampliationes, restrictiones, formalitates, heccetitates, quidditates* and those other kinds of monstrous names." Moslems and Jews, Pirckheimer continued, studied their sacred laws every day, but Christians found abstract speculation more exciting than the Scriptures. As a result, after years of study and contemplation, Christian theologians were only capable of writing commentaries on Donatus or Alexander Villedieu.

Pirckheimer went on to outline what he considered a proper course of theological study. First the prospective theologian had to master the three scholarly languages: Latin, "so that he will not seem more a barbarian than theologian"; Greek, "so that he might be able to understand Aristotle and the cyclic teachings"; and Hebrew, "since in Hebrew letters all the mysteries of the Old and New Testament are hidden." Although he warned that ostentatious use of logic's technical vocabulary "put people asleep," the study of the discipline "within restricted limits" was acceptable. Rhetoric, a means of teaching the unlearned and stirring emotions, was comparatively more important. The theologian also had to know philosophy—"not only that which Aristotle has accurately set forth but also that more divine philosophy in which most excellent Plato holds the honor." He reminded the reader that Cicero had called Plato divine, that Augustine chose him as his guide, and that the "Latin and Greek fathers agree with one voice that Platonic theology agrees most completely with the Christian religion." Because of Plato's importance, the

---

[43] *Ibid.*, b v.

theologian must have skill in mathematics, "for without geometry, arithmetic, music, and astronomy, Platonic philosophy cannot be completely learned." History was also demanded because it helped theologians understand the past and foretell the future; finally, a knowledge of civil and canon law was required so, if needed, theologians could be effective administrators.[44]

Did a knowledge of the great scholastic *doctores* have any role for Pirckheimer's ideal theologian? He approved the moderate study of "Saint Thomas, subtle Scotus and all the other writings of the speculative theologians." But he also warned of the dangers of such pursuits. He had seen how some men "displaced the evangelical teachings of Christ with dialectic, the Old Testament with physics, the dogmas of the apostles with metaphysics, and the writings of the pristine theologians with logic."[45]

Pirckheimer concluded by reaffirming that a theologian's greatest obligation was to make his own life a model of Christ's teaching. Good works and truthfulness were more important than erudition and mere talk. The theologian must substitute "humility for pride, calmness for contentiousness, charity for hatred, and virtue for moral failure." Without this even the most thorough knowledge of Aristotle and Plato was worthless.

To summarize: although Pirckheimer criticized scholasticism in general terms, he was nonetheless drawn to the writings of certain scholastics such as Aquinas. He had no desire to purge the schools completely of scholastic theology and logic. Platonic philosophy should be taught, however, as should Greek and Hebrew. Pirckheimer also criticized the scholastics for neglecting the religious needs of the Christian laymen. To the Nuremberg patrician, the theologian must not only be learned but also be an inspiring teacher and a model of piety and virtue.

[44] The summary and the quotes included are based on Pirckheimer's discussion in *ibid.*, b vi-b viiii.
[45] *Ibid.*, b x.

REUCHLIN

As many historians have pointed out, it is ironic that Johannes Reuchlin was the humanist who provoked the wrath of the Cologne theologians and thus lent his name to the controversy reputed to be the classic confrontation between humanism and scholasticism. During most of his life Reuchlin's criticisms of scholasticism were mild and infrequent. He did have definite ideas about needed reforms of scholastic theology, but he offered them in a spirit of humility and honest piety.[46]

Reuchlin was by training a lawyer, and he pursued an active career serving the government of Württemberg as a jurist, councillor, and diplomat. His major works mainly appeared after 1500, even thought he was born in 1455. Northern universities provided his formal education, if not the inspiration for his scholarship. He began his university training at Freiburg-im-Breisgau, later studied at the University of Paris, and finally received his Master of Arts from Basel in 1478. Although an interest in Nicholas of Cusa in these early years hints at the intellectual path he later would follow, more decisive were several visits he made to Italy. Especially significant were his trips to Florence in 1482, when he met Marsilio Ficino, and in 1490, when he met Pico della Mirandola. His interest in Pythagorean philosophy and the Jewish Cabala can safely be traced to the influence of these two illustrious Italians.

His contemporaries considered Reuchlin the most learned German of their age. Although others talked bravely of learning the three scholarly languages—Greek, Hebrew, and Latin—

---

[46] Reuchlin scholarship still rests on the pioneering work by Ludwig Geiger, *Johann Reuchlin, sein Leben und seine Werke* (Leipzig: 1871). Max Brod, *Johannes Reuchlin und sein Kampf* (Stuttgart: 1965), adds little new information. Manfred Krebs, ed., *Johannes Reuchlin, 1455-1522* (Pforzheim: 1955), is a good collection of essays. See also Lewis Spitz, "Reuchlin—Pythagoras Reborn," *Religious Renaissance* . . . , 61-80. Reuchlin's letters have been published in *Johann Reuchlins Briefwechsel*, ed. Ludwig Geiger (Tübingen: 1875); several other letters can be found in Adalbert Horawitz, ed., *Zur Biographie und Correspondenz Johannes Reuchlins* (Vienna: 1877).

he was one of the few who mastered all three tongues. Actually his accomplishments as a Latinist were unspectacular. They were limited to a single *Jugendarbeit*, a Latin dictionary entitled *A Brief Vocabulary*, published in 1475 when Reuchlin was twenty years old.[47] Occasionally he boasted of having studied grammar and rhetoric under Robert Gaguin and William Tardif,[48] but he took little pride or interest in his own Latin style. In the opinion of Erasmus, he was "a great man, but his speech is redolent of his age, which was still somewhat rough and unpolished." Erasmus had no reservations about Reuchlin's proficiency in Greek.[49] Reuchlin learned the rudiments of the language during early student days at Paris and polished his skills through independent study. Among his published translations from the Greek were works by St. Athanasius, Demosthenes, Hippocrates, and Homer.

It was above all as a master of Hebrew that Reuchlin assured his reputation as a great scholar. And it was Hebrew that aroused the greatest enthusiasm in Reuchlin himself. In *On the Wondrous Word*, a work on the Cabala published in 1494, he defended Hebrew against the "barbarians" who did not consider it a worthy tongue. It did not, he admitted, have much elegance or grace, but "its speech is simple, pure, uncorrupted, holy, brief and consistent, the language by which God spoke to men and men with angels."[50] Later in his career, he likened the reading of Hebrew to a true religious experience. In a letter to his friend Nicholas Killen, he wrote that he had studied many languages, but none brought him closer to God than Hebrew: "Always in fact, while reading Hebrew, I seem to see God himself speaking, for I know this was the language in which God and the angels described their merits

---

[47] *Vocabularius breviloquus* (No place: 1478); it was frequently republished during the next forty years.

[48] Reuchlin, *Briefwechsel*, 199.

[49] Erasmus, *Ciceronianus*, English translation by Izora Scott, in *Controversies over the Imitation of Cicero* (New York: 1911), 107. For a summary of Reuchlin's Greek scholarship see Geiger, *Reuchlin*, 97-101 and the recent work, Holzberg, *Pirckheimer*, *passim*.

[50] *De Verbo mirifico* (Basel: 1494), C 5 b. (Facsimile reprint, Stuttgart: 1964.)

to men."[51] The experience, he related, was at once terrifying and joyful.

Reuchlin's most lasting achievement as a Hebraist was to lay the groundwork for further Hebrew studies by writing two fundamental works on Hebrew grammar. In 1506 he published his lengthy *On the Rudiments of Hebrew* along with an edition of several psalms to be used as study aids.[52] Twelve years later, in 1518, he published a more specialized work on Hebrew pronunciation, *On the Accent and Orthography of the Hebrew Language*.[53] More fascinating to Reuchlin was his work on the Cabala, that esoteric body of Hebrew mysticism dating from around 1200. The Italian philosopher, Pico della Mirandola, was the inspiration for this important aspect of Reuchlin's work. Both men were attracted to the Cabala because of its close affinity to certain Pythagorean and neo-Platonic doctrines such as contemplation, hierarchy, emanation, and spiritualism.[54] They were convinced that, when properly studied, the Cabala not only confirmed important Christian truths but also unlocked mysteries of the Bible and even the universe itself. The key to its use was knowledge of the special qualities of Hebrew words and letters, which to the Cabalist had esoteric meanings and magical powers.[55] Reuchlin wrote two long and difficult works on the Cabala, *On the Wondrous Word* (1494) and *On the Cabalistic Art* (1518).

Before the clash with the Cologne theologians, Reuchlin could not be characterized as a harsh critic of scholasticism. A lawyer rather than a university professor, his writings and correspondence convey little interest in reforming Latin in-

[51] Reuchlin, *Briefwechsel*, 123.

[52] *De Rudimentis Hebraicis* (Pforzheim: 1506).

[53] *De accentibus et orthographia linguae Hebraicae libri tres* (Hagenow: 1518).

[54] The common attraction of Platonism and Cabalism has been discussed in Jean-Louis Viellard-Baron, "Platonisme et Kabbale dans l'oeuvre de Johann Reuchlin," *L'humanisme allemand (1480-1540)*, ed. Joël Lefebvre and Jean-Claude Margolin (Paris: 1979), 159-67.

[55] On the Cabala, see F. Secret, *Les kaballistes chrétiens de la Renaissance* (Paris: 1964) and G. G. Scholem, *Major Trends in Jewish Mysticism* (Jerusalem: 1941).

struction or forging a place for classical literature in the scholastic curriculum. He was enough of a realist to know that the arcane and controversial wisdom of the Cabala had no chance of acceptance at the universities. In fact he seems to have admired the writings of some scholastics. Like many German humanists, he praised Albertus Magnus, and he dedicated one of his Greek translations to his realist teacher at Paris and Basel, Johann Heynlin of Stein.[56] He was well-acquainted with Aristotle and in one work even adopted the formal scholastic method of argumentation. While defending the usefulness of Hebrew writings in the *Augenspiegel* (Eye Mirror) (1512) he set forth fifty-two propositions, presented the *pros* and *contras* on each and then presented his own *conclusiones*. Reuchlin himself called it "arguments in the scholastic style."[57]

Nonetheless, even before the eruption of the conflict with Cologne, his works contained some anti-scholastic rhetoric. In *Henno* (1498), a play written for the edification of Bishop Johann Dalberg of Speyer and his circle, one of the characters makes an impassioned speech against the detractors of poetry, whom he calls "wild beasts and donkies." Reuchlin had made more explicit criticisms of the scholastics four years earlier in *On the Wondrous Word*. In one passage he criticized them for neglecting the sacred wisdom of ancient sages and poets. The people considered philosophy to be "the knowledge of all things human and divine," but today, Reuchlin wrote, philosophers did nothing but "ravel and unravel the perplex questions of the schools." As a result, "the name of philosophy was a name of scorn," and philosophers are considered "mad and foolish rather than wise."[58] In a similar vein he chided theologians for spending their time on the "sophistical dialectic of Aristotle" and other matters of "human invention." Thus "heavenly instruction is neglected," and "human loquacity drowns out the word of God."[59]

[56] See citations in Geiger, *Reuchlin*, 154.
[57] *Augenspiegel* (Tübingen: 1512), F-H iv.
[58] *De verbo mirifico*, D iv, D iv b.
[59] *Ibid.*, E iv a.

On the positive side, Reuchlin was convinced that the teaching of Hebrew, which he championed, would improve theology by giving theologians the ability to read the original words of the Old Testament. Reuchlin wrote in 1513 that so great was his "enthusiasm for the idioms and properties of languages" that he could not study any writing unless it was an exact copy of the original."[60] He stressed the necessity of knowing the Old Testament in Hebrew in the introduction to his *On the Rudiments of Hebrew*. He urged theologians to learn the language "so that the universal disdain for all the interpretations could be removed."[61] In the text he pointed out approximately two hundred passages in the *Vulgate* that did not agree with the Hebrew original. He noted that any one of these errors might cause theological errors. Reuchlin himself was careful to draw no theological conclusions from his philological inquiries. After showing an error in a passage in *Chronicles*, he remarked in a typical statement, "I am not discussing the meaning as a theologian, but the words as a grammarian."[62]

Elsewhere Reuchlin asserted that "our doctors and teachers of the Holy Bible" would also benefit from studying scriptural commentaries and other works of previous Hebrew scholars; among those he named were Rabbi Solomon, Moses of Garona, Rabbi Levi, Joseph and David Kimchi.[63] Reuchlin made these suggestions without scorn or arrogance. Ignorance of Hebrew was lamentable, but it was no reason to dismiss all scholastics as barbarians. Reuchlin was no revolutionary. His pious wish was to serve the cause of theology and the church.

MUTIAN

Conrad Mutian, recognized leader of Erfurt humanism in the early sixteenth century, was nothing if not a man of contra-

[60] Reuchlin, *Briefwechsel*, 189.
[61] *Ibid.*, 89.
[62] *De rudimentis hebraicis*, 123.
[63] *Augenspiegel*, XII v.

dictions. He was a prodigious intellectual who never published a word; he was a lover of classical literature who was quick to condemn prideful poets; he was a harsh critic of the priesthood but was himself a cleric who avidly pursued benefices and admitted writing several letters "good and drunk." A similar paradox colored his attitude toward scholasticism. Although deeply alienated from scholastic philosophy and theology, he refrained from openly attacking them and occasionally denounced others who did. In his unwillingness to reveal his true beliefs, Mutian shows the inner tensions that humanism's new boldness after 1500 had the capacity to engender.

In contrast to the complexity of his personality and the subtlety of his thought, Mutian's life was simple and uncluttered.[64] Born of a prosperous Homberg family in 1471, he received his early education at local schools. At the age of ten he entered the renowned school of the Brethren of the Common Life at Deventer. Five years later he enrolled at the University of Erfurt, where by his own account he heard and was impressed by the lectures of Conrad Celtis.[65] After receiving his Master of Arts in 1492 he remained at Erfurt for two more years as a teacher in the arts course. Then in 1495 he left Erfurt for Italy, where he remained until 1502. He visited the major Italian cities, received a law degree from Bologna, and, most importantly, deepened his appreciation of classical literature and Platonic philosophy. When he returned to Germany he briefly worked in the Hessian chancellery. But in 1503, at the age of thirty-two, he became a canon in the Chapter of Mary in Gotha; there he remained until his death in 1526. In those

---

[64] Mutian has yet to receive the sound scholarly treatment he deserves; the best analysis of his religious ideas is Lewis Spitz, "Mutian, Intellectual Canon," in *Religious Renaissance* . . . , 130-55; Fritz Halbauer, *Mutianus Rufus und seine geistesgeschichtliche Stellung* (Leipzig: 1929), is poorly organized and barely readable. See also Jean-Claude Margolin, "Mutianus Rufus et son modèle erasmien," *L'humanisme allemand (1480-1540)*, ed. Lefebvre and Margolin, 169-202. His correspondence has been collected in Carl Krause, ed., *Der Briefwechsel des Mutianus Rufus* (Kassel: 1885).

[65] Mutian, *Briefwechsel*, 655.

years he devoted himself to his studies, observation of Germany's religious scene, and the cultivation of many friendships, especially with humanist sympathizers at the University of Erfurt. Despite occasional urgings from friends, however, he never committed anything to print. Fortunately he was an active correspondent, and although many of his letters have been lost or destroyed, enough have been preserved to allow us at least a glimpse into the mind of this extraordinary man.

As one reads through Mutian's letters, one is struck by his consistent pessimism about Germany's cultural and religious situation. There are exceptions, of course. In 1505, for example, he enthused that his countrymen were freeing themselves from ignorance and entering a golden age.[66] And four years later he exulted that "young masters at Erfurt were freeing themselves from barbarism."[67] But long gaps separate such expressions of optimism. For all his bold mockery of monkish ignorance and scholastic obscurity, Mutian, in a spirit reminiscent at times of Erasmus, sensed the vulnerability of humanism and the cause of intellectual revival. Even before the Reuchlin affair must have confirmed many of his fears, he felt surrounded by dark forces ready to strike and snuff out advances that he and like-minded men had made.

These forces of darkness had two strongholds—the priesthood and the universities. From his first arrival in Gotha, Mutian's letters reveal his scorn for the ignorant clerics surrounding him. None of them had any sympathy for his reading of the poets and ancient philosophers: "Barbarians, proud and contentious, prevail among the barbarians, and those who should especially revere and respect me give vent to their anger. Yesterday abusive, threatening and bitter words flared up. There is little chance that they might pride themselves in Mutian; they already want me far away from them."[68] But scholasticism was by far the greater barrier to good learning.

Attacks on the universities' scholastic curricula were es-

---

[66] *Ibid.*, 21.
[67] *Ibid.*, 113.
[68] *Ibid.*, 19.

pecially common in 1509, the year when his friend and correspondent, Heinrich Urban, began work on his Bachelor of
Arts degree at the University of Leipzig. Because Urban had
already made substantial progress in his knowledge of ancient
literature and philosophy, Mutian thought it tragic that he
must now go back to the trivial fare of the arts course. In
October he wrote Urban that he could never think about his
situation without breaking into tears;[69] he warned his friend
that he would have to forget every worthy thing he knew.
"These inept and arrogant men," he complained, "are accustomed to draw good talents away from worthwhile studies
and pull them off course to their distorted prison, just like so
many blind donkeys."[70] Mutian continued: "Why is this so?
Encumbered by errors, overwhelmed with opinions, surrounded by darkness, they are not able to attain a notion of
truth even if those old men cared to. But it is not for me to
dispute against the barbarians. You will see to how great an
extent lamentable ignorance and error holds them."[71] In another letter he refused to discuss the lectures Urban had to
attend, since that "kind of babbling offers shadows and inane
absurdities."[72] At other times he urged his friend to study
good authors privately and practice his Greek whenever time
allowed.[73]

Mutian's attacks on scholastic theology were steeped in
similar rhetoric. He complained, among other things, that
these men ignored Greek and Hebrew, scorned the Church
fathers and other good authors, closed their minds to any
spirit of change, and in general were useless to the Church.
Indeed, most of the inadequacies of the universities could be
ascribed to the conservatism of scholastic theologians. They
maintained the status quo, and their prestige was such that
others hesitated to oppose them. Referring to the University

[69] *Ibid.*, 118.
[70] *Ibid.*, 117.
[71] *Ibid.*, 118.
[72] *Ibid.*, 146, 147.
[73] *Ibid.*, 135.

of Erfurt in 1513, he lamented that "the apes of the theologians seize the whole school, forcing upon the students the teachings of Donatus and the 'little logicals,' sheer nonsense, exercises of all kinds, and other trifles."[74]

What alternatives did Mutian suggest? In 1513 he jokingly wrote Urban about his conception of a good university: "It would be enough . . . if there were one sophist, two mathematicians, three theologians, four jurists, five physicians, six orators, seven Hebraists, eight Graecists, nine grammarians and ten right-minded philosophers."[75] Perhaps this was another letter Mutian wrote while *bene inebrius*; even if this was the case, in certain respects it faithfully reflects his intellectual position.

The low rank accorded to dialectic, for example (one sophist on a faculty of fifty-five!), underlines his low regard for scholastic logic. At times he rejected scholastic logic entirely, dismissing it as a method for twisting arguments to support even the most preposterous propositions. In 1506 he complained to Urban about the stupidity of the modern philosophers who had no concern about the writing of good Latin, but who were "well-instructed in raillery and fallacies." With their syllogizing, he complained, they defend any argument, no matter how foolish. He cited two examples: "The apostles of God are twelve; Peter and Paul are apostles of God, therefore Peter and Paul are twelve; Furthermore: God is everywhere, i.e., in every place. The sewer is a place, therefore God is in the sewer."[76] At other times, he took a more moderate position on logic's usefulness. In 1514, for example, he quoted the famous French humanist, Jacques Lefèvre, to defend the position that logic was necessary for rational discourse, but that the medieval logicians had made the discipline "insolent and fruitless." As a result, Mutian continued, natural and rational philosophy, mathematics and philosophy all suffered. In the same letter he went on to attack the numerous scholastic

[74] *Ibid.*, 331.
[75] *Ibid.*
[76] *Ibid.*, 67.

compendia on logic, specifically the *Short Summary of Logic*, published in 1512 by the Erfurt nominalist, Jodocus Trutvetter. To Mutian it was sufficient for a true philosopher to learn logic by reading Aristotle himself. By their long commentaries, men like Trutvetter only turned "gems into pickles." Thus in Mutian's opinion, logic was worthwhile only if studied in moderation and from original Aristotelian sources.[77]

Compared to logic, the other two trivium subjects had a higher status at Mutian's "ideal university," which was to have six orators and nine grammarians. Mutian no doubt approved the attempts of his fellow humanists to improve grammar teaching and bring poetry and rhetoric into the universities of Germany. In 1510, for example, he berated a Benedictine monk who had claimed that "the poets are ruining the universities," and he would discourse at length about the faulty Latin found in much medieval writing. But Mutian differed from the rhetorical humanists and grammar reformers of the previous generation. He took little pride in his Latin style and frankly admitted, "in me there is certainly nothing of Cicero."[78] He was angered when anyone referred to him as a "mere poet."

Mutian actually shared many of Wimpfeling's reservations about poetry. He felt there was nothing more ludicrous than the wordy pride of men who boastfully fashioned themselves as "poets." In 1506 he wrote about the visit of three such men:

> What can I say about inept poets? Three of them came to me. Which of them was more boastful I cannot express in words. One is a noxious thief and a plagiarizer of Ovid, the second a barbarian babbler, the third a little man with such a dull mind, that no one knows what he says besides himself. They set before me four badly-written and ridiculous verses. All are bad imitatiors and like leeches

[77] *Ibid.*, 444, 445.
[78] Mutian's comment on the Benedictine and on his own style can be found in *ibid.*, 212.

sucking bad blood, leave behind the good in the poets. They have read like a small boy and searched into the books of collections, but they found lumps of coal and not treasures. But I am neither a public censor, nor the preceptor of any man."[79]

Like Wimpfeling, Mutian's favorite poet was Baptista Mantuanus, the Italian Carmelite, who composed verses on pious themes.[80] He also feared poetry's nefarious effect on morals: young boys should read only "chaste poets," priests none at all. To support this view he quoted the famous passage from Jerome, "What has Horace to do with the Psalms, Virgil with the Gospels, Cicero with the apostles?"[81]

If Mutian declined the titles of "poet" and "Ciceronian," he never complained when someone called him "philosopher." His ideal university was a school of philosophy more than anything else; it included ten "right-minded philosophers" and what might be called a supporting cast of fifteen—eight professors of Greek and seven of Hebrew. It included only three theologians, but Mutian's philosophers would no doubt have been expected to say a good deal about the workings of God.

Mutian never produced a well-constructed theological or philosophical synthesis. His philosophy is scattered in numerous passages throughout his letters. But all these scraps do show one common pattern: his consistent interest in the neo-Platonism of the speculative humanists of late fifteenth-century Italy. He often expressed interest in Ficino and praised Pico as "a divine man among the most noble, a great miracle among the most learned of his age."[82] Mutian's tendency toward "spiritualization of the Judaeo-Christian theological heritage,"[83] his stress on love as the binding force in the uni-

---

[79] *Ibid.*, 33.

[80] *Ibid.*, 52.

[81] *Ibid.*, 189.

[82] *Ibid.*, 174.

[83] According to Lewis Spitz, Mutian's emphasis on the spirit over flesh drove him not only to denounce relics but also to question transubstantiation

verse, and the idea of man existing at the mid-point of the Great Chain of Being can be traced back without exception to the influence of the two Florentines.

All of Mutian's disparagements of scholasticism were limited to his private correspondence. He never publicly attacked the scholastics, and he strongly disapproved when others did so. It was especially repugnant to see "a mere poet" attack theologians. In a possible reference to the conflict between Jacob Locher and George Zingel,[84] he wrote in 1510 that he could "hardly stand" the stupidity of the crowned poets who felt they were lovers of eternal truth." These men, he complained, attacked the theologians and renounced the sacred scriptures. They said good things badly and judged bad things good.[85] He expressed similar sentiments in 1513 when a young humanist, Tillmann Conradi, insulted the scholastics at Erfurt. He said to Urban that it was wrong to attack "holy masters just for personal greatness and grandeur." Although the sophists offered little that was valuable for Christian living, they were wise at "solving perplexities and questions, in confirming truth and refuting error."[86] Versifiers had no business attacking them.

Why was Mutian reticent about openly criticizing the scholastics? His reticence partly resulted from his views about the august nature of philosophy and theology; even when poorly done the disciplines demanded respect. It also resulted from the same convictions that led to his decision to publish no books. He once defended his aversion to publishing by citing the examples of Christ and Socrates, who of course left behind no written works.[87] But the true reason lay in Mutian's beliefs that it was important to protect the common people from radical philosophizing, attacks on tradition, and criticisms of

---

and Christ's passion. He was, Spitz notes, "on the thin edge of historic Christianity." See *Religious Renaissance*, 141, 142.

[84] See the following chapter for a discussion of this controversy.

[85] Mutian, *Briefwechsel*, 189.

[86] *Ibid.*, 328.

[87] *Ibid.*, 112.

authority. Mutian and his friends might jest about ignorant priests and dull-witted theologians, but to express these thoughts openly would only confuse the people and weaken the Church. He wrote in 1505, "we know certainly that mysteries must not be popularized, but are to be suppressed in silence or else treated under the coverings of fables or riddles, nor should pearls be thrown to pigs."[88]

Thus the humanist whose thought was most deeply estranged from both the method and content of late scholasticism never publicly attacked the practices he deplored. Nonetheless through his correspondence and wide circle of friends, his influence was considerable. His significance lay in the fact that he was among the first of his generation to transcend the grammatical and rhetorical interests of the early humanists; he looked to antiquity not for a reform of Latin speech, but for a renewal of Christian philosophy and theology. Hesitant in his recommendation of the classical poets, Mutian was convinced that only a recovery of the ancient *pia philosophia* could revivify the thought and culture of his age.

~ ~ ~

THIS CHAPTER might very well have explored the thought of other early sixteenth-century German humanists: Ulrich von Hutten, the fiery nationalist; Jacob Locher, the controversial successor of Conrad Celtis at Ingolstadt; Hermann Buschius, the latter-day wandering poet; Eobanus Hessus, the first salaried humanist at Erfurt; Peter Mosellanus, the prodigy in Greek who died in 1524 at the age of thirty-one; Johann Murmellius, the Westphalian schoolmaster who introduced Greek to the Münster schools; Philip Melanchthon, Reuchlin's young nephew destined to become known as *praeceptor Germaniae*. Each was a unique individual whose approach to the religious and intellectual issues of the day bore his own personal stamp.

Nonetheless, the criticisms of scholasticism offered by Bebel, Reuchlin, Pirckheimer, and Mutian are representative of

[88] *Ibid.*, 13.

the fundamental changes that took place in humanist polemics after 1500. Although Bebel did so only in a limited way, all four broke not only with contemporary scholasticism but also with their humanist predecessors. Stimulated by the speculations of the Florentine neo-Platonists and equipped with new skills in Greek and Hebrew, Mutian, Pirckheimer, and Reuchlin sought the wisdom of antiquity in the Jewish Cabala, the Greek Church fathers, and the non-Aristotelian heritage of ancient Greece. They also stressed the importance of utilizing original Greek and Hebrew texts or at least updated Latin translations. Most importantly, all four humanists shared a sense that the approach to theology then dominating the universities was deficient. Mutian criticized theologians for their ignorance of Plato, and Pirckheimer deplored their inability to convey the precepts of moral philosophy and Christian ethics. Reuchlin urged them to master Greek and Hebrew, while Bebel called on them to write in more elegant Latin. Taken together they envisioned the ideal theologian as a pious and learned individual not only versed in logic and Aristotelian metaphysics but also in Platonism, rhetoric, biblical studies, and the Greek and Hebrew languages.

Their rejection of scholasticism's traditions were, however, by no means total. Aristotle continued to be admired; the value of logic, if studied in moderation, was confirmed; and the theological *doctores* of the past still merited a certain restrained respect. But there is no mistaking the fact that given humanism's new orientation, the occasionally precarious coexistence with scholasticism before 1500 would now be more difficult to maintain.

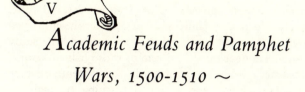

Academic Feuds and Pamphet Wars, 1500-1510 ~

ANYONE with even the faintest knowledge of the history of German humanism is acquainted with the famous Reuchlin affair, that war of words that convulsed much of learned Germany in the years before the Reformation. Indeed, the prominence of the Reuchlin affair is so great that it has tended to obscure two earlier controversies in which humanism was an issue. Between 1500 and 1504 a short but bitter pamphlet war erupted between two Leipzig academics, Conrad Wimpina and Martin Polich of Mellerstadt, on the relationship of poetry and theology. Between 1503 and 1510, Celtis's successor at Ingolstadt, Jacob Locher, became embroiled in a prolonged debate on the merits of scholastic theology. Although neither attained the continent-wide significance of the Reuchlin affair, each nevertheless provides important insights into the relationship of German humanism and scholasticism in the first decade of the sixteenth century.

CONRAD WIMPINA VS. MARTIN POLICH OF MELLERSTADT (1500-1504)

The first conflict began in 1500 with the publication in Leipzig of a work entitled, *Apology and Defense of Sacred Theology against those who have Strived to Establish that Poetry is its Well-*

173

Spring, Source and Patron.[1] The author of this formidable-sounding tome was Conrad Wimpina, a Leipzig academic just entering his fortieth year.[2] Born in Buchen, in the diocese of Würzburg, he had matriculated at Leipzig in 1479 and received his Bachelor of Arts and Master of Arts in 1481 and 1485, respectively. He then remained at Leipzig, where he embarked on a career that combined teaching of the arts and the study of theology. He developed into one of those half-humanist, half-scholastic hybrids, so common in late fifteenth-century Germany. His publications included teaching manuals on rhetoric, suggesting an interest in humanism, but also on logic, showing a continuing absorption with traditional subject matter. Having written a lengthy versified description of Leipzig and an "epic" that recounted deeds of the dukes of Saxony, he was also a published poet.[3] Thus, despite his thorough scholastic training, he seemed an unlikely author of a book which denounced the pretensions of poets.

In the introduction to his *Apology*, Wimpina offered an explanation, accepted by most scholars, of how the book came to be written. An unnamed poet in Leipzig had composed some verses that claimed that poetry was the *fons sacratae sophiae* or the "source of sacred wisdom." When denounced from the pulpit, he "slandered the preachers of God's word, both privately and publicly, with sneers and unseemly ref-

[1] *Apologeticus in Sacretheologie defensionem, Adversus eos qui nixi sunt eidem fontem Caput et patronam Poesim instituere: ac per hoc nec sacram theosim: jure religionis nostre monarchum et architectonicam habituum scientialium agnoscere revererique* (Leipzig: 1500).

[2] Gustav Bauch, *Geschichte des Leipziger Frühhumanismus* (Leipzig: 1899) 105-69, is the most thorough treatment of the controversy; see also, Theodor Grüneberg, "Martin Pollich von Mellerstadt, der erste Rektor der Universität Wittenberg," *450 Jahre Martin-Luther Universität* (Leipzig: 1956), 87-93; Joseph Negwer, *Konrad Wimpina* (Breslau: 1909), 47-69.

[3] *Precepta coaugmentande Rethorice oracionis comodissima* (Leipzig [?]: 1486); *Congestio Textus Nova Proprietatum logicalium cum commentatione non vulgari A. M. Conrado ex Buchen dicto Wimpina theologo* (Leipzig: 1498); *Alme universitatis Studii lipzensis et urbis liptzg descripcio* (Leipzig: 1488); *Bellorum illustriumque actorum Principis Alberti Ducis Saxonie Epithoma* (Leipzig: 1497); see Negwer, *Konrad Wimpina*, 200-37, for a complete list of Wimpina's publications.

erences" and "defiled the whole city with his abusive verse."[4]
Local clergymen demanded the refutation of his outrageous
ideas, and Wimpina took up the challenge. The result was his
Apology in Defense of Sacred Theology.

Wimpina stated at the outset that he did not intend to demean all poetry but only to assign it to its proper place among
the scholarly disciplines. Specifically, he sought to refute the
contention that poetry was the source of sacred wisdom and
therefore "higher" than theology. Such a contention could
only have been made by an "impertinent man who from
youth has studied myths and made verses but knows nothing
of philosophy and theology."[5] Wimpina drew his main arguments from passages in Aquinas and Aristotle on the hierarchy of the various disciplines. He pointed out that Aristotle, "easily the monarch of all things knowable," considered
poetry the lowest of all the arts because it had no set methodology. He also quoted the passage from Aquinas's *Summa
theologica* where the theologian had stated that "sacred doctrine
transcends all other disciplines, whether speculative or practical."[6] He also alluded to Aquinas's commentary on the *Posterior analytics*, where he accorded poetry a rank below logic
and rhetoric; in other words, poetry was not the peak of
theology, but the tail (*cauda*) of logic.

The Leipzig theologian also offered a number of arguments
from his own experience. He had studied poetical theory in
Horace and had read many poems, but in all his years he had
never learned even the most paltry scrap of theology from
poetry. What, he asked, do comic poets have to say about
"the notion of the trinity, of concepts, attributes, relations,
and special characteristics?" Who, among the dramatic, lyric,
and epic poets, has never treated questions such as "whether
pious deeds (*sacramentalia*), as distinct from individual sacraments, contain one essential grace?" Wimpina therefore rec-

---

[4] Quoted in Bauch, *Geschichte*, 105; his detailed summary provides the
basis for the following discussion.

[5] *Ibid.*, 106.

[6] Negwer, *Konrad Wimpina*, 51.

ommended that future theologians and philosophers avoid too much contact with poetry. Alluding to a comment of Aristotle in the *Metaphysics*, he warned that a preoccupation with fables, stories, and literary froth dulled the mind and weakened its ability to grasp the essence of reality. He conceded that some great Christian thinkers, most notably Augustine and Jerome, had been deeply versed in rhetoric and poetry; their excellence as theologians, however, stemmed from their training in philosophy, not literature. It was also true that biblical writers expressed themselves in verse; but poetry inspired only the form, not the content of their writing. The singing of hymns in praise of the saints showed that poetry had some usefulness for the Church. Nonetheless, this failed to prove that poetry was the source, head, and patroness of theology.

Finally, Wimpina advanced the argument that theology was superior to poetry, and to all other disciplines, because it was created first. Utilizing an argument hinted at in Augustine's *City of God*, he alleged that when on the first day of creation God had said "Let there be light," light symbolized "holy, speculative theology." Then, taking a chronological scheme from Eusebius, Wimpina placed Abraham before any poet, philosopher, or historian and placed Moses some three hundred fifty years before the Trojan War and even the deeds of Zeus! Thus the great antiquity of these two religious patriarchs showed the precedence of theology.

He reiterated in closing that he was not attacking all poetry but only its alleged superiority to theology. Theology held a fourfold preeminence over all other disciplines—primacy of duration, perfection, direction, and correction. It was the alpha and omega of all knowledge, the final goal and purpose of every intellectual endeavor.

Wimpina's book created something of a stir in Leipzig, where poetical and rhetorical studies had steadily grown in the 1480s and 1490s. Although few local humanists were prepared to defend the assertion that poetry was the source and wellspring of theology, some undoubtedly were offended by Wimpina's snipes at poetry. For despite his oft-repeated denial of any attempt to demean poetry, his arguments unquestionably reduced its importance. And the phrases he occasionally used to describe poetry—"a false frothing of words," "a vulgar and tawdry art," "shallow vanity"—were clearly offensive. Wimpina must have sensed that a rebuttal was in the offing and may very well have been uncomfortable about the prospect. His *Apology*, obviously written in haste, had been repetitive, disjointed, and notably lacking in logical rigor. Hence when he published in late 1500 his *Pallilogy for the Preeminence of Theology*, he repeated and clarified many of his arguments. He also depicted himself as theology's defender; anyone 'who attacked him was the enemy and despiser of theology and Christ himself.[7]

But Wimpina's warnings were too late. Just as the printing house of Landsberg was preparing his *Pallilogy*, another Leipzig firm, that of Johannes Thanner, was setting the type for the expected counterattack. The identity of the author is surprising. He was neither a poet nor rhetorician, but a physician trained in scholastic philosophy who had shown no real interest in humanism before 1500. His name was Martin Polich of Mellerstadt.[8] Polich, like Wimpina, had spent his academic life at Leipzig. Having received his Master of Arts in 1476, he taught in the arts faculty while studying medicine. As a professor, his specialties appear to have been logic and physics; he composed two handbooks on these subjects, both published after his death.[9] In the mid 1480s he became the personal physician and court astrologer for Frederick the Wise. From then on, he divided his time between lecturing at the university and attending the elector. He became acquainted

---

[7] The full title of the work was *Pallilogia de theologico fastigio. Ex nobilitate objecti eius Christi reparatoris et glorificatoris nostri sumpta* (Leipzig: 1500). The work is summarized in Bauch, *Geschichte*, 113, 114; Negwer, *Konrad Wimpina*, 54, 55.

[8] On Mellerstadt see the article by Grüneberg cited above; also U. Hirsch, "Martin Pollich von Mellrichstadt," *Allgemeine Deutsche Biographie*, 26 (Leipzig: 1888), 393-95.

[9] *Cursus Logici commentariorum . . .* (Leipzig: 1514); *M. Polichii . . . exquisita cursus physici collectanea* (Leipzig: 1514).

with Conrad Celtis when the poet taught at Leipzig in 1486. From his interests and inclinations, however, he was an unlikely candidate to defend poetry against the denigrations of Wimpina.

Polich's entry into the fray seems to have resulted from a bitter grudge he was harboring against Wimpina. Polich, clearly not a man of serene temperament nor one to flinch from an argument, had just wound up four years of acrimonious controversy with another Leipzig physician, Simon Pistoris, over the cause of syphilis. Polich, abandoning an earlier interest in astrology, sought to refute Pistoris's contention that the constellation of the heavens was causing the epidemic. The two men publicly debated the issues in 1496 and soon published works defending their views. In the next four years Polich published four treatises on the subject and Pistoris three. Typically, both men became more personal and vindictive as the dispute went on. For reasons that are unclear, Wimpina sided with Pistoris and even helped him polish the Latin of his last two polemics. Polich neither forgave nor forgot this treachery. Thus when Wimpina published his controversial *Apology*, it was an irascible physician, not a poet, who responded. Toward the end of 1500 Polich's *Brief and Hurried Statement in Defense of Poetry against a certain Theologian* appeared.[10]

Polich did not even attempt to defend the notion that poetry was the source and wellspring of theology. Instead, he claimed his intent was to define poetry as one of several sources of "sacred wisdom," a broader term, he felt, than "theology." In defending this proposition, the physician made several humanist-like arguments. In the introduction dedicated to the dukes of Saxony, for example, he expressed hope that his treatise would help preserve poetical studies at the University of Leipzig. He feared that if the "sickening and nonsensical" arguments of Wimpina went unanswered, poetry would be brushed aside, and students would be deprived of instruction

---

[10] *Laconismus tumultuarius Martini Mellerstad ad illustrissimos saxonie Principes in defensionem poetices contra quendam theologum editus* (Leipzig: 1500/01). The work is summarized in Bauch, *Geschichte*, 114-29.

in disciplines that all the Church fathers had enthusiastically approved. Polich also advanced "humanist" arguments when he attempted to refute Wimpina's assertion that the poets offered nothing that served religion. Claiming that this confirmed his opponent's ignorance, he noted the numerous poets who had written on religious subjects. Included were David, Lactantius, and Prudentius among the ancients, Baptista Mantuanus, Johannes von Dalberg, and Conrad Celtis among the moderns. Furthermore, even pagan poets were capable of teaching valuable lessons about virtue and right living. Virgil, in his character Aeneas, presented a man who was a model of bravery, dedication, and virtue. Horace, Persius, and Juvenal all warned against lust, pride, gluttony, and other diseases of the soul; Plautus and Terence revealed the faults and affectations of humans from infancy to old age.

Aside from the arguments, however, Polich, the physician well-trained in scholastic argumentation, showed through in most of the *Brief and Hurried Statement*. The treatise was largely a statement-by-statement examination of Wimpina's arguments in which the author pointed out definitional flaws and logical inconsistencies. He questioned Wimpina's use of Aristotle and Aquinas, extensively criticized his interpretation of the *Genesis* story and belittled his understanding of poetry and natural philosophy. The arguments Polich offered to defend the majesty of poetry would have struck most humanists as mere sophistry. He proposed, for example, that rational philosophy was the basis of theology, and since poetry was a part of rational philosophy, it was therefore a source of theology. He also argued that speculative theology was not always clear and accurate; therefore poetry's lack of a set methodology did not negate its value.

Wimpina answered Polich's book in 1502 with his *Response and Apology against the Brief and Hurried Statement of a certain Physician*.[11] It added nothing to the arguments already set forth

---

[11] *Responsio et Apologia Conradi Wimpine contra laconismum cuiusdam medici pro defensione Sacretheologie, et veritatis fidei* (Leipzig: 1502).

in the *Apology*. In the introduction Wimpina reiterated that his book was not against all poetry but only against the assertion that it was nobler than theology. He then proceeded to list all the errors he had found in Polich's book. At the top of the list was Polich's contention that "the source of sacred theology is the art of poetry invented by human beings." This was followed by ninety-one other errors of varying gravity. Among them were:

19. Our schools of theology are indistinguished in design.
23. Poetry confirms the articles of faith.
24. Poetry strengthens the articles of faith.
25. Articles of faith are not more worthy than poetry.
28. To believe is not more worthy than to pass judgement.
39. To clearly explain and proceed knowledgeably is not suitable to theology.
42. Not to believe with Augustine in the antiquity of theology and divine wisdom.
65. Natural knowledge of angels is not occasional (*successivam*).
66. To reckon it an error that the knowledge of the saints is discussive, against Scotus.[12]
85. Cimbrians were not Flemish, against Tartellius.[13]
86. Moses was not more ancient than the Egyptians.
92. To argue that the *Apology* called evangelical teaching obscurities.

The text was an explication of the most important of these errors. The major scholastics—Aquinas, Bonaventure, Scotus, Henry of Langenstein, and Capreolus—were marshaled

[12] 65. Angelorum noticiam naturalem non esse successivam, contra Egidium.
66. Errorum putare scientiam Beatorum esse discursive, contra Scotum. *Responsio* . . . , A vii.
[13] 85. Cimbos non esse Flamingos, contra Tartellium, *ibid.* The Cimbrians were an ancient German tribe; how this fit into the controversy is difficult to fathom.

to buttress Wimpina's arguments. The arguments themselves are basically those of the *Apology*. At the close he challenged Polich to debate the issue before the local bishop, the chancellor of the university, the Leipzig faculty, or even the inquisitor-general of Germany. He also offered a prayer to the Virgin, asking her to make Polich "see his errors and desist from them."

Before 1502 was over, Polich, now residing in Wittenberg, responded to Wimpina's *Response* with his *Against Wimpina's Insults and Denigrations of Sacred Theology*.[14] Once again old arguments were revived, new authorities were cited and the opponent's attacks parried. Substantial effort was lavished on such irrelevancies as the difference between *sacramenta* and *sacramentalia* and the question of whether Adam and Eve had indulged in sex before the fall. The book's main claim to originality rested in the imaginative names bestowed on the physician's opponent. Among them were "that lowest and paltriest of all men"; "that fox and barking hound"; "most beggarly ape"; "superstitious hypocrite"; "corpse-bearer"; and "two-legged donkey." Then in early 1503 Polich offered yet another brief pamphlet. *A Golden Proposition for Men studious of Philosophy and Theology*.[15] After an introductory poem informed the reader that his opponent's books were worthy of being burnt to ashes or plunged into a sewer, Polich's treatise offered a detailed discussion of Wimpina's interpretation of the Genesis creation story and comments on Wimpina's list of errors.

The last words in the dispute were Wimpina's. In the middle of 1503 he published an oration he had delivered in January 1503 in connection with his promotion to the doctorate. Entitled *On the Excellence of Theology*, he distilled the familiar arguments on theology's primacy among the disciplines.[16] A

---

[14] *In Wimpinianas offensiones et denigrationes Sacretheologie* (Wittenberg: 1502).

[15] *Theoremata aurea pro studiosis philosophie et theologie* (Wittenberg: 1503).

[16] *Oratio in commendationem Sacretheologie habito ab Egregio Sacretheologie professore Magistro Conrado Wimpine de Fagis In Aula sua doctorali* (Leipzig: 1503).

short time later appeared his *Response and Apology against Mel-lerstadt's Insults and Denigrations of Sacred Theology.*[17] With this effort, both combatants realized they had nothing more to say. Mercifully, the controversy between Conrad Wimpina and Martin Polich over the relationship of poetry and theology came to an end.

What seems at first glance to have been the first pamphlet war between the principles of humanism and scholasticism was nothing of the sort. Essential humanist convictions such as the value of classical literature and the usefulness of rhetorical and poetical studies were peripheral issues in the feud. On the other hand, the notion that poetry was the wellspring of theology was a doctrine that few humanists cared to defend. The "defender of humanism" was a physician who wrote treatises on logic and physics and whose methods of argumentation reflected his thorough scholastic training. The "detractor of humanism" was a theologian who had written two works of poetry and a treatise on rhetoric. Personal animosity and the apparent inability to drop an argument seem to provide the most plausible explanations for the duration of the conflict. Did the contemporaries of Polich and Wimpina see it any differently?

The intellectual world outside of Saxony was largely indifferent to the affair. None of the leading humanists came to Polich's defense; none of them seems even to have mentioned the feud in their letters or writings. The only person outside of Saxony who commented on the conflict was Bohuslaus of Hassenstein, a Bohemian humanist who had been a friend of both adversaries while studying and teaching at Leipzig in the 1480s. He also concluded that personal rivalries precipitated the affair. In a letter to Wimpina in 1502, he did not question the theologian's judgment in attacking good learning or poetry. Instead he expressed sorrow that the two "brightest lights in Leipzig" were now bitter enemies because

---

[17] *Responsio et Apologia . . . ad Mellerstatinas offensiones et denigrationes Sacretheologie* (Leipzig: 1503).

of their short tempers. He asked, "What will be the talk of people in the future if Conrad and Martin, who to this point have been models of virtue and modesty, now loose the reins of their passions, and in the way of those driven like the wind by their emotions, struggle fiercely between themselves."[18] He urged them to end their search for glory and renew their friendship.

Within the narrower arena of Leipzig, Polich and Wimpina each had supporters. After the publication of Wimpina's *Response* in 1502, an otherwise unknown friend of his, Johannes Seicius, wrote a short pamphlet that praised the learning and arguments of the Leipzig theologian.[19] The book was a superficial summary of Wimpina's previous arguments. At the end he called on all theologians, bishops, and monks of Germany, France, England, Italy, and Spain to denounce Polich's impieties. On behalf of Polich, Sigismund Fagilucus, the poet whose statements about theology and aspersions on monks apparently had sparked the controversy, contributed three poems that were published with Polich's *Brief and Hurried Statement*. One depicted Polich as fighting on behalf of the muses, another praised poetry in general terms, while a third celebrated Polich's "victory" over his opponent. He also composed several epigrams against Wimpina which questioned his learning and called him a "huge, boorish dog, an infernal worm, a delirious wasp, and a dung-eating pig.[20]

Another humanist who took a hand in the dispute was Hermann Buschius, the much-traveled poet who was teaching at Leipzig when the controversy began. After the publication of Polich's *Brief and Hurried Statement*, he composed a pamphlet entitled "To Martin of Mellerstadt, a Man of Remarkable and Rare Erudition and most Inclined to all Good Let-

[18] Josef Truhlar, ed., *Listár Bohuslava Hasisteinskéko z Lobkovic* (Prague: 1893), 43.

[19] *Ad Prestantem et magne eruditionis virum Magistrum Conradum Wimpine pro defensione sacre theologie et theologice veritatis* (no place or date); undoubtedly the book was published in Leipzig in 1502.

[20] Bauch, *Geschichte*, 131.

ters."[21] Buschius described how Polich's book had reached him at carnival time, and that he had found it so pleasurable that he had given up celebrating to read and study it. For Buschius, renowned for his love of "celebrating," this was high praise indeed. He went on to laud Polich's Latin, acclaim his defense of poetry, heap scorn on Wimpina's style, and in general to attack the theologian's barbarism. He added nothing to the scholarly aspect of the debate.

Buschius's ardent defense on Polich does suggest, however, that the relative merits of humanism and scholasticism were involved in the controversy. But by 1503 the humanist had completely reversed himself and was supporting Wimpina! When in that year Wimpina published his *Oration on the Excellence of Theology*, it included no less than five laudatory poems by Buschius. He praised Wimpina's erudition and "cursed his hand" for having attacked the theologian. Buschius's about-face is a clear case of the triumph of self-interest over principle. When he wrote his first pro-Polich pamphlet, the object of his praise had just left Leipzig for Wittenberg where he was directing the establishment of the university soon to open under the auspices of Frederick the Wise. Buschius coveted a position at the new institution, and this ambition undoubtedly contributed to his decision to side with Polich. Subsequently, Buschius did become the first salaried humanist at Wittenberg and delivered a festive oration at the university's opening ceremonies. But within months he left Wittenberg and returned to Leipzig, where he remained until 1508. His willingness to contribute laudatory poems to a work by Wimpina seems a transparent effort on his part to ingratiate himself with an important individual at the institution he had recently abandoned.

It is difficult, therefore, to view seriously the conflict between Polich and Wimpina as a major or even minor example of humanist-scholastic confrontation. One humanist, Bohuslaus of Hassenstein, clearly viewed it as a result of personal

---

[21] *Prestabili et rare eruditiones viro Martino Mellerstat alias Policho ducaliphisico et litteratorum omnium favissori* (Leipzig: 1502).

spite. Buschius saw so little substance in the issues that he freely changed sides when it suited him. It is safe to say that if Wimpina had never lifted his pen to correct the Latin prose of Samuel Pistoris, he and the world would have been spared his protracted conflict with Martin Polich of Mellerstadt.

Jacob Locher Philomusus vs. George Zingel, Jacob Wimpfeling, Ulrich Zasius and Others (1503-1510)

The second "humanist-scholastic" controversy of the early sixteenth century began in 1503 when the salaried lecturer at the University of Ingolstadt, Jacob Locher Philomusus, abruptly resigned from the post he had held since 1497.[22] He immediately assumed a new position at Freiburg-im-Breisgau, where on arrival he hastily composed an outrageous personal attack on the venerable Ingolstadt theologian, George Zingel. In so doing he set off a controversy that swirled back and forth between Freiburg and Ingolstadt for eight years. Before it ended in 1510, it had involved several prestigious humanists, numerous academics of all stripes, and even the dukes of Bavaria. It included battles waged in print, from the podium, and occasionally with fists. Allegedly, even hired assassins became involved. It produced the era's only published defense of scholastic theology, which as it turned out, was written by a leading humanist. It was both a monument to human folly and an important indicator of the tensions generated by the new tendencies and personalities in German humanism after 1500.

When he resigned his post at Ingolstadt, Locher was in his early thirties and had already made a mark for himself as one

---

[22] There is no single account of this controversy; see however, Dr. J. Hehle, *Der Schwäbische Humanist Jakob Locher Philomusus* (Ehingen: 1875), originally printed in *Programm des Königlichen Gymnasiums in Ehingen*, 1871-1872; 1873-1874; 1874-1875; Joseph Schlecht, "Zu Jakob Wimpfelings Fehden mit Jakob Locher und Paul Lang," *Festgabe Karl Theodor von Hiegel* (Munich: 1903), 214-46.

of Germany's most energetic and productive humanists. Even before coming to Ingolstadt, he was a widely published author whose works included manuals for teaching grammar and rhetoric, an oration in honor of Emperor Maximilian, and the *Theologica emphasis*, which sought to show the superiority of the Church fathers over the theologians of his own day. His fame spread across the continent when his Latin translation of Sebastian Brant's *Narrenschiff* was published in 1497. In that same year he also became the second German humanist after Conrad Celtis to receive the poet's laurel crown from Emperor Maximilian.

At Ingolstadt his career continued to move rapidly forward. In 1498 he published a handsome edition of the *Odes* of Horace, replete with illustrations and commentary.[23] This was followed in 1500 by his *Extemporaneous Oration concerning the* Studia Humanitatis *and in Praise of the Poets*,[24] in which Apollo awakes him and leads him to the Elysian fields, where he meets the great poets of antiquity. His interest in religion, already evident in his *Theologica emphasis*, also continued. In 1500 he edited a translation, previously published in Italy, of the poetical works of Phocylidis, the Greek Christian poet of the sixth century.[25] And in 1501, he published a collection of poetry and other "elegant phrases" from the Psalms and a few other books of the Old Testament. In the introductory letter to Conrad Wiblingen, a local Benedictine abbot, he referred to himself as *sacrae theologiae cultor* and castigated modern theologians for ignoring the Old Testament and frittering away their lives on "obscure, garrulous and moldy matters of slight utility to the Church."[26] In Locher's eyes, however,

---

[23] *Horatii Flacci Venusini poete lirici opera cum quibusdam annotationibus imaginibusque pulcherrimis aptisque ad Odarum concentus et sententius* (Strassburg: 1498).

[24] *Oratio de studio humanorum disciplinarum et laude poetarum Extemporalis* (Freiburg-im-Breisgau: 1500). He had delivered and published the same speech at Freiburg in 1496.

[25] *Poema Nutheticon phocylidis greci poete christianissima a Jacobo Locher Philomuso ad Latinos Elegos traductum* (Freiburg-im-Breisgau: 1500).

[26] *Tetrastichon ad Lectorem . . . Magni Athanasii . . . in psalmorum effectus . . . sequestratio* (no place: 1500), A ii.

the capstone of his career came in 1502, when two of his plays were performed at Ingolstadt before crowds of luminaries including, in one case, no less a person than Duke George of Bavaria. The first play, presented on February 13 with a cast of eleven students, was entitled, "An Elegant Drama in the Tragic Manner, concerning the Christian Kings and Princes who took up Arms against the Insults of the Turks and Settled their Feuds." This was followed in the summer of 1502 by the performance of "The Judgment of Paris concerning the Golden Apple, depicting three Goddesses and the threefold Life of Man." In it three goddesses—Juno, Pallas, and Venus—present arguments in favor of the active, contemplative, and "voluptuous" life. Although Paris ultimately rejects the voluptuous life, Venus, it must be said, stated her case bluntly and eloquently. Before the year was over, both plays were published, along with dedicatory letters to Duke George.[27]

What did the *magistri* and *doctores* of Ingolstadt think of this energetic young poet who had burst into their world? Did they object to his salary of forty guldens, higher than any received by a professor of the arts?[28] Did they find it deplorable that a mere poet without even a bachelor's degree chided the theologians, published religious books, and adopted the title *sacrae theologiae cultor*? Did they raise their eyebrows about his passion for pagan poets and his histrionic lectures, which began by sounding a loud bell? Although it would be surprising if his welcome was universally cordial, neither Locher's writings nor university records hint of opposition until 1502. In that year the dedicatory letter to Duke George that accompanied the publication of his plays referred to the "infernal madness" of certain unnamed critics who had attempted to stifle his plays and "destroy his happiness." He thanked the prince for closing his ears to their "babbling words" and

---

[27] *Spectaculum more tragico concinnatum de regibus et principibus christianis, qui contra Thurcorum insultus arma parant foedusque constituunt* (Ingolstadt?: 1502); *Judicum Paridis de pomo aureo, de tribus deabus et triplici hominum vita* (Ingolstadt?: 1502).

[28] Gustav Bauch, *Die Anfänge des Humanismus in Ingolstadt* (Munich: 1901), 71.

assured him that "God the avenger of evil would punish them in Hell."[29]

Then in 1503 Locher resigned. From his ensuing behavior, it is safe to conclude that the poet considered his departure a humiliation. But university records contain only two terse references to the event: first, an official resignation in which Locher renounced all claims to his salary; and second, a note signed by Locher that confirmed his debt to the university treasury of fifteen Rhenish guldens.[30] By mid-year Locher had moved to Freiburg, where he had studied and taught before going to Ingolstadt. He signed a three-year agreement to teach poetry and rhetoric at an annual salary of fifty-two guldens. Meanwhile at Ingolstadt the salaried lectureship was filled by Sebastian Sprenz, a friend of Celtis and an Ingolstadt Master of Arts, who had been director of the St. Lorenz School in Nuremberg since 1499.[31]

It was at Freiburg that Locher composed the work entitled *The Apology of Jacob Locher Philomusus against the most Passionate Enemy of the Poets, George Zingel, Theologian*.[32] Who was this "passionate enemy"? Zingel was a seventy-five-year-old gentleman who had left Vienna in 1475 to teach theology at the newly opened University of Ingolstadt. There he remained until his death in 1508. Although he never published anything, he was nonetheless a respected figure within the university. Four times elected rector, he was dean of the theology faculty thirty-one out of his thirty-three years at the Bavarian institution. It is puzzling why Zingel provoked Locher's wrath, for the theologian seems to have had some sympathy for humanism. His relationship with Celtis, for example, was apparently friendly. Celtis even wrote a flattering ode in praise of Zingel in which the virtue and erudition of the theologian were extolled.[33] And after the poet departed for Vienna, Zin-

---

[29] *Judicum Paridis* . . . , 90.

[30] Hehle, *Der Schwäbische Humanist*, II, 8.

[31] Bauch, *Die Anfänge*, 72, 73.

[32] *Apologia Jacobi Locher Philomusi contra poetarum acerrimum Hostem Georgium Zingel Theologum Ingolstadiensem* (Strassburg: 1504).

[33] Ad Georgium Cygnum theologum se contra jurisperitos ob artes li-

gel wrote a letter to Celtis which, while wishing him good fortune, also reminded "his special friend" about the unpaid balance on a loan the theologian had extended.[34] Another sign of Zingel's sympathy for humanism came in 1507, when he was among the Ingolstadt reformers who recommended the adoption of Nicholas Perotti's text for grammar instruction.[35]

There is also evidence that at first Locher and Zingel were on good terms, for like Celtis, Locher successfully borrowed money from the aged theologian.[36] But things had deteriorated by 1503. Unquestionably, Locher's remarkable eight-page pamphlet is the most scurrilous in all of German humanist writing. The list of imaginative and descriptive names applied to Zingel was almost endless; Zingel was called an "old dog," "a raving Occamist," "an invidious horned snake," "hissing viper," "the son of the devil" and much else. Locher promised that Zingel would be punished by a thousand devils for "vomiting lies against the innocent and saintly." He contended that Zingel was endangering the entire University of Ingolstadt. The theologian, so he claimed, had slandered the faculty and had made the professors laughable in the eyes of students; he had called "the poets foolish, the philosophers sorcerers, the jurists trouble-makers and 'law merchants' and the physicians murderers."[37] Not surprisingly, in Locher's mind, Zingel's most heinous acts had been his attacks on the poets, i.e., Jacob Locher. He had, claimed Locher, opposed innovations in grammar instruction and persisted in the belief that Latin was best learned through "posterior and prior analytics, the suppositions of Marsilius, and through contraposition."[38] Furthermore, Zingel's deceit and trickery had driven him from Ingolstadt. He had interfered with his courses,

---

berales non discendas opponentem," in Celtis, *Libri Odarum Quattuor*, ed. Pindter, 53, 54.

[34] Celtis, *Briefwechsel*, 292.

[35] Prantl, *Geschichte der Ludwig-Maximilians-Universität*, I, 104-106; Bauch, *Die Anfänge*, 89.

[36] Bauch, *Die Anfänge*, 72.

[37] *Apologia*, A ii.

[38] *Ibid.*, A ii c; "Marsilius" was undoubtedly Marsilius of Inghen, the noted nominalist who was first rector of the University of Heidelberg.

incited the university council against him, demeaned his learning before Duke George, and accused him of corrupting morals and causing disturbances. Worst of all, Zingel had hired sixty-six men to murder him! Locher did not relate how he managed to fend off this small army. Perhaps he had beguiled them with a poem.

The *Apology* also hints that Zingel's disregard for Locher's two dramatic performances brought matters to a head. Locher argued that Zingel's attacks were completely unjustified. "What improper," he asked, "what illicit, finally what of unfitting or improper appearance was shown, what did we tell of the Anti-Christ?" Everyone else who had seen the performances applauded and approved.[39]

Zingel, preserving his record of non-publication, did not personally respond to Locher's pamphlet. Instead he did two things. First, against an unpaid two-gulden debt of Locher's, he entered a suit for the confiscation of some of the poet's property left in Ingolstadt with the poet's jurist friend, Hieronymus von Croaria.[40] Second, he petitioned the university council to publish a rebuttal to Locher's pamphlet. His lawsuit came to nothing, but his request came before the faculty senate in late 1504. There it sparked some disagreement. The faculties of law and medicine recommended that the university take no action. The jurists pointed out that since Locher had composed his treatise at Freiburg, *that* institution should take any disciplinary steps. But finally, on the recommendation of the faculties of arts and theology, the rector decided that the university should publish an official defense of Zingel that would clear him of Locher's accusations. The jurists opposed the decision, but it was not reversed.[41]

The university's defense of Zingel appeared in early 1505 with the imposing title, *Vindication of the Venerable and Famous University of Ingolstadt on behalf of George Zingel against the Invective unjustly and impiously Composed by Jacob Locher under*

[39] *Ibid.*, A iii.
[40] Bauch, *Die Anfänge*, 72.
[41] Hehle, *Der Schwäbische Humanist*, II, 11.

cover of an Apology.[42] No author was named, but internal evidence such as the recurring use of the phrase *nos theologi* suggests it was the work of younger members of the theology faculty. Compared to Locher's outburst, the *Vindication* was a mild composition with little mud-slinging. The author or authors did call Locher a liar and criticized his outrageous language. It was noted that such language was especially unseemly "for a person who called himself a theologian." In contrast, Zingel's life was praised for its probity, moderation, and dedication to the university.

Most of the eight-page pamphlet was given over to refuting Locher's various accusations. Zingel was a friend of good learning who had slandered no one. Certainly he had not hired sixty-six armed men to dispatch Locher; as a man of intelligence he would have realized that only two or three men would have been more effective. The only anti-humanist remarks consisted of well-worn attacks on pagan poetry. Christian poets such as Prudentius and Baptista Mantuanus were sufficient models for eloquence, so there was no need to study Greek and Roman poets; also offered was the oft-heard argument that Plato in the *Republic* called for the expulsion of poets from the city.

By the fall of 1505 Locher replied to the university's defense of Zingel with his *Compendious Response in Rebuttal to the Rector and Senate of the Ingolstadt School.*[43] Locher claimed at the beginning that he had considered making no response, since his reputation among scholars was already secure and because his "windbag opponents" had offered up mere chaff. He also stated that Zingel's jealousy was understandable, since the theologian had never won fame and recognition, whereas "Philomusus, renowned throughout the world for his sound

---

[42] *Expurgatio rectoris et consilii almi ac celebris gymnasii Ingolstadiensis pro Domino Georgio Zingel sacrae theologiae magistro ordinareo et vicecancellorico in eodem Gymnasio . . . contra invectivam sub velamine apologiae a Jacob Locher Ph-O* (no place or date). Copy in Bavarian State Library, Munich.

[43] *Jacobi Locher Ph-i in anticategoriam rectoris cuiusdam et conciliabuli Gymnasii Ingolstadiensis responsio compendiosa cum declaratione Zingelensis factionis* (no place or date); probably published in September or October, perhaps at Basel.

character, does not blush to have received the poet's crown from lord Maximilian." Nonetheless, since his opponents' pamphlet was "deceitful, bombastic, putrid, meager, filthy, rotten, and shitty" (*dolosa, bullata, subrancida, strigosa, lutulenta, putida, merdosa*), it deserved a reply. As this string of adjectives shows, Locher exceeded the high rhetorical standards achieved in his earlier attack on Zingel. This time Ingolstadt's university council became an added target. Its members were labeled, among other things, as "three-headed dogs," "vipers," "an obscene and envious faction of babblers," and "a diabolical conspiracy." In fact, the main point of Locher's work was that the Ingolstadt faculty had by no means been united in its decision to publish the *Vindication*. He pointed out, with apparent accuracy, that the faculties of law and medicine had opposed the step; he also asserted that even a majority of the arts masters spoke on his behalf. Thus he concluded that the "*Vindication* was not conceived out of an agreement of the university but by two or perhaps three who belched forth poison against me and good letters."[44]

Until this point Locher's dispute with Zingel had followed a course one might expect in a conflict between humanism and scholasticism. Obviously the feud had been sparked by more than a simple disagreement about the merits of humanism, but at least a poet and a scholastic theologian were the main antagonists. In 1505, however, the lines blurred considerably. In that year the conflict spread to the University of Freiburg, where Locher acquired two new enemies. And they were not "raving Occamists" like Zingel, but two well-known Rhineland humanists—Ulrich Zasius, the learned jurist, and Jacob Wimpfeling. Zasius of course was still a professor on the Freiburg law faculty; Wimpfeling, having recently failed to receive a hoped-for benefice in Basel, was also in Freiburg, where he was tutoring local children in Latin. At one time all three men had been on good terms. Locher had even written poems and letters which Wimpfeling had published in several

[44] Hehle, *Der Schwäbische Humanist*, II, 12.

of his works, among them *Integrity, Adolescence,* and *Apology for the Christian Commonwealth*[45] Locher, in turn, had chosen Zasius to play the role of his conversant in the dialogue section of the *Theologica emphasis.*

But in 1505 all signs of friendship evaporated. The reasons for the rupture can be found in a brief satire composed and circulated that year by Wimpfeling among friends at the university. It purported to be a transcript of statements made by Locher to Wimpfeling during confession.[46] In the course of the "confession," Locher naturally admits to a host of outrageous sins. He repeatedly asks forgiveness for having "dismembered and denigrated" the fame of George Zingel in a crude and impious way. He admits to having stained the reputation of an honorable man and having unjustly demeaned his learning.

It is clear from this "confession" that, to Wimpfeling, two other qualities made Locher obnoxious. First there was his unbridled love of pagan poetry. Locher asked forgiveness, for example, for his lavish praise of Ovid: "I have proclaimed and written that the filthiest and most impure poet, Ovid, was very temperate, unblemished, chaste, and of virtuous mind." Furthermore he had slandered "angelic Politian" and "holy Petrarch," who both agreed that Ovid had been "dangerous, licentious, and lecherous." Locher also "confessed" to claiming that the writings of Juvenal were just as "credible" as those of Paul and the rest of Scriptures.

According to Locher's fictional confession, his second major "sin" was pride, vanity, and a "libertarian" personality. Locher confessed he had demanded a place in university processions in front of the dean of the arts faculty and the licentiates of the other three faculties. Such behavior, he admitted, was particularly unsuitable since "I am no true scholar

---

[45] Charles Schmidt, *Histoire littéraire de l'Alsace,* 2 vols. (Paris: 1879), I, 58, 59.

[46] "Jacobus Wimphelingus Selestatinus Jacobo Philomuso poete laureato presens Confessionale dicat," in Joseph Schlecht, "Zu Jakob Wimpfelings Fehden," 239–42.

but only a poet laureate, having no degree except in poetry, i.e., in the art of metrification, in telling stories of the gentiles and expouding certain poets—things teachers in local schools do every day." Furthermore, he was a poor teacher: he had "babbled away" on the writings of Ovid for six months without finishing. Worst of all, admitted Locher, "I have through filthy words scandalized young boys by speaking of the venereal act; through this I have incited and inflamed them to lust in saying, while naming that act like a peasant, that they couldn't toil and sweat in their loins even though chastity was impossible."

Wimpfeling left Freiburg late in the summer, but Zasius and his followers continued to harass Locher. Zasius, for example, began to lecture on Plautus at the same hour Locher was lecturing on Ovid and Virgil.[47] A bitter feud ensued in which the two men traded insults in lectures and slandered each other in poems circulated within the university community.[48] On September 30, 1505, the university council ordered both men to end their verbal brawling. But Locher refused to settle down. He allegedly urged his students to attack supporters of Zasius, and he continued to lecture on Sundays and holy days even after the rector had ordered him to desist.[49] When Wimpfeling was informed of Locher's behavior and received word of several scornful verses the poet had written against him, he again took a hand in the affair. In December 1505 he wrote to the university council to complain of Locher's continued outrages. He threatened that unless Locher was silenced, he would publish one of Locher's letters "in which he disgracefully described Bavarian women, and more disgracefully the society and pleasure he boasted to have had with them." Finally, he would tell how, most disgracefully of all, he had "provoked, incited, and inflamed five

---

[47] Schmidt, *Histoire littéraire de l'Alsace*, I, 61.

[48] Several of these poems have been published in *ibid.*, I, 60.

[49] "30. Sept. 1505. Fuit mandata pax poetae Philomuso et Zasio, in forma communi ut moris est." Heinrich Schreiber, *Geschichte der Albert-Ludwigs-Universität zu Freiburg-im-Breisgau* (Freiburg: 1868) I, 77.

youths to sexual longing and dissipation with words more salacious than Martial and Catullus had ever used."[50]

Locher's days at Freiburg were obviously numbered. On March 30, 1506, the university council announced that Locher's salary would be suspended on April 23. Until that time, he was ordered to stop lecturing and "live in peace."[51] Then, in what surely is the most perplexing event in the whole controversy, the University of Ingolstadt rehired Locher as its salaried poet! Only a year and a half earlier, this same university in the name of her "rector and council" had published a stinging rebuke of Locher; Zingel, though one year before his death and seventy-eight years old, was still active in university affairs.

Locher, however, still had powerful friends in the Bavarian government. When he realized that his welcome at Freiburg had worn thin, or more accurately had disappeared altogether, he apparently contacted well-placed supporters in the ducal government and university about the possibility of returning to the scene of his earlier endeavors. His efforts were successful, for on March 16, 1506, the university received an order from Duke Albert announcing that "he had arranged and disposed that Jacob Locher should be admitted to the lectureship in poetry and that he should be paid per year as much as Celtis had received, namely eighty Rhenish guldens."[52] For several reasons—Locher himself, his generous salary, and the fact the lectureship was already filled by Sebastian Sprenz—the princely mandate sparked several months of debate and negotiations. On May 12, however, the council accepted Locher, agreed to pay him eighty guldens, and even voted him a stipend of four guldens for his trip from Freiburg to Ingolstadt. Later in the summer, the unfortunate Sprenz,

---

[50] Letter printed in Josef Riegger, *Amoenitates Literareae Friburgenses* (Ulm: 1774), II, 170.

[51] Schreiber, *Geschichte*, I, 81.

[52] Bauch, *Die Anfänge*, 74, 75, is the source for this quote and for what follows.

now referred to as *olim poeta in nostra universitate*, was voted a sum of five guldens to dull the pain of his forced departure.[53]

Even after this triumphal return to Ingolstadt, Locher refused to end his feud with Zingel. In late 1506, he published another bitter slander against Zingel and scholastic theology in general. It was entitled *Invidious Comparison of the Sterile Mule to the Muse, the aforementioned dewy with Elegance*.[54] The book began with a familiar ring. In the introductory poems and dedicatory letter Locher repeated the now familiar slanders against the "loquacious old theologian, ignorant of the Christian faith and Catholic doctrine, who had babbled that the sacred poets are mules."[55] The "old theologian" is not identified, suggesting perhaps that Locher intentionally sought to raise a question in the reader's mind whether Zingel (seventy-eight years old) or Wimpfeling (fifty-six years old) was the intended target. We are informed, however, that the mouth of the person in question was "stuffed with stinking dung and fetid muck." We are also told that the person had "numerous followers and disciples who know nothing beyond the rude little verses of Alexander Gallus, the modes of signifying and worthless offensive grammar rules."[56]

Soon the work became less an *ad hominem* attack than a general criticism of scholastic theology. A unique feature of the work was the utilization of several anonymous woodcuts to illustrate the themes of the text.[57] The first two (see Plates I and II) show the comparison made throughout the book between the "sterile mule theologian" and the eloquent and productive muses. In the first, the artist has shown the muses

---

[53] As things turned out, Locher's unexpected return to Ingolstadt may have been a blessing in disguise for Sprenz. He went on to study canon law, served in a variety of government positions and became bishop of Brixen in 1521. Bauch, *Die Anfänge*, 76.

[54] *Vitiosa sterilis Mulae ad Musam roscida lepiditate praedictam Comparatio* (Nuremberg: 1506).

[55] *Ibid.*, A iv a.

[56] *Ibid.*, A iv b.

[57] Woodcuts in Locher's work have been attributed to Wolf Traut (d. 1520); see Campbell Dodgson, *British Museum Department of Prints and Drawings. Catalogue of Early German and Flemish Woodcuts*, I (London: 1903), 505.

I "Poet and the Nine Muses," from Locher, *Mulae ad Musam Comparatio*

attentively sitting around Apollo in a scene of pastoral seren-
ity; on the next, a dour scholastic theologian is following a
seedy mule named "master." A "squawking magpie" perches
on the mule, and the theologian follows behind, holding a
basket the mule is filling with excrement. In an obvious reference to the contents of the basket, the theologian states "I
have ravenously devoured the turds" (*Ich hab die Feigen fres-
sen*). The title of the woodcut reads, "The number of dullards

Tardorum infinitus eft numerus.

Ich hab die fey gen Ereffen

Pica loquax

herre

II "Mule Theologian," from Locher, *Mulae ad Musam Comparatio*

is infinite." Later, a larger woodcut (see Plate III) depicted "queen theology riding in a triumphal chariot." She wears a crown, it is explained, which symbolizes the seven liberal arts. Moses drives the wagon, which is drawn by five horses symbolizing the biblical books he wrote. Three Old Testament poets, David, Solomon, and Jeremiah, sit alongside her. The prophets, the four evangelists, Gregory, Jerome, Augustine, Ambrose, and figures symbolizing the books of the Bible surround the central figures. In contrast, another woodcut (see Plate IV) shows five theologians, Sophisaster, Mostophagus, Misophoebus, Microsius, and Logicorax, who are in a field flailing away at several bundles of straw. In the accompanying dialogue the reader learns that these are theologians who know nothing of the Bible, cite Paul only over their

III "Queen Theology's Triumph," from Locher, *Mulae ad Musam Comparatio*

wine cups, scorn the Church fathers, rely on confused and worthless sources, and make more difficulties than they solve.[58]

In the text itself, Locher used several literary devices to express his ideas. Among the poems in the work, one exhorted the poets of all of Europe to combine against the "mule theologian," while another exempted all "sound theologians" from his attacks.[59] At the end of the work he printed the four poems in praise of Jerome, Augustine, Gregory, and Ambrose already published in his *Theologica emphasis*.

The most imaginative section of the work, and the one that contained the most direct attacks on scholasticism, was the "Mutual Exhortation of Calliope and Apollo," in which the deities discuss in verse the attack on poetry made by that ever-

[58] *Vitiosa sterilis.*, A iii.
[59] "Philomusi Clamor ad poetas ubique gentium degentes de Mulotheologo"; "Excusatio Philomusi apud sinceros theologos," *ibid.*, A iv, A iv b.

IV "Five Theologians," from Locher, *Mulae ad Musam Comparatio*

present "slanderous" and "stinking" old man. Apollo began
by singing the praise of the great poets of antiquity: Homer,
Orpheus, Hesiod, Democritus, Virgil, Lucan, Statius, Horace, Ovid, Plautus, and Terence. All were in a sense theologians, since they "taught the rewards of virtue and the penalties of vice." He added that no Christian could deny this,
except certain theologians whose only interests were "minute
trifles, foolish words, and logical traps," and who debated
such inanities as "whether the first Adam defecated in the
Garden of Eden." He also argued that no theologian could
be truly learned without a knowledge of poetry and added

that the usual authorities—Occam, Buridan, Scotus, Marsilius, Holcot, Bricot, and others—only taught the theologian how to "dispute in words" and "ply their logical nets."[60] In the concluding section of his poetical oration, Apollo compared the benefits offered on the one hand by the muses and on the other by "mule theology." From the latter, nothing is gained but "stinking filth, from which a crude and garrulous theologian is born, who swells with spite, who always spreads strife, and who is ruined by dark furies."[61] In comparison the muses "gain powerful kings for peace, instruct magistrates in justice, cause pleasant speech," and have produced inspiring religious leaders such as David, Solomon, the holy prophets, Saint Bernard, and Jean Gerson, a "worthy but abandoned theologian."

With this final burst of wrath against the "mule theologians," Locher brought his role in the feud to an end. Soon Zingel did the same. He drew up a list of twenty-five articles from Locher's works that were heretical or "highly suspect." He may have considered sending the list to Rome, but apparently never did.[62] Both men were consulted in connection with the wide-ranging statute review and reform conducted by the Bavarian government in 1507. Zingel spoke in favor of requiring the Latin grammar of the Italian humanist, Perotti, and either the *Bucolics* or *Georgics* of Virgil.[63] When the government issued its *Nova Ordinatio*, Locher, as salaried poet, was granted a permanent seat on the university council. In

[60] Non est theologus perfectus semine phoebi
    Castalio pariter qui ne furore caret
  Non est theologus si quem Buridanus & Ockan
    Aut scotinus tantum digladiano parit.
  Marsilius, Maufelt, Burleus, Brulifer, Holkot
    Atque Bricot logices retia sola ligant.

Ibid., B ii a.

[61] Mula aliquid gignit. quid? stercora foeda, quid inde?
    Theologus crudus nescitur atque loquax.
  Qui livore tumet, qui toto tempore lites
    Seminat & furiis precipitatur atris.

Ibid., B iii.

[62] Schlecht, "Zu Wimpfelings Fehden," 243, 244.
[63] Bauch, *Die Anfänge*, 89.

April 1508 George Zingel died at the age of eighty. Three months later Locher was sent to the University of Tübingen on an unsuccessful mission to recruit a successor.[64]

But the feud Locher had called into being refused to die. That formidable controversialist, Wimpfeling, continued to snipe at him in works published in 1507 and 1509.[65] Then in 1510 Wimpfeling published the era's sole *apologia* for scholastic theological methods: *Against the Foul Pamphlet of Philomusus. A Defense of Scholastic Theology and the Moderns.*[66] The frontispiece (see Plate V) showed Christ entering Jerusalem on a mule, an obvious response to Locher's "mule theme."

Wimpfeling's work was in part designed to further discredit Locher. In Chapter Two, "That the Sterile Opinions of Histrionic Poets are not to be greatly Valued," he expressed approval of Virgil, Baptista Mantuanus, and other Christian poets. But he vilified versifiers such as Philomusus "who read something of the poets for a stipend, and who in the space of a whole hour scarcely read six or eight lines with any useful result." They offer only "trifles, bombast, and filth" that endanger the youthful innocence of their listeners.[67] What is worse, they filled their lectures with "wild gestures and effeminate shrieking"—behavior that encouraged large crowds, but was "utterly unsuitable for serious men." Chapter Four was also clearly directed against Locher. It criticized the emperor for bestowing the laurel crown on "despised poets" and with it, a supposed academic degree. In an obvious reference to Ingolstadt's *Nova Ordinatio* of 1507, it branded as extraordinarily foolish the practice of admitting "mere poets" to the university council.[68]

Predictably, in Chapter Six Wimpfeling stressed that he had no intention of rejecting all poets. As proof, he compiled a

[64] Hehle, *Der Schwäbische Humanist,* II, 35.

[65] Schmidt, *Histoire,* I, 61, 62.

[66] *Contra turpem libellum philomusi, theologie scholastice & neotericorum defensio* (Nuremberg: 1510). The Weissenburg firm, which published the work, had also published Locher's *Mulae ad Musam Comparatio.*

[67] *Ibid.,* A ii b.

[68] *Ibid.,* A iii.

V "Christ Entering Jerusalem on a Mule," frontispiece from Wimpfeling, *Contra turpem Libellum Philomusi*

long list of contemporaries who cultivated poetry but who were nonetheless acceptable. Included were Johannes Reuchlin, Dyonisius Reuchlin, Sebastian Brant, Hermann Buschius, Johannes Aesticampianus, Eobanus Hessus, Beatus Rhenanus, and even Ortwin Gratius, the unfortunate victim of the *Letters of Obscure Men*. These men, claimed Wimpfeling, used their poetical talents for eradicating corruption, commending virtue, extolling saints, praising writers of honorable things, and composing the epitaphs of famous men."[69]

Despite his protestations, Wimpfeling's arguments did tend

[69] Discussed in Chapter VI of the *Defensio*.

to deny poetry's usefulness. Such was the main thrust of Chapter Three, entitled "That poets are entirely worthless to the state and the Christian commonwealth in every matter." He pointed out that many great leaders and thinkers of the past had never studied poetry and that poetry offered no useful preparation for law or medicine. His main argument was that poetry lacked any practical value:

> if someone is weak in body, he calls a physician, not a poet; if the work is to plead a lawsuit a jurist is present, not a poet; if someone in the cure of souls or in confession must be counseled, a learned theologian is sought, not a poet; if someone desires the judgment of a priest or a censor of morals, he summons a lawyer trained in sacred letters; if a legate must be sent somewhere, an eloquent, pure and truthful orator or speaker is chosen, not a mangy and trifling poet and teller of stories. If an appropriate teacher is sought for the sons of princes and nobles, no libidinous, proud, irascible, and raving poet must be chosen, but rather a modest moral philosopher, an unassuming historian or theologian, serene and humble in spirit.[70]

Wimpfeling offered his arguments in defense of scholastic theology at the end of the book, especially in Chapter Seven, entitled "In which is defended scholastic theology against the mule-poet who hates dialectic, scorns philosophy, and compared theology proceeding through *questiones* to mules and mule dung." His main point, constantly repeated, was that logic and dialectic were rightfully the foundation for theological discourse. Without sound training in these two disciplines, refutation of heresy was impossible. To show the respectability of dialectical argumentation, Wimpfeling cited several biblical authors who in his opinion used the scholastic *modus quaestionum* in their writings. One example he cited was the opening verses from the twentieth chapter of Luke. It relates the episode in which the chief priests and scribes con-

[70] *Ibid.*, A iii.

front Jesus with the question, "Tell us by what authority you do these things, or who it is that gave you this authority?" Christ responded with another question: "Was the baptism of John from heaven or from men?" Then the following exchange ensued:

> And they discussed it with one another saying, "If we say, 'From heaven,' he will say, 'Why did you not believe him?' But if we say, 'From men' all the people will stone us; for they are convinced John is a prophet." So they answered that they did not know whence it was. And Jesus said to them, "Neither will I tell you by what authority I do these things."

Wimpfeling also cited a passage from Malachi I:6 to prove that biblical authors used dialectical forms of argumentation: "A son honoreth his father, and a servant his master: if then I be a father, where is mine honor? and if I be a master, where is my fear? saith the Lord of hosts unto you." With all due respect for Wimpfeling, these are not the strongest of examples. Surely he knew that the use of a question mark was not at the heart of scholastic methodology. For the remainder of his defense, he catalogued a long list of scholastics from Lombard to Gabriel Biel who had been "columns" of the Church. The scholastics criticized by Locher received special praise. Frequently interspersed were attacks on the "ape-like lovers of poetry."

Locher offered no response. In fact, sometime after 1510, when he heard that a Nuremberg printer, probably Weissenburg, was planning to republish Wimpfeling's *Against the Foul Pamphlet*, he wrote to the Nuremberg humanist Willibald Pirckheimer and urged him to make an effort to prevent the appearance of another edition.[71] Whether Pirckheimer intervened is uncertain; in any case no second edition was published.

Locher remained at Ingolstadt until 1522, where he contin-

---

[71] Pirckheimer, *Briefwechsel*, 52, 53.

ued to publish texts on rhetoric and editions of classical texts. But he played a minor role in university affairs and launched no further attacks on scholasticism. After several years of poor health, he died in apparent obscurity in 1528 at the age of fifty-seven. For his part, Wimpfeling continued to live in Strassburg, where he supported himself through a modest benefice and by offering Latin instruction to local children of good family. In 1515 he retired to his native town of Schlettstadt. There he continued to publish on a moderate scale and was occasionally consulted by princely governments on ecclesiastical and academic matters. He played no role in the Reuchlin affair but began to speak out in 1519 against both Luther and Zwingli, whose attacks on the Virgin Mary he particularly deplored. At the age of seventy-eight, he, like Locher, died in 1528.

~ ~ ~

IT IS TEMPTING to view the controversies described in this chapter as nothing more than bits of academic comic opera, proving nothing beyond the deplorable tendency of late medieval scholars to abuse the new medium of print. Such a dismissal, however, would be a mistake, for in certain important ways each feud adds to our understanding of post-1500 humanism and its relationship to scholasticism. First of all, both controversies show how personality conflicts often preceded intellectual combat. Wimpina and Polich were already spiteful enemies before they began to exchange diatribes about poetry and theology. And one can think of no greater contrast than the flamboyant Locher and the squeamishly puritanical Wimpfeling, who had once warned young boys against curling or dyeing their hair because "it makes the hair fall out, insults God the Father and frightens away guardian angels."[72] Second, the controversy surrounding Locher clearly reveals the changes in humanism after 1500 and the gap that now existed between "the new humanism" of Locher and the

---

[72] Wimpfeling, *Pädagogische Schriften*, ed. and tr. Joseph Freundgen, 342.

ideas of older humanists such as Zasius and Wimpfeling. Even Zingel seems to have had no objections to humanism as long as it essentially represented grammar reform through the selective use of suitable ancient authors. But all three men found Locher's extravagant enthusiasm for pagan authors dangerously subversive to morality and the Church. Most importantly, both controversies show the difficulty, perhaps the impossibility, of neatly dividing the intellectuals of the age into clear-cut humanist-scholastic camps. This is readily apparent when one finds a "scholastic" like Martin Polich defending the majesty of poetry and a "humanist" like Wimpfeling producing the era's sole defense of scholastic theology.

VI

Humanism at the Universities, 1500-1515: The Prelude to Reform ~

THE OPENING YEARS of the sixteenth century were in many ways the golden age of northern European humanism. It was a time when powerful princes—Henry VIII, Francis I, and Emperor Maximilian, to name only the most prominent— lent their enthusiastic support to the "revival of letters"; when printing houses from Alcala to Cracow were producing handsome editions of the classics and publishing texts and manuals that made possible both the mastery of Greek and Hebrew and the widespread diffusion of humanist culture; when eminent humanists such as Reuchlin, Budé, Lefèvre, and especially Erasmus reached the peak of their careers. To many, the appearance of Erasmus's Greek New Testament in 1516 culminated a decade of fruitful biblical and patristic scholarship that promised a new era of religious enlightenment. For the disciples of humanism, it was a time of great achievement and high expectations.

It was also a time when the German universities faced a number of perplexing and controversial questions about their response to this new and dynamic intellectual movement. Would humanism remain what it had been in the late fifteenth century: a presence that was tolerated, but was peripheral to the universities' academic priorities? Or should the *studia hu-*

manitatis become an integral part of the curriculum? If so, how would professors of poetry and rhetoric fit into the established faculty structure? Would traditional scholastic courses need to be limited or modified? Was it the universities' responsibility to offer instruction in Greek and Hebrew? What should be the response to those who demanded fundamental changes in the teaching of theology? None of these questions received a definitive answer before 1515. But they were continually asked and debated, making the years from 1500 to 1515 an era of special importance in the history of humanist-scholastic relations.

THE SLOW PACE OF CURRICULAR CHANGE

The boldest experiment involving humanism's academic status was made at the University of Vienna in the opening years of the century. It will be recalled that after nearly a decade of pro-humanist pressure applied to the university by Hapsburg officials, the thoroughgoing reforms proposed in 1499 had foundered, and their main sponsor, Bernard Perger, had resigned amid controversy. This setback seems to have been a revelation to the university's salaried poet, Conrad Celtis, who now perceived that, given the traditional structure of the faculties, humanist studies had little chance to flourish. Thus in 1501 he made a radical proposal to Emperor Maximilian I. He petitioned the emperor to support the establishment of a special College of Poets and Mathematicians, which would be part of the university but independent of any of the four existing faculties.[1] The emperor and his advisers were agreeable, and in the fall of 1501 Celtis received the imperial charter for the founding of the college.[2] The charter stated that the emperor, always thinking of the honor of Germany and the

---

[1] On the background of the founding, see Lewis Spitz, *Conrad Celtis, the German Arch-Humanist* (Cambridge, Mass.: 1957), 68, 69.

[2] The charter is printed in Conrad Celtis, *Briefwechsel*, ed. Hans Rupprich (Munich: 1934), 456-60.

Austrian homeland, thought it wise to found a school of Roman literature, "from whence would result so many excellent leaders and statesmen for the state." It continued, "Therefore by our arrangements in the manner of our imperial forebears, we have directed the foundation of a college of poets at our school in Vienna, to restore the lost eloquence of the previous age, since until now we have done nothing for the poetic and rhetorical arts."

The makeup of the college reflected Celtis's educational ideals. Of the four professors, two taught "eloquence"—poetry and rhetoric—and two taught "wisdom"—mathematics and astronomy. The number of students was to remain small. On completion of their course of study, graduates did not receive a conventional degree but instead became eligible to receive the poet's crown from the emperor. Celtis's enterprise was self-governing and free from financial dependence on the university. The emperor provided salaries and also paid rent on the house Celtis had acquired for the college's use. The superintendent of the college, Celtis, was solely responsible for determining the lecture schedule.

The career of Celtis's brainchild was short and undistinguished.[3] It opened in February 1502 but with only three-quarters of the proposed faculty. Celtis and his friend Vinzenz Lang were the two poets, and Andreas Stiborius was the lone mathematician. It originally enrolled a dozen students, none of whom attained any literary, mathematical, or scientific distinction. The high point of the college's existence came in 1504 with the performance of Celtis's drama, *Rhapsody*, written to celebrate the emperor's victory over the Bohemians in the War of the Bavarian Succession. Performed by Celtis's students, the play mainly consisted of a series of laudatory speeches addressed to the emperor by Heroldus, Paresiphanus, Phoebus, and the muses. It also featured dancing and singing by Bacchus and a troop of satyrs, who called for

---

[3] Spitz, *Conrad Celtis*, 72-82; also Joseph Ritter von Aschbach, *Geschichte der Wiener Universität*, 2 vols. (Vienna: 1865, 1877), II, 221, 222.

victory over the Turks and the expulsion of Poles, Swedes, and Bohemians from the empire. When the text of the *Rhapsody* was published one year later, Celtis's introduction provided the only description of the college's activities. Its goal, explained Celtis, was the achievement of wisdom and eloquence. He added that he gave lessons on the best authors and required his students to give declamations and perform in dramas. He failed to mention lectures on mathematics.

Even at the time of the performance of the *Rhapsody*, the college was beginning to languish. A severe blow was the death in early 1504 of Lang, who was not replaced. Celtis, who himself was suffering from syphilis, carried on, but his poor health and his travels away from Vienna limited his effectiveness. When the archhumanist died in 1508 his College of Poets and Mathematicians had already disappeared. Celtis did not even mention it in his final testament.[4]

The Poets' College, even before its demise, was a setback for the real progress of humanism within the university. Having failed in 1499 to attain an integral place in the arts curriculum, poetry, rhetoric, and mathematics were now relegated to a special college without degree-granting powers. Traditional practices in the faculty of arts could continue unchanged, and governmental pressure for reform was temporarily defused.[5]

Opportunities for creative innovation in the early 1500s were also afforded by the foundation of two new universities in northeast Germany: the University of Wittenberg in 1502 and the University of Frankfurt an der Oder in 1506. But the founders and organizers of the new institutions showed little imagination. Although humanist teaching was encouraged, in most respects the structure and curricula of both universities

---

[4] Celtis, *Briefwechsel*, 603-609.

[5] "In dieser Gründung liegt eine Verurteilung der bestehenden Ordnung der Universität und der Verzicht auf den Versuch einer tiefergriefenden Reform." Georg Kaufmann, *Geschichte der deutschen Universitäten*, 2 vols. (Stuttgart: 1888, 1896), II, 547.

adhered to long-familiar patterns. They were in a sense the last expression of Germany's scholastic age.

Elector Frederick the Wise of Saxony, the founder and patron of the University of Wittenberg, chose two men to direct the establishment of the new institution.[6] The first, Martin Polich of Mellerstadt, was the Leipzig physician then in the midst of his stormy debate with Conrad Wimpina over the relative merits of theology and poetry. The second, Johann von Staupitz, was a prominent Augustinian who had taught theology at Tübingen before coming to Wittenberg.[7] Neither man was truly a humanist, but each was familiar with humanist ideas and harbored no hostility toward them.

Staupitz's Tübingen background explains the almost literal adoption of the Tübingen statutes by the new Saxon institution. The requirements for degrees in the faculty of arts included the same material that German university students had studied for more than a century.[8] Candidates for the bachelor's degree were required to hear five lectures, all on logic: the *Isagoge* of Porphyry, and the *Predicaments, Posterior Analytics, Prior Analytics,* and *Topics* of Aristotle; they also were required to attend exercises on Aristotle's *Physics* and Peter of Spain's *Parva logicalia.* Candidates for the master's degree had to hear lectures on the remaining major Aristotelian writings: the *Physics, De caelo et mundo, De generatione et corruptione, De anima,* the *Metaphysics, Ethics,* and the *Parva naturalia*; additional exercises were required on the *Ethics* and the *Parva naturalia.*

---

[6] On the early history of the university, see: Walter Friedensburg, *Geschichte der Universität Wittenberg* (Halle: 1917); Gustav Bauch, "Wittenberg und die Scholastik," *Neues Archiv für Sächsische Geschichte,* 18 (1897), 285-339; Maria S. Grossmann, *Humanism in Wittenberg, 1485-1517* (Nieuwkoop: 1975); Max Steinmetz, "Die Wittenberger Universität und der Humanismus," *450 Jahre Martin-Luther-Universität,* I (Leipzig: 1952), 103-40; Walter Friedensburg, ed., *Urkundenbuch der Universität Wittenberg,* I (Magdeburg: 1926).

[7] Schulte, "Johann von Staupitz," *Allgemeine Deutsche Biographie,* 35 (Leipzig: 1893), 529-33.

[8] Theodor Muther, ed., "Die ersten Statuten der Wittenberger Artistenfakultät," *Neue Mitteilungen aus dem Gebiet historisch-antiquarischer Forschungen,* 12 (1874), 176-208.

Although humanist courses were not required, the founders
assured their availability to students. A salaried lectureship
for poetry was established, with Hermann Buschius as the
first incumbent.[9] Buschius had most recently taught at
Leipzig, where he had sought and apparently won Polich's
favor by publishing a brief treatise on his behalf during the
feud with Wimpina. Buschius delivered an oration to high-
light the university's opening ceremonies and began to lecture
on Ovid's *Metamorphoses* once classes began; then inexplica-
bly, he abandoned Wittenberg in the spring of 1503 and returned to Leipzig.

Nothing indicates that opposition to humanism caused
Buschius's departure. Lectures on the *studia humanitatis* certainly continued after he left. This is clearly shown in the
Rotulus doctorum Vittemberge ("Roll of Wittenberg Doctors"),
a document drawn up in 1507 by Christoph Scheurl, a professor of law and at the time the university's rector.[10] The
Rotulus was distributed throughout Germany with the intent
of publicizing the university and attracting students. In addition to proclaiming Wittenberg's non-academic virtues (its
benign climate and low prices), Scheurl catalogued the university's lectures and their subjects. The *Rotulus* listed three
men who lectured *in humanis litteris*. The first was a Hessian,
Balthasar Phaccus, who had received his Master of Arts degree
from Wittenberg in 1503. He had apparently inherited the
salaried lectureship abandoned by Buschius. Scheurl's *Rotulus*
listed him as lecturing twice a day on three authors, Virgil,
Sallust, and Valerius Maximus. Although Ulrich von Hutten

---

[9] Friedensburg, *Geschichte*, 69, 70.

[10] The most accessible version of the *Rotulus* is Kaufmann, *Geschichte der
deutschen Universitäten*, II, 572-80; also in J.C.A. Grohmann, ed., *Annalen der
Universität Wittenberg* (Meissen: 1801), II, 79-84; for commentary on the *Rotulus*, see Gustav Bauch, "Zu Christoph Scheurls Briefbuch," *Neue Mitteilungen aus dem Gebiet historisch-antiquarischer Forschungen*, 19 (1898), 400-56;
and "Christoph Scheurl in Wittenberg," *Neue Mitteilungen aus dem Gebiet
historisch-antiquarischer Forschungen*, 21 (1903), 33-42; see also Grossmann, *Humanism in Wittenberg*, 64-72.

later called him the "glory of the fatherland,"[11] Phaccus was a minor figure with no publications to his credit. He did become a fixture at Wittenberg, however, teaching there until his death in 1541. Two others were listed as lecturing on the *studia humanitatis*. Scheurl himself was noted as lecturing on Suetonius in addition to offering courses in the faculty of law. Finally, Georgius Sibutus, designated as *poeta et orator laureatus*, lectured on Silius Italicus's *Punica*, a book on the Punic War, and on his own *Silvula (Little Woods)*, a dialogue describing the town of Wittenberg.

Although the university slightly modified its statutes in 1508,[12] the original degree requirements remained intact. But this did not prevent innovation on the part of individual professors. In 1507, for example, Johannes Crispus began giving grammar lessons based on the text of the Italian humanist, Johannes Sulpitius. Crispus published the text and in the dedication expressed satisfaction that, after three hundred years of barbarism, students were at last receiving sound grammatical training.[13] In 1509, Kilian Reuther published and adopted for his courses the new translation of Aristotle's *De anima* by the Greek scholar, John Argyropulos.[14] In the introduction, he claimed to have chosen this version "because it was written in the pristine splendor of Roman eloquence." Interestingly, the book also contained a commentary on *De anima* by Thomas Aquinas. For Reuther, utilizing a new humanist translation along with a traditional scholastic commentary was not contradictory. It was also possible for Wittenberg students to receive informal training in Greek in the early 1500s. Nicholas Marschalk, a law student, gave private lessons between 1502 and 1505. He had come to Wittenberg from Erfurt, where he

[11] Ulrich von Hutten, "Ad poetas germanos," *Opera omnia*, III, ed. Eduard Böcking (Leipzig: 1862), 67.

[12] Steinmetz, "Die Wittenberger Universität und der Humanismus," 120.

[13] *Posterior editio Sulpitiana in partes tres divisa* . . . (Wittenberg: 1506); discussed in Bauch, "Wittenberg und die Scholastik," 309, 310.

[14] *Liber de anima Aristotelis, nuper per Johannem Argrilopilum de graeco in latinum sermonem elegantissime traductus cum commentariis divi Thome Aquinatis* . . . (Wittenberg: 1509).

had already edited a number of works on poetry and Greek and Latin grammar.[15] After his departure, two others, Hermann Trebelius and Tillmann Conradi, also privately taught Greek.[16]

Less is known about the early years of the University of Frankfurt an der Oder, founded under the aegis of Elector Joachim I, duke of Brandenburg in 1506.[17] Even the earliest statutes of the institution have been lost. Scholars have assumed, however, that they were modeled on the statutes of the University of Leipzig. This seems reasonable since Conrad Wimpina, the Leipzig theologian, was responsible for organizing the university, and more than two-thirds of Frankfurt's original faculty had been recruited from Leipzig. If the practices of the venerable Saxon institution had in fact been followed, it means that Frankfurt students, like the Wittenbergers, faced degree requirements that followed long-established patterns.

It is also known, however, that Frankfurt's original faculty included two humanists whose salaries were provided by Duke Joachim. The first, Publicius Vigilantius, came to Frankfurt from Erfurt; he delivered an oration during the opening ceremonies and lectured on Horace once the university began its formal academic life.[18] The second salaried humanist was Johannes Aesticampianus, who remained at Frankfurt for two years before moving to the University of Leipzig. He lectured not only on poetry and grammar but also on moral philosophy.[19] On his departure he was replaced by Hermann Trebelius.

The status of humanism at Frankfurt and Wittenberg typ-

---

[15] F. X. Wegele, "Nicholas Marschalk," *Allgemeine Deutsche Biographie*, 20 (Leipzig: 1884), 431, 432.

[16] Steinmetz, "Die Wittenberger Universität und der Humanismus," 117.

[17] Paul Reh, ed., "Die allgemeinen Statuten der Universität Frankfurt an der Oder, 1510-1610," *Jahresbericht der Schlesischen Gesellschaft für vaterländische Cultur*, 75 (1897), 2-102; Gustav Bauch, *Die Anfänge der Universität Frankfurt a. O.* (Berlin: 1900).

[18] Bauch, *Die Anfänge*, 98.

[19] On Aesticampianus, see below, 238-41.

ified its standing throughout the empire. At these new universities, and elsewhere, there were, on the one hand, unmistakable signs of humanism's continued growth and vitality. Even at those institutions where humanism had previously had little impact, enthusiasm for the new learning took hold. Greifswald and Rostock, for example, established salaried lectureships for the *studia humanitatis* in 1514 and 1515, respectively.[20] While humanism gained no official recognition at the University of Cologne, there were now ample opportunities for the study of oratory, poetry, and even Greek. Prominent among the Cologne humanists were Ortwin Gratius, who delivered and later published in 1508 a festive oration in praise of the *studia humanitatis*;[21] Johannes Caesarius, who taught Greek; and Hermann Buschius, the well-traveled poet, who managed to stay put at Cologne for almost a decade after his arrival in 1508.[22] At other institutions, the offerings of the poets and humanist grammarians increased in numbers and popularity; individual masters increasingly adopted new humanist translations of Aristotle for their lectures; opportunities for the study of Greek expanded.

These innovations took place, however, within universities that like Wittenberg and Frankfurt an der Oder remained attached to educational practices that proved stubbornly resistant to change. The persistence of traditional scholastic methods resulted in part from academic inertia; but it also reflected the emergence of a body of opinion within the universities that sought to curb further humanist progress. It is apparent that some German academics had been willing to tolerate humanism only so long as it remained an "ornament" decorating a curriculum that remained essentially scholastic. Some perceived that further acceptance of humanism threatened the

[20] Johann Kosegarten, *Geschichte der Universität Greifswald mit urkundliche Beilagen* (Greifswald: 1857), I, 167; Otto Krabbe, *Die Universität Rostock im fünfzehnten und sechszehnten Jahrhundert* (Rostock: 1854), 270.

[21] James V. Mehl, "Ortwin Gratius' *Orationes Quodlibeticae*: humanist apology in scholastic form," *The Journal of Medieval and Renaissance Studies*, 11 (1981), 57-69.

[22] Hermann Keussen, *Die alte Universität Köln* (Cologne: 1934), 191-96.

universities' very nature. They worked, therefore, to block the acceptance of reforms favored by supporters of humanism. As a result, curricular reforms were often discussed between 1500 and 1515, but nothing substantial was accomplished. Courses on the *humaniora* proliferated, but the *poetae* and *magistri* who offered them received scant institutional recognition. The situation was conducive to friction and tension. At one institution, the University of Leipzig, it resulted in a series of major confrontations that convulsed the academic corporation for close to a decade.

The clearest sign of the uneasy balance between innovators and traditionalists was the ongoing and generally futile debate over curriculum reform that went on at many German universities. Between 1500 and 1515, we know of at least seven institutions where curriculum reforms were either formally debated or implemented. But the results must have been disappointing to those who saw humanism as the best hope for Germany's intellectual and spiritual rejuvenation. Concrete gains were few, and were more than balanced by efforts at several institutions to limit and curtail humanist teaching.

Early evidence that traditional methods would not simply evaporate in the face of humanist criticisms is provided by the experience of Jacob Wimpfeling at Heidelberg around the turn of the century. Wimpfeling had returned to his alma mater in 1497, undoubtedly nurturing the hope that he could influence the university to adopt the new methods of grammar instruction he had championed in his recent writings. Thus in 1499 he delivered an oration that pointedly denounced the teaching of speculative grammar and called for the study of the classics in the *bursae*.[23] But the response was negative. The rector of the *Nova bursa*, Johannes Hosser, denounced Wimpfeling's proposals in a public letter posted shortly after the speech. Poetry and rhetoric were of little value, Hosser argued; much more useful were logic and the precepts of spec-

[23] On the brief exchange, see Gustav Knod, "Wimpfeling und die Universität Heidelberg," *Zeitschrift für die Geschichte des Oberrheins*, N.F., I (1886), 328, 329.

ulative grammar learned in Scotus, especially for future theologians and ecclesiastics.[24] Wimpfeling responded in a public letter of his own, but it had no effect. Disillusioned with the resistance he encountered, he soon left the university and briefly lived in a Strassburg monastery before going to Basel in 1503.[25] Without its main spokesman, humanism made little progress at the Rhenish university. When Philip Melanchthon later described his studies at Heidelberg between 1509 and 1511, he recalled, "nothing was taught there except that garrulous dialectic and small portions of physics." What he had learned of the poets, orators, and historians, he added, had resulted solely from his own private reading.[26]

Stronger evidence of devotion to medieval grammar methods is provided by events at the universities of Tübingen and Freiburg-im-Breisgau. In 1505 both institutions adopted statute revisions that while mainly dealing with organizational and administrative issues, also touched upon Latin instruction. At Tübingen, in an edict entitled "Against Departures in the Pedagogium," it was stipulated that all Latin instructors were to swear to use the familiar texts of Donatus and Alexander Villedieu. Only after these authors had been thoroughly covered could other texts be considered.[27] Such a step was clearly a setback for Heinrich Bebel, an outspoken critic of the *Doctrinale*, and his younger colleague, Johann Heinrichmann, who had been teaching grammar according to humanist methods for the past three years. In fact, at the time of the edict, Heinrichmann was just about to publish a Latin grammar of his own, the *Grammatical Principles*, which appeared in early 1506.[28]

A conservative policy concerning grammar instruction was

---

[24] The thirteenth-century *Grammatica speculativa*, long thought to be the work of Scotus, is now known to be the work of Thomas of Erfurt.

[25] Charles Schmidt, *Histoire littéraire de l'Alsace*, 2 vols. (Paris: 1879), I, 29.

[26] Philip Melanchthon, *Opera omnia*, IV, ed. Charles Bretschneider (Halle: 1837), 715.

[27] Rudolf Roth, ed., *Urkunden zur Geschichte der Universität Tübingen* (Tübingen: 1877), 416, 417.

[28] *Grammaticae institutiones* . . . (Pforzheim: 1508). The first edition also included a section by Bebel on poetry writing.

also adopted at the University of Freiburg-im-Breisgau in 1505. Accompanying a number of minor statute changes was a formal denunciation of innovation in grammar teaching: "Strange authors and teachings had confused the students, and this was the mother of error." Therefore teachers were ordered to use Alexander and Donatus exclusively.[29]

The experience of the universities of Vienna and Ingolstadt also show the difficulties of breaking loose from familiar and time-honored practices. Both institutions had been lively centers of humanist interest and activity. But reform attempts at each institution yielded only meager results.

The government of Bavaria undertook a review of the University of Ingolstadt shortly after the accession of Duke Albert IV in 1504.[30] Although details are sparse, it is known that a faculty committee was formed in 1506 to investigate and discuss a variety of issues, including curriculum reform. The committee included representatives from all faculties, in addition to the recently rehired salaried poet, Jacob Locher. Among the issues discussed was the advisability of retaining the commentary on Priscian by Peter Helias, a thirteenth-century modistic grammarian whose work had been required at Ingolstadt since 1476.[31] Several members of the committee, including the "enemy of poets," George Zingel, recommended that it be replaced with the grammar of Nicholas Perotti and collateral reading in Virgil or Cicero. Certain members of the arts faculty objected, however, and when Albert released his *Nova ordinatio* in 1507, no mention was made of new grammatical texts. In fact, except for the provision that the *via antiqua* be represented in the faculty of theology, the *ordinatio* contained no curricular changes at all.[32]

At the University of Vienna, the ambitious but futile reform

---

[29] H. Ott and J. M. Fletcher, eds., *The Medieval Statutes of the Faculty of Arts of the University of Freiburg-im-Breisgau* (Notre Dame, Ind.: 1964), 119.

[30] Carl von Prantl, *Geschichte der Ludwig-Maximilians-Universität zu München* (Munich: 1872), I, 104-106; Bauch, *Die Anfänge des Humanismus in Ingolstadt,* 86-89.

[31] Bauch, *Die Anfänge,* 86, 87.

[32] The *Nova ordinatio* has been published in Arno Seifert, *Die Universität Ingolstadt im 15. und 16. Jahrhundert* (Berlin: 1973), 58-67.

attempts of the previous decade finally gained some concrete results in 1509. In comparison to Perger's bold dreams, however, the results were unimpressive. They were restricted to grammar teaching alone, and even then old methods were not completely discarded. The reforms, which again were initiated by the Hapsburg government, were approved by both the faculty of arts and the university senate.[33] The new regulations required the teaching of the grammar of Nicholas Perotti for eighteen weeks during every academic year. Lectures on Alexander's *Doctrinale* were to be discontinued altogether. Nonetheless, candidates for the Bachelor of Arts degree were still required to attend *resumptiones*, or review classes, on the first three parts of the *Doctrinale*. In a concession to humanism, instructors were urged to minimize detailed logical analysis. They were to treat the work with "clear and simple explanation" and were not to mention "logical and metaphysical concepts or the maddening and perplexing opinions about vocatives and gerunds." Also to be avoided were "long and erroneous commentaries, metaphysical *modi significandi*, and the obscure meaning of rules." For what it was worth, instructors were advised to treat the *Doctrinale* the way "a bee gathers from the flowers."

Two other universities, Frankfurt an der Oder and Erfurt, adopted statute revisions that more fully reflected humanist ideas. But the changes were modest and by no means granted full recognition to humanism's role within the university.

The results of the changes at Frankfurt are preserved in two documents dating from 1512.[34] The *Nova ordinatio* listed the time of day and lecturer for all offered courses, while the *Ordinatio pro gradibus* listed courses required for degrees. Both documents show that the traditional Aristotelian texts served as the basis for instruction. The *Nova ordinatio*, however, listed courses on grammar and rhetoric, and the *Ordinatio pro gra-*

[33] Printed in Rudolf Kink, *Geschichte der Kaiserlichen Universität zu Wien*, II (Vienna: 1854), 315, 318.
[34] Gustav Bauch, *Acten und Urkunden der Universität Frankfurt a. O.*, 6 (Breslau: 1906).

dibus confirms that both subjects were mandatory for all students. Cicero and Aristotle were the authorities used for rhetoric; the texts of Perotti or Sulpitius, rather than the *Doctrinale*, were used for Latin grammar. The *Ordinatio pro gradibus* also listed several courses on poetry; but each was followed by the phrases, *Quod est placiti*—"to the extent it is agreeable"—or *si licet*—"if it is pleasing"—which suggests that students could attend or not at their pleasure.[35] Regular members of the arts faculty taught the required courses on grammar and rhetoric, not Frankfurt's two salaried humanists, Publicius Vigilantius and Hermann Trebelius. The lectures of these two men were listed separately from the other arts faculty courses and took place in the lecture room of the jurists.[36] In other words, the faculty of arts had adopted certain limited segments of the humanist program, but the salaried poets themselves were still not part of the faculty's formal structure.

Erfurt was another university that abandoned standard medieval grammatical texts. But this was accomplished only in 1515, after a decade in which curricular reform had been debated constantly in meetings of the arts faculty council.[37] Until 1515, however, despite the presence on the council of several humanist sympathizers, nothing had been accomplished. In that year a thoroughgoing reform of grammar instruction was approved. Donatus was replaced by the *Donatus melior (Improved Donatus)* of the Italian grammarian Antonius Mancinellus (1452-1503); the section of the *Doctrinale* on syntax was replaced by the *Syntax* of Johann Brassicanus; Priscian was abandoned in favor of the *Orthography* of George Valla, the *Quantity of Syllables* of Heinrich Bebel and *The Figures of Speech* of Mancinellus; finally, the *Laborinthus* of Eberhard of Bethune was set aside for rhetorical works by Cicero and Quintilian and *The Introduction to Letter-Writing* of Johannes Sulpitius.[38]

[35] On this issue, see the introductory comments by Bauch, *ibid.*, X, XI.
[36] *Ibid.*, 39, 40.
[37] Erich Kleineidam, *Universitas Studii Erffordensis*, 2 vols. (Leipzig: 1964, 1969), II, 181, 183, 187.
[38] *Ibid.*, 214.

The final institution that grappled with the problem of curriculum reform in the early sixteenth century was the University of Leipzig, where statute revisions were considered and approved in 1502, 1508, and 1511. All three episodes are richly documented: available to the historian are not only the reform statutes themselves but also the record of much of the debate that preceded their adoption. Taken together, the events at Leipzig offer extraordinary insights into the nature of humanist-scholastic tensions in the early 1500s.

Leipzig, founded in 1409, was among the oldest, largest, and most prestigious universities in the empire. But the late fifteenth century found the university in the grip of an institutional malaise. In 1496, convinced that the university had "declined into a state of sluggishness," the government of ducal Saxony had promulgated a series of edicts designed to tighten discipline, ensure industry among professors, and effect a number of minor curricular changes.[39] The results were deemed unsatisfactory, and concerns about the institution deepened, especially when in 1502 the richly funded University of Wittenberg began its academic life in nearby electoral Saxony. Thus in October 1502 the ducal government initiated another review of the university's statutes and operations. As a first step, Duke George himself visited Leipzig and ordered faculty members to submit reports to him on their perceptions of the university's problems. Forty-five professors responded by the deadline of October 25.[40]

The results must have afforded little comfort to the duke. They conveyed a picture of a university dulled by lassitude, wrent by factionalism, and filled with an extraordinary amount of personal animosity. There were few signs of happiness at the University of Leipzig in 1502. Many *magistri* complained about the high cost of living, with the price of beer eliciting the greatest concern. Nicolaus Kleynschmidt grumbled that it was "no small hardship" that he had to pay five *pfennig* for

[39] On the 1496 Leipzig reforms, see Chapter III, 157-59.
[40] The forty-five responses have been printed in Emil Friedberg, *Die Universität Leipzig in Vergangenheit und Gegenwart* (Leipzig: 1898), 95-148.

"good tasty beer,"[41] while Johannes Sperber testily pointed out that in Erfurt beer was a whole penny cheaper.[42] Others denounced the undisciplined behavior of students in the colleges and *bursae*. It was deplorable, noted Conradus Imhoff, that pious folk sent their children to study at Leipzig only to find that they learned "lewdness and rascality." The *fursten collegium*, he added, should more accurately be named the *buben collegium*.[43] Another common complaint was the paucity of lectures in the higher faculties, especially the faculty of theology. Benedict Staetz, a physician, claimed he knew of one theologian who had taken twenty-four years to cover eight chapters of Jeremiah and others who "in ten years had delivered only fifteen lectures on holy writ."[44] Laurentius Zcoch added that the theologians offered so few lectures, that he would need the "years of Methuselah" to complete his degree.[45] Andreas Boner, another theology student, complained there were "few lectures and fewer disputations," and as a result, "theology at Leipzig grows like grass in winter."[46]

The consensus was, however, that the university's sorest spot was the faculty of arts, which Andreas Boner characterized as the scene of "great factions, deceitful trickery, fierce avarice, gross jealousy, and secret conspiracy.[47] The root of the problem was a conflict between masters who were members of the arts faculty council and a larger, younger group that was excluded. As elsewhere, the arts faculty council at Leipzig wielded powers that affected the academic and economic status of every teaching master. It determined the distribution of lectures, controlled private teaching in the *bursae*, set lecture hours, and chose examiners. Leipzig also followed the general pattern of German university history in that, by the end of the fifteenth century, membership on the council

[41] *Ibid.*, 98.
[42] *Ibid.*, 132.
[43] *Ibid.*, 127.
[44] *Ibid.*, 114.
[45] *Ibid.*, 130.
[46] *Ibid.*, 144, 145.
[47] *Ibid.*, 145.

had become narrow and restricted. According to the revised 1496 statutes,[48] the council was limited to sixteen members, four from each of Leipzig's four nations.[49] Membership was for life and could be lost only through resignation or the attainment of a doctorate in law, theology, or medicine. When an infrequent vacancy did occur, only masters with seven years' teaching experience were eligible. Such a system left younger masters powerless and guaranteed that faculty affairs would be controlled by a small group of older, established professors.

The reports submitted to the duke in 1502 revealed how bitterly young masters resented their impotence and subservience. Eighteen non-council members responded, and to a man they denounced the selfishness and greed of the *Fakulisten*. Singled out for special abuse was the so-called "Swabian *Bund*," a faction of six or seven council members whose leader was Johannes Werdea. They were accused of a variety of crimes, among them scandalous love affairs known to "all doctors, masters, and students"[50] and so insatiable an avarice that they would "graduate a donkey" if the price was right.[51] Most deplorably, they were accused of monopolizing lucrative offices, manipulating faculty affairs, and subverting the career of any master not in their favored circle. Laurention Helbigk maintained that as long as they had authority, "good policy and profitable reform at this holy university is unthinkable."[52]

[48] The 1496 revisions can be found in Friedrich Zarncke, *Die Statutenbücher der Universität Leipzig* (Leipzig: 1861), 16-27.

[49] Leipzig and Vienna were the only universities in the empire that followed the tradition established in the Italian and French universities of dividing into nations. At Leipzig the four nations were Polish (Silesia and all eastern lands); Meissen (Thuringia, east German lands, subjects of the Meissen margraves and of the bishop of Meissen); Saxon; and Bavarian (Bavaria, Westphalia, Rhineland, and other lands of western Europe). Their leaders, known as proctors, participated in the election of the rector, and various offices were to be divided equally or rotated among the four corporations. Otherwise, they had little importance within the university. See Pearl Kibre, *The Nations in the Medieval Universities* (Cambridge, Mass.: 1948), 175, 176.

[50] Friedberg, *Die Universität Leipzig*, 128.

[51] *Ibid.*, 145.   [52] *Ibid.*, 139.

What solutions were offered by the disgruntled arts faculty members? They all demanded that the seven-year requirement for council membership be shortened. Many called for an eight, ten, or twelve-year limit on council membership. Others proposed regular salaries for teachers of exercises and review classes or recommended new procedures for naming lecturers to required courses.

Did humanism play a part in the young masters' dissatisfaction? Several complained that the council members prevented them from offering courses that would attract enough students to produce an adequate income. These "popular" courses seem certainly to have been humanist offerings on poetry and rhetoric. Andreas Boner of Lindeus (also known as Arnold Woestfeld) complained in his report about the difficulty of attracting young students to exercises on works such as the *Physics, Topics*, and *Sophisms*.[53] Since Boner had in 1500 and 1501 published for classroom use editions of Cicero's *Paradoxa* and works by the recently deceased Italian poet, Cleophilus of Fano, it is clear where his interests lay.[54] Similar sentiments were expressed by Bartoldus Ganderscheim, who deplored that "young masters were hindered by council members so they could not teach what the students willingly heard."[55] The most explicit references to humanism were made by Andreas Meynhart. He defended the young masters against the charge of council members that they neglected required subjects and taught only poetry and rhetoric. In response, he claimed that courses on logic and philosophy were being offered, but more was being done on literary studies because of their popularity with students. He stated, "a person must give *resumptiones* on those things for which a teacher has listeners; most listeners are young boys (*Knaben*), to whom po-

[53] *Ibid.*, 146.

[54] *Marci Tullii Ciceronis Paradoxa scitu jucundissima. Finis Paradoxorum Tullii per Magistrum Arnoldum Wostfeldes pro virili sua emandatorum* (Leipzig: 1500); *Octavii Cleophili Phanensis poete venutissime de cetu poetarum Libellus* (Leipzig: n.d. [1501]).

[55] Friedberg, *Die Universität Leipzig,* 102.

etry is more beneficial than the books of *Physics, Ethics,* and *Metaphysics.*[56]

Thus, although there were no proposals for specific curriculum reforms in the reports submitted to the duke, humanism's place within the university was definitely an issue. If statute changes favored the young masters, it would mean that humanistically inclined individuals could expect more freedom to offer courses on poetry and rhetoric. If, on the other hand, the powers of the faculty council remained intact, the restrictions alluded to by Boner, Ganderscheim, and Meynhart could be expected to continue.

Having deliberated only a scant two weeks, Duke George made public his mandated reforms on November 8.[57] His decisions concerning the arts faculty reflected a decisive victory for the young masters. The faculty council was expanded from sixteen to twenty-four members; the eligibility requirement was decreased from seven to two years; council membership was limited to fifteen years, with exemptions to existing members. The reforms also stripped the council of its most important power, namely its control over the distribution of required salaried lectures. Instead, a five-man committee was established to exercise this important function. For one semester it would include three members of the faculty council and two non-members; in the next, the non-members would have a three-to-two majority. Significantly, the committees were to be chosen by all masters, irrespective of their council membership. The system was designed to insure that the interests of young masters would be well-protected. On another issue young masters also prevailed. The duke's decree gave masters freedom to offer extraordinary lectures and *resumptiones* on any subject as long as they were offered at five, six, seven, or eleven o'clock in the morning or four in the afternoon. They could also teach at other hours, but only on required subjects.

Another sign of Duke George's support of humanism was

[56] *Ibid.,* 147, 148.
[57] Printed in Zarncke, *Die Statutenbücher,* 27-33; Bruno Stübel, *Urkundenbuch der Universität Leipzig* (Leipzig: 1879), 262-72.

his decision in 1503 to provide funds for a salaried lecturer on poetry. The first recipient was Hermann Buschius, the wandering poet who had changed sides in the Polich-Wimpina feud and most recently had held the position of salaried lecturer at Wittenberg.[58] Thus was created the awkward situation where on the one hand the rhetorical lectures mandated by the 1496 statute revisions were offered by a master of arts who was a regular member of the arts faculty. On the other hand, poetry and rhetoric were now also to be taught by Buschius, who was paid directly by the duke and was not part of any faculty. After Buschius left in 1505, he was succeeded by Johannes Aesticampianus, who remained at Leipzig from 1508 to 1511. Both humanists became involved in controversy, and each left Leipzig amid acrid debate. Their dramatic departures will be discussed later in this chapter.

The year of Aesticampianus's arrival, 1508, also saw a number of basically conservative decisions by the faculty of arts on the role of humanism in the curriculum. On St. Luke's Day, October 18, the dean, Nicholas Apel, recorded that the faculty had "harmoniously with no one speaking against them,"[59] approved several decrees. It decided, first of all, that for public lectures new humanist translations of Aristotle could be used only for moral philosophy; otherwise, especially for natural philosophy and logic, traditional versions were mandated. Another effort to uphold tradition was the requirement that only Donatus and the *Doctrinale* of Alexander Villedieu should be used for public grammar teaching, and that for elementary logic only the *Parva logicalia* of Peter of Spain should be taught. "This is done," stated the dean, "so that students may not be troubled by novelties and too much variety nor be distracted from their usual studies." Anyone who failed to comply would ipso facto be considered a private teacher, and another would take his place. It was also resolved

---

[58] Gustav Bauch, *Geschichte des Leipziger Frühhumanismus* (Leipzig: 1899), 168, 169.

[59] Printed in Georg Erler, *Die Matrikel der Universität Leipzig*, II (Leipzig: 1897), 444.

"that no one among the masters in his public statements vex another with insults, reproaches and annoyances." Finally, masters were warned to avoid "irreligious public statements" and in private to say nothing "strongly suspect to the Christian religion."

Although university records reveal nothing about the events leading to these decisions, an analysis of the document itself points to several conclusions. It is first of all important to note what the document exactly intended. The old Aristotelian translations and the use of Donatus, Alexander, and Peter of Spain were stipulated only for *public* lectures, that is, lectures officially required for degrees and offered in the faculty's lecture hall by professors presumably chosen by the five-man committee established in 1502. No effort was made to regulate private teaching in colleges or *bursae*, which in any case was outside the faculty council's jurisdiction according to the 1502 statutes. The document also reveals continuing divisiveness within the faculty, warned to avoid "insults, reproaches and annoyances." It also suggests that groups within the university were still pressing for the acceptance of new humanist texts for arts faculty instruction. Most importantly, it discloses the emergence of another, and seemingly more powerful faction that opposed innovation and was in a sense telling humanist sympathizers, "this far and no farther." Finally, the warning against "irreligious" statements suggests a reference to Aesticampianus, the new poet who on arrival published an edition of Jerome's letters, the preface of which strongly criticized contemporary theologians.[60] In fact it is possible to speculate that the arrival of Aesticampianus was the spark which prompted the adoption of this essentially antihumanist decision.

All of the arts faculty's tensions—innovators versus traditionalists, council members versus non-council members, young versus old—resurfaced with a vengeance in 1511. In that year

[60] *Septem divi Hieronymi epistole cum Johanni Aesticampiani epistola et Sapphico Carmine* (Leipzig: 1508).

Duke George and his advisers undertook another review of the university. As a first step, the deans of the four faculties were required to submit reports on the effectiveness of the 1502 reforms. The dean of the arts faculty responded with a broad denunciation of the changes, which he claimed had done nothing but cause "disobedience, divisiveness, and disorder."[61] Young and inexperienced masters, he complained, were now choosing lecturers, and as a result men without learning were teaching even the most difficult subjects. The examiners they chose were often only one or two years older than the students they tested. More disastrous had been the decision to strip the faculty council of its powers to control extraordinary lectures. As a result, "the foreign poets as well as masters not enrolled in or obedient to the faculty of arts have like an epidemic privately and publicly taught all hours of the day, whenever it pleased them." Certain members of the faculty council had attempted to control this epidemic, but they had been frustrated by the "poets and their disciples." Poetry had become so popular that the teaching of logic, philosophy, and physics had been all but abandoned by the young masters. Except for the "faculty council members, especially the oldest," the study of philosophy would have completely collapsed. The dean concluded by reminding the duke "that Leipzigers had for a long time received praise from other universities because they were good philosophers." He pointed out that no less than three universities had been established under the direction of "learned Leipzig philosophers"—Ingolstadt by Johann Permeter, Wittenberg by Martin Polich, and Frankfurt an der Oder by Conrad Wimpina. Now Leipzig's foundation was being uprooted and destroyed: the poets

---

[61] The response is printed in Stübel, *Urkundenbuch*, 307-19, with the sections relevant to the arts faculty on pp. 309 to 313; a problem in tracing the course of the 1511 reform is the lack of clarity about the dating and author of some of the documents, most of which are vaguely listed by Stübel as coming "sometime between 1506 and 1537." I have largely followed the datings and analysis of Felician Gess, "Leipzig und Wittenberg," *Neues Archiv für Sächsische Geschichte und Altertumskunde*, 16 (1895), 43-94, especially 82-94.

and the jurists had the upper hand and Leipzig's prestige was plummeting.[62]

Although the other deans had fewer complaints, they showed enough dissatisfaction to convince Duke George that his review should continue. Consequently he again decided to solicit faculty opinion and requested each faculty council to submit proposals. The arts faculty council, despite the infusion of eight new members after the 1502 reforms, still was a stronghold of traditionalism. Reflecting the opinion of its dean, its report complained of "the great disrespect and disobedience in our university that has begun among the young masters."[63] It recommended that the seven-year requirement for council membership be reinstated and that the fifteen-year limit on membership be abandoned. It also demanded that the council be given stricter controls over the extraordinary lectures.

Duke George, well aware of the deep divisions within the arts faculty, also requested a report from arts masters who were non-council members.[64] Not surprisingly, this group expressed approval of the provisions on council membership in the 1502 reforms. Their report also revealed strong support for certain aspects of the humanist program. They recommended that new translations of Aristotle be utilized for all arts courses. They argued that students were abandoning philosophy because they found the "inelegant Latin" of the old translations "unpleasant and wasteful to listen to."[65] They also attacked the theologians for stubbornly teaching nothing but the commentaries of Aquinas and Capreolus. As a result, "lectures on Augustine and other authors and the books of the prophets are completely ignored."[66]

By October 1511, the beginning of the winter semester, a decision by the duke was imminent. Several groups and corporate bodies within the university submitted recommenda-

---

[62] Stübel, *Urkundenbuch*, 318, 319.
[63] *Ibid.*, 277-80; this specific quotation is to be found on 278.
[64] *Ibid.*, 280-83.
[65] *Ibid.*, 282.
[66] *Ibid.*

tions, some of which contained strong anti-humanist statements. Such was the case with the report of four unnamed members of the arts faculty council.[67] It pointed out that the faculty's original organization and methods had been modeled on the practices of Prague and Paris. But recently, it continued, "a few men who have spent some time in Italy and who do not know the custom of our university," have begun to call for reforms and "have scorned the university's practices and professoriate."[68] The report also denounced the new vogue of poetry and rhetoric. In previous years, Leipzig lecturers were "undoubtedly considered learned in all of Germany and Italy." But in recent years, "poetical teaching has gotten the upper hand, and the arts have become very much depressed." According to the authors, poetry and rhetoric were popular because students found them simple and because they prepared them for "worldly work and professions." Consequently, young masters no longer taught "good and difficult subjects" and concentrated on poetry, from which resulted "inobedience, misbehavior, and divisiveness." Continuing their attacks, the four *magistri* argued that poetry and rhetoric were not true disciplines because they dealt with "words not things": "Whoever knows words, he is a grammarian; but he is therefore neither a learned man nor a philosopher, on which the university was founded; for to know words is something proper to young boys."[69] The solution was to follow the example of Paris and Cologne and take steps to "limit and decrease" the lectures on poetry. Concluding with a probable reference to the progress of humanism at Wittenberg and Frankfurt, the four masters stated that too much attention was being paid to the "new universities."

The other group that submitted a strongly anti-humanist report in 1511 was the leadership of the Polish nation,[70] which included masters from Silesia and all eastern lands. The small-

[67] *Ibid.*, 289-93.
[68] *Ibid.*, 290.
[69] *Ibid.*
[70] *Ibid.*, 285-89.

est of Leipzig's four nations, it was a stronghold of academic conservatism. It recommended that the traditional translations of Aristotle be maintained, since they were "genuinely accurate" and well-known within the university. New translations should be used sparingly and only to "clarify and interpret" the old texts. Another demand was that the arts faculty council "act diligently that everywhere the study of philosophy and good arts prosper and the study of lascivious poetry decline, from which young boys are damaged rather than edified." Finally the Poles suggested that the best way to treat "complainers and trouble-makers" was "to isolate them and drive them away." Otherwise, their "sparks would surely burst once more into flame."

Other groups that submitted extant recommendations were the faculties of medicine and law and the Saxon nation. The report of the jurists was brief and inconsequential. The physicians requested more financial support and also recommended reforms in grammar instruction. Noting that "a small error in the beginning often becomes huge in the end," it recommended the rejection of "Alexander and other unuseful grammar and logic texts, which are scorned by all learned men." Instead, "suitable and more illustrious books, already utilized in other countries and universities," should be introduced.[71] The Saxons demanded rigorous discipline and a return to pre-1502 practices within the arts faculty. Misgovernment was a plague, "because unskilled masters have been accepted into the council, while the learned have been excluded."[72]

Having been inundated with proposals and counterproposals that on many points were irreconcilable, the duke and his advisers adopted a course of compromise; when this was impossible, they simply maintained the status quo. Nothing, for example, was specified about replacing the *Doctrinale* of Alexander, academic requirements in the arts faculty remained

[71] *Ibid.*, 341.
[72] *Ibid.*, 378, 379.

intact, and no innovations were proposed for the faculty of theology. Lecturers in the arts faculty were permitted to use either the new or old translations of Aristotle.[73] The procedure for choosing lecturers in the arts faculty was again altered. The five-man committees were abandoned, and the powers of choice returned to the faculty council. The council, however, was broadened to include all masters of good character who had taught for six years. The council was obligated to include among the lecturers at least four young masters not yet eligible for council membership.[74] Finally, the position of the salaried poet was clarified. He was to reside and exclusively lecture in the former *pedagogium*, or Small College, which as a result of the 1511 reforms was given to the jurists to house their students and carry on their academic exercises. He came under the jurisdiction of the *ordinarius*, who was to oversee his teaching so that "nothing indecent or wicked was taught."[75] He could lecture only twice a day, at eleven in the morning or, if he wished, at four in the afternoon.

On balance, the duke's 1511 reforms favored the old masters over the young, the traditionalists over the innovators. Old requirements were maintained, and the activities of the salaried poet were relegated to the *Juristenschul*, where they would be closely regulated. The regained powers of the arts faculty council over lectures undoubtedly meant that humanist teaching in the *bursae* and colleges would also be more rigorously controlled. The hopes of certain faculty members that poetical teaching would be "limited and decreased" were largely fulfilled.

The events at Leipzig and elsewhere suggest two important reasons for the slow pace of humanist reforms in the early sixteenth century. First, it is apparent that at least some German scholastics now had abandoned the belief of the previous generation that the humanists' laudable efforts to improve Latin style had no implications for the rest of the university's

[73] *Ibid.*, 326.
[74] *Ibid.*, 326.
[75] *Ibid.*, 321.

academic programs. By now it was evident that such a faith had been illusory. For the medieval grammars and commentaries, filled as they were with metaphysical discussions and the logical analysis of language, had provided young students with an invaluable and irreplaceable introduction to scholastic methodology. For a young boy who learned grammar from one of the modistic commentaries on the *Doctrinale*, it was a short and easy step to Peter of Spain, and from Peter to the full panoply of scholastic logic and philosophy. Such a step would be much more difficult and perhaps might never be taken by a student whose grammatical training was limited to a grammar by Perger, Perotti, or some other humanist author. An appreciation of the importance of basic grammar instruction explains the efforts made at Freiburg, Tübingen, and Leipzig to enforce the teaching of Alexander's *Doctrinale*; it was now sensed that without the continued use of this venerable authority, further erosion of academic tradition was inevitable.[76]

Second, the other main obstacle to reform was the system of governance within the universities themselves. The Leipzig experience revealed that humanism found its strongest support among "young masters" and students, who, as the defenders of scholasticism themselves admitted, were deserting traditional courses for the offerings of the poets and orators. But the sources of power—the arts faculty council, the faculty of theology, the university senate, and at Leipzig the four nations—were still dominated by older men who had comparatively little interest in humanism and were more resistant to change. Given time, of course, as leadership within the university changed, the disciples of humanism would gain the power to implement the reforms they favored. At Leipzig and several other universities this movement was close at hand. Meanwhile, in the early 1500s, political realities determined that humanist progress would be slow or nonexistent.

[76] This argument is convincingly presented in Terrence Heath, "Logical Grammar, Grammatical Logic and Humanism at Three German Universities," *Studies in the Renaissance*, 18 (1971), 9-64.

Leipzig was not the only university that demonstrated such a "generation gap." At Cologne in 1508 the powerful and conservative faculty of theology issued a strong attack on the widespread teaching of unacceptable pagan and certain modern poets;[77] noting the moral dangers of such authors, it recommended that only Virgil and early Christian poets be utilized. Although university records are lacking, the efforts of the theologians to limit humanist teaching were successful. It will be recalled that in 1511 a report submitted to Duke George urged Leipzig to follow the model of Paris and Cologne to "limit and decrease" poetical teaching.[78] Similar political/generational divisions are evident at the University of Heidelberg. In 1513, the faculty of arts, now won over by humanism, petitioned the university senate to hire a salaried lecturer on the *studia humanitatis*, claiming that such a step had already brought "fame and advantage" to other universities.[79] But the senate, controlled by doctors of the higher faculties, refused to act, and Heidelberg was fated to remain the only German university other than Cologne that failed to hire a salaried humanist in the pre-Reformation era.

HUMANISTS AND THE ACADEMIC CORPORATION: THE CASE OF SIX "EXPULSIONS"

Another sign of the universities' difficulties in absorbing humanism between 1500 and 1515 was the controversy that engulfed several university-based "poets" and salaried humanists in these years. University records reveal no less than six episodes in which a poet was either "expelled" or resigned as a result of real or imagined opposition. Two of these cases have already been discussed: Jacob Locher's abrupt resignation

[77] Hermann Keussen, ed., "Regesten und Auszüge zur Geschichte der Universität Köln," *Mittheilungen aus dem Stadtarchiv von Köln*, 36-37 (1918), 337.
[78] Stübel, *Urkundenbuch*, 282.
[79] Eduard Winkelmann, *Urkundenbuch der Universität Heidelberg* (Heidelberg: 1886), II, 70, 71.

from Ingolstadt in 1503 and his expulsion from Freiburg-im-Breisgau in 1506. The others are as follows: the controversial departures of Hermann Buschius from the University of Leipzig in 1505 and from the University of Erfurt in 1506; the resignation and subsequent banishment of Johannes Aesticampianus from the University of Leipzig in 1511; and finally, the forced departure of Tillmann Conradi from the University of Erfurt in 1514. The resignation of the Italian jurist, Peter of Ravenna, from the University of Cologne after a bitter dispute with several university theologians was in certain respects similar to the previous episodes.[80] But since Ravenna was a jurist, and because the disputed points involved legal, not humanist-scholastic issues, this clash and Ravenna's ensuing "expulsion" will not be considered.

Comparatively little information is available concerning the problems encountered by Hermann Buschius. Buschius had become Leipzig's first salaried poet in 1503, when he signed a three-year contract. In 1505, however, it was reported by the rector in the records of the university senate that he had fined the poet for frequently insulting students, other masters, and especially the rector himself. Buschius refused to pay and appealed to the university senate. After lengthy debate, the senate waived the fine but only after it was assured that Buschius was planning to leave. Only the representatives of the Bavarian nation disagreed, demanding that the poet first be forced to humble himself before the rector.[81] Buschius next attempted to establish a career at the University of Erfurt, where in 1507 he received permission from the faculty of arts to lecture on the *ars poetica*. He commenced to lecture on the first six books of Virgil's *Aeneid*. But he seems to have quickly outworn his welcome. Entries in the *Dekanatsbuch* began to refer to his "outrageous boasting" and "frivolous and shame-

---

[80] Charles Nauert, Jr., "Peter of Ravenna and the 'Obscure Men' of Cologne: A Case of Pre-Reformation Controversy," in *Renaissance Studies in Honor of Hans Baron*, ed. Anthony Molho and John Tedeschi (DeKalb, Ill.: 1971), 609-640.

[81] Bauch, *Geschichte des Leipziger Frühhumanismus*, 169.

ful talk." Then in early 1508 Buschius left. The dean reported with satisfaction, "again he has disappeared, for our people could hardly stand such a fellow."[82]

Between 1501 and 1508, Buschius's career had been spotty to say the least. He had taught at Leipzig, resigned to go to Wittenberg, quickly left Wittenberg to return to Leipzig, and finally departed from Leipzig in 1506 and Erfurt in 1508 amid controversy. Without necessarily resorting to any complicated psychoanalytical theory, one might surmise that the humanist, now in his mid-thirties, was experiencing some kind of personal or career crisis. In any case he was having no luck remaining sober. In 1506, his friend, the abbot Trithemius wrote him:

> Flee everything that leads to ruin, the excessive enjoyment of wine and all sordid behavior. For this cripples every strength, deludes the mind and brings your profession in danger. Preserve your eyes which through excesses of both evils have been almost completely destroyed through sickly drunken discharges and redness. If you are to protect your possessions and property, you must earn it through industrious teaching; take care you are not forced into beggary in your old age.

And his nineteenth-century biographer, Hermann Liessem, conceded that, "the irregularity of his life style endangered his career and gave his enemies reasons for attacks."[83] Undoubtedly, much of the poet's "outrageous boasting" and "frivolous and shameful talk" took place after his tongue had been well-loosened by wine.

The forced departure of Tillmann Conradi from Erfurt resulted from a blatant defiance of the faculty of arts.[84] Conradi had studied at Erfurt but completed his arts training at Wittenberg, where he received his Master of Arts in 1509 and

---

[82] Kleineidam, *Universitas Studii Erffordensis*, II, 186, 187.

[83] Liessem's comment and the quotation from Trithemius both are from Hermann J. Liessem, *Hermann von dem Busche* (Nieuwkoop: 1965), 26.

[84] For the following, see Kleineidam, *Universitas* , II, 199-201.

subsequently remained to offer private lessons on Greek. In 1513, however, he traveled to Erfurt and petitioned the arts faculty council for permission to lecture publicly on the *ars poetica*. Perhaps recalling its difficulties with Buschius, the council turned him down. Undaunted, Conradi rented a house and commenced to lecture anyway. The faculty reacted by ordering him to cease teaching, reminding him that according to his matriculation oath of 1502, he had sworn to follow the statutes and practices of the university. He continued to lecture, however, and appealed to the faculty to change its decision. He was denied again. At the same time the poet became involved in a brief but typically scurrilous bout of name calling with a group of Erfurt scholars, including several humanists. It began when a young master, Johannes Femel, posted a satirical poem that mocked the humanist's early lectures for their errors and halting style. He was soon joined by Conrad Mutian's close friend, Euricius Cordus, who harbored a grudge against Conradi that went back to the early 1500s when both had been young students at Erfurt. Conradi must now have realized his prospects of a successful teaching career at Erfurt were unpromising to say the least. He left in early 1515 for Wittenberg, where he resumed his former career as a private tutor of Greek, and beginning in 1516, Hebrew.

Of all these "expulsions," by far the most dramatic was the exodus of Johannes Aesticampianus from the University of Leipzig in 1511.[85] The controversy began in September, when the humanist presented an inflammatory "farewell speech" to the academic community.[86] It was a farewell speech with

----

[85] On Aesticampianus, "Johannes Rhagius Aesticampianus," *Allgemeine Deutsche Biographie*, 1 (Leipzig: 1875), 133, 134; Gustav Bauch, "Die Vertreibung des Johannes Rhagius Aesticampianus aus Leipzig," *Archiv für Litteraturgeschichte*, 13 (1885), 1-33; W. Friedensburg, "Die Berufung des Johannes Rhagius Aesticampianus an die Universität Wittenberg," *Archiv für Reformationsgeschichte*, 21 (1924), 146-48; several of his letters have been published in Karl and Wilhelm Krafft, *Briefe und Documente aus der Zeit der Reformation* (Elberfeld: 1875).

[86] Printed in H. Pescheck, "Erinnerung an zwei einst sehr berühmte Niederlausitzer," *Neues Lausitzisches Magazin*, 20 (1842), 187-99; German trans-

little grace and no reminiscing about happy times and pleasant memories. As the humanist warned in his opening lines, his listeners were not to expect "soft and pleasant words, for the tormenting which increases daily has destroyed all my good humor." He expressed confidence, however, that this "would please his listeners, for surely they were all lovers of truth." He began by describing his teaching accomplishments at Leipzig. He recounted how "in an unprecedented short period of time, I have commented on those authors who had a two-fold usefulness: they were the wisest and most virtuous which Greece and Rome had ever seen." He hoped that as a result his students had become "both learned and virtuous, prizes to their parents and ornaments of the Christian religion."

Then Aesticampianus reached what he termed the most difficult part of his speech—the section where he "gave thanks" to various individuals in and around the university. He praised God for giving him health, thanked Duke George for providing his salary, and expressed his appreciation to the townspeople for shelter and sustenance. Then he sarcastically "thanked" his enemies:

> those who have pursued me with hate and jealousy, who have envied my position, who have never dined or even talked with me, who have closed off their lecture halls, who have kept their students away from my lectures and who have otherwise criticized their value. I have not brought this on myself for I have vexed and insulted no one; instead you have been driven by your very own nature, your perverted customs (for a long time rusty and dilapidated) and your own evil will.

He declined to name his enemies, for he claimed that everyone in the audience knew their identity. The theologians, he claimed, hated poetry the way the "pharisees had hated sin." The jurists had deprived him of lecture rooms and called him a teller of

---

lation in Otto Clemen, "Aesticampianus Leipziger Abschiedsrede," *Neue Jahrbücher für Pädagogik*, 2 (1899), 236-40. The summary of the farewell speech is based on Clement's German translation.

fairy tales. The physicians had treated him coldly while continuing to practice their "sordid and poisonous cures." Within the faculty of arts he had managed to find some admirers and friends, but most masters had ignored him. He again thanked all his detractors because as a result of their "jealousy and disparagement," they had driven him to deliver this "manly speech."

He then offered his farewell. He claimed he was leaving, "not because of intellectual impotence or scandalous behavior (accusations which hypocrites are accustomed to bring against the poets), but because of the disfavor and evil of a few men who greedily plunder you and through their imbecilic speech and voluptuous feasting draw you away from the path of true eloquence and the norms of virtuous behavior." Leipzig, he added, had remained true to its tradition. He recalled, "you hunted Conrad Celtis as a fiend, you tormented Hermann Buschius and expelled him, and now you have made war on Aesticampianus with all kinds of intrigues." As a result Leipzig would be doomed to barbarism and intellectual emptiness, for no poet would again lecture in its halls. Then Aesticampianus concluded: "Have pity then, Germans, for my righteous sorrow and provide only the tiniest space for truth, so that God almighty might forgive your sins! Amen! Live well and remember Aesticampianus in your pious prayers, for now he again takes hold of his wanderer's staff!"

It would have been too much to expect the sensitive and volatile academics of the early 1500s to accept the humanist's speech with equanimity.[87] Members of the faculties of the-

[87] Aside from the speech of Aesticampianus, three other documents shed light on his expulsion: several terse statements in the records of the Leipzig university senate, printed in Friedrich Zarncke, *Die urkundliche Quellen zur Geschichte der Universität Leipzig* (Leipzig: 1857), 692; a short satirical summary of the episode in which the author has parodied John's scriptural account of Christ's passion (in the "last judgment" scene the members of the arts faculty gather around and shout, "Crucify him, crucify him"). Printed in Carl G. Brandis, ed., "Passio Esticampiani secundum Joannem," *Zeitschrift des Vereins für Thüringische Geschichte und Altertumskunde*, N.F., Beiheft 8 (1917), 1-11; finally, another satirical account can be found in Epistle 17 of the *Letters of Obscure Men*, from "Magister Hipp to Ortwin Gratius." Because

ology and medicine reacted immediately.[88] They demanded that the poet appear before them and apologize. When he refused, the theologians and physicians demanded action by the university council. A meeting was called on October 2, at which Aesticampianus was to appear with a copy of his oration. The humanist arrived with a lawyer and a train of followers but in the tumultuous proceedings refused to recant. The rector then appointed a committee, made up of representatives from Leipzig's four nations, that was charged with adjudicating the case. In early October, on the recommendation of the Polish nation, Aesticampianus was banned from Leipzig for ten years; the university also took it upon itself to inform other universities of the circumstances of the poet's departure. Not surprisingly, Aesticampianus refused to let the matter drop. In fact he took the bold step of traveling to Rome and directly appealing to no less a figure than Pope Julius II! His holiness must have had more pressing matters to consider, but he nevertheless heard and took action on the poet's complaint. Henning Gode, a Wittenberg jurist, was named the pope's *judex delegatus*, with the authority to gather information and decide the case. Several hearings were held with Leipzig officials, but when Julius died in 1513, Leipzig withdrew, claiming that the *judex* had lost his authority. The case had still not been decided in 1520 when Aesticampianus died in Wittenberg, where he had taught poetry and rhetoric at the university since 1517.

What then do these episodes reveal about the state of humanist-scholastic relations in the first decade and a half of the sixteenth century? They confirm, first of all, how personality conflicts and the combative and sensitive natures of early sixteenth-century academics contributed to "humanist-scholastic conflict." As Chapter V has shown, Locher's dismissal from

---

it is satire this, too, is a rather dubious historical source. Nonetheless, Ulrich von Hutten, the probable author, was a friend and former student of Aesticampianus and was undoubtedly acquainted with the affair. In any case, his account fits well with other known facts.

[88] The following is based on Bauch, "Die Vertreibung."

Freiburg was almost inevitable, considering the gap between his values and those of the staid Wimpfeling and Zasius. Like Locher, Conradi's apparently lusty personality might have disturbed some conservative Erfurt academics. His publications, after all, did include a poetical work, *The Triumph of Bacchus* (1511), which according to the historian of Wittenberg humanism, Maria Grossmann, was "a collection of erotic poems, calling for the orgiastic enjoyment of life and telling of his amorous ventures in Wittenberg."[89] And Buschius's frequent drunkenness must certainly have contributed to his inability to restrain his tendency to disparage colleagues.

But to dismiss these episodes as merely "clashes of personality" would be an oversimplification. One cannot ignore the importance of the uneasiness that at least some scholastics and conservative humanists were feeling about humanism's growing strength and changing nature after 1500. Locher's enemies deplored not only his personality but also his blind devotion to pagan literature and his scorn of contemporary theologians. The opponents of Aesticampianus might also have objected to the bold attacks on the theologians found in several of his works.[90] Furthermore, the problems of Buschius and Aesticampianus at Leipzig cannot be divorced from the decade-long debate on humanism's place in the curriculum that went on between 1502 and 1511. The role of the two salaried poets must have been openly criticized and questioned by those traditionalists who were attempting to protect the university's curriculum from further humanist inroads. Such criticisms would have been particularly sharp in the year of Aesticampianus's farewell oration, 1511, as the debate on curriculum approached a climax. In fact, without naming him, several reports submitted to Duke George in that year clearly referred

---

[89] Grossmann, *Humanism at Wittenberg*, 97.

[90] Aesticampianus had denounced scholastic theology in the introductions to two edited works: the letters of Jerome, published at Leipzig in 1508, and Augustine's *De doctrina christiana*, published in Paris in 1510. The introductions to both works have been published by Gustav Bauch, "Biographische Beiträge zur Schulgeschichte des XVI. Jahrhundert," *Mitteilungen der Gesellschaft für deutsche Erziehungs-und-Schulgeschichte*, 5 (1895), 8, 9.

to the humanist. The arts faculty dean complained how "outside poets not enrolled in or obedient to the faculty of arts have like an epidemic privately and publicly taught all hours of the day, whenever it pleased them."[91] Later, the four members of the arts faculty council denounced "a few men who have spent some time in Italy and who do not know the custom of our university," but nonetheless mocked the university and demanded reforms.[92] Most ominous was the suggestion of the Polish nation that trouble-makers be "isolated and driven away."[93] One can surmise that Aesticampianus, finding such hostility intolerable, decided to leave, but not before delivering his "manly"speech of farewell.

Finally, and most importantly, all six episodes reveal the incomplete assimilation of humanism within the German universities. The difficulties of all four humanists resulted in large measure because they were "outsiders." Not one of them was an integral part of the academic corporation. They were part of no faculty and subject to no dean. Buschius and Aesticampianus at Leipzig and Locher at Freiburg and Ingolstadt were special salaried humanists paid directly by a princely-patron or else on order from the prince from general university funds. At Erfurt, Buschius and Conradi attempted in vain to maintain an independent academic existence by offering courses neither required nor otherwise offered by any other master. The result was a situation unsatisfactory to all parties. It is easy to see how other faculty members might resent the humanists' freedom to lecture on any subject, at whatever hour pleased them. On the other hand the poets must have encountered numerous aggravations, especially when it came to ascertaining suitable lecture rooms for their courses. The farewell speech of Aesticampianus shows that one of his major frustrations was the unwillingness of various deans to allow him use of facilities under their control.

The status of the humanists was particularly awkward at

---

[91] Stübel, *Urkundenbuch*, 310.
[92] *Ibid.*, 282.
[93] *Ibid.*, 285.

institutions that had made provisions for rhetorical or poetical lectures by members of the faculty of arts. At Erfurt, for example, beginning in the early 1500s, Maternus Pistoris was regularly referred to in faculty records as *lector ordinarius* on the *studia humanitatis*.[94] At Leipzig, Andreas Delitzsh, a regular member of the faculty of arts, performed a similar function, lecturing every semester in the early 1500s on some classical or humanist text.[95] In such a situation, the activities of salaried or itinerant poets must have been resented by many. In fact, shortly after Buschius arrived at Leipzig, the faculty of arts questioned Duke George on the necessity of hiring an outsider without a master's degree when the university itself had so many "eloquent men."[96] Stronger evidence of such resentment is found in the account of Aesticampianus's departure from Leipzig in Epistle 17 of the *Letters of Obscure Men*. In that letter the supposed author, "Magister Hipp," names only one enemy of the embattled poet. It turns out to be no theologian, no feverish defender of Alexander's *Doctrinale*, but rather Andreas Delitzsch, the Master of Arts who lectured on poetry and rhetoric. He is quoted as saying that "Aesticampianus was like a fifth wheel of a coach—for he thwarted the other faculties so that students could not graduate therein."[97]

One final episode that reveals humanism's status within the universities took place at the University of Ingolstadt in 1506. In that year, the university showed remarkable forbearance when, on the urging of Duke Albert, it allowed Jacob Locher to return to the university after his expulsion from Freiburg. Locher was even made a member of the university senate and was accorded a position in university processions alongside the dean of the faculty of arts. But in another decision, the poet was firmly put in his place. The university council man-

[94] Kleineidam, *Universitas Studii Erffordensis*, II, 196.

[95] Delitzsch's teaching activity between 1505 and 1511 is recorded in Erler, ed., *Die Matrikel der Universität Leipzig*, II, 419, 423, 429, 437, 441, 445, 451, 455, 460, 463, 468.

[96] Stübel, *Urkundenbuch*, 272.

[97] Hutten et al., *The Letters of Obscure Men*, ed., Hajo Holborn (New York: 1964), 37, 38.

dated that Locher's main lectures, along with those of the astronomer, were to be restricted to the vacation period in late summer and early fall between the summer and winter semesters.[98] It was a time when the university was largely deserted, and the only teaching was offered by recent recipients of the bachelor's degree. Humanist teaching was to remain secondary to the university's main academic concerns.

~ ~ ~

THIS CHAPTER should not leave the impression that in the early 1500s peaceful coexistence and fruitful cooperation between humanists and scholastics never occurred. Heinrich Bebel taught at Tübingen for close to twenty years without experiencing undue friction with university officials. Other salaried humanists such as Balthasar Phaccus at Wittenberg, Ulrich Zasius at Freiburg, and Angelo Cospi,[99] the Italian who succeeded Conrad Celtis in 1506 at Vienna, had teaching careers free of controversy or any signs of "scholastic opposition." Even embattled poets whose careers at some point had been engulfed by major controversy were capable of settling into a more placid academic groove. Buschius, perhaps heeding Trithemius's advice to moderate his alcoholic intake, overcame the instability of his early career and taught without major incident at Cologne between 1508 and 1518. Contentiousness was also absent during Locher's second tenure as salaried poet at Ingolstadt between 1506 and 1522. He continued to publish actively and remained a popular teacher, but the excesses of his early years were abandoned. On September 17, 1517, at age 45, he married a young woman named Ursula in a celebration attended by many local dignitaries and academics. The couple soon produced a son, Johann Paul. When the poet died in 1528, the faculty senate of the University of Ingolstadt voted to send the widow the sum of ten florins, "with many speaking on the poet's behalf."[100]

---

[98] Bauch, *Die Anfänge*, 78, 79.
[99] Aschbach, *Geschichte der Universität Wien*, II, 278-81.
[100] Hehle, *Der Schwäbische Humanist Jacob Locher Philomusus*, Part 2, 49.

But by the time the Ingolstadt senate made this gesture, the academic and intellectual atmosphere had fundamentally changed, not only at this Bavarian institution but throughout Germany. Nor should the examples of peaceful coexistence be allowed to cloud the condition of most German universities in the early 1500s, which at best can be described as one of uneasy tension between traditionalists and humanist innovators. The universities of Germany were no longer the purely scholastic institutions they had been throughout much of the fifteenth century. Humanism had by now gained a recognizable niche in German academic life. But it was as yet unclear whether its role would continue to expand; it was still uncertain if the revered scholastic authorities would be maintained or abandoned. Issues such as these would soon be resolved, but only after Germany had witnessed one of the most celebrated intellectual controversies of the pre-Reformation era: to historians it is known as the Reuchlin affair.

*T*he Reuchlin Affair ~

NOTHING has had more impact on modern interpretations of German humanism than Johannes Reuchlin's vehement and protracted controversy with the theologians of the University of Cologne. Since the nineteenth century, most historians have viewed the Reuchlin affair as the classic confrontation between humanism and scholasticism. Here was undeniable proof that humanism and scholasticism were irreconcilable opposites, and their proponents implacable enemies. It is true, of course, that the feud was long and bitter. It is true that it produced the greatest anti-scholastic masterpiece of the Renaissance, *The Letters of Obscure Men*. It is also true, however, that the clever mockeries of works like *The Letters* have misled many historians, resulting in distorted assessments of both the nature and extent of the controversy.[1]

THE COURSE OF THE CONFLICT

The events of the Reuchlin affair are well known and require only a brief summary.[2] It began in 1504, when at age thirty-

[1] This chapter is based on the author's previously published article, "A New Look at the Reuchlin Affair," *Studies in Medieval and Renaissance History* 8 (1971), 167-207.

[2] Accounts of the events are contained in Ludwig Geiger, *Johann Reuchlin, sein Leben und seine Werke* (Leipzig: 1871), 203-454; Max Brod, *Johannes Reuchlin und sein Kampf* (Stuttgart: 1965), 178-270; Salo Wittmayer Baron, *A Social and Political History of the Jews*, 2nd ed., 14 vols. (New York: 1952-1969), XIII, 182-91; Heinrich Graetz, *Geschichte der Juden*, 4th ed., IX (Leipzig: 1907),

six a Moravian Jew, Joseph Pfefferkorn, converted to Catholicism along with his wife and children. Changing his name
to Johann and moving to Cologne, he became a religious
zealot obsessed with converting his former co-religionists to
Christianity. In 1507 he began to publish a series of slanderous
anti-Jewish pamphlets, which among other things argued that
confiscation of Jewish books would facilitate conversions to
Christianity.[3] In 1509 he managed to gain a hearing with
Emperor Maximilian, at which he sought imperial approval
for a campaign to confiscate and examine Jewish books for
possible anti-Christian statements. At the urging of his wid-
owed sister, the pious Abbess Kunigunde, the emperor readily
complied. Thus on September 28, 1509, Pfefferkorn, along
with three priests and two municipal officials entered the syn-
agogue in Frankfurt-am-Main, seized all Hebrew books and
transferred them to the city hall for examination. In the following weeks, similar confiscations took place in Mainz and
several smaller towns.[4] But in 1510, Archbishop Uriel von
Gemmingen of Mainz, who considered Pfefferkorn's campaign an infringement of his jurisdiction, temporarily ordered
an end to the convert's activities. In the same year Maximilian
withdrew his original mandate and ordered the archbishop of
Mainz to seek out several expert opinions before the confis-

63-195; English translation without footnotes, *History of the Jews*, IV (Philadelphia: 1897), 383-422. A thorough bibliography of the works written in
the controversy can be found in Ulrich von Hutten, *Operum Supplementum*,
ed. Eduard Böcking, 2 vols. (Leipzig: 1864, 1869); hereafter cited as Böcking,
Supplement.

[3] Among these early works were *Speculum adhortationis judaice ad Christum*
(Cologne: 1507); *Ich heyss eyn Buchlyn der Juden beicht* (Cologne: 1508); *Ich
bin ain Buchlinn der Juden veindt ist mein namen* (Cologne: 1508); *Libellus de
Judaica confessione sive sabbato afflictionis* (Cologne: 1509); *In disen Buchlein vindet
Jer ain entlichenn fürtrag wie die blinden Juden yr Ostern Halten unnd besunderlich
wie das Abentmal gessen wirt* (Cologne: 1509); Böcking, *Supplement*, II, 55-69,
lists the full titles of Pfefferkorn's books and the various reprints and translations.

[4] On Pfefferkorn and his activities around Frankfurt, see Meier Spanier,
"Zur Charakteristik Johannes Pfefferkorns," *Zeitschrift für die Geschichte der
Juden in Deutschland*, 6 (1893), 209-29; I. Kracauer, "Die Konfiscation der
hebraichen Schriften in Frankfurt," *Zeitschrift für Geschichte der Juden in
Deutschland*, 1 (1886), 160-76, 230-48.

cations continued. In the summer of 1510 the archbishop asked for written statements on the issue from the theologians of four universities—Cologne, Mainz, Erfurt, and Heidelberg. He also sought opinions from three individuals—Jacob von Hochstraten, a Dominican theologian from Cologne and the Inquisitor of Heretical Pravity in Germany; Victor Karben, a converted Jew who had become a priest; and finally Johannes Reuchlin, the famous Hebrew scholar.

Of the seven responses, only Reuchlin argued against the suppression of Hebrew writings. As a result, in 1511 a specially appointed imperial commission recommended that the confiscation and examination of Jewish writings be resumed. But a close friend of the emperor, Duke Eric I of Brunswick-Kalenberg, encouraged Maximilian to halt Pfefferkorn's activities. The duke, it seems, owed money to certain Frankfurt Jews and in the hope of gaining an extension of his loan, took their side in the dispute over confiscation.[5] In any case, the emperor rejected the commission's recommendation. His campaign frustrated, in 1511 Pfefferkorn published another pamphlet, entitled *Hand Mirror against and opposed to the Jews, and Jewish Talmudic Writings.*[6] It contained the usual anti-Jewish calumnies but also something new: personal attacks on the scholarship and character of Reuchlin. Blaming him for the emperor's unfavorable decision, Pfefferkorn argued that the humanist had damaged the Church and given comfort to the Jews. It also claimed that Reuchlin had accepted Jewish bribes and that a Jewish imposter had written his scholarly books. In response, Reuchlin published a book of his own, the *Augenspiegel (Eye Mirror)*, which contained his original opinion on confiscation and brief rebuttals to fifty-two statements in Pfefferkorn's book.[7]

At this point the Cologne theologians further entangled

[5] Baron, *A Social and Religious History of the Jews*, XIII, 186, 187.

[6] *Handt Spiegel wider und gegen die Juden, und Judischen Thalmudischen schrifftenn* (Mainz: 1511).

[7] *Doctor J. Reuchlins . . . warhafftige entschuldigung gegen und wider ains getaufften juden genant Pfefferkorn vormals getruckt ussgangen unwarhaftigs schmachbüchlin. Augenspiegel* (Tübingen: 1511).

themselves in the controversy. Pfefferkorn sent them the *Augenspiegel* for examination, and, after Reuchlin refused to recall published copies of the work, one of the theologians, Arnold of Tungern, published a book that described "forty-four errors" in the *Augenspiegel*.[8] Reuchlin countered with yet another work, *Defense against his False Accusers of Cologne*.[9] He reiterated his position on confiscation and harshly berated Pfefferkorn and his supporters in Cologne.

With the publication of Reuchlin's *Defense* the controversy rapidly escalated. Upon the urging of the Cologne theologians the emperor suppressed Reuchlin's *Augenspiegel* and his *Defense*. The Cologners also sent copies of the *Augenspiegel* to the theology faculties of Louvain, Mainz, and Erfurt. Concurring with Cologne, all three faculties condemned the work.[10] In the fall of 1513, Hochstraten called Reuchlin before his court of inquisition in Mainz; but before any decision was reached, the archbishop of Mainz halted the trial on the grounds of several legal technicalities. Meanwhile Reuchlin had appealed to Leo X, who in turn passed the matter to the Bishop of Speyer. In March 1514 the bishop decided in Reuchlin's favor. He denied that the *Augenspiegel* was heretical and ordered Hochstraten to stop his harassment of Reuchlin.

Now it was Hochstraten's turn to appeal to the pope; he spent several years lobbying in Rome for the condemnation of the *Augenspiegel*. Meanwhile in northern Europe, interest

---

[8] *Articuli sive propositiones de judaico favore nimis suspecte ex libello theutonico domini Joannis Reuchlin legum doctoris . . . cum annotationibus improbationibus venerabilis et zelosi viri magistri nostri Arnoldi de Tungeri* (Cologne: 1512).

[9] *Defensio Joannis Reuchlin contra calumniatores suos Colonienses* (Tübingen, 1513).

[10] According to an excerpt from the records of the Cologne theology faculty, the theologians of the universities of Ingolstadt and Frankfurt an der Oder also condemned the *Augenspiegel*. This may have been an error or wishful thinking on the part of the Cologne theologians, since there is no mention of these added condemnations in any source. Furthermore, if the condemnations had actually occurred, Reuchlin's opponents would undoubtedly have publicized them as they did with every other anti-Reuchlin proclamation. See A. Kober, "Urkundliche Beiträge zum Reuchlinischen Streit," *Monatsschrift für Geschichte und Wissenschaft des Judentums*, 67 (1923), 113.

in the controversy intensified. Following the publication of his *Defense* in 1513,[11] Reuchlin published *Letters of Distinguished Men written in Latin, Greek, and Hebrew, sent to Johannes Reuchlin* in 1514.[12] This was a collection of flattering letters received by Reuchlin during his scholarly career and of course was the inspiration for the more renowned *Letters of Obscure Men*, the first edition of which was published anonymously in late 1515. Meanwhile, the University of Paris condemned the *Augenspiegel* in August 1514. Even powerful rulers became involved: Charles of Hapsburg, having just inherited the Netherlands, and Francis I both wrote the pope recommending suppression of the *Augenspiegel*; Emperor Maximilian wrote the pope on Reuchlin's behalf. With powerful men on both sides, the pope temporized by appointing another commission to examine the various arguments. Meanwhile in Germany the war of words continued, as Reuchlin's supporters and detractors kept dozens of printers busy publishing satires, slanders, arguments, and counterarguments. The controversy was finally settled only in 1520, when Pope Leo X formally condemned the *Augenspiegel*. By then Hochstraten had already turned his attention to combatting a more dangerous foe, the Augustinian friar from Wittenberg, Martin Luther. Reuchlin quietly accepted the decision and two years later, shortly after having been ordained as a priest, died at age sixty seven.

Although the Reuchlin affair has been described in countless books and articles, there has been surprisingly little disagreement about its significance. Most historians have assumed that the attack on Reuchlin was a veiled strike at humanism and that the controversy in essence was a conflict between humanism and scholasticism. The Cologne theologians were the leaders of a scholastic campaign to discredit not just Reuchlin but the whole humanist enterprise. Hatred of Jews and the questions involving the Jews' books were merely side issues. Ludwig Geiger, in his biography of Reuchlin, argued that

[11] See note 9, above.
[12] *Clarorum virorum epistolae latinae, graecae et hebraicae missae ad Johannem Reuchlin* (Tübingen: 1514)

anti-Jewish fanaticism was an important consideration only at the beginning, but that once Reuchlin and the theologians became involved, the affair became a battle for "free expression" on the part of the humanists.[13] Another nineteenth-century historian of German humanism, Carl Krause, wrote: "It was soon recognized that it was really barbarism, intolerance and fanaticism which were struggling for victory with learning and a freer way of thinking, that with the intended attack on Reuchlin, every branch of knowledge not buttressed on Church authority—and that in principle was humanism—was threatened."[14]

More recently, Paul Joachimsen has argued that the matter of Jewish books was insignificant, and that the controversy was a pure struggle of humanism against the "scholastic monks' faction."[15] And Hajo Holborn has written, "what embittered the theologians and evoked the condemnation of the universities of Germany" was not Reuchlin's opinion on Jewish books, but his use of philology "for a new interpretation of Biblical passages." In Holborn's opinion, "the humanists were endangered. Basically the question was not simply as to the retention of the Jewish books, but as to something much more fundamental. Should the humanists have a voice in the Church?"[16]

A few Jewish writers have stressed the prominence of religious fanaticism in the controversy, but their views have been largely ignored. As a result, textbooks and popular accounts routinely depict the controversy as a conflict between two ideologies in which the status and even survival of humanism was at stake. In a typical fashion, the most recent

[13] This is the argument developed in Chapter 6 of Geiger, *Johann Reuchlim*, 321-67.

[14] Carl Krause, *Helius Eobanus Hessus, sein Leben und seine Werke*, I (Gotha: 1879), 167, 168.

[15] Paul Joachimsen, "Der Humanismus und die Entwicklung des deutschen Geistes," *Deutsche Vierteljahrsschrift für Litteraturwissenschaft und Geistesgeschichte*, 8 (1930), 460, 461.

[16] Hajo Holborn, *Ulrich von Hutten and the German Reformation* (New York: 1965), 56.

edition of the *Encyclopedia Britannica* states, "The dispute aligned the entire European liberal and Humanist community against the speculative doctrine of the university Scholastics."[17] Of course it would be foolish to argue that tension between humanism and scholasticism played no part in making the Reuchlin affair the long and acrid controversy that it was. But it would be equally foolish to argue that the relationship between humanism and scholasticism was the only or overriding issue in the feud. In this chapter we will reassess the Reuchlin affair. The first section will examine the writings of the actual participants—Reuchlin and his opponents; it will show that, for most, the status of the Jews and their books was a more important issue than the status of humanism or scholasticism. The second section will attempt to clarify the nature of German humanist involvement in the controversy and to show that humanist support for Reuchlin was less universal and less enthusiastic than most writers have assumed.

An Anti-Jewish or Anti-Humanist Crusade?

It should be clear, even from the brief preceding summary, that the Reuchlin affair can be understood only in the context of the deep current of anti-Jewish prejudice that ran through late medieval society.[18] Pfefferkorn and his allies, for example, were hardly original when they demanded the examination and destruction of Hebrew writings. Burning Jewish books had been a time-honored custom among zealous friars and vigilant inquisitors since the 1230s, when thousands of Hebrew books were fed to the flames in Montpellier and Paris. For medieval man, Jews were objects of frustration because of their stubborn rejection of Christianity; they were also

[17] "Johann Reuchlin," *The New Encyclopedia Britannica. Micropaedia*, 15th edition (Chicago: 1980), Vol. 8, 535.

[18] Baron, *A Social and Political History*, vols. IX-XIII, is the best treatment of this subject. See also Wilhelm Grau, *Antisemitismus in späten Mittelalter* (Berlin: 1939) and Edward A. Synan, *The Popes and the Jews in the Middle Ages* (New York: 1967).

objects of fear and resentment because of their ability to survive, and sometimes prosper, despite their spiritual blindness
and the hatred of their Christian neighbors. For some, wild
fantasies developed in which the Jews came to be viewed as
semi-humans capable of the grossest immoralities, the deepest
hatreds, and the blackest crimes.[19] According to this perverted
vision, Jews emitted a fetid stench, had tails and horns, and
suffered from grotesque diseases, curable only by Christian
blood. They were a "demonic" people, immersed in sorcery
and magic, arts they mastered through pacts with the devil
or the Antichrist. Especially distressing was their obsessive
hatred of all things Christian. They were mockers and blas-
phemers, desecrators of the host, allies of heretics, murderers
of Christian children. As Joshua Trachtenberger has stated,
"The only Jew whom the medieval Christian recognized was
a figment of his imagination."[20] It is hardly surprising that in
times of religious frenzy, such as the Crusades, or of psy-
chological tension, such as the Black Death, people vented
their hatreds by attacking the "demonic" Jews.

Several aspects of late medieval anti-Jewish sentiment are
particularly significant for understanding the Reuchlin affair.
First, sentiment for persecuting Jews had always been especially strong within the Dominican order, to which Hochstraten and Tungern belonged. A Dominican, for example,
had inspired the mass burning of Jewish books in France in
1233.[21] The Dominicans, in their role as inquisitors, had also
been largely responsible for bringing the Jews under the jurisdiction of the Inquisition, despite the fact that the Jews were
not true heretics, i.e., fallen Christians. The zeal of the friars
occasionally provoked the censure of high Church officials
and secular rulers, who for practical or humanitarian reasons,
sought to protect the Jews and their property. In 1448, for
example, Pope Nicholas V warned the inquisitors to ignore

---

[19] See Baron, *A Social and Political History*, XI, 122-191, and Joshua Trachtenberger, *The Devil and the Jews* (New Haven: 1945), *passim*.

[20] Trachtenberger, *The Devil and the Jews*, 216.

[21] *Ibid.*, 178.

the Jews except in clear cases of blasphemy or anti-Catholic activity.[22] Second, one of the great centers of anti-Jewish activity had always been the German Rhineland. Rhineland Jews had suffered fearfully during the Crusades, and Rhineland towns had been among the first in Germany to expel their Jewish populations.[23] A spawning ground for mystics, demonology, witch-mania, and magic, this area also produced Pfefferkorn's small circle of anti-Jewish disciplines. Finally, attacks on Jews, after decreasing in the early 1400s, revived dramatically at the end of the fifteenth century.[24] German Jews experienced renewed harassment, and many German towns that had not already done so banished the Jews and confiscated their property.[25] This new wave of anti-Jewish sentiment provides the background for Pfefferkorn's campaign and goes far in explaining the support he received from universities, rulers, and the Dominican order.

Early in the controversy, only one person, Reuchlin, was concerned that Christian scholarship might be affected by Pfefferkorn's campaign. For the converted Jew and his supporters—Hochstraten, Karben, and the universities—support for confiscation grew out of simple prejudice toward the Jews. The anti-Jewish opinions submitted to the emperor by the

---

[22] *Ibid.*, 180.

[23] Norman Cohn, *The Pursuit of the Millennium* (New York: 1961), 50, 51.

[24] H. R. Trevor-Roper, "The European Witch-Craze of the Sixteenth and Seventeenth Centuries," in *The European Witch-Craze of the Sixteenth and Seventeenth Centuries and Other Essays* (New York: 1968), 90-192, points out that the Dominicans were the instigators and leaders of the anti-witch and anti-Jew mania that bloomed in the late fifteenth century. In 1484, in his bull *Summis desiderantes affectibus*, Innocent VIII authorized two Dominican inquisitors, Heinrich Institor and Jacob Sprenger, to halt the spread of witchcraft in Germany, especially in the Rhineland (*ibid.*, 101-102). These same German Dominicans, writes Trevor-Roper, were responsible for extending the anti-witch, anti-Jew mania "down the Rhine" after 1450 (p. 111).

[25] Baron, *A Social and Political History*, XI, 275, provides a partial list of the cities that expelled Jews between 1432 and 1520. Few Rhineland towns are included, simply because they had done thorough jobs in previous purges. Having been all but annihilated in rioting following the Black Death, the Jews in Cologne reestablished a small community in the late 1300s. They were expelled, however, in 1424. *Ibid.*, IX, 176.

universities in 1510 showed no hint of anti-humanism, no hint of opposing Hebrew for biblical studies.[26] In each of them the expressed motive was to strike at Jewish "perfidy" and "blind stubbornness." This can be seen most clearly in the opinion of Cologne, which recommended not only confiscation, but also that Jews be forced to refrain from usury, engage in manual labor, hear Christian sermons, and wear distinctive badges. Later in 1510, when the imperial commission recommended in favor of Pfefferkorn's crusade, it specifically made a point of protecting Christian scholars by stipulating that all condemned Jewish books be copied on parchment and placed in a "Christian library."[27]

Although those who supported Pfefferkorn did so to damage the Jews, Reuchlin must have viewed the anti-Jewish crusade as a threat to his personal intellectual commitments. He must have known that fanatics like Pfefferkorn would be unlikely to bother with copying manuscripts before feeding them to the fire. He must have nurtured the fear that valuable Hebrew manuscripts would be destroyed needlessly. Thus to a certain extent Reuchlin believed that humanism, or more accurately, Christian Hebrew scholarship, might be damaged by mass confiscations.

It would be wrong, however, to assume that Reuchlin defended the Jews' right to keep their books simply to protect himself as a humanist and Hebrew scholar. He opposed Pfefferkorn's campaign not only because it threatened his work but also because it offended his lawyer's sense of justice and equity. Although he disdained the Jews' religion, he considered them to be fellow human beings whose legal rights and

---

[26] Pfefferkorn printed the opinions of Mainz, Cologne, and Hochstraten in his *Defensio . . . contra Famosas obscurorum virorum Epistolas* (Cologne: 1516). I have used the nineteenth-century edition printed at Leipzig in 1864. The opinions can be found on pp. 27-43. He claimed that the opinions of Karben and Erfurt agreed with the others and were not printed because of their length. Brief summaries of the opinions favoring confiscation may be found in Graetz, *History of the Jews*, IV, 444, and Baron, *A Social and Political History . . .* , XIII, 187.

[27] Geiger, *Reuchlin*, 239.

religious practices should be protected as long as they lived peacefully. In explaining his position in 1513, he wrote:

> I favor the Jews to the extent that they do no injustice and are also subjected to no injustice. I deem it the natural bond of life and human decency that we are required to treat a man, who is even a sinner, as not excluded from or denied the law. For injustice is beastliness, banishing all human feeling. Those who strive for it, driven by base greed or hateful arrogance, are such monstrous beasts that they differ not at all from the nature of wild animals.[28]

He argued that Jews, like Christians, "are the lambs of Christ, for whom he died." They were also fellow citizens (*concives*) of the empire who should have protection from injustice. Finally, they were human beings and were to be respected as such. He wrote: "Since I say that the Jews are our brothers, brothers of Arnold of Tungern, brothers of all the Cologne 'theologists,' not only because we have the same heavenly father from whom all come, but also because they are descended from the same parent on earth as we are; although they may not be members with us, nevertheless they are our brothers."[29]

Most historians have assumed that Reuchlin's enlightened attitude derived from his interest in Hebrew literature and his desire to protect the interests of Christian humanists like himself. At least as important, however, were his training and

[28] "Ita faveo judaeis ut injuriae non subjeceant & injuriam non faciunt, haec mihi visa est naturalis vitae societas & human consyderatio, qua hominem etiam peccatorem a jure non expulsum neque prohibitum tractare jubemur. Injusticia enim est immanitas omnem humanitatem repellens, cuius qui sunt appetentes vel turpi quaestu vel odiosa superbia moti, tanquam immanes beluae nihil absunt a natura ferarum." *Defensio Joannis Reuchlin contra calumniatores suos Colonienses* (Tübingen: 1513), H. iiiib.

[29] ". . . quia dico judaeos esse fratres nostros, fratres Arnoldi, fratres omnium thelogistratum Coloniensium, non tum quia unum patrem omnium habeamus in caelis, unde omnis paternitas, verum etiam qui ex eodem nobiscum parente in terris generati sunt, qui licet non sint nobiscum membra, tamen sunt nobiscum fratres. . . ." *Ibid.*, I.

long practice as a lawyer and judge.[30] Unlike most of his fellow humanists, who taught or lived on patronage, Reuchlin was an active lawyer who had served as adviser to the dukes of Württemberg, as judge on the supreme court of the Swabian League, and as legal counsel for, of all people, the German Dominicans. Significantly, law was one aspect of medieval life where Jews were generally treated with objectivity, equality, and fairness.[31] As a graduate of the University of Orleans and as a practicing lawyer, Reuchlin was well acquainted with this tradition of justice for Jews. And his devotion to this tradition substantially contributed to his opposition to confiscation and his abhorrence of Pfefferkorn's motives and tactics. In much that he wrote and did in the long controversy, it was Reuchlin the lawyer, not Reuchlin the humanist, who spoke.

In the opinion he submitted to the emperor in 1510, Reuchlin took his strongest arguments against confiscation from civil and canon law.[32] He maintained that Jews, as subjects of the emperor, had the same legal rights as Christians. Among those rights was protection against seizure of property either by force or without due process of law. In addition, Reuchlin cited passages from civil and canon law that stated that Jews could maintain their synagogues and perform their ceremonies without interference. The core of his argument was that the confiscation and destruction of Hebrew literature was illegal. The law stipulated that Jews should be able to keep all

[30] Guido Kisch, *Zasius und Reuchlin* (Constance: 1961), 23-36, is one of the few books to argue that legal training rather than scholarly interests inspired Reuchlin to defend the Jews.

[31] Guido Kisch, "The Jews in Medieval Law," in *Essays on Anti-Semitism*, ed. Koppel S. Pinson (New York: 1946), 103-111; Kisch, *The Jews in Medieval Germany* (Chicago: 1949).

[32] The original copy of Reuchlin's opinion is no longer extant. But Reuchlin published it in an extended and modified form in his *Augenspiegel* (Tübingen: 1512), B-E ii c; a facsimile has been printed in *Quellen zur Geschichte des Humanismus und der Reformation*, ed. Bernhard Wendt, 5 (Munich: 1964); also printed with a modern German translation in Johannes Reuchlin, *Gutachten über das Jüdische Schriftum*, ed. Antoine Leinz-von Dessauer (Stuttgart: 1965); for a discussion of Reuchlin's general attitudes toward the Jews, see Kisch, *Zasius und Reuchlin*, particularly 23-36.

their writings except those which mocked or slandered Christ, the Virgin, the apostles, or saints. Reuchlin agreed that according to law, such books should be destroyed, and that after a fair trial, their owners punished. But he added that in all Jewish literature, only two such blasphemous books existed.

Thus Reuchlin's 1510 opinion on confiscation was not a humanist manifesto or even an *apologia* for his own intellectual pursuits. He did, it is true, utilize a few "humanist" arguments to oppose Pfefferkorn. He insisted that Christian scholars should study Hebrew and Jewish biblical commentaries to deepen their understanding of the Old Testament. Furthermore, the Talmud and the Cabala were also worthy of study, for they explained many divine mysteries, and in some passages even confirmed Christian beliefs. But these discussions did not make up a significant part of Reuchlin's opinion.[33] More important were the legal arguments, previously mentioned, and others based on Scripture, Church authority, and common sense. Reuchlin was skeptical, for example, that confiscating Hebrew literature would cause Jews to denounce their faith and flock to the Church. If anything, it would strengthen Jewish resentment and make their conversion more unlikely. He proposed that Christians should study, not burn, Hebrew literature, so they could convince Jews of their errors. He quoted Aristotle that "a wise man not only speaks the truth, but is capable of opposing falsehood." He added that a knowledge of Hebrew literature would prevent Christians from carrying on "beer-table" debates, where "fist-pounding takes the place of knowledgeable argumentation."[34] Furthermore, he was perplexed over the sudden need to convert all Jews; after all, the Church had existed fourteen centuries and the Jews had never seriously damaged it.[35]

---

[33] Quantitatively, in Von Dessauer's modern version of Reuchlin's opinions, three or four pages out of fifty are devoted to these "humanist" arguments.

[34] Reuchlin, *Gutachten*, 43.

[35] "Und das hat die cristenlich kirch also by den 14 hundert jar gelitten und geduldt und hat es nie für kainen schmach angenommen." *Ibid.*, 87.

Reuchlin expanded these arguments in the *Augenspiegel*. It is clear in this work that Reuchlin sought to combat anti-Jewish fanaticism, rather than scholasticism or anti-humanism. He directed his arguments against Pfefferkorn and the misguided zeal that had inspired the anti-Jewish campaign. In fact, Reuchlin was shocked when he learned in October 1511 that the Cologne theologians had decided to examine the *Augenspiegel* for errors. To trade arguments with the uncultured Pfefferkorn was one thing; to contend with the powerful Dominicans at Cologne was quite another.

For several months Reuchlin sought to avoid a conflict with the Cologne scholastics. Just two days after receiving news of the impending examination, he sent off flattering, obsequious letters to two members of the Cologne theology faculty. To Arnold of Tungern he wrote that he was joyous because "such a learned and skilled man" was to direct the examination of the *Augenspiegel*; he added that he was looking forward to seeing his criticisms. He expressed his respect for scholastic theology and assured Tungern that he had no grudge against any university, especially "the most splendid University of Cologne." He conceded that he was a lawyer, not a theologian, and that "whatever therefore the Holy Church, which is the column and foundation of truth, believes, and however it believes, I will also believe the same."[36] He warned, however, that "no law, no canon, no public decree, no rule of the universal church" sanctioned the burning of Jewish books. In his letter to Conrad Collin, another Cologne scholastic, he was equally humble.[37] But Reuchlin's letters failed to placate the theologians. After quickly "examining" Reuchlin's book, they demanded a retraction, claiming that the *Augenspiegel* was "scandalous, ill-sounding, and offensive to pious

---

[36] "Fateor enim: in scholis theologiam non didici, sed civiles leges, quare vestram disputandi rationem ignoro. . . . Quisquid igitur sancta ecclesia quae est columna et firmamentum veritatis credit, et qualitercumque credit idem ego et taliter credo." Johannes Reuchlin, *Briefwechsel*, ed. Ludwig Geiger (Tübingen: 1875), 139.

[37] *Ibid.*, 140-44.

ears."[38] Reuchlin refused to acquiesce, and now chances for compromise became remote.

The possibility of compromise all but disappeared in the spring of 1512, when both Tungern and Pfefferkorn published books against the *Augenspiegel*. Pfefferkorn's *Fire Mirror* (*Brandspiegel*) included the usual anti-Jewish, anti-Reuchlin slanders, and was not in any way anti-humanistic. Tungern's work, entitled *Articles or Propositions suspected to be too favorable to the Jews* lacked the *Brandspiegel*'s crudeness, but in theme and motive the two books were similar: both were products of their authors' aversion for the Jews. Despite its subtle argumentation and its copious citations from Scripture, the Church fathers, and previous scholastics, Tungern's long discourse was basically an exercise in hate. The stereotype of the demonic Jew had penetrated Tungern's mind. Jews' synagogues are "witches temples," full of impiety;[39] Jews are "clever, cunning snakes" who blaspheme God, Christ, the Virgin, and the sacraments;[40] they are avaricious usurers, "murderers and destroyers of the poor";[41] they are sordid and unhappy men, "despised even by pagans."[42] In countless passages the Talmud is depicted as immoral, blasphemous of the Church, and filled with magic, sorcery, and other sources of Jewish wickedness. To Tungern, Jews were despicable and deserved no forbearance or sympathy. Certainly they should not be permitted to keep their books.

The most important part of Tungern's work consisted of a discussion of forty-four erroneous statements that the theologian had discovered in the *Augenspiegel*. None of his criticisms can be construed as anti-humanistic.[43] He even con-

---

[38] *Ibid.*, 146-48.

[39] Arnold von Tungern, *Articuli . . .* , B i.

[40] *Ibid.*, B iii.

[41] *Ibid.*, E iii b.

[42] *Ibid.*, B i.

[43] Although little is known about Tungern's life, there is evidence that he sympathized with at least some humanist ideas. In 1525, while rector, he initiated steps at the University of Cologne which, if successful, would have

ceded that an acquaintance with Hebrew grammar and Jewish commentaries might benefit Christian biblical scholarship. He merely complained that Reuchlin overemphasized the need for such knowledge; he stressed that the issue was not whether Christians should use Jewish books, but whether Jews could keep them.[44] He presented no strong arguments against studying the Cabala, except to deny Reuchlin's assertion that Alexander VI had openly approved it.[45] Otherwise, Tungern's forty-four "errors" had no connection with humanism. Many of them challenged Reuchlin's legal opinion that Jews held legal rights as imperial subjects. Others rejected Reuchlin's argument that the Jews were not heretics since they had never been members of the Church. He also accused Reuchlin of misunderstanding the nature of the Talmud (Tungern eagerly pointed out that Reuchlin admitted never having read it); of misinterpreting previous authorities (Aquinas had urged only the study of the Old Testament, not the Talmud and other rabbinical writings); and of erroneously claiming that the Church had no right to pass judgment on non-Christian writings. Tungern also attacked Reuchlin's interpretation of certain biblical passages. He did this not because the humanist had used "philology to change their meaning," but because he had used them to oppose confiscation. For example, the two men disagreed over the interpretation of *Matthew* XIII in which Christ compared the kingdom of heaven to a field where weeds were planted along with grain. In the parable, the owner told his servants to let the weeds grow, "lest in gathering the weeds you root up the wheat along with them." Reuchlin argued that the parable might be applied to the confiscation controversy, with the "weeds" symbolizing Jewish

---

introduced certain humanist precepts into Cologne's scholastic curriculum. See Franz Joseph von Bianco, *Die älte Universität Köln*, I (Cologne: 1855), 470-74.

[44] "Et forte parum videretur si solum christiani hec legerent, sed quod judei qui nunc libellos in manibus habent, hoc judicium de scriptoribus nostris legere debeant ex viro christiano an expediat pensent quorum maxime interest." *Articuli*, E ii.

[45] *Ibid.*, E i b.

books. Tungern naturally disagreed, claiming that the "weeds" symbolized human beings rather than books.[46]

That Tungern was motivated by anti-Jewish prejudice rather than anti-humanism becomes even more apparent in the second section of his work. Neglecting Reuchlin and the *Augenspiegel* completely, it contained a list of slanders against the Jews, replete with commentary, and for the sake of convenience, arranged in alphabetical order. On reaching Z, he arrived at the climactic conclusion: "Let the princes and prelates of the church be more strongly fired by their Zeal for the faith than is necessary, so that they should do enough to root out from their districts all errors regarding the divine, heresies and insults to the almighty God, to the extent that on the dreaded day of strict judgment they may be able to give account of themselves that their opportunities (*talenti*) were excellently committed."[47] Clearly, Tungern's *Articles or Propositions* shows that the author attacked Reuchlin not because he was a humanist, but because Tungern considered him a patron and protector of the Jews.

This can also be said of the condemnations of the *Augenspiegel* by the Universities of Mainz, Louvain, Erfurt, Cologne, and Paris between 1512 and 1514. Nothing in the condemnations suggests that the book was condemned because its author was an eminent humanist who recommended Hebrew for biblical study. The judgment of Louvain stated, "we are unanimously of the opinion that that book has been sprinkled here and there with various errors and assertions somewhat suspect to the faith and especially contains agreements with the perfidious stubbornness of the Jews."[48] The Mainz

---

[46] *Ibid.*, D iiii c, D iiii d.

[47] "Zelo idcirco fidei (quo oportet) fortuis accensi principes ac ecclesiae prelati exterminare satagant ab area divini errores, hereses et contumelias omnipotentis die quatenus in expavendo die districti judicii rationem reddere valeant talenti sibi magnifice commissi." *Ibid.*, R iii a.

[48] Pfefferkorn, *Defensio*, 112. In the *Defensio* Pfefferkorn included the condemnations of the *Augenspiegel* in addition to other anti-Reuchlin letters and documents. There is no reason to suspect that Pfefferkorn attempted to alter the wording or change the sense of the various documents.

theologians wrote, "we have found opinions offensive to pious ears and producing scandal among the young, disgorging irreverence for the sacred doctors, nourishing approval for the perfidious Jews, and otherwise suspect of heresy."[49] The Cologne theologians condemned the *Augenspiegel* because it argued that the "Talmud and certain other books of the Jews should not be burned," and because it was "favorable to Jewish falsehood."[50] The Paris condemnation of 1514 called the book "false, temerarious, scandalous, erroneous, offensive to pious ears, contumelious, and blasphemous to the Church." Why? Because it defended the Talmud and was "manifestly favorable to the Jews."[51] Not one of these opinions referred to Reuchlin's connection with humanism. In fact, the condemnation by the University of Erfurt went out of its way to praise Reuchlin's piety and humanistic learning. It called him "a most learned man of singular and pre-eminent erudition, capable of three languages—Hebrew, Greek and Latin— widely famed by the integrity of his life and morals, a good and Catholic Christian, submitting himself and his case to the Roman Church, and practiced in the free discourse of the orators and philosophers."[52] Hardly the language one might expect from scholastic theologians launching a "veiled attack on humanism!" Nevertheless Erfurt condemned the book: although it was beyond the intention of the author, the book scandalized simple Christians and "gave comfort to the perfidious Jews in their blindness." Nor did the condemnation of the *Augenspiegel* by Hochstraten differ from those of the universities; he asserted, "it smells of heresies, contains many

[49] *Ibid.*, 121.

[50] *Ibid.*, 114.

[51] *Ibid.*, 126-29.

[52] ". . . invenimusque auctorem ipsius alioquin singularis ac preeminentis eruditionis virum doctissimum, triplicis linguae, hebraice, graece, atque latine peritissimum celebri fama de vite ac morum integretate nobis multipliciter commendatum, et prout commendabilis sua testatur protestatio, quam consultationi sue et premisit et subjexuit, bonum ac catholicum christianum, se sua que Romane ecclesie determinationi humillime subiicentem, forensium philosophorumque more liberis verbis usum. . . ." *Ibid.*, 118.

errors more favorable to the perfidious Jews than is fitting, is injurious to the Church, irreverent to the holy doctors and highly scandalous to the simple members of the faith."[53]

The anti-Reuchlin pronouncements by "non-scholastic" parties, namely Emperor Maximilian, Francis I, and the future emperor Charles of Hapsburg, also support the contention that Reuchlin's alleged favoritism for the Jews rather than his association with humanism was the main issue for his opponents. All three rulers had humanist sympathizers among their councilors and were generous patrons of the humanist movement. They, like the universities, condemned the *Augenspiegel* because of its alleged favoritism to the Jews. When, for example, Emperor Maximilian banned the sale of the *Augenspiegel* in 1512, he did so because it contained many articles "useful for the sale of Jewish books" and "strengthened the Jews in their obstinate blindness."[54] Charles's letter to the pope urged the condemnation of Reuchlin's book because "it quite clearly contained knowledge to help and strengthen the Jews."[55] The letter of Francis I to the pope cited the condemnations by Cologne and the other universities and alleged that the *Augenspiegel* helped Jews in their stubbornness and contained "heresies against our holy Catholic faith."[56]

Thus for the first four years of the Reuchlin affair, the relative merit of humanism and scholasticism simply was not an issue. Neither Reuchlin nor his adversaries attacked each other's learning or scholarly preferences. But as the dispute dragged on, restraint wore thin, especially for Reuchlin's supporters. Even the pious, soft-spoken Reuchlin found it impossible to avoid invective, name-calling, and attacks on his opponents' intellectual interests. This becomes apparent in

---

[53] ". . . pronunciamus, decernimus et declaramus memoratum libellum hereses sapientem, et errores multos continentum perfidis Judeis plus quam deceat favorabilum ecclesie die injuriosum, ac sacris ecclesiae doctoribus irreverentialem, christefidelium maxime simplicum scandalisatinum. . . ." *Ibid.*, 124-25.

[54] *Ibid.*, 100.

[55] *Ibid.*, 146.

[56] *Ibid.*, 144, 145.

1513, when in response to Tungern's *Articles*, he published his *Defense of Johannes Reuchlin against his False Accusers of Cologne*.[57] In this work, Reuchlin combined a repetitious defense of the *Augenspiegel* with personal attacks on the learning and motives of his opponents. In the case of Tungern, Hochstraten, and the other Cologne theologians, this meant a denunciation of scholastic theology, the first meaningful attack the aging humanist had made.

It was, nevertheless, a moderate and unoriginal attack. Only in one passage, where he mocked the Cologner's obsession with logic and dialectic, did Reuchlin censure scholastic methodology in general. Taking his arguments from St. Jerome, he stated that "the dialecticians, it is said, including Aristotle, who is their prince, are accustomed to spread their nets of argumentations and compress the unrestricted freedom of rhetoric into the thornbushes of syllogism."[58] Reuchlin insisted that logic should have a place in everyone's education. It was one of several methods of discourse, and it was useful in teaching young boys to differentiate truth from falsehood. But it was lamentable for grown men to devote all their energy to such matters. After a person had studied the liberal arts, philosophy, and theology, it was laughable "to sink back to elementary things, to play as boys with their babblings and show themselves learned in foolish and inquisitive sophisms."[59]

Except for this brief swipe at the scholastics' predilection for logic, Reuchlin was careful to aim his attacks not against scholastic theology in general, but only against the small handful of theologians from Cologne who were his opponents. Speaking of theologians elsewhere, he wrote:

---

[57] See above, note 9.

[58] "Dialectici, ait & Aristoteles qui Princeps est solent argumentationum retia tendere, & vagam rhetoricae libertatem in syllogismorum spineta concludere." *Defensio* . . . , C ii b.

[59] "Sed hoc turpe duco, post artes & philosophiam viro ad sublimem illam theologiae facultatem evecto, relabi ad elementa, & cum pueris balbutiendo ludere, ac se ingeniosum in vanis & curiosis sophismatibus ostentare." *Ibid.*

Knowledge of true theologians is a divine light descended from the Father above—something which the outstanding doctors and masters of theology of other universities have: through their heavenly wisdom the world is enlightened, through their piety, brotherly love is enhanced and cherished; nature has fashioned them to honesty, seriousness, temperance, justice, learning, and humanity; by their learned authority and example of good living human society is strengthened and peace in the body and members of Christ is kept indivisible.[60]

But Reuchlin denied that the Cologners deserved the title "theologians." "I refuse," he wrote, "to call my false accusers of Cologne theologians; they are false theologians, rejected counterfeits." He referred to his adversaries as "theologists," so that "none of the true theologians of other universities will bear a grudge against me."[61] He argued that Hochstraten and Tungern had usurped the name theologian either through "robbery or trickery": "Puffed up with human learning, they do not blush to deceive both in life and talk; they offer work only in contentions and quarrelsome disputes, for which they are all armed with a language of trickery; they have turned their backs on good actions."[62] In other words, there was a wide chasm between theologians and theologists—a difference

[60] ". . . sed verorum theologorum scientia est divina desursum a patre lumens descendens quam habent aliquarum universitatum praeclarissimi doctores & magistri theologiae, quorum caelesti sapientia mundus illustratur, quorum pietate fraterna caritas incenditur & incensa fovetur, quos natura ad honestatem finxit, gravitatem, temperantiam, justiciam & benevivendi exemplo societas humana confirmatur & pax in christi corpore atque memoris indissoluta custoditur." *Ibid.*, C iii.

[61] ". . . quos equidem solos calumniatores meos Colonienses nequeo vere theologos appellare, sed falsos theologos sicut nummos reprobos . . . ego posterius notiore vocabulo theologistas appellabo, ne mihi quisquam aliarum universitatum de sancto coetu virorum theologorum succenseat." *Ibid.*, C i b.

[62] "Cuius rei tam sanctum nomen vel de rapina vel furto sibi calumniatores mei arrogant, etiam quacunque humana scientia inflati, qui & vita & lingua mentiri non erubescunt, qui solis operam dant contentionibus & rixosis disputationibus, ad quod artificium linguas armant, longe a tergo bonarum actionum relicitis officiis." *Ibid.*, C ii.

between "virtue and vice, between good and bad, between the false and the true."[63]

Significantly, Reuchlin made all his comparisons between the scholastic theologians of Cologne and scholastic theologians of other universities. He did not compare them to humanists like Erasmus, Lefèvre, and himself, whose scholarly interests touched on religious matters. Furthermore, these attacks on the learning of his opponents took up only a few paragraphs in a book of more than one hundred pages. In most of it, Reuchlin reiterated his arguments in favor of preserving Jewish books.

As the controversy continued, the issue of Jewish books diminished in importance for Reuchlin. He did not even answer the later works of Hochstraten and Pfefferkorn that recommended confiscation. For a time in 1513 and 1514, he even wondered if the attack on himself was part of a larger "conspiracy" to subvert and discredit humanism. In 1513 he suggested to Jacques Lefèvre that his opponents attacked him simply because he knew Greek and Hebrew. "The pure pride of my barbarian adversaries," he wrote, "could not bear with calm mind that posterity, imbued with more honorable teaching, might condemn their puerile studies and anile disciplines."[64] And in November 1514, after the Paris theologians condemned the *Augenspiegel*, he wrote a friend that a plan was afoot at the University of Louvain to attack Erasmus; he feared that as soon as he and Erasmus were suppressed, all humanists would be endangered.[65] But Reuchlin's suspicions about a developing anti-humanist plot were short-lived. He saw that Louvain did not suppress Erasmus, that the German universities did not move against their humanists, and that his own opponents did not grow beyond the small band of Co-

---

[63] "Magnum igitur chaos, maxima intercapedo, & notissima inter theologos & theologistas differentia est, qualis inter virtutem & vitium inter bonum et malum inter fucatum et veram, tam & si nullo discrimine omnes vulgo theologi appellantur." *Ibid.*

[64] Reuchlin, *Briefwechsel*, 199.

[65] *Ibid.*, 231.

logners. After 1514, he abandoned the "conspiracy theory" altogether.

Instead, Reuchlin's behavior after 1514 shows that his first priority was to defend his own reputation rather than the goals and ideals of humanism. After all, his opponents had accused him of spreading heresy, confusing simple Christians, favoring the Jews, intellectual dishonesty, and much else. To bolster his reputation was the main purpose of the *Letters of Distinguished Men* (1514). In 1519 he produced a similar volume, *Letters of Illustrious Men*, which contained letters written to him during the conflict with the Cologners.[66] Reuchlin wrote nothing after 1514 designed to discredit scholasticism or to defend humanism. In his *Concerning the Cabalistic Art* (1517) and *Concerning Accents and Orthography of the Hebrew Language* (1518), critical references to scholasticism were rare and restrained—as they had been before the controversy began.

Among the anti-Reuchlinists, Pfefferkorn continued to be the most energetic pamphleteer after 1513. Apparently he hoped that, once Reuchlin had been discredited, he could resume his campaign against the Jews. In 1514, he published a brief pamphlet, *Alarm Bell (Sturm Glock), about and against the Jews*. Its purpose was to publicize the condemnation of the *Augenspiegel* by the University of Paris.[67] In 1516 he published a more extensive work, *Defense of Johannes Pfefferkorn against the Notorious and Criminal Letters of Obscure Men*.[68] Although he repeated his attacks on Reuchlin's learning (saying that Reuchlin paid Jews to write his books) and denounced the *Letters of Obscure Men*, which had just been published, Pfefferkorn did not condemn humanism. He recounted the history of the controversy, defended his own actions, and printed numerous

---

[66] *Clarorum virorum epistolae latinae, graicae & hebraicae . . . missae ad Joannem Reuchlin* (Tübingen: 1514); J. Reuchlin, *Illustrium virorum epistolae* (Hagenau: 1519).

[67] *Sturm Glock Johannis Pfefferkorns uber und wider die Juden . . .* (Cologne: 1514).

[68] See above, note 26.

mandates and opinions against Jewish books and the *Augen-spiegel*. Then in late 1516 or early 1517, he published another pamphlet, *Little Book of Quarrel (Streitbüchlein)*, whose specific goal was to refute the slanders against him in the *Letters of Obscure Men*.[69] The last of Pfefferkorn's anti-Jewish compositions appeared in 1521,[70] almost a year after the papal condemnation of the *Augenspiegel* had, for all other parties, brought the controversy to a close.

It is not surprising that zealous Pfefferkorn, who was neither an intellectual nor an academic, failed to attack humanism and restricted himself to defending his plan to confiscate the Jews' books. But what of the theologians? How did they react to the attacks on scholasticism contained in the *Letters of Obscure Men* and some of the other pro-Reuchlin writings? With one exception, they remained silent. Only Jacob von Hochstraten took an active part in the pamphlet war after 1514. He entered the literary battle in 1518, after having spent several years in Rome unsuccessfully urging Leo X to condemn the *Augenspiegel* and its author. His failure in Rome and the mockery of the humanists must have stung a man like Hochstraten. As doctor of theology at the prestigious University of Cologne, as inquisitor-general for Germany, and as a prominent Dominican, he was used to having his own way on religious questions.[71] Furthermore, he seems to have relished intellectual combat. Before his involvement with Reuchlin, he and Peter of Ravenna had carried on a protracted controversy that forced the Italian jurist to give up his position at the University of Cologne. The conflict involved Ravenna's assertion that German princes were wrong to allow the corpses of executed criminals to rot on the gallows for extended periods.[72]

---

[69] *Streydt peuchlyn vor dy Warheit und eyner warhafftiger Joannis Pfefferkorn Vechtende* (n.p.: n.d.).

[70] J. Pfefferkorn, *Ein mitleydliche claeg uber alle claeg an unsern aller gnedlichsten Kayser und gantze deutsche Nation* (n.p: 1521).

[71] Hochstraten has attracted little scholarly interest. See, however, Hubert Cremans, *De Jacobi Hochstrati Vita et Scriptis* (Bonn: 1869).

[72] H. Heindenheimer, "Petrus Ravennas in Mainz und sein Kampf mit den Kölner Dunkelmännern" *Westdeutsche Zeitschrift für Geschichte und Kunst,* 16

And as previously mentioned, with the onset of the Reformation, Hochstraten quickly became the major anti-Lutheran writer in northwestern Germany and the Low Countries.

It would thus appear that his aversion to the Jews, an inability to accept defeat, and an earnest desire to uphold traditional sources of ecclesiastical authority drove Hochstraten doggedly to seek the condemnation of the *Augenspiegel* long after his fellow theologians had let the matter drop. His objections to Reuchlin's *Augenspiegel* were succinctly stated in a small pamphlet, *Erroneous Assertions in Reuchlin's Augenspiegel*, published in Rome in 1517.[73] In the pamphlet, Hochstraten argued that Reuchlin's defense of Jewish literature was as damnable as the hersey of the Hussites.[74] For proof, Hochstraten listed nineteen erroneous statements from the *Augenspiegel* and offered brief rebuttals. Most of the errors had already been noted in Tungern's *Articles or Propositions*. But Hochstraten bore down especially hard on Reuchlin's defense of the Talmud. He must have known that his case against the Talmud was strongest; after all, Gregory IX and Innocent IV, urged on by Dominicans, had ordered its burning in the thirteenth century.[75] In all, about half of the alleged errors dealt with Reuchlin's defense of the Talmud, a work in which Reuchlin had no real scholarly interest. The others concerned Reuchlin's interpretation of civil and canon law, his assertion that the Church had no power over works by non-Christians, and his claim that the Apostles, especially Paul, were well-versed in rabbinical literature.

Having failed to quash his opponent in Rome, Hochstraten took to the printed page when he returned to Germany, pro-

---

(1897), 223-256; Theodor Muther, *Aus dem Universitäts-und Gelehrtenleben im Zeitalter der Reformation* (Erlangen: 1866), 95-128; Charles G. Nauert, Jr., "Peter of Ravenna and the 'Obscure Men' of Cologne: A Case of Pre-Reformation Controversy" in *Renaissance Studies in Honor of Hans Baron*, ed. Anthony Molho and John Tedeschi (DeKalb, Ill.: 1971), 609-640.

[73] *Erronee assertiones in oculari Speculo Jo. Reuchlin verbatim posite & conclusiones per magistrum Jacobum de alta platea eisdem obiecte* (Rome: 1517).

[74] *Ibid.*, A iii d.

[75] Synan, *The Popes and Jews in the Middle Ages*, 11.

ducing no less than three lengthy books in 1518 and 1519. His first *Apology* censured a pro-Reuchlin dialogue written by an Italian ecclesiastic, George Benignus. His *Second Apology* answered criticisms of the first, and his third, *Destruction of the Cabala*, disparaged Reuchlin's cabalistic studies.[76] For the most part, the three books rehashed the old objections to the *Augenspiegel* that the Cologne faction had repeated with tiresome regularity since the feud began: Reuchlin twisted the sense of the Scriptures; he encouraged Jewish perfidy; he offended the Catholic Church; he misinterpreted previous writers. He was berated for defending the Talmud and for asserting that Jews were subjects of the emperor (if this was so, Hochstraten pointed out, pigs and donkeys must also be subjects).[77] In his smaller *Second Apology*, Hochstraten answered criticisms of his first work and republished the nineteen "erroneous assertions" that had already been printed in Rome. Little in either *Apology* referred to humanism. In the introduction to his first *Apology*, he deplored the anti-scholastic taunts of Reuchlin and his supporters, but in the body of the work, he stuck to the issue of confiscation. And in the *Second Apology* his only reference to humanism occurred when he answered a critic who had mocked his Latin style. Rejecting the humanist ideal of eloquence, he contended that as long as a book defended Christ, its literary form was irrelevant.[78]

Even Hochstraten's *Destruction of the Cabala* can hardly be construed as a general attack on humanism. It is true that it rejected the arcane Hebraic studies that intrigued Reuchlin. Its main argument was that since Jews refused to accept Christ, they had only an imperfect conception of God; therefore their writings were erroneous, heretical, and dangerous. To study their books served to strengthen the Jews by weakening the

---

[76] Jacob von Hochstraten, *Apologia . . . contra dialogum Georgio Benigno Archiepiscopo Nazareno in causa Joannis Reuchlin ascriptum* (Cologne: 1518); *Apologia secunda contra defensionem quandam in favorem Joannis Reuchlin* (Cologne: 1518); *Destructio Cabale seu Cabalistice perfidie ab Joanne Reuchlin* (Cologne: 1519).

[77] *Apologia . . . contra dialogum*, B biv b.

[78] *Apologia secunda*, A vi a.

faith of Christians. In Book IV he argued that the best approach to theology was not through the Cabala, but through traditional scholastic methods: the analysis of Scripture and other authorities by dialectic and logic. Arguments such as these were definitely aimed at one aspect of the humanist program for the rejuvenation of philosophy and theology. But it was an aspect of humanism that interested only Reuchlin and a handful of others. The interests of most humanists— the pursuit of Latin eloquence, the reform of grammar teaching, the revival of Greek—were not even mentioned in the *Destruction of the Cabala*. It was largely a compilation of isolated statements from Reuchlin's works that Hochstraten criticized as erroneous or contradictory. Furthermore, its goal was no different from the purpose of the previous anti-Reuchlin literature: by denigrating Reuchlin's scholarship and his enthusiasm for Hebrew studies, he sought to undermine the argument that Jewish books should be preserved because of their value for Christians.

Only one book in the entire controversy was directed against humanism rather than Reuchlin's arguments against confiscation. This was the *Lamentations of Obscure Men*, a collection of satirical letters that first appeared in March 1518 and was republished in an extended version several months later.[79] It was not written by Hochstraten, Tungern or any other scholastic theologian, but rather by Ortwin Gratius, the ill-fated Cologne humanist who had sided with Pfefferkorn. As is well known, Gratius received a vicious lambasting in the *Letters of Obscure Men*; less well known is the fact that he was a skilled Latinist and a supporter of humanist ideas. Having studied at the school of the Brethren of the Common Life in Deventer, he went to Cologne, where after receiving his Master of Arts he served as an editor for a local publisher and taught poetry

---

[79] *Lamentationes obscurorum virorum* (Cologne: 1518); several further editions were published in the sixteenth and seventeenth centuries; I have used the version printed in *Defensio J. Pfefferkorn contra famosas Obscurorum Virorum Epistolas* (Leipzig: 1864).

and rhetoric at the university.[80] In an oration delivered in 1507, Gratius, with his copious praise for classical literature, sounded no different from any young humanist launching his academic career.[81] Older humanists felt he had great promise. Wimpfeling called Gratius one of Germany's best poets,[82] and even Erasmus remarked that he was "endowed with great genius."[83]

But Gratius shared Pfefferkorn's aversion for Judaism and was the convert's ally from the start. He translated Pfefferkorn's early pamphlets into Latin and later composed a poem that embellished Tungern's *Articles or Propositions*. In it he attacked Reuchlin, claiming that because of the *Augenspiegel*, a great crime had been perpetrated: the forces of Hell triumphed, the Virgin wept, and Jesus again suffered his wounds.[84] In 1514, he edited an anti-Reuchlinist book of his own.[85] Sandwiched between his preface and conclusion were several documents (the condemnations of the *Augenspiegel* by the universities and Tungern's forty-four "errors") and an account of Reuchlin's trial at Mainz. Like the Erfurt theologians, he praised Reuchlin's learning and linguistic accomplishments. But he deplored Reuchlin's defense of Hebrew literature; repeating arguments advanced by the universities, he warned that Reuchlin's opinions confused Christian laymen and gave support to the Jews.

Gratius paid dearly for opposing Reuchlin. In the *Letters of Obscure Men*, he was accused of everything from writing bad

[80] Dietrich Reichling, *Ortwin Gratius, sein Leben und Wirken* (Heiligenstadt: 1901); James Mehl, "Ortwin Gratius, Cologne Humanist," Diss., University of Missouri, 1975.

[81] Ortwin Gratius, "Orationes quodlibeticae," in Hans Rupprich, ed., *Humanismus und Renaissance in den deutschen Städten und an den Universitäten* (Leipzig: 1935), 149-57; James Mehl, "Ortwin Gratius' *Orationes Quodlibeticae*: humanist apology in scholastic form," *The Journal of Medieval and Renaissance Studies*, 11 (1981), 57-69.

[82] Jacob Wimpfeling, *Contra turpem libellum philomusi*, Chap. 6.

[83] Francis M. Nichols, ed., *The Epistles of Erasmus*, 3 vols. (New York: 1962), III, 416.

[84] Reprinted in Böcking, *Supplement*, II, 78, 79.

[85] Ortwin Gratius, *Hoc in opusculo contra speculum oculare Joannis Reuchlin Phorcensius hec in fidei et ecclesie tuitionem continentur* . . . (Cologne [?]: 1514).

poetry to sleeping with Pfefferkorn's wife. The *Lamentations* was an attempt by a bruised humanist to beat the Reuchlinists at their own game. In his collection of letters, the "humanists"—Hans Leverworst, Petrus Olfontianus, Pultronus Sycophanta, Guilhelmus Capniolambius, and many others—are the "obscure men" whose correspondence makes them appear ridiculous.

As the title suggests, most of the letters concocted by Gratius were simply "lamentations"—expressions of despair and confusion on the part of the Reuchlinists because of supposed setbacks.[86] In letter after letter, correspondents painfully recount their disappointments: Leo X has condemned the *Letters of Obscure Men*, and the great Erasmus has criticized it; Pfefferkorn has sent a letter to the pope "full of sound arguments"; Hochstraten has written an *Apology* "very damaging to Reuchlin's cause." In the second edition of the *Lamentations*, the "humanists" complain about the drubbing they took in the first edition! Other letters tell how Jews were rejoicing because of Reuchlin and his followers. In one epistle, Trullus Pomivendulus relates that the Jews were reading Reuchlin's works in their "diabolical synagogues"; they mocked Christians and rejoiced because they could retain their blasphemous books.[87]

Gratius also depicted the Reuchlinists as pagans and enemies of the Church. Several "lamentors" admit being in league with the Anti-Christ, while others correspond with Gog and Magog, their "princes." In return, Gog and Magog urge them to keep up their "rashness, arrogance, impudence, blindness, obstinance, foolishness, heresy, and blasphemy."[88] In one letter, Simprianus concedes that Reuchlinists are "irrational and degenerate Christians," who debase "both good and wise men and Christ and the Virgin."[89] In another, Johannes Peltzflicker

---

[86] Examples of the "lamentation" type of letter are numbers 1, 7, 9, 10, 11, 17, 26, 33, 37, 42, from the first edition; 1, 9, 10 from the second.

[87] *Lamentationes*, 265.

[88] *Ibid.*, 274.

[89] *Ibid.*, 259.

describes a meeting of Reuchlinists where Christ had been blasphemed and the cross defiled.[90] Many letter writers boast of their love of sorcery and magic.

In a few letters, Gratius belittled the intellectual interests of the humanists. In one exchange Schelmo demands some information from Genselinus, a "very learned grammarian," so he could "overshadow the theologians in debate." Specifically, he wants to know what kinds of birds were mentioned in the grammar text by Donatus; he also wants to know what the birds ate and where they flew. Genselinus responds that Donatus mentions three birds—sparrow, eagle, and hawk— all of which "ate fruit" and "flew in the forest." After conveying this information, he warns: "Beware my dearest Schelmo, that you do not make manifest these occult mysteries of Minerva to the theologians, since such remarkable things are not to be found in commentaries on the *Sentences*."[91] Another writer boasts that theologians could never best the Reuchlinists in debate, for "they do not know the poets or the mysteries of our letter writing, nor have they studied the fifteenth book of Aristotle's *Physics*, the *De anima* of Porphyry, or the metaphysics of Aesop."[92] Of course the *Physics* contained only eight books, Porphyry had not written *De anima*, and Aesop was no metaphysician. In another exchange, Johannes Grap, a "new poet," writes to Armulphus Codrianus that he had read in Aristotle that the three principles of physics were "matter, privation, and form." Grap feels this is ridiculous, since he could not find these principles "in the epigrams of Martial, the satires of Horace or the work of any other poet." Codrianus responds that whoever prefers the "old philosophers to the poets, knows only smoke and rancid fat." Furthermore, Aristotle had made a "horrendous mistake" in naming the principles of physics. Codrianus argues they were actually "air, earth, and sea": "From the air in fact rain falls to the earth, which again and again produces inebriating drinks,

[90] *Ibid.*, 210.
[91] *Ibid.*, 238, 239.
[92] *Ibid.*, 264, 265.

lions, wild boars, cows, bulls and other necessary brute beasts. And the sea grants fish so we do not drop dead in the road during Lent." He added that Grap should not worry if he could not find such information in Scotus or Albertus Magnus.[93]

But as Gratius made clear, his satire was not intended to discredit all humanists. In a lengthy letter published at the end of the *Lamentations,* he denied that he wanted to offend either Reuchlin or most of his supporters. He conceded that there were many good poets, or humanists, in Germany, and that many good and honorable men had sided with Reuchlin. Reuchlin had blundered by supporting the Jews; yet he was a "Catholic man and a distinguished poet." As for Reuchlin's supporters, he wrote: "Johannes Reuchlin surely has on his side noble, learned, erudite and eloquent men who are very devoted to him; some of them have disputed on the field of battle (something we cannot curse). In addition, he has for himself many worthy young men and several studious professors of the arts whom we all honor and venerate."[94] Only the Reuchlinists who had composed the *Letters* were worthy of hatred and reproach.

In summary, opposition to humanism was not a prime motive for Reuchlin's detractors, and their writings offer no suggestion that they viewed the controversy as a show-down between the principles of humanism and scholasticism. What they sought from the outset was a justification for confiscating Jewish books. If after 1514, they attacked or satirized certain limited aspects of humanist scholarship, it was because the humanists had provoked them and because one humanist, so they thought, had thwarted their original plans. Humanism, however, was never the central issue. If Reuchlin had been a physician or philosopher, there is no reason to believe that Pfefferkorn and his learned allies would have pursued him with any less vigor.

[93] *Ibid.,* 290.
[94] *Ibid.,* 352.

The fact that opposition to Reuchlin was centered entirely at Cologne also supports this interpretation. Several other universities—Paris, Louvain, Erfurt, and Mainz—condemned the *Augenspiegel*, but only because of its favoritism to the Jews. Even after the appearance of the *Letters of Obscure Men*, no scholastic outside Cologne published anything against Reuchlin or his humanist supporters. No other German university gave financial support to the Cologners to help pay the costs of the various judicial processes. Nor did the passions raised during the Reuchlin affair cause any reaction against humanists teaching at the German universities. On the contrary, in the final years of the Reuchlin affair the humanists began to attain many of the reforms of scholastic education for which they had worked since the 1450s.

German Humanists and the Reuchlin Affair

Another commonplace assumption in most accounts of the Reuchlin affair has been that humanist support for Reuchlin was universal and overwhelmingly enthusiastic. For most historians, it was unthinkable that any self-respecting German humanist could remain silent while the forces of scholastic barbarism threatened to undermine the whole humanist enterprise. But this premise about humanist participation in the Reuchlin affair also demands close scrutiny. In fact, humanist support for Reuchlin developed slowly; it was often tentative, and it was never universal.

The behavior of Reuchlin's fellow humanists before 1514 further supports the contention that the status of humanism was not an issue in the early years of the controversy. With few exceptions, humanists ignored the squabble over confiscation. Conrad Mutian, Willibald Pirckheimer, and several Viennese humanists wrote to Reuchlin after the appearance of the *Augenspiegel*. Rather than offering their support for Reuchlin, they expressed dismay that the humanist had bothered with Pfefferkorn at all. Writing in 1512, Joachim Vadianus, a Viennese humanist, wished Reuchlin well, but added that he hardly felt it necessary to spend so much time refuting a mere "baptized Jew."[95] Pirckheimer expressed similar sentiments early in 1513. He scolded Reuchlin for ever answering the "semi-Jew." In so doing Reuchlin had lent Pfefferkorn a measure of fame he never would have attained on his own merits.[96]

Two humanists even gave public support to Reuchlin's antagonists. Ortwin Gratius has already been mentioned; the other was Hermann Buschius, then teaching poetry and rhetoric at Cologne. He later became Reuchlin's ardent supporter, but in 1512 he composed a poem that was printed with Tungern's *Articles*. Entitled "Elegy to the Jews and the Perverted Jew-lovers," it described the faith's triumph over the Jews and their benefactor, Reuchlin.[97] As late as January 1514, Buschius still had doubts about the advisability of supporting Reuchlin. At that time he wrote to Johannes Murmellius that he regretted Reuchlin's involvement in the conflict.[98] Only in March 1514, after meeting with Reuchlin, did he finally come over to the Hebrew scholar's side.

Extensive humanist support for Reuchlin did not develop until 1514, and even then it was never unanimous. The better-known Rhineland humanists—Wimpfeling, Sebastian Brant, and Ulrich Zasius—all remained aloof from the controversy. Reuchlin tried to enlist the support of Wimpfeling and Brant in 1513 by writing Wimpfeling a long, plaintive letter that described the conflict.[99] But neither responded, and their writings during the 1510s fail to mention Reuchlin's difficulties. Nor did Wimpfeling's other close friend, Zasius, ever publicly support Reuchlin. In 1513 a Viennese Reuchlinist sent Zasius a copy of Reuchlin's *Defense*, but Zasius, who had strong anti-

---

[95] Reuchlin, *Briefwechsel*, 169.

[96] *Ibid.*, 167.

[97] ". . . in Judaeos Judaeorumque amatores praeposteros Elogium." Printed by Geiger, *Reuchlin*, 361.

[98] Karl and Wilhelm Krafft, *Briefe und Documente aus der Zeit der Reformation im 16. Jahrhundert* (Elberfeld: 1876), 129.

[99] Reuchlin, *Briefwechsel*, 200-207.

Jewish sentiments, never did anything on Reuchlin's behalf.[100] Others too remained silent. Among them were two veterans of previous conflicts with scholastics—Johannes Aesticampianus and Jacob Locher. Nor is there any evidence that Reuchlin's fellow Swabian, Heinrich Bebel, ever expressed support for Reuchlin's cause.

Some humanists publicly sided with Reuchlin but privately questioned his actions. This was the stance of Conrad Mutian, the Erfurt humanist often depicted as one of Reuchlin's strongest defenders. Considering his intellectual interests, one would certainly have expected him to be an enthusiastic Reuchlinist. He detested scholasticism and, like Reuchlin, was a speculative humanist, interested in the revival of the *prisca theologia*. But Mutian's correspondence shows that he actually disapproved much that Reuchlin did in the controversy.

Mutian began following the dispute in 1510, when Reuchlin, Hochstraten, Karben, and the four universities submitted their opinions on confiscation. At the time, Mutian observed it was foolish to consult the universities, since the theologians could never catch the "truths of the Talmud" or the "mysteries of the Cabala in their dialectical nets." He added that he opposed the suppression of Hebrew literature, agreeing with "a whole crowd of learned men that it was a Christian thing to tolerate the quibblings of nonconformists." Besides, if Jewish literature was condemned, "you would have to give up the writings of the prophets, the reading of which is rather frequent in the churches, no one can deny."[101]

In 1512 and 1513, Mutian frequently referred to the controversy. In the fall of 1512, when the Cologne theologians

---

[100] *Ibid.*, 209. Kisch, *Zasius und Reuchlin*, describes Zasius's anti-Jewish sentiments; Brant and Wimpfeling may have shared his prejudices but, in all likelihood, their intellectual and religious conservatism sufficed to keep them from participating in the affair.

[101] "Sed Bessarion et omnis eruditorum coetus conset ex re esse christiana tolerare recutitiae gentis cavillationes; quibus accedo. Nam si aliter facias, relinquare prophetas necesse habes, quorum lectio quam sit in aede sacra frequens, nemo est qui nesciat." Konrad Mutian, *Briefwechsel*, ed. Carl Krause (Kassel: 1885), 194.

condemned the *Augenspiegel*, he complained that Reuchlin was being harassed by "men uncultivated in Greek and Latin, not to say Hebrew."[102] When in May 1513, the emperor banned the sale of Reuchlin's *Defense*, he wrote excitedly, "Alas! Alas! Truth is with no protector. It has been overcome by barbarism. The unlearned judge the learned!"[103] But Mutian hesitated to support Reuchlin openly. Although he urged his young disciples to write Reuchlin, he had no correspondence with the embattled humanist until the summer of 1516. His failure even to send Reuchlin a letter was an embarrassment to his younger followers. Heinrich Urban made excuses for him, informing Reuchlin in October 1513 that Mutian could not write because "he was busy working in the vineyards."[104] In 1513, when the *Augenspiegel* was submitted to the University of Erfurt for examination, Mutian seemed about to take a more active role. On September 10, he asked Urban to send him the names of the Erfurt rector and deans. He promised he would "urge, warn, ask, and implore" them to do justice for Reuchlin.[105] Whether Mutian carried through is uncertain. In any case, it would have been a meaningless gesture, for Erfurt had already condemned the *Augenspiegel* on September 3. When Mutian finally wrote Reuchlin, his letters were bland and noncommittal. In one he expressed sympathy over the death of Reuchlin's friend, Eitelwolf von Stein.[106] In another, he congratulated Reuchlin after the temporary suspension of the Roman trial in 1516 and assured him that he had numerous young supporters at Erfurt.[107]

Why was Mutian so reserved? The answer is that he had serious doubts about Reuchlin's behavior in the controversy. As early as October 1512, he asserted that Reuchlin had "erred

---

[102] *Ibid.*, 225.
[103] "Heu, Heu! Veritas patrono caret. Barbaria dominantur. Indocti de doctis judicant." *Ibid.*, 296.
[104] *Ibid.*, 386.
[105] *Ibid.*, 375.
[106] *Ibid.*, 562, 563.
[107] *Ibid.*, 645.

here and there" in the *Augenspiegel*.[108] In March 1514, he objected to the language of a handsheet distributed by Reuchlin at Mainz during his heresy trial. Although Reuchlin had been seriously attacked, Mutian noted that he had spoken "not without anger and madness" and had sinned for "too bitterly defaming his adversaries." He decided that Reuchlin must now be considered a man skilled in five languages—Greek, Hebrew, Latin, Swabian, and "slander-Latin" (*malelatina*).[109] Mutian expressed his doubts most thoroughly in a letter written at the time of the imperial ban of Reuchlin's *Defense*. In Mutian's opinion, Reuchlin had erred by expressing doctrines "offensive and confusing to the unlearned laymen of the Church." Mutian had always believed that the arcane secrets of philosophy and theology should be reserved for the learned and not exposed to the common people. He had written in 1510, "we know in fact that mysteries must not be popularized, but are to be suppressed in silence or else treated under the coverings of fables or riddles."[110] Reuchlin, he felt, had ignored this rule in both the *Augenspiegel* and the *Defense*: "He should have acted more moderately to spare the ears of the cloistered, not to offend the pious ears of the simple people and the beliefs of the crowd; he should not have placed his own honor before these considerations. To refute the authority of the Church, even if you are detecting errors, is contumelious and full of impiety when you are a member of the body."[111] In no way, he continued, should a learned man do anything to weaken the beliefs of the multitude, for when this happened, anarchy and chaos would be the certain result.

Erasmus's behavior also fails to support the usual generalizations about humanist participation in the Reuchlin af-

---

[108] *Ibid.*, 259.

[109] *Ibid.*, 404.

[110] *Ibid.*, 13.

[111] "Modestius igitur agere debuit, monastarum auribus parcere, non offendere pias aures simplicium et vulgi opinionem propriis honoribus anteferre. Aucoritatem ecclesiae refellere, cum sis hujus corporis membrum, et contumeliosum est et plenum impietatis, etiamse errores deprehenderis." *Ibid.*, 353.

fair.[112] He, like Mutian, was reluctant to support Reuchlin openly; and again like Mutian, his reluctance is at first surprising. He knew and admired Reuchlin's work, and in fact, shortly after Reuchlin's death in 1522, he composed a brief colloquy in his honor, *The Apotheosis of the Incomparable Worthy Johannes Reuchlin.*[113] Erasmus described how the angels and saints, led by St. Jerome, welcomed Reuchlin into heaven, while "the sky overhead parted asunder, displaying an inexpressible majesty." But while Reuchlin was living, Erasmus was hesitant to utilize his prestige and literary talent to further Reuchlin's cause. His activity was limited to 1515, when, after Hochstraten had appealed Reuchlin's case to Rome, he briefly mentioned Reuchlin's problems in letters to two Italian cardinals. In both of these long epistles—one to Cardinal Domenico Grimani, the other to Cardinal Raphael Riario—Erasmus restricted his brief comments on Reuchlin to the concluding paragraphs.[114] He expressed admiration for Reuchlin's scholarship and sorrow that the humanist's old age was being disturbed. He hoped that the two cardinals could do something to end the dispute. Now that European monarchs were at peace, he noted, "how absurd it is for men of learning to carry on war with books and controversies, and that while the former have their weapons sheathed, the latter should be stabbing each other with books and poisons."[115]

Writing these two terse paragraphs was the extent of Erasmus's involvement on behalf of Reuchlin. After 1515, his activity was motivated by two concerns. First, he hoped to end the controversy by convincing the participants of its triv-

---

[112] For a brief summary of Erasmus's role in the affair see Werner L. Gundersheimer, "Erasmus, Humanism and the Christian Cabala," *Journal of the Warburg and Courtauld Institutes,* 26 (1963), 38-52; also important is Guido Kisch, *Erasmus' Stellung zu Juden und Judentum* (Tübingen: 1969).

[113] Erasmus, *De incomparabili heroe Joanne Reuchlino in divorum numerum relato*; English translation in Craig R. Thompson, ed., *The Colloquies of Erasmus* (Chicago: 1965), 79-86.

[114] The two letters are printed in Francis Nichols, ed., *The Epistles of Erasmus,* II, 183-194, and in P. S. Allen, ed., *Opus epistolarum Des. Erasmi Roterdami,* 11 vols. (Oxford: 1907-47), II, 68-79.

[115] Nichols, *Epistles of Erasmus,* II, 193-94.

iality and by imploring them to exercise moderation. Second, he hoped to convince the learned world that he had no interest or stake in Reuchlin's cause. He might admit a sympathy for Reuchlin, but he stressed repeatedly that the disputed issues had nothing to do with himself or his own intellectual activities.

From the start, Erasmus found the controversy upsetting and distasteful, especially the harsh language and name-calling of some of the polemicists. After reading Reuchlin's *Augenspiegel* and *Defense* in 1514, he wrote Reuchlin a letter praising the two books' "spirit and eloquence" and "exuberance of learning." But like Mutian, he urged Reuchlin to avoid crude language: "I should have liked you to be more sparing of digressions found in commonplaces, and moreover, to have abstained from outright invective."[116] Later, in 1517, he tried to convince Reuchlin that little could be gained by continuing the dispute. After attacking the "half-Jew, half-Christian" Pfefferkorn, he advised Reuchlin to ignore him, for "it is for us, my dear Reuchlin, to turn our backs upon such portents, and to find our pleasure in Christ."[117]

Erasmus expressed similar sentiments to other Reuchlinists. In November 1517, he wrote Pirckheimer about a composition in which the Nuremberg patrician had assailed Reuchlin's detractors. He praised Pirckheimer's eloquence but then stated that Pirkheimer should have avoided the controversy. "It was calamitous," he wrote, "to carry on warfare with a sordid and disreputable foe" like Pfefferkorn and the Dominicans. He concluded, "while you are scouring the field against the dialecticians and philosophers, I should have preferred to see you give your whole attention to the matter in hand, and leave other persons and other things to the care of themselves."[118] He was also critical of the younger Reuchlinists, especially Ulrich von Hutten and the other contributors to the *Letters of Obscure Men*. He claimed, for example, to have

[116] *Ibid.*, 156-58.
[117] *Ibid.*, III, 149.
[118] *Ibid.*, 113-15.

"taken pains" in 1515 to suppress publication of Hutten's poem, *Reuchlin's Triumph.*[119] He expressed his strong disapproval of the *Letters of Obscure Men* in two letters written in August 1517. He wrote Johannes Caesarius, a Cologne humanist, that "their pleasantry might amuse at first glance," but that their offensive language and personal invective were both indefensible.[120] He reiterated his disapproval of the satire in a letter to Count Hermann of Neuenar; he called it a bit of "trifling nonsense."[121] He urged both correspondents to suppress further editions if they could.

In his campaign to mitigate or to end the controversy, Erasmus appealed not only to Reuchlin's supporters but also to his opponents. In 1518 he expressed sorrow in a letter to Perckheimer that men like Gratius and Hochstraten were ruining themselves through their anti-Reuchlin campaign. Gratius, he wrote, "seemed endowed with such a genius as, judiciously and rightly exerted, might have placed him in the ranks of learned and eloquent men."[122] He continued, "how often have I wished to advise Hochstraten not to risk upon this controversy the fruit of so many years' study, or to lower the character which he holds among the learned by the pamphlets he is issuing." Shortly afterward he did write both Gratius and Hochstraten. In the shorter letter to Gratius, he praised the humanist's Latin style but admonished him for using his gifts in a controversy which should not have concerned him.[123] In the letter to Hochstraten he began by praising Hochstraten's learning and his favorable opinion of "good letters." He also apologized for the rudeness of Reuchlin and his supporters. He claimed to have read Reuchlin's *Defense* with "sadness of mind," and he deplored "the violent and

[119] *Ibid.*, 20; Hutten published the poem in 1519.

[120] *Ibid.*, II, 610-12; Gratius printed the letter in his *Lamentationes.* The story mentioned in some works that Erasmus laughed so hard while reading the *Letters* that an abscess in his throat opened and was healed, is certainly apocryphal.

[121] Nichols, *Epistles of Erasmus*, III, 19-21.

[122] *Ibid.*, II, 415-17.

[123] Allen, *Opus epistolarum*, IV, 85, 86.

cruel mockeries" written on Reuchlin's behalf. But, Erasmus
continued, Hochstraten's works were blemished by similar
shortcomings. He particularly deprecated the *Destruction of the
Cabala*, which he felt maligned Reuchlin in an especially vicious way. He hinted that Hochstraten was using his position
as inquisitor to further his own ambition and pursue a private
feud. He told the powerful Dominican that he should have
left the decision to the pope or a bishop, for "it is not necessary
for you to mix up heaven and earth and to raise up so many
tragedies." Hochstraten should have devoted himself to
preaching Christ; as it was, he was hated, and the whole
Dominican order was in disrepute. He urged Hochstraten to
end the affair, claiming there was no reason why theology
and good letters could not be compatible.[124]

Erasmus's attempts to mitigate the controversy failed. He
was hardly more successful in convincing others of his own
neutrality. In fact, both sides used his name to advance their
cause. Gratius, Pfefferkorn, and Hochstraten all publicized
the letter to Caesarius, which attacked the *Letters of Obscure
Men*; and the Reuchlinists all assumed Erasmus was on their
side, despite his repeated denials. Typical protestations of neutrality can be found in two letters he wrote in 1519. In the
first, to Cardinal Wolsey, he lamented that the Reuchlin affair
had been mixed up with his own cause—the "cause of Good
Letters—whereas they have no proper connection with each
other." He admitted that he had a "passing acquaintance"
with Reuchlin and that he had carried on some "friendly correspondence" with him. But he denied having ever supported
his cause. All he had done, so he claimed, was advise him to
abstain from those "plain terms of abuse . . . in which after
the German fashion he indulges in his *Apology*."[125] Later in
the year he repeated his position in a letter to Albert of Bran-
denberg. He stated flatly, "I am not involved in any way with

---

[124] *Ibid.*, 42-51.
[125] *Ibid.*, III, 587-93; Nichols, *Epistles of Erasmus*, III, 378-86, improperly
dated.

the cause of Reuchlin and Luther. For what has literary study to do with a matter of faith?"[126]

Erasmus's well-known aversion to controversy partly explains his stance in the Reuchlin affair. He believed that political, intellectual, and theological tranquility was a prerequisite for the reforms in European life that he envisioned. The Reuchlin affair obviously was doing nothing to attain this tranquility.

It is also clear that Erasmus never considered the affair as a showdown between the principles of humanism and scholasticism. As he stated in his letter to Wolsey, the Reuchlin affair and the cause of "Good Letters" has "no connection with each other." Although he occasionally insisted that theologians should know Hebrew, such statements carried little conviction, for he actually had little interest in Reuchlin's Hebrew studies. Erasmus's aim was the revival of the Church fathers and a return to the philosophy of Christ as expressed in the New Testament. To this goal Reuchlin's work on the Old Testament and the Cabala were irrelevent. Erasmus never expressed this belief to Reuchlin himself, but his correspondence contains many derogatory references to Judaism and Hebrew literature and scholarship.[127] He expressed his sentiments most clearly in a letter to Wolfgang Capito in March 1518. He wrote that "though I find no fault" with Hebrew studies,

---

[126] Allen, *Opus epistolarum*, IV, 96-107; English translation in John C. Olin, ed., *Christian Humanism and the Reformation* (New York: 1965), 134-45.

[127] The sophisticated Erasmus did not share the fantastic conception of the Jews typical of the popular imagination. He opposed the Jews because he conceived Judaism as a religion based on meaningless ceremonies and rites; accordingly it was a religion diametrically opposed to the inner piety demanded by the "philosophy of Christ." Any Catholic, therefore, who emphasized the "ceremonial" aspects of Catholicism was a "Judaizer," according to Erasmus. For example, when Aleander came through northern Europe bearing the papal bull against Luther, Erasmus labeled him a "Jew" (Allen, *Opus epistolarum*, IV, 399). He seems actually to have feared that renewed interest in Hebrew studies would inject a new element of ceremonialism into the Church. In 1517, he wrote to Capito, "I am afraid . . . that the restoration of Hebrew learning may give occasion to the revival of Judaism. This would be a plague as much opposed to the doctrine of Christ as anything that could happen." *Ibid.*, II, 508.

he wished that Capito were more inclined to Greek than Hebrew. He continued:

> Talmud, Cabala, Tetragrammaton, Portae Lucis—empty names! I had rather see Christ infected by Scotus than by that rubbish. Italy has a multitude of Jews; while Spain has scarcely any Christians! And I fear that this may lead to the revival of that plague which was put down in former days. It were well if the Christian Church did not attribute so much to the Old Testament, which given as it was for a time, consists of shadows, and is nevertheless almost preferred to the Christian writings, while we somehow or other are turning our steps away from Christ, who was formerly our one sufficient guide.[128]

It is easy to see why Erasmus was able to view the issue in the controversy—whether the Jews should keep their books— as a matter that did not concern him, "something that in my judgment is more trifling than an ass's shadow."[129] Thus the villain in the piece was not the scholastic theologians but the "brazen-faced buffoon," Pfefferkorn, whose fanaticism had destroyed the concord of the learned world. He wished that "he were a Jew all over, and that his circumcision extended to his tongue and hands."[130] He even surmised that Pfefferkorn's conversion was a sham, and that his goal was to benefit Jews by sowing Christian discord. In a letter to Johannes Caesarius, he wrote:

> But what, if the world understood his treachery, and perceived that the man under the pretext of defending the Christian faith, is in fact proceeding to its subversion? He will then have gained the gratitude of his circumcised friends, to whom he will have done the same service as Zopyrus did to Darius. . . . And what would be more desired by the Jews—whose cause this fellow is for-

---

[128] Nichols, *Epistles of Erasmus*, III, 308-310.
[129] *Ibid.*, II, 193.
[130] *Ibid.*, III, 122; Allen, *Opus epistolarum*, III, 124-26.

warding, while he pretends to oppose it—than such a serverance of Christian concord?

Erasmus added that, as long as the New Testament was preserved, he would prefer to see the Old Testament abolished rather than "that the peace of Christendom should be broken for the sake of the books of the Jews."[131]

The final factor that affected Erasmus's behavior in the Reuchlin affair was its timing. Erasmus believed that the years between 1514 and 1520 were decisive ones for himself and for his campaign to renew the spiritual and intellectual life of Europe. He had already gained recognition as a wit and a gifted Latinist, but only now did his patristic and biblical studies begin to bear fruit. In 1516, for example, he published his New Testament and his edition of St. Jerome. If only he and his disciples could continue their work, he was convinced that a golden age of peace and piety would certainly dawn.[132] But his optimism was always tempered with apprehension— apprehension that the forces of monkish conservatism might close in on him and snuff out the light of true religion, apprehension that harsh words and meaningless polemics might cause discord and interrupt his scholarly work. Events after 1514 deepened these apprehensions. The Cologne theologians attacked Reuchlin for his opinions on Hebrew literature or perhaps, as Erasmus occasionally surmised, simply because he knew Greek and Hebrew.[133] Erasmus could never shake the fear that he might suffer the same fate, especially while living under the eyes of the theologians of the University of Louvain between 1517 and 1521. One of them, Edward Lee, had attacked his version of the New Testament. At the same time, Hochstraten, in *Destruction of the Cabala*, had questioned

---

[131] Nichols, *Epistles of Erasmus*, III, 125; Allen, *Opus epistolarum*, III, 126, 127.

[132] See John Huizinga, *Erasmus and the Age of the Reformation*, trans. F. Hopman (New York: 1957), 99.

[133] Erasmus supposed this was also the reason for early opposition to Luther; see letter to Albert of Brandenburg in Olin, *Christian Humanism*, 134-45.

the views on marriage Erasmus had expressed in his New Testament commentary. Worst of all, it was now being rumored that Erasmus was the author of *Julius exclusus*, the satire in which the warrior pope is excluded from heaven. In other words, Erasmus had good reasons for believing that monkish-scholastic interference might interrupt his scholarship. He felt it would have been foolish to plunge in on Reuchlin's side and risk further ill-will between himself and Dominicans and theologians. Thus, while Mutian withheld his support for Reuchlin out of his concern for common Christians, Erasmus withheld his support, at least in part, out of concern for himself.

Aside from Mutian, Erasmus, and the other humanists mentioned previously, most of the German humanists supported Reuchlin. Few of them shared Reuchlin's concern for protecting the Jews. Like Erasmus, they cared little if Pfefferkorn and the Dominicans burned Jewish books. A few may have feared that the goal of Reuchlin's opponents was to discredit humanist scholarship. Little evidence, however, suggests this was the case. The humanists rarely showed concern that their own intellectual interests might be threatened if Reuchlin was crushed by the Dominican juggernaut. They were aroused by the fact that a pious scholar, whom they revered, was being maligned by uncultured Dominican monks, whom they despised. Thus most German humanists viewed the controversy as an unfortunate struggle between one individual, Reuchlin, and several other individuals, Hochstraten, Pfefferkorn, Gratius, and the others. Only one or two viewed the Reuchlin affair as a life and death struggle between the principles of humanism and scholasticism.

Hence, for most German humanists, participation in the Reuchlin affair was limited to sending encouraging letters to Reuchlin and perhaps defending him in classrooms or over wine cups. The young disciples of Mutian around Erfurt—Eobanus Hessus, Heinrich Urban, Eurycus Cordus, and Crotus Rubeanus—all wrote letters to Reuchlin that praised his learning and damned his barbarian opponents. Others who did the same were Joachim Vadianus, Johannes Cuspianus and Simon Lazius of Vienna, Johannes Caesarius and Heinrich Glareanus, humanist teachers at Cologne, Conrad Peutinger of Augsburg, and Philip Melanchton, Reuchlin's great-nephew.[134] But only a few humanists openly stated their support for Reuchlin in published books. Crotus Rubeanus, Mutian's most radical follower, wrote much of the *Letters of Obscure Men*, and was a main inspiration for the work. Willibald Pirckheimer attacked Reuchlin's detractors in the prefaces to three translations he published in 1517 and 1518.[135] Count Hermann of Neuenar, a Cologne patrician and humanist dilettante, edited and helped publish two pro-Reuchlin works.[136] Standing far above the others in rage and bitterness was Ulrich von Hutten. He wrote the second part of *Letters of Obscure Men*, published a lengthy poem, *Reuchlin's Triumph*, and in 1520 even convinced his fellow noble, Franz von Sickingen, to declare a feud against the German Dominicans.

With the notable exception of the *Letters of Obscure Men*, humanist polemics were repetitious and unimaginative. Only a few humanists took note of the issues involved in the confiscation debate. Two scholars wrote books that included defenses of Reuchlin's Hebrew studies, but they were both Italians, Petrus Galatinus and George Benignus.[137] Among the Germans, only Pirckheimer defended Reuchlin's Hebrew scholarship. In the preface to his translations of Lucian's *Fish-*

---

[134] All these letters replete with their repetitious rhetoric, can be found in Geiger's edition of Reuchlin's *Briefwechsel*. A smaller collection of letters can be found in Adalbert Horawitz, *Zur Biographie und Correspondenz Johannes Reuchlins* (Vienna: 1877).

[135] See especially, Willibald Pirckheimer, ed., *Luciani Piscator seu Revivi-scentes* (Tübingen: 1518), a-ciii; this work was discussed in Chapter IV.

[136] These were, first, a work by an Italian ecclesiastic, George Benignus, *Defensio praestantissimi viri Joannis Reuchlin* . . . (Cologne: 1517); Benignus had been a member of the commission which had investigated the charges against Reuchlin. Second, Neuenar edited *Epistolae trium illustrium virorum* (Cologne: 1518); this contained letters of Reuchlin, Hutten, and Buschius against Hochstraten's first *Apologia*.

[137] Petrus Galatinus, *Opus* . . . *de arcanis catholicae veritatis* (Basel: 1516); on Benignus, see previous note.

erman, he affirmed that "many recondite doctrines lay hidden in the Talmud and Cabala."[138] Otherwise, no German humanist made a serious effort to answer the anti-Jew, anti-Reuchlin arguments of the scholastics. Their weapons were mockery and satire.

A typical humanist response can be seen in the letters of Buschius and Hutten, published by Hermann of Neuenar in his *Letters of Three Illustrious Men.* The book was designed by its editor to answer Hochstraten's first *Apology,* which had dealt with the confiscation issue in great detail. But Hutten's letter was filled with fiery denunciations of Hochstraten's impudence and "slanderous language," and made no pretense of answering the Dominican's arguments. Buschius's letter also denounced Hochstraten in general terms and derided his childish, un-Ciceronian Latin.[139] The anonymous editor of the *Ornaments or Elegencies* adopted the same approach.[140] He compiled a long series of particularly awkward sentences from Hochstraten's *Destruction of the Cabala* to show the scholastic's stylistic barbarism.

In addition to demeaning the Latin style of Hochstraten, Tungern, and the others, the humanists also attempted to utilize their rhetorical gifts to compare the countless merits of Reuchlin with the abject worthlessness of the Cologners. In *Reuchlin's Triumph,* for example, Hutten described Reuchlin's opponents as ambitious, superstitious, barbarous, ignorant, and hateful; but Reuchlin was brave, innocent, learned, industrious, truthful, and immortal.[141] He also included personal attacks on each of the anti-Reuchlinists; for Hochstraten, he wrote: "Are God and religion spoken of? At once he cries to the fire, to the fire! Does one write a book? To the fire with the book and its author! Do you speak truth? To the

[138] Pirckheimer, ed., *Luciani Piscator,* B iii.
[139] Geiger, *Reuchlin,* 413-17.
[140] *Flores sive Elegentiae ex diversis libris Hochstrati Magistri nostri haeretice . . .* (n.p.: n.d.); copy in the British Museum, London.
[141] Ulrich von Hutten, *Opera omnia,* ed. Eduard Böcking, 7 vols. (Leipzig: 1859-1870), III, 428, 443.

fire! Do you utter falsehood? To the fire! Do you commit injustice? To the fire! He is all over fire! To the fire! To the fire! Such is his first and last word."[142] Pirckheimer made similar comparisons in the preface to his translation of Lucian's *Orator*. The supporters of Reuchlin were "polished, calm, firm, suitable, acute, erudite and ignorant of no proper branch of learning"; his opponents were "barbarous, inert, rude, inept, stupid, illiterate, and unknowledgeable in whole disciplines."[143]

Another characteristic of humanist writing in the controversy was its restricted nature. There was much talk about sophists, barbarians, and "theologists," which, read out of context, seem to be general attacks on all scholastic theology. But as was the case with Reuchlin's *Defense*, such slanders were usually directed against specific men—Hochstraten, Tungern, Pfefferkorn, and the others who had actually attacked Reuchlin. Surprisingly, the Reuchlin affair stimulated little serious writing among the humanists about the reform of scholastic theology. Once again, Pirckheimer was an exception. During his defense of Reuchlin in the preface of Lucian's *Fisherman*, he outlined his program for the education of the "ideal theologian."

One work—the *Letters of Obscure Men*—and one author—Ulrich von Hutten—do not fit the pattern of humanist response during the Reuchlin affair.[144] No humanist matched Hutten's hatred for Reuchlin's detractors; no work matched the *Letters'* bitter sarcasm. Three elements in Hutten's background made him the most passionate Reuchlinist. First, largely

---

[142] *Ibid.*, 431, 432.

[143] Willibald Pirckheimer, *Opera politica, historica, philologica*, ed. Melchior Goldast (Frankfurt: 1610), 246.

[144] On von Hutten the following works are most useful: Lewis Spitz, "Hutten—Militant Critic," in *The Religious Renaissance of the German Humanists* (Cambridge, Mass.: 1963), 110-29; Hajo Holborn, *Ulrich von Hutten and the German Reformation* (New Haven: 1937); Paul Held, *Ulrich von Hutten. Seine religiös—geistige Auseinandersetzung mit Katholizismus, Humanismus, Reformation* (Leipzig: 1928). Böcking's collection of von Hutten's major works remains invaluable; see note 141.

from his studies under Aesticampianus at Leipzig and Frankfurt, he had a strong antipathy for scholastic theology. Second, he was an intense nationalist, who yearned for the empire's revival and the loosing of Rome's grip on the German
Church. Third, he was an ardent anti-cleric who blamed ignorant, immoral priests and monks for the corruption he perceived in the Roman Church.

Reuchlin's opponents incarnated everything that Hutten
hated—they were scholastic theologians, Dominican monks,
allies of the hated Italian papacy. He came to see the Reuchlin
affair as a cosmic battle between good and evil in which the
honor of Germany was at stake. To Hutten, Reuchlin's detractors symbolized the worst features of an ecclesiastical system that kept Germany in intellectual and religious darkness.
In the preface to his poem *Nemo* (1518), he reflected on three
hundred years of damage wrought on Christendom by scholastic theology: true theology was abandoned, religion declined, good studies were lost, and worst of all, superstition
emerged that "so beclouded pure worship that one could not
know whether many things belonged to Christ, or some new
God reserving for himself the last age of the world."[145] In the
preface to *Reuchlin's Triumph*, he proclaimed that the scholastic theologians were more detestable than the Turks: "These
are the ones by which good studies are destroyed to the det-
riment of the age, by which letters are trampled on, divine
theology reduced to useless loquacity, pure nonsense, and
superstitious absurdities."[146] Germany, he continued, had la-
bored under their yoke for centuries. But now, because they
had attacked Reuchlin, Hutten could prophesy their imminent
demise: "Germany has opened her eyes; the veil has fallen
away; she sees you now at full length! You have conspired
against Reuchlin. Germany can no longer remain deluded
when she saw you attack such a man. She felt his honor
threatened and rose to defend it. The scholastics had wrapped

[145] Hutten, *Opera omnia*, I, 182.
[146] *Ibid.*, 237.

294

religion in darkness, but we have poured on light! The gospel has seen the light of day, Jerome has reappeared, Greek and Latin authors have been published." He urged all his countrymen to close ranks against the sophists: "Our chains are broken. The die is cast. To fall back is impossible."[147]

The greatest monument to Hutten's fury was his contribution to the famous *Letters of Obscure Men*, which first appeared in the fall of 1515 and subsequently in an expanded edition in 1517. Actually Crotus Rubeanus, another fiery young humanist, conceived the idea for the *Letters*, but Hutten was his ally from the start. He composed several epistles for the first edition and wrote almost all those added in the second. The format of the work is well known: monks, theologians, scholastic logicians and philosophers, and anti-Reuchlinists of all kinds write letters to Ortwin Gratius in which they reveal themselves as moral degenerates and intellectual buffoons. Although the work is well-known,[148] a few comments are in order here.

First, the criticisms of scholasticism were far more sweeping than those in other pro-Reuchlin writing. Other humanists restricted their attacks to the scholastics of Cologne. But for Hutten and Rubeanus, the target was all of scholastic theology and philosophy. Medieval Latin grammars, foolish syllogizing, theological quibbling were all mocked unceasingly. Second, the *Letters* contained much material that was clearly irrelevant to the Reuchlin affair or even to a book designed to denigrate scholasticism: it satirized the Roman curia, the pope, indulgences, relics, religious orders (not just the Dominicans), and Church dietary rules. Clearly, Hutten and Rubeanus wanted more than a victory for Reuchlin; they sought a fundamental transformation of Germany's ecclesiastical and religious life.

---

[147] *Ibid.*, 237, 238.

[148] Hutten et al., *On the Eve of the Reformation*, ed. Hajo Holborn (New York: 1964) is an edition of the original English translation by Francis Stokes published in London in 1909. Translations have also been made into French and German: *Lettres des Hommes obscurs*, trans. V. Develay, 3 vols. (Paris: 1870); *Briefe von Dunkelmännern*, trans. W. Binder (Stuttgart: 1876).

There is little evidence to support the often-heard assertion that, except for dull-witted scholastics, learned Germany greeted the *Letters of Obscure Men* with gleeful enthusiasm. Eminent humanists like Beatus Rhenanus[149] and Erasmus strongly disapproved the *Letters*; and although they never mentioned the work in their writings, it is likely that Wimpfeling, Mutian, and even Pirckheimer felt the same way. Reuchlin never commented on the *Letters*, but his biographer, Ludwig Geiger, concedes that he probably disapproved of them, since they were "far removed from his character."[150] Hutten, not surprisingly, mentioned the *Letters* favorably in his correspondence, and Thomas More expressed amusement with the work in a letter to Erasmus.[151] Otherwise the humanists responded to the work with near total silence. Even for Reuchlin's defenders, the *Letters of Obscure Men* was excessively rude.

In conclusion, most historians have erred by depicting the Reuchlin affair as essentially a conflict between humanism and scholasticism. It is true that the Reuchlinists were largely humanists (though by no means all of them). But the anti-Reuchlinists were a disparate group of individuals from many walks of life: they included some scholastics, but also a few humanists and even several kings. Furthermore, the relative worth of humanism and scholasticism was not the main issue in the controversy. No evidence supports the contention that the Cologne scholastics wanted to discredit humanism by attacking Reuchlin. Hochstraten and the others did not attack Reuchlin because he was a famous humanist who wanted to use "philology to change the meaning of the Scriptures." As they made abundantly clear in page after page of repetitious argumentation, they attacked him because of his "favoritism" to the Jews and his refusal to approve their plans for the confiscation of Jewish books. The humanists supported Reuchlin because they admired his piety and scholarship, and because they hated to see his old age ruined by what they considered improper

[149] Nichols, *Epistles of Erasmus*, II, 555, 556.
[150] Geiger, *Reuchlin*, 378.
[151] Nichols, *Epistles of Erasmus*, II, 426.

and erroneous attacks on his character and learning. Only one person, Ulrich von Hutten, conceived the Reuchlin affair as a climactic showdown between humanism and scholasticism. His interpretation, however, has been the one which most historians have chosen to accept.

VIII

The Transformation of German Scholasticism ~

HAVING BEEN MALIGNED, scorned, and occasionally defended for the previous seven decades, medieval scholasticism lost its hold on Germany's universities in the two decades between 1515 and 1535. One institution after another adopted comprehensive statute changes that implemented the major curricular goals of the humanists. Not all vestiges of scholasticism were obliterated, of course: Aristotle remained a revered authority, and logic continued to be studied. Nor did the full spectrum of humanist interests gain acceptance: Platonic philosophy and cabalistic mysticism, for example, won no recognition within the universities. Nonetheless, old authorities disappeared; former controversies ceased to be divisive; once-popular texts were no longer printed; disputations ceased. A curriculum based on the *studia humanitatis* and the mastery of ancient languages came to be established. Although universities continued to provide professional training in theology, medicine, and law, their major function now became the introduction of large numbers of students to a breadth of disciplines ranging from poetry to physics. It is not an exaggeration to say that with these changes an educational revolution occurred, ending Germany's scholastic era.

THE PATTERN OF CURRICULAR CHANGE

The movement toward comprehensive curriculum reform first centered in the northeastern universities of Erfurt, Leipzig, and Wittenberg, with the newest of the three, Wittenberg, providing the spark.[1] The Wittenberg reforms were initiated in the spring of 1516 when the faculty senate in a memorandum to the university's patron, Frederick the Wise, outlined the institution's weaknesses and petitioned for additional financial support. Frederick did not respond immediately, but in the year and a half that followed he requested several detailed reports from the faculty senate and sent a number of councillors to the university to evaluate the institution's needs and performance.[2] By early spring 1518, a consensus emerged within the government and university that a general reform was preferable to piecemeal changes. George Spalatin, the elector's chaplain, secretary, and unofficial adviser on academic affairs, was appointed to oversee the reform process. He solicited advice from several professors, the most prominent of whom was his close friend, the dean of the faculty of theology, Martin Luther. This man was to become the driving force behind the changes that took place in the years that followed.

Luther can hardly be called a humanist. His intellectual and spiritual interests were far removed from the humanists' enthusiasm for ancient literature and their preoccupation with stylistic elegance. But he shared much in common with "Christian humanists" such as Erasmus, Reuchlin, and Jacques Lefèvre and found their work indispensable aids in his quest for religious enlightenment. Like these older and, at least for the moment, more illustrious contemporaries, he was convinced that religious truth must be sought directly in the scriptures rather than scholastic commentaries. He was also convinced that a sound knowledge of Greek and Hebrew was a prerequisite for precise scriptural understanding. Thus from

[1] On the Wittenberg reforms, the following works are useful: Walter Friedensburg, *Geschichte der Universität Wittenberg* (Halle: 1917), 107-135; Max Steinmetz, "Die Wittenberger Universität und der Humanismus (1502-1521)," *450 Jahre Martin-Luther-Universität Halle Wittenberg* (Leipzig: 1956), 103-140; Maria Grossmann, *Humanism at Wittenberg, 1485-1517* (Nieuwkoop: 1975), 76-85.
[2] Relevant documents printed in Walter Friedensburg, *Urkundenbuch der Universität Wittenberg*, I (Halle: 1926), 74-87.

the beginning of his biblical lectures at Wittenberg Luther freely utilized whatever linguistic and philological aids humanist scholarship could offer. Among the texts he employed were Jacques Lefèvre's editions of the Pslams and the Epistles and Reuchlin's *On the Rudiments of Hebrew*. As is well known, he also utilized Erasmus's *Annotations on the New Testament* when it appeared in 1516.[3]

Luther also shared the humanists' deep aversion for the scholastics' rational-dialectical approach to theology. Luther's spiritual struggles had by the mid 1510s fully revealed the chasm between his evangelical theology and the methods of the scholastic *doctores*. His disillusionment with old methods found its fullest expression in the ninety-seven theses—known as the "Disputation against Scholastic Theology"—which he prepared for a disputation held at Wittenberg in September 1517. Although most of the theses expressed Luther's reservations about the theology of grace in the works of Occam, Biel, and Pierre d'Ailly, theses forty-three through fifty-three questioned scholastic methodology rather than specific doctrines. Luther denounced the intrusion of logic and philosophy into matters of belief and called for the liberation of theology from Aristotle:

43. It is an error to say that no man can become a theologian without Aristotle. This is in opposition to common opinion.

44. Indeed, no one can become a theologian unless he becomes one without Aristotle.

45. To state that a theologian who is not a logician is a monstrous heretic—this is a monstrous and heretical statement. This is in opposition to common opinion.

46. In vain does one fashion a logic of faith, a substitution brought about without regard for limit and measure. This is in opposition to the new dialecticians.

47. No syllogistic form is valid when applied to divine terms.

[3] Grossmann, *Humanism at Wittenberg*, 78.

50. Briefly, the whole of Aristotle is to theology as darkness is to light. This is in opposition to the scholastics.

53. Even the more useful definitions of Aristotle seem to beg the question.[4]

Similar attacks were common in Luther's correspondence during 1517 and 1518. In February, 1518, in a lengthy letter to Spalatin, for example, he attacked dialectic as an obstacle to true theology: "Maybe it could be play and useful exercise for the minds of youngsters, but in Biblical studies, where only faith and inspiration from above are desired, all syllogism must be left behind."[5] A short time later he wrote his old philosophy professor from Erfurt, Jodocus Trutvetter, that "it is impossible to reform the Church unless canon law, scholastic theology, philosophy and logic that we now have are eradicated and new studies instituted."[6]

At the time these letters were written, Luther and his fellow theologian, Andreas Karlstadt, were drafting their proposals for reforms, which they sent to Spalatin on March 11, 1518. In the accompanying letter, Luther predicted great fame for the elector and university if their recommendations were adopted. "Here is offered an opportunity," he wrote, "to reform all the other universities, indeed, to drive away all barbarism and to improve all our education in the widest range."[7] Unfortunately the theologians' proposals have been lost. But a letter of Luther's written to Johannes Lang on March 21 probably gives an accurate idea of the contents. Luther enthusiastically wrote, "Our university progresses; we can expect in a short time to receive lectures on two, maybe even three languages, also on Pliny, mathematics, Quintilian and other worthy authors; and to reject those worthless lectures on Peter of Spain, Tartaretus and Aristotle. Already the

---

[4] "Disputation Against Scholastic Theology," trans. Harold J. Grimm in *Luther's Works*, 31, ed. Harold J. Grimm (Philadelphia: 1957), 12, 13.

[5] Martin Luther, *Werke*, I (Weimar: 1930), 170.

[6] *Ibid.*, 150.

[7] *Ibid.*, 153, 154.

Elector has been won over, and the matter has been sent before his council."[8]

After almost two years of discussion, a new lecture schedule for the arts course was adopted in spring 1518. The impact of humanism is obvious. Peter of Spain and Alexander Ville-dieu were both excluded; logic was to be taught from the original Aristotelian texts, and grammar instruction was to be based on Priscian. Although traditional Aristotelian writings continued to be taught, humanist translations replaced old versions. Stipends for two more lectures on classical authors—Quintilian and Pliny—were established. Also founded was a pedagogium where beginning students learned grammar and studied rhetoric and poetry. Most importantly, lectureships were established for both Greek and Hebrew.[9]

The first professor of Greek was the twenty-one-year-old prodigy, Philip Melanchthon, destined to exert inestimable influence over German Protestant education in the sixteenth century. On his arrival in Wittenberg, in August 1518, he delivered an oration on the reform of university education that Luther called "extremely learned and absolutely fault-less."[10] Summarizing seventy years of humanist opinion, Melanchthon deplored the one-sided nature of scholasticism, denounced traditional authorities and called for the study of ancient languages and a return to original Aristotelian texts.[11] Through no small effort of his own Melanchthon was to see the thorough implementation of his program at Wittenberg during the next decade. Within the year his lectures on Greek were attracting overflow audiences of more than five hundred students.[12] And partly because of his influence, scholastic commentaries were gradually abandoned. In December 1518, Luther wrote Johannes Lang that the university was giving

[8] *Ibid.*, 155.
[9] Friedensburg, *Urkundenbuch*, I, 85, 86.
[10] Luther, *Werke*, I, 192.
[11] Philip Melanchthon, "De corrigendis adolescentiae studiis," *Opera Omnia*, XI (*Corpus Reformatorum*, ed. Charles Bretschneider), 17-40.
[12] *Ibid.*, 407, 408.

up Aquinas's commentaries on logic and on Aristotle's *Physics*; both were superfluous because professors were utilizing original texts.[13] Melanchthon's greatest contribution, however, was the publication of a wealth of pedagogical material on a wide range of subjects, which became the basis for instruction in the Wittenberg arts faculty and many other Lutheran institutions.[14] They included manuals for instruction in Greek and Latin, texts on dialectic, rhetoric, moral philosophy, arithmetic, and etymology; commentaries on Aristotle's *Politics, Ethics*, and *De anima*; and editions of works by dozens of ancient writers, among them Cicero, Plutarch, Demosthenes, Pliny, Virgil, Xenophon, Aristophanes, Ptolemy, and Lycurgus.[15] His publications reflect the themes of his Wittenberg inaugural oration: the importance of Greek, the inadequacy of traditional scholastic authors, and reverence for an Aristotle freed of medieval accretions. Perhaps his most influential texts were his various manuals on dialectic;[16] strongly influenced by Agricola's *Dialectical Invention*, they emphasized close ties between logic and rhetoric and omitted medieval supposition theory altogether.

Although extant lecture schedules from 1521 and 1526[17] reconfirm the changes in the arts faculty, university records contain no reference to formal changes in theological instruction. Unquestionably, however, old scholastic methods were abandoned. Luther and other faculty members focused their lectures on the Bible, with the writings of the Church fathers and Luther himself becoming the primary aids in exegesis. After its publication in 1521, Melanchthon's *Loci communes*

[13] *Ibid.*, 262.

[14] The most thorough treatment of Melanchthon's pedagogical writings and activities remains Karl Hartfelder, *Philipp Melanchthon als Praeceptor Germaniae* (Berlin: 1889) (*Monumenta Germaniae Pedagogica*, VII).

[15] A chronological listing of Melanchthon's works can be found in Hartfelder, *Melanchthon*, 577-620.

[16] *Compendiaria Dialectices ratio* (Wittenberg: 1520); *Dialectices Libri Quatuor* (Hagenow: 1528); *Dialecticae praeceptiones collectae* (Wittenberg: 1544); *Erotemata dialectices* (Wittenberg: 1547).

[17] Friedensburg, *Urkendenbuch*, 116, 117, 148.

became an important introductory text for theological discussion.[18]

Luther was correct when he predicted in his letter to Frederick the Wise that once Wittenberg altered its plan of studies other universities would soon follow suit. In fact, within a year after Wittenberg adopted new statutes in 1518, similar steps were taken by her academic neighbors, Erfurt and Leipzig. Although Erfurt had fostered a considerable amount of humanist teaching ever since the 1490s, humanism had received little formal recognition. Time-worn scholastic requirements remained intact, and the university had never hired a salaried poet. This changed in 1518 and 1519.[19] One reason for the turnabout was the timely election of humanist sympathizers to several pivotal offices within the university. Most importantly, Maternus Pistoris, who had lectured on humanist subjects since the early 1500s, was chosen dean of the arts faculty in 1518; one year later, Justus Jonas, another ardent disciple of the new learning, was chosen rector. These elections revealed the broad support for humanism within the university and enhanced the feasibility of reform. Another important factor was the inspiration provided by Wittenberg. The Wittenberg curriculum reforms had been followed closely by several of Luther's correspondents, most notably the young theologian and teacher of Greek, Johannes Lang. He and other Erfurt masters undoubtedly realized that Erfurt's enrollments would be threatened unless their institution kept pace with its nearby competitor.

The first concrete step toward the official recognition of humanism was taken in 1518, when the university established a stipend for lectures by the poet Eobanus Hessus, something that Conrad Mutian and others had been urging for the pre-

---

[18] See Karl Bauer, *Die Wittenberger Universitätstheologie und die Anfänge der Reformation* (Tübingen: 1928).

[19] For the Erfurt reforms, see Erich Kleineidam, *Universitas Studii Erffordensis*, II (Leipzig: 1969), 227-57; Georg Oergel, "Die Studienreform der Universität Erfurt vom Jahre 1519," *Jahrbücher der Königlichen Akademie gemeinnütziger Wissenschaften zu Erfurt*, N.F., 25 (1899), 83-96.

vious four years.[20] Thus the practice of delegating lectures on poetry and rhetoric to "part-time" humanists such as Pistoris came to an end.

More important were the steps toward curriculum reform taken in early 1519 when an eight-man committee, representing all faculties but medicine, was formed to make proposals. One suspects that the most influential figures on the committee were the two theologians, Lang and Pistoris, both strong supporters of humanism. The committee's proposals were presented and adopted in late spring 1519. Both Peter of Spain and Alexander Villedieu were dropped from the curriculum; grammar was to be studied from Priscian, while logic was to be taught on the basis of the original Aristotelian texts. Most importantly, lectures on the *studia humanitatis* and on Greek were now required for both the Bachelor and Master of Arts. Although these changes were moderate, Erfurt humanists were enthusiastic. Justus Jonas, who was absent from Erfurt when the reforms were accepted, was both astounded and jubilant when he learned of the changes. In June 1519 he wrote to a Nordhausen churchman, Melchior von Aachen,

> Hear and be astonished! You must read this in awe and worship it as almost something heaven-sent. You certainly know our old Erfurt school, where the sophists have so well dominated things that the whole republic of letters seems to have been reduced to a few feeble dialectical arguments . . . I have been gone six weeks. In this short time everything has been reformed. I found the school completely different from when I left. The study of the three languages, of true philosophy and true theology have been introduced.[21]

Supporters of humanism at Leipzig also had reason to rejoice in 1519, when that university also adopted substantive curriculum changes. After having been stymied in 1511 by

[20] Kleineidam, *Universitas*, II, 234.
[21] Justus Jonas, *Briefwechsel*, ed. Gustav Kawerau (Hildesheim: 1964), 25.

Duke George's conservative statute revisions and by the expulsion of Aesticampianus, humanism once again began to make progress in 1515. In that year the faculty of arts encouraged the teaching of Greek by voting ten florins to subsidize the printing costs of teaching material then being used by the English professor of Greek, Richard Crocus.[22] In the same year Alexander Villedieu's *Doctrinale* was formally removed from the curriculum. This was done, according to faculty records, because "students had completely rejected it and because it was no longer utilized in neighboring *gymnasia* or even trivial schools.[23] More thoroughgoing changes took place in 1519. In that year the government of Ducal Saxony, always conscious of developments at rival Wittenberg, initiated yet another review of Leipzig's academic practices.[24] After having again solicited faculty opinion, the duke issued a new lecture schedule in early summer.[25] The preamble confirmed that philosophy was still the basis of instruction in the faculty of arts and that Aristotle was the best authority. It warned, however, that when treating Aristotle, masters were to avoid "foolish and intricate questions"; furthermore, since it was "most wretched for the mind to learn things from commentaries," they were to rely on original texts and utilize one of the "new translations."[26] Unlike the statute revisions at Erfurt and Wittenberg, which abandoned Peter of Spain altogether, his *Summulae logicales* continued to be required at Leipzig. The statutes stipulated, however, that to prevent discouragement on the part of beginners, "complex questions of the first and second intention and those wanderings of Scotus's formalities

[22] Georg Erler, *Die Matrikel der Universität Leipzig*, II (Leipzig: 1897), 510; on the activity of Crocus and his successor, Peter Mosellanus, see Felician Gess, "Leipzig und Wittenberg," *Neues Archiv für Sächsische Geschichte und Altertumskunde*, 16 (1895), 43-94.

[23] Erler, *Die Matrikel*, II, 511.

[24] On the 1519 reforms, see Herbert Helbig, *Die Reformation der Universität Leipzig im 16. Jahrhundert* (Gütersloh: 1953), 29-32.

[25] Published in Friedrich Zarncke, *Die Statutenbücher der Universität Leipzig* (Leipzig: 1861), 34-43; faculty opinions, if written down, have been lost.

[26] *Ibid.*, 39.

should be avoided."[27] Classical literature had a prominent place in the new lecture schedule. At eleven o'clock lectures were given on Cicero, at one, on Quintilian, and at four, on Virgil.

The Leipzig reforms also initiated some minor changes in the teaching of theology. Of the five daily lectures, two were set aside for instruction on the Bible, and one for the study of the writings of Augustine, Jerome, or one of the other Church fathers. Only one lecture was devoted to Lombard's *Sentences*, and one to a "scholastic of the sacred page," preferably Aquinas.[28]

Incremental change continued at Leipzig in the 1520s. Lectures on Greek and Hebrew, although not mentioned in the 1519 reforms, were regularly offered from the early 1520s onward.[29] Another important step was taken in 1524 when the faculty of arts approved their dean's proposal to discontinue the use of Peter of Spain.[30] In his place the handbook by Johannes Caesarius, simply entitled *Dialectica* (later *Dialectices libri decem*), was now to be used. Caesarius (1460-1551),[31] who had taught Greek at Cologne in the 1510s, first published his treatise in 1520.[32] It later went through dozens of editions and was adopted for use at many northern universities. Similar in many ways to Melanchthon's dialectical manuals, Caesarius's treatise was a summary of Aristotelian logic that purported to be even clearer than the Aristotelian texts themselves. It also abandoned medieval supposition theory and drew heavily on the dialectical ideas of Rudolph Agricola.

---

[27] *Ibid.*, 40.

[28] *Ibid.*, 36.

[29] Lecture lists for the faculty of arts from 1519 to 1555 are listed in Erler, *Die Matrikel*, II, 542-753.

[30] *Ibid.*, 591.

[31] Friedrich Eckstein, "Johannes Caesarius," *Allgemeine Deutsche Biographie*, 3 (Leipzig: 1876), 689-91.

[32] The first printed version of Caesarius's *Dialectica* appeared in Cologne in 1520; some subsequent editions were given the title, *Dialectices . . . Libri decem*.

It would be surprising if the fourth university of north-eastern Germany, Frankfurt an der Oder, did not at this time emulate the reforms of Wittenberg, Leipzig and Erfurt. But there are no records of any formal curriculum revisions until 1541, after the Brandenburg elector, Joachim II, accepted Protestantism and enlisted Melanchthon to bring his university in line with Lutheran academic practices. The following schedule shows the arts faculty lectures offered at Frankfurt as a result of the 1541 reforms.[33] It is notable for its stress on literature and languages and its near exclusion of Aristotle:

5 A.M.	Dialectic from the work of either Melanchthon or Caesarius.
6 A.M.	Poetry from Virgil or Ovid.
6 A.M.	Hebrew.
7 A.M.	Greek literature from Homer, Demosthenes or occasionally Aristotle.
7 A.M.	Latin grammar from the text of Melanchthon.
8-9 A.M.	Left open for lectures in theology.
11 A.M.	Music.
Noon	Latin literature from Terence, Plautus, Tacitus.
1 P.M.	Moral philosophy from Aristotle and Cicero.
1 P.M.	Mathematics from Euclid.
2 P.M.	Oratory from various works by Cicero.
3 P.M.	Greek grammar from text of Melanchthon.
3 P.M.	Letter writing from Cicero.
4 P.M.	Rhetoric from text of Melanchthon, *Ad Herennium* of Cicero or *Copia rerum et verborum* of Erasmus.

No set plan of lectures was established for theology, although it was stipulated that professors should concentrate on the exposition of the Bible.

Outside of northeast Germany, the first university to un-

[33] Printed by Bauch, *Die Anfänge der Universität Frankfurt a.O.* (Berlin: 1900), 144, 145; also by Ernst Friedländer, "Aktenstücke zur Geschichte der Universität Frankfurt an der Oder," *Forschungen zur Brandenburgischen und Preussischen Geschichte*, 8 (1895), 213-15.

dertake curriculum revision was the University of Ingolstadt. In fact, although formal statute changes were approved only in late 1518 or early 1519, the beginnings of reform can be traced back to 1515, at least two years before revisions were seriously considered at Wittenberg.[34] Ingolstadt's priority is not surprising. The university had provided for a salaried humanist ever since 1476; prominent humanists such as Celtis and Locher had taught there; most importantly, the Bavarian dukes had shown a continuous interest in the institution and had often assumed an active role in university affairs.

The transformation of Ingolstadt began in the fall of 1515 when the prestigious ducal councillor, Leonhard Eck, arrived to assume the role of *patronus* or *dominus* of the university. A graduate of Ingolstadt (M.A., 1493), Eck had studied law in Italy and since 1511 had been one of Duke William IV's closest advisers. In 1514, however, he ran afoul of the Bavarian estates and became tutor and general steward for the duke's younger brother, Ernest, who matriculated at Ingolstadt in 1515. Eck would play an important role in university affairs for the next thirty years.[35]

On his arrival in 1515, Eck consulted various faculty members and, having been advised by three ducal councillors, Sebastian Ilsung, Johann Aventinus, and Augustin Kölner, issued a reform decree, or perhaps a series of them, during the fall.[36] By December 4, he was able to write Duke William pridefully, "I have carried out with great effort a reform within the university and with such skill (if I may celebrate myself with truth) that the order of both teaching and studying at the venerable institution has never been as sound since its very

[34] Arno Seifert, *Die Universität Ingolstadt im 15. und 16. Jahrhundert. Texte und Regesten* (Munich: 1973), 80.

[35] F. Oppenheim, "Leonhard Eck," *Allgemeine Deutsche Biographie*, 5 (Leipzig: 1877), 604-606.

[36] For a discussion of Eck's early activity in Ingolstadt, see Arno Seifert, *Statuten-und Verfassungsgeschichte der Universität Ingolstadt, 1472-1586* (Munich: 1971), 88-98, 429-38; Prantl, *Geschichte der Ludwig-Maximilians-Universität zu München* (Munich: 1872), I, 168, 211.

beginning."[37] It is difficult to evaluate Eck's boastful claims, since whatever decrees he issued have been lost. Their essential elements, however, can be ascertained from faculty records and the revised statutes of 1518-1519, which officially incorporated the innovations he had proposed earlier.

One of Eck's major goals was to reduce the confusion caused by the proliferation of scholastic commentaries and the contending claims of the various schools and *viae*. With its divided faculty of arts, Ingolstadt had always been plagued by the *Wegestreit*; it had resurfaced most recently in 1511, when government officials proposed certain changes in the election methods for university offices. Eck responded by abolishing all special rules and privileges concerning the *via antiqua* and *via moderna*. The words *antiqui, moderni, realistae*, and *nominales* were no longer to be used, and all masters in the arts faculty were to be known simply as *artistae*.[38] Thus, by Eck's command, Ingolstadt's version of one of medieval Europe's great intellectual controversies came to an abrupt and permanent halt.

Eck's wish to sweep aside old authorities and standardize instruction also led to one of the true virtuoso performances of Germany's closing scholastic era. This was the production between 1515 and 1520 of a complete new series of logical texts and Aristotelian commentaries for classroom use by the bright young Ingolstadt theologian, Johannes Eck. Having received an eclectic education, which included studies at Tübingen, Cologne, and Freiburg and an introduction to nominalism, realism, and humanism, Eck became professor of theology at Ingolstadt in 1510.[39] With his diverse academic background and his already impressive list of publications, it

[37] Seifert, *Texte und Regesten*, 77.

[38] This was the wording from the statutes of 1518-1519; see Prantl, *Geschichte*, II, 156.

[39] On Eck's call to Ingolstadt and his later activity there, see Klaus Rischar, "Professor Dr. Johannes Eck als akademischer Lehrer in Ingolstadt," *Zeitschrift für bayerischen Kirchengeschichte*, 37 (1968), 193-212; see also Erwin Iserloh, *Johannes Eck (1486-1543) Scholastiker, Humanist, Kontroverstheologe* (Münster: 1981), 14-20.

is not surprising that on November 11, 1515, Eck became the choice of the arts faculty to compose commentaries on both Peter of Spain and the texts of Aristotle.[40] Eck worked quickly, and his first treatise, a commentary on Peter of Spain, appeared in May 1516. The same year also saw the appearance of his lengthy commentary on the *Organon*. By 1520 he had also produced his own introduction to logic, *Elements of Dialectic*, and commentaries on Aristotle's *Physics, De anima* and *De caelo et mundo*.[41] In 1520 he proposed to the arts faculty yet another text on arithmetic, but nothing came of this plan.[42]

In his correspondence and in the introductions to his various works, Eck claimed to be striking a bold new path for teaching the arts. In April 1516 he wrote that he was busy "forging a new course of everything in philosophy, which labor I assumed on appeal from the faculty of arts." He claimed that his course would be stripped of the "rubbish of the sophists" and would be written in a style "loftier than that which to this point most philosophers of our age have utilized."[43] But it is difficult to see exactly what Eck had in mind when he proclaimed the novelty of his works. It is true that he utilized updated translations of Aristotle by Argyropulos; it is also true that humanism is evidenced by the literary references in his flowery introductions and by the inclusion of laudatory verses by Heinrich Bebel and others. Otherwise Eck produced works of a traditional nature. Passages from Aristotle are followed by sections of commentary in which opinions of the great scholastic *doctores* are compared and criticized. Representatives of both *viae* are cited, with the opinions of the nominalists usually winning Eck's approval. Nor did Eck's

---

[40] Seifert, *Texte und Regesten*, 80, 81.

[41] *In summulos Petri Hispani . . . explanatio pro superioris Germaniae scholasticis* (Augsburg: 1516); *Aristotelis Dialectica . . . facili explanatione declarate* (Augsburg: 1516); *Elementarius Dialecticae* (Augsburg: 1517); *Aristotelis Physicae libri VIII . . . Adjectis J. Eckii adnotationibus* (Augsburg: 1518); *Aristotelis Stagyritae libri de caelo IV . . . adjectis Eckii commentariis* (Augsburg: 1519); *Aristotelis de Anima libri VIII . . . adjectis Eckii Commentariis* (Augsburg: 1520).

[42] Seifert, *Texte und Regesten*, 89.

[43] *Ibid.*, 81, note 8.

logical commentaries and text show particular originality or any of the humanist's reservations about supposition theory or the stylistic deficiencies of Peter of Spain. As Arno Seifert has remarked, "Eck's job of clearing away was limited in general to incidentals, without questioning the substance of tradition."[44] Nonetheless, when Ingolstadt's statutes were officially revised in 1518-1519, the *cursus Eckianus* became the basis for teaching in the arts faculty, replacing those "long and useless commentaries of the past."[45]

These new statutes also reveal the second major result of Leonhard Eck's reforming efforts. This was the inclusion of the *studia humanitatis* as a recognized part of Ingolstadt's curriculum. Lectures on Terence, Cicero, and the Italian humanist, Filelfo, became required, and the *Rudiments of Grammar* by the Bavarian humanist and ducal councillor, Johannes Aventinus, replaced the *Doctrinale*. The statutes also required that new translations by Argyropulos or Bruni be used exclusively when dealing with an Aristotelian text.

Although the new Ingolstadt statutes did not require instruction in Greek, lectures on both Greek and Hebrew became available soon after Eck became patron of the university. Johannes Böschenstein gave a course on Hebrew, and Johannes Agricola lectured on Greek.[46] Then in 1520, Eck attracted his friend, Johannes Reuchlin, to Ingolstadt to lecture on the two ancient tongues. Reuchlin's presence was a source of much pride on the part of the faculty. On Reuchlin's arrival, Johannes Gussubelius delivered an oration that praised Reuchlin as a man knowledgeable in three languages and pure theology and philosophy.[47] He predicted that "idleness, barbarism, darkness, ignorance, and malicious sophistry" would disappear, to be replaced by "diligence, virtue, light, and true

[44] Arno Seifert, *Logik zwischen Scholastik und Humanismus. Das Kommentarwerk Johann Ecks* (Munich: 1978), 51.

[45] Carl von Prantl, *Geschichte der Ludwig-Maximilians-Universität*, II, 160; he includes the complete text of the reforms.

[46] *Ibid.*, I, 138, 139, 205, 206.

[47] Joannes Gussulebius, *Oratio . . . coram Universitate Ingolstatensi per D. J. Capnionem . . . cum in lingua Hebraica et Graeca ludum literarium ex conducto aperiret* (Augsburg: 1520).

learning." Reuchlin received the generous salary of two hundred guldens, half paid by the university, half by Duke William. He lectured twice a day, in the morning on Hebrew, and in the afternoon on Greek. The plague drove Reuchlin from Ingolstadt to Tübingen in 1521, but in succeeding years other less illustrious figures took his place.[48]

The Ingolstadt statutes were revised again in 1526.[49] The principal innovation was the founding of a pedagogium, where young students were instructed in Aventinus's grammar, the poetry of Virgil and Babtista Mantuanus, and the elements of Greek. Lectures on oratory and letter writing were also added to the list of required courses for arts students. Finally in 1535, Peter of Spain and Eck's dialectic were replaced by the increasingly popular manual of Caesarius.[50]

University reform reached the Rhineland in 1520 and 1521, at an institution that till then had given scant recognition to humanism. This was the University of Heidelberg, where after an early introduction by Peter Luder in the 1450s, humanism had withered in the face of governmental indifference and the intransigence of the university senate. But by the 1510s dissatisfaction with the institution's conservatism had become widespread within the faculty of arts. As already noted, the faculty had in 1513 unsuccessfully petitioned the university senate for a salaried lectureship in the *studia humanitatis*.[51] Seven years later, in 1520, the same faculty of arts voted on its own initiative to assume the cost of publishing revised translations of Aristotle for their students' use. The dean, who recorded the decision, noted that there had been many complaints about the old renderings, and added that "for the most part all the other universities had abandoned obsolete methods and amended their studies."[52]

In August 1521, the arts faculty again petitioned the uni-

---

[48] Prantl, *Geschichte der Ludwig-Maximilians-Universität*, I, 208-10.

[49] *Ibid.*, II, 177-81.

[50] *Ibid.*, II, 181-82.

[51] See above, 303.

[52] Eduard Winkelmann, *Urkundenbuch der Universität Heidelberg* (Heidelberg: 1886), I, 213.

versity senate to take action to halt the downward slide of the faculty of arts and the university as a whole. Their petition stated that at one time the faculty of arts had been one of Germany's most flourishing centers of learning, but now suffered "contempt and disdain" because it had become "flabby and enfeebled."[53] A major cause, asserted the faculty, was the lack of qualified teachers of Greek and Hebrew. This deficiency became particularly glaring when a neighboring institution such as Tübingen was able to attract as prestigious a scholar as Reuchlin.[54] The faculty recommended that the university senate, in cooperation with the elector, do Tübingen one better by bringing Erasmus to Heidelberg. Not surprisingly, nothing came of the faculty's appeal. As the dean flatly stated in his report, "to this letter there simply was no reply." He added that as a result, "the more studious among the students, . . . loathing our university's way and order of teaching and treating the arts," had left for Tübingen or other schools, "in search of improving their studies."

Although the university failed to lure Erasmus to its lecture halls, cooperation among the four faculties did enable Heidelberg to attract a teacher of Greek and Hebrew at least for a short time in 1521-1522. Johannes Böschenstein, who also came from Ingolstadt, received a salary of just under forty guldens; the university treasury, the faculties of arts and theology each donated ten guldens, while the jurists contributed five or six guldens and the physicians only one or two. But Elector Louis V declined to add any further support, and in the spring of 1522, Böschenstein left, *ob stipendii tenuitatem.*[55]

Later in the year, however, bending perhaps to pressure from within the university itself, the elector decided to investigate the possibility of reforming all four faculties. He appointed his chancellor, Florentinus of Venningen to take

---

[53] Johann Friedrich Hautz, *Geschichte der Universität Heidelberg* (Mannheim: 1862), I, 369, 370.

[54] After he left Ingolstadt because of the plague in spring, 1521, he went to Tübingen, where he remained for the few remaining months of his life.

[55] Hautz, *Geschichte*, I, 371.

charge of the proceedings. The chancellor, in turn, invited three Heidelberg alumni to submit suggestions for reforming the institution. They were Jacob Wimpfeling, now 72 years old; Johannes Sturm, the Strassburg pedagogue; and Jacob Spiegel, an imperial official.

All three agreed that the main obstacle to reform was the faculty of theology.[56] Spiegel plainly stated that "the reform of study at Heidelberg must begin with the theologians, although they will fight against it harder than anyone." They also agreed that instruction on the Bible and Church fathers should replace the emphasis on medieval authorities. Sturm and Spiegel both suggested that members of the mendicant orders should be given the task of teaching authors such as Aquinas and Scotus. For the faculty of arts all three men called for an improvement in grammar instruction and recommended the reading of classical literature as an aid to teaching. Sturm and Spiegel both stressed the need for salaried professors of Greek and Hebrew. The three men disagreed about the writings of Aristotle. Sturm and Spiegel recommended the retention of his works, but only if one of the new translations was utilized; Wimpfeling, however, advised the abandonment of lectures on Aristotle's *Physics* and *De generatione*, asserting that the time would better be spent on Cicero's works on moral philosophy. There was also disagreement concerning the teaching of logic. Sturm recommended the use of Agricola's *Dialectical Invention*, but Wimpfeling urged the retention of Aristotle and Peter of Spain, claiming that Agricola's work was "too subtle."

Having weighed the various suggestions, the elector announced new statutes in December 1522; but since they were destroyed in the late seventeenth century, the specifics of the reforms are unknown.[57] For the faculty of arts, however, it can safely be assumed on the basis of three appointments made

---

[56] The three reports have been published in Winkelmann, *Urkundenbuch*, I, 214-19.

[57] August Thorbecke, *Statuten und Reformationen der Universität Heidelberg vom 16. bis 18. Jahrhundert* (Leipzig: 1891), introduction, p. ii.

in 1523, that the statutes provided for regular lectures on Greek, Hebrew, and ancient literature. In that year, the university employed Hermann Buschius to lecture on the *studia humanitatis*. He was paid sixty florins, to be raised to eighty florins if he refrained from giving private lessons. At the same time, Simon Grynaeus was hired away from the University of Basel to teach Greek, and Sebastian Münster, a Franciscan, was contracted to teach Hebrew.[58] Ominously, however, all three had left by the mid-1520s, reflecting what appears to have been Heidelberg's chronic penury. In the late 1520s, arts faculty records refer to the difficulty of implementing reforms, citing *tenuitas fisci* as the cause.[59] And even if fully implemented, the 1522 reforms fell short of changes elsewhere. The division between the *via antiqua* and *via moderna*, for example, was formally ended only in 1546.[60]

The importance of fiscal health and a stable political environment to university reform, hinted at in the sparse Heidelberg records, is more explicit in the experience of several other institutions. This was certainly the case with the University of Vienna, which experienced particularly difficult times in the 1520s. An outbreak of the plague in 1521 and the constant threat from the Turks caused a drastic decline in enrollment. A year after the Turkish attack on Vienna in 1529, there were only about thirty students in the whole university, and the faculties of law and theology had ceased functioning.[61] To compound the financial crisis, the presence of numerous troops in the area caused a marked increase in prices.

In 1524 the Hapsburg government under Duke Ferdinand, responding to what the prince referred to as "the extraordinary lack of lecturers and learned men, the daily decreases in students and general decline," issued a list of reform propos-

---

[58] Hautz, *Geschichte*, I, 372, 373.
[59] Thorbecke, *Statuten und Reformationen*, iv, 92.
[60] *Ibid.*
[61] Rudolf Kink, *Geschichte der kaiserlichen Universität zu Wien* (Vienna: 1854), I, part 1, 255.

als.[62] Most dealt with administration and discipline, but one demanded that the university establish lectureships in both Greek and Hebrew. The eighteenth-century chronicler of the school, Sebastian Mitterdorfer, claimed that after 1524, no one could be promoted in the faculty of arts without having studied Greek.[63] But the lack of money prevented the hiring of the necessary teachers, so his assertion was certainly inaccurate. In 1528 the university admitted to Ferdinand that financial difficulties had made the implementation of the 1524 proposals impossible.[64]

Thus in 1528 Ferdinand appointed another commission to find measures for the school's revival. The commission recommended the adoption of the reformed statutes proposed for Tübingen in 1524, which envisioned broad curricular changes.[65] They also set forth several plans to strengthen the university's financial position, a prerequisite for academic reform. They proposed that Austrian prelates be encouraged to offer more money for the university's support and also suggested confiscating the property of two monasteries that had suffered war damage and were no longer occupied. But the Turkish siege in 1529 prevented action on the proposals.[66]

In the 1530s conditions finally stabilized, and with the support of the Hapsburg government, the University of Vienna again became an active and flourishing institution with a strong commitment to humanism. In 1533 Ferdinand took several steps that successfully addressed the institution's administrative and financial problems.[67] Four years later, a thorough reform of teaching was implemented. For the faculty of arts, the government promised to subsidize twelve professors.[68]

[62] Arthur Goldmann, *Die Wiener Universität, 1519-1740* (Vienna: 1917), 17, 18.

[63] Sebastian Mitterdorfer, *Conspectus Historiae Universitatis Viennensis*, II (Vienna: 1724), 117.

[64] Goldmann, *Die Wiener Universität*, 19.

[65] On the nature and fate of these proposals, see below, 318, 319.

[66] Goldmann, *Die Wiener Universität*, 19, 20.

[67] Kink, *Geschichte*, II, 332-39.

[68] *Ibid.*, II, 342-70.

The first was to teach Latin grammar from Priscian, with the aid of Valla's *Elegancies of the Latin Language* or Erasmus's *On the Copiousness of Language*. Another taught Greek and was to lecture on authors such as Aristophanes, Lucian, Demosthenes, Homer, and Euripides. A third taught Hebrew grammar either from the text of Reuchlin or David Kimchi. The fourth salaried professor taught dialectic, in part from Aristotle, but also from Agricola, Valla, Cicero's *Topics*, Porphyry, and Politian. The *studia humanitatis* received three lectureships, one each in poetry, rhetoric, and history. The latter was to examine works of Sallust, Livy, Cicero, Curtius, Tacitus, and Valerius Maximus. Mathematics received two professors, as did moral philosophy and natural philosophy. The teaching of natural philosophy was to be grounded on Aristotle in proper translation, while the teaching of moral philosophy was to be based on Aristotle along with a number of other "acceptable" works such as Plato's *Republic* and Cicero's *On Friendship* and *On Old Age*.

The new statutes also altered the faculty of theology. It was to consist of three professors, each lecturing once a day on the Bible. As aids in interpretation, the writings of the Church fathers were recommended exclusively. The statutes added, almost as an afterthought, that one professor might lecture on a scholastic writer if the students found it desirable.[69]

Political instability and social upheaval also slowed the pace of reform at the University of Tübingen. In the late 1510s, Duke Ulrich of Württemberg, the university's patron, quarreled with the Swabian League, whose forces expelled him from his lands in 1519 and sold them to the recently elected Emperor Charles V; the emperor, in turn, gave control of the territory to his brother, Ferdinand. The Hapsburgs, whose territories already included the universities of Freiburg and Vienna, were not indifferent to their new academic inheritance. In fact, as was the case with Vienna, the 1520s witnessed several governmental efforts to strengthen the institution

[69] *Ibid.*, II, 344.

through curricular and administrative reforms. As early as 1521, the government offered the university a stipend to hire Reuchlin as a lecturer on Greek and Hebrew. It also assumed the expenses for the purchase of Hebrew Bibles, which were to be sold to students for two florins.[70]

Reuchlin's presence caused a brief upsurge of enrollments, but when he died in June 1522 matriculations again declined. Thus in 1525, "prompted by the calamities of the present century," and knowing that "fragile and tottering subtlety had taken the place of solid and admirable teaching of truth and that the perplex opinions of philosophy had supplanted the heavenly mysteries of eloquence," Ferdinand appointed a five-man commission to consider a thorough reform of the university.[71] Included on the commission were Ambrose Wydman, a Tübingen prelate and university chancellor; Paul Riccius, a converted Jewish physician who had previously attended Maximilian; Jacob Spiegel, a former student of Wimpfeling and now an imperial secretary; Johannes Paul, a jurist in the service of the Hapsburg government; and Martin Plantsch, a professor of theology, and the only academic representative.

Spiegel, who had already contributed to the reformation of the University of Heidelberg, drew up the final reform document and probably exercised the greatest influence on its content. The proposed statutes were an incongruous amalgam of innovation and traditionalism. As had been done at Ingolstadt, the reformers sought to abolish the division of the arts faculty between nominalists and realists. The new statutes asserted that there was "only one way to truth" and that the old schism had caused nothing but dissension and "pernicious factionalism." The paraphrases of Jacques Lefèvre on logic and physics were to be substituted for the old translations, which the students "generally loathed." The statutes added that teachers could, if they wished, utilize "old interpreters

---

[70] Rudolf Roth, ed., *Urkunden zur Geschichte der Universität Tübingen* (Tübingen: 1877), 66.

[71] Ferdinand's *Ordinatio* is printed in *ibid.*, 141-52.

and commentators who offered fewer sophistical and superfluous matters." Surprisingly, the list of these "approved"
authorities included most of the great medieval scholastics—
Robert of Lincoln, Albertus Magnus, Aquinas, Scotus, Occam, and Egidius of Rome.[72] Peter of Spain's work was also
recommended as a possible text on logic, along with the paraphrases of Lefèvre. The statutes added that if these two works
still "disgusted" the students, the dialectic of either Agricola
or Trapezuntius could be substituted. Special provision was
made for the study of moral philosophy, since it offered good
preparation for law and theology and was pertinent to the
"teaching of right living." All professors were urged to avoid
"the insipid and crude teaching" found in commentaries and
to adhere more closely to original texts.

The new statutes also sought to regularize teaching in the
faculty of theology. Provision was made for four professors,
each one of whom was to be competent to teach a certain
number of biblical books and one of the sections from Lombard's *Sentences*. Although the *Sentences* was to be retained,
professors were warned to avoid overly complicated analysis.
The statutes stated, "while nevertheless interpreting the text
of the master of the *Sentences*, they should solve the difficulties
rising from the text rather briefly and clearly, since we are
made sons of God through faith and not through inane and
frivolous questions."[73]

It is questionable if Ferdinand's *ordinatio* had much impact
on the university. As Heiko Oberman has observed "the times
were not propitious for a programmatic renewal."[74] Aside
from the unsettled political situation, academic life in Tübingen was halted in 1525 by the Peasants' War and again in
1530 by plague. As a result, a visitation committee sent to
the university in August 1531 found that the old divisions

---

[72] Also mentioned were Averroes, Avicenna, Themistius, Simplicius,
Alexander and Theophrastus. *Ibid.*, 147.

[73] *Ibid.*, 143.

[74] Heiko Oberman, *Masters of the Reformation*, trans. Dennis Martin (Cambridge, Eng.: 1981), 251.

between nominalists and realists persisted. The committee noted that in dialectic the realists taught Peter of Spain, while the nominalists used Agricola's *Dialectical invention*.[75] Since Agricola's work had little in common with traditional nominalist texts and moreover on the question of universals defended realism,[76] its use shows how meaningless the old labels from the *Wegestreit* had become.

In any case, more thoroughgoing and effective reforms took place between 1534 and 1537, after Duke Ulrich's return to power in 1534 and his conversion of Württemberg to Lutheranism. The duke immediately confirmed the university's privileges but at the same time appointed Ambrosius Blarer and Simon Grynaeus to reform the institution. It was not an easy task, particularly in view of the fact that "reform" meant not only curricular and administrative change but also the dismantling of Roman Catholicism. Curricular changes were outlined in an order of Duke Ulrich dated January 30, 1535.[77] Following the example of several other universities, a pedagogium was established in which beginning students learned Latin grammar, music, and choir singing. Older students in the pedagogium continued their grammatical studies and covered works by Terence and Virgil, the letters of Pliny and Cicero and the *Colloquies* of Erasmus. Finally, the highest class in the pedagogium learned the elements of Greek.

Candidates for degrees in the faculty of arts were required to continue their study of Greek and to hear regular lectures on rhetoric. A stipend was established for a teacher of Hebrew, but his course was not mandatory, since as the statutes stated, the language was useful mainly for later students of theology.[78] The elements of dialectic were to be taught from the manual of Caesarius, Melanchthon or another similar au-

---

[75] Johannes Haller, *Die Anfänge der Universität Tübingen* (Stuttgart: 1927), II, 182.

[76] August Faust, "Die Dialektik Rudolf Agricolas," *Archiv für die Geschichte der Philosophie*, N.F., 34 (1922), 126.

[77] Roth, *Urkunden*, 176-85.

[78] *Ibid.*, 181.

thor. Aristotle was to be studied from one of the new translations, and teachers were required to make frequent references to the original Greek texts. In keeping with the precepts
of Protestant piety, students were also required to attend classes
in Bible study where the Scriptures were read in the original
languages.

The new statutes also proposed to alter the teaching of
theology. Medieval commentaries and texts were completely
abolished. The faculty was now to consist of two professors,
one lecturing on the New, and the other on the Old Testament. It was ordered that each should utilize the original
Greek or Hebrew texts, and that the lecturer on the New
Testament should comment on a *summa* of Christian teaching,
perhaps Melanchthon's *Loci communes*.

No institution had more difficulty incorporating humanist
ideas than the University of Cologne. The unsparing satire
directed against the university during the Reuchlin affair undoubtedly caused some anti-humanist sentiment, particularly
among the theologians. To some Cologners the rejection of
their traditional curriculum in favor of the humanist program
would have been a public admission that the picture drawn
in the *Letters of Obscure Men* was essentially accurate. But this
should not be seen as the only cause for the slow pace of
reform at this venerable institution. Even during the Reuchlin
affair's most passionate moments, humanists continued to teach
at Cologne. Buschius lectured on poetry, rhetoric, and moral
philosophy; Johannes Caesarius, a regular correspondent of
Erasmus, gave lessons on Greek while preparing his manual
on dialectic; and Johannes Phrysemius became the first German *magister* to utilize Agricola's *Dialectical Invention*. Thus
hostility to humanism engendered by the Reuchlin affair was
only one cause of Cologne's curricular inertia; more important
was the institution's inability to cooperate fruitfully with its
patron, the Cologne city council.

In 1523 the faculty of arts adopted new statutes that made
a few concessions to the humanist program.[79] Cicero's rhet-

[79] Printed by Franz Josef von Bianco, *Die alte Universität Köln* (Cologne:

oric was listed among the required lectures, and Cicero and Virgil were recommended as grammatical aids, as were "books on the elegancies of words and sentences by proper authors." To carry out the lectures on rhetoric, the Cologne city council agreed to pay the salary of a professor of oratory, Johannes Sobius.[80] But the new statutes made no mention of using new translations of Aristotle; the *Doctrinale* of Alexander Villedieu continued to be used for the teaching of Latin; and the *Summulae* of Peter of Spain was retained as the main text for logic.

In 1525, under the rectorship of Reuchlin's former nemesis, Arnold von Tungern, a more thorough reform of the university was undertaken. Each faculty was to agree upon a list of recommendations and then appoint deputies to make proposals to the Cologne city council. This task was accomplished on April 24, 1525.[81] But the "reformers" showed little taste for curricular innovation. Instead, their petition blamed the university's declining enrollments on non-academic factors: "by the destiny of God, through war and dissension, by which lands and peoples are armed and militarized, through multitudinous deaths, through changes and troubles with the coinage, through uncertainty of roads and through many other things which lie not in the hands of man but with God."[82]

The proposals showed no concern that traditional teaching methods at Cologne might in any way be deficient. For the most part they were nothing more than demands for the confirmation of various privileges. Among other things, they recommended that the city council suppress trivial schools in the nearby areas, control the "presumptuous townspeople who pelt the students with rocks and mud and pull their hair,"

1856), I part 2, 288-316, though with the incorrect date of 1522; see Hermann Keussen, "Regesten und Auszüge zur Geschichte der Universität Köln," *Mittheilungen aus dem Stadtarchiv von Köln*, 36, 37 (1918), 375.

[80] Keussen, "Regesten und Auszüge," 376.

[81] Printed by von Bianco, *Die alte Universität Köln*, I, part 2, 316-26; also printed in G. Eckert, ed., "Rector, Decane, Doctoren und Meister der Universität zu Köln ersuchen den Rath ihnen zur Reformirung u. zur Hebung der Universität zu reichen," *Annalen des historischen Vereins für den Niederrhein*, 17 (1865), 219-27.

[82] von Bianco, *Die alte Universität Köln*, I part 2, 316.

halt the flow of "satirical and heretical" literature, prevent druggists from practicing medicine, and end all tolls and special taxes for students and faculty. There was no request for hiring new instructors for any of the humanist disciplines. In fact, one of the demands seems to have been directed against the humanists. It called for the limitation of extraordinary lectures, which according to the authors of the petition interfered with required course work, drew students away from good teaching, inspired indifference to the "good arts," and filled the students' minds with "frivolous matters." These accusations were standard anti-humanist complaints, reminiscent of those set forth by the opponents of humanism at Leipzig in the early 1500s.

Several men connected with the university rejected the conservatism of the "reformers'" petition and submitted separate proposals of their own. Quirinus von Wilich, for example, a suffragan bishop in the Cologne archdiocese, wrote the council that the main cause of the university's decline was its outdated curriculum. Regaining privileges was important, but he added that the university could collapse if it continued to reject curricular innovations that other institutions had already adopted. He remarked that if this advice had been followed twenty years ago there would have been no decline at the University of Cologne. Count Hermann von Neuenar and Arnold von Wesel, a student in theology, also sent the council letters agreeing with von Wilich.[83]

The city council took no action on any of the proposals, claiming that other business was keeping it occupied. By the summer months, students in the faculty of arts were disgusted that the old curriculum had not been altered. As a result, disturbances broke out in the student quarter of the city. The records of the faculty of arts read,

> In the same time, a tumult sprang up among the students in the faculty of arts; for they loathed to hear only the old commentaries according to the teaching of Thomas

[83] Printed in L. Ennen, *Geschichte der Stadt Köln*, IV (Cologne: 1875), 214-17.

and Albertus Magnus; they considered these things blown up, rather prolix, unuseful and fruitless, and appealed that the text of Aristotle be interpreted according to a more polished translation; also, that not just Aristotle, but all the liberal arts be taught, so that the title by which they are called masters of the liberal arts will not lose all its meaning.[84]

The students also sent a petition to the dean of the faculty of arts complaining about their education. They pointed out that their parents had sent them to the university to be schooled in the seven liberal arts. But they complained that of the arts, only dialectic was lectured on thoroughly, and this in a barbarian manner. They demanded that, besides dialectic, they also receive instruction in rhetoric, music, arithmetic, astronomy, geometry, physics, and logic, "all arranged by most acceptable men and translated by the most learned." They mentioned Agricola as an excellent authority for dialectic.[85]

The student agitation had a definite impact. On August 12, 1525, university officials again met with the city council, and again they asked for a confirmation of the privileges they had sought in April. But they also promised to draw up a new lecture schedule for teaching in the faculty of arts. One month later, on September 9, they presented their outline to the government.[86] The proposals certainly would have satisfied the disgruntled students. A Latin grammar written by Perotti or another Italian humanist would replace Alexander's *Doctrinale*; the logic manual of Jacques Lefèvre would replace Peter of Spain. Regular times were to be set aside for courses on letter writing, oratory, and moral philosophy, the latter to be taught from Cicero. The writings of Aristotle were to be

---

[84] "Eodem tempore alia tumultatio in Facultate Artium in suis suppositis et discipulis suborta est; nam commentaris antiqua secundum doctrinam Thomae et Alberti Magni conflata, quasi prolixa, inutilia et infructuosa fastidiebant audire solum petentes textum Aristotelis secundum politorem traductionem eis interpretari, et non solum Aristotelis doctrinam, verum omnes artes liberales, ne evacuaretur titulus quo Magistri Artium liberalium appellantur." von Bianco, *Die alte Universität Köln,* I, part 1, 409.

[85] *Ibid.*

[86] *Ibid.*, part 2, 326-28.

studied in the best Latin speech, in translations by Argyropulos, Trapezuntius, or Boethius. But final agreement proved
illusive. The university, so it claimed, could not implement
the curriculum reforms without financial support from the
city; and the city was unwilling to underwrite the costs as
long as the university insisted on the confirmation of the
various privileges. Finally after October 11, the two groups
stopped meeting entirely. University officials conferred several times in succeeding months to decide on a course of
action, but with no results.

In 1526, however, the city council took the initiative in
another attempt to reform the curriculum. It appointed Johannes Sobius, the salaried professor of oratory, to take charge
of the process. But he was elderly and half-blind, hardly the
man to carry out a general reform of the university. On October 26, 1526, he wrote to the city council that he was giving
up his efforts because of the extensive opposition he had encountered.[87] The university and the city council tried to get
together again in 1528 and 1532, but they were unable to
resolve their differences. As a result, there was no formal
curriculum reform at Cologne until the 1540s and 1550s.[88]

Details about curricular change at the remaining universities
of Germany are sparse, and non-existent for the University
of Mainz. It is known that the University of Freiburg-im-
Breisgau began regularly to support lectures on Greek and
Hebrew in 1520 or 1521.[89] It is also known that the Hapsburg
government, as it was also doing at Tübingen and Vienna,
attempted a thoroughgoing revision of studies in 1524-1525.[90]
That it had some concrete results is suggested by Ulrich Zasius's undoubtedly exaggerated complaint from the time that
"they have reduced Aristotle in rank, since his work is neither
lectured on or taught; Peter of Spain is gone; all logic is gone
except that some offer a little work of Melanchthon, others

---

[87] Ennen, *Geschichte*, IV, 217, 218.
[88] Keussen, *Die alte Universität Köln*, 371.
[89] Schreiber, *Geschichte der Albert-Ludwigs-Universität zu Freiburg-im-Breisgau*, 2 vols. (Freiburg: 1857), I, 193-97.
[90] Oberman, *Masters of the Reformation*, 248, 249.

the book of Rudolph Agricola."[91] But extant university records yield no details about this or subsequent curriculum
changes. In 1521 the University of Greifswald began to require
courses on poetry and rhetoric for all students in the arts, and
in 1543, when the duke of Pomerania formally adopted Protestantism for his lands, another reform of curriculum and
statutes took place.[92] Humanist reforms were fully implemented at Rostock in the 1520s, when, after having overcome
severe fiscal and enrollment problems, it gradually came under
the influence of Melanchthon and several of his students.[93]

With the realization of the humanists' aims, a distinctive
chapter of Germany's academic and intellectual history ended.
Humanist attacks on the sterilities of scholasticism, which in
previous decades had provided the theme of countless orations, treatises, and polemics, lost all purpose and relevance.
In 1518 Hermann Buschius, then at the University of Cologne, published a treatise, *The Defense of Culture*, which once
again assailed the scholastics and rehashed the well-worn arguments for the study of good letters and the ancient tongues.[94]
But his treatise was the last of a dying breed. A more accurate
gauge of humanist opinion was a comment made by the Erfurt
humanist, Eobanus Hessus, in a letter to Johannes Lang in
1524. He remarked that there was no longer any need to attack
the sophists, since so few sophists remained.[95]

Humanists and Scholastics

At the end of this survey of some seventy years of German
intellectual and academic history, three observations may be
emphasized. First, it is important to note the extraordinary

[91] Cited in Seifert, *Logik zwischen Scholastik und Humanismus*, 75.

[92] Johann S. Kosegarten, *Geschichte der Universität Greifswald* (Greifswald: 1857), I, 171; II, 126.

[93] Otto Krabbe, *Die Universität Rostock im fünfzehnten und sechszehnten Jahr-hundert* (Rostock: 1854), 712, 713; Hartfelder, *Philipp Melanchthon*, 522-24.

[94] *Vallum humanitatis* (Cologne: 1518).

[95] Carl Krause, *Helius Eobanus Hessus, sein Leben und seine Werke* (Gotha: 1879), II, 364, 365.

importance of Germany's governments, especially her princely governments, in fostering humanism within the universities. In a sense of course, the princes, as general patrons of universities, supported all kinds of academic and scholarly pursuits, from the study of introductory logic to lectures on Lombard's *Sentences*. But from the mid-fifteenth century onward humanism increasingly attracted their attention and favor. Several probable reasons can be suggested for this support: the influence of Italian-educated advisers; a conviction that the *studia humanitatis* offered better preparation for princely service than traditional scholastic fare; the ambition to enhance their personal prestige and that of their university. Perhaps they were also reflecting the educational interests of their noble subjects, a group that had scorned the medieval universities, but in the early sixteenth century was turning to the universities in greater numbers to gain the polish and training deemed necessary to attract princely favor. It is significant that notable upsurge of aristocratic matriculations took place in the wake of the humanist curriculum reforms of the early sixteenth century.[96]

Whatever their motives, involvement of the princes was a precondition for humanist progress, and at institutions where it was lacking, such as Cologne and Heidelberg, humanism stagnated. In addition to offering financial support to salaried poets and encouraging their efforts in various ways, princely governments assumed the role of prodding the universities to accept statute revisions and new humanist requirements. The universities themselves were incapable of changing from within. What Arno Seifert has written about statute reform at Ingolstadt could equally apply to Germany's other pre-Reformation universities: "The university rarely showed . . . the inclination to reform its old statutes or replace them with new ones. Initiative and urgent warning from the state preceded each reform, while the university, dully and without ideas,

[96] See Overfield "Nobles and Paupers at the German Universities to 1600," *Societas—A Review of Social History*, 7 (1974), 175-209.

complied."[97] Nowhere was such princely inspiration and pressure more important than in the general humanist reforms of the late 1510s through 1530s. It would not be an exaggeration to say that humanism became an established part of German academic life largely as a result of an act of state.

A second conclusion that derives from this study is that humanist-scholastic relations were certainly not marked by the titanic and never-ending struggles imagined by the humanists and repeated in much historical writing. Scholastic opposition to humanism was late in developing, limited in time and place, and only briefly effective. It was also inarticulate: the only two published works that defended scholasticism or attacked humanism in a broad sense were written by two men with close ties to humanism, Jacob Wimpfeling and Ortwin Gratius. It seems that while some German academics might have felt uncomfortable about certain features of humanism, others sensed that much of what the humanists were saying was valid: that medieval logic had become monstrously complex; that grammar instruction had lost touch with its true purpose; that there was a better path to philosophical and theological truth; that literary studies did have merit and value. Significantly, the widespread curricular innovations described in this chapter elicited no apparent opposition. Where the traditional curriculum lingered, unsolved financial or religious problems or unsettled political conditions provide the explanation. In its final hour, medieval scholasticism passed into history undefended and unmourned.

On the other hand it would also be unwarranted to describe the relationship of humanism and scholasticism as one of "peaceful coexistence."[98] Humanists did encounter opposition, and their experiences within the universities were often

---

[97] Seifert, *Statuten-und Verfassungsgeschichte der Universität Ingolstadt,* 417, 418.

[98] The term "peaceful coexistence" has been used to describe humanist-scholastic relationships by several authors, most notably Gerhard Ritter, "Die Geschichtliche Bedeutung des deutschen Humanismus," *Historische Zeitschrift,* 127 (1923), 393-453.

far less than peaceful. The universities assimilated humanism, but not without a certain amount of tension and unease. This was in large measure the result of the fact that for many years humanists taught on the periphery of the universities and lacked clear status within the academic corporation. Furthermore, by the 1490s, their courses became increasingly popular but still were not required. Such anomalies were conducive to conflict, particularly if the humanist was a foreigner, received a high princely stipend, had an abrasive personality, or aggressively denounced the university's academic traditions.

Third and most important, this study reveals the danger of characterizing the academics and intellectuals of pre-Reformation Germany according to simple dualisms—humanist or scholastic, progressive or conservative, reformer or reactionary. Such stereotypes, when applied to all but a few individuals, had little meaning. Many "humanists" saw value in certain aspects of scholasticism and perceived dangers in the rejection of tradition and the unbridled pursuit of pagan literature, for which some of their fellow humanists were calling. Many "scholastics" cultivated an interest in ancient literature and encouraged the humanists' effort to improve grammar instruction and bring eloquence to Germany. Controversies and academic conflicts abounded in this era, but the participants' enthusiasm for "humanism" or "scholasticism" rarely caused them or determined their outcome. Personal ambitions, devotion to the Church, loyalties to a region or perhaps a religious order, antagonism toward foreigners or Jews, uneasiness over social and political change, and much else were things Germans were thinking and worrying about in the closing years of the medieval era. Their enthusiasm or disdain for humanism or scholasticism was but one factor among many which shaped their values, ideals and actions. An appreciation of such subtleties certainly complicates the task of historians who study the period; just as certainly it will deepen their understanding of the age.

INDEX

Demosthenes (*cont.*)
thon's treatises on, 303; role in
scholastic curriculum, 27-35. *See
also* logic
Dialectical Invention, see Agricola,
Rudolph
Dietrich, Archbishop of Cologne,
54
Dinckelsbühl, Nicholas, 122
disputations, importance at German
universities, 43, 44
Doctrinale of Alexander Villedieu,
115, 121, 153, 244, 323; approach
to grammar instruction, 36-39;
humanists criticize, 78-79, 84,
157, 196, 232; place in universities' curricula, 36-39, 114, 138-
39, 218-19, 220, 221, 227-28,
234, 302, 305, 306, 312, 323, 325
Dominicans, influence on University of Cologne, 54; support for
schools, 4; anti-Jewish traditions,
254
Donatus, *Ars Grammatica*, 36, 79,
148, 167, 218, 219, 221, 227,
228, 276
Duns Scotus, *see* Scotus
Dürer, Albrecht, 152

Eberhard the German, 40
Eberhard the Bearded, Count of
Württemberg, 100, 113
Eck, Johannes, 47; texts and com-
mentaries for use at University
of Ingolstadt, 310-13
Eck, Leonhard, 309-11
Egidius of Rome, 150, 320
Eichman, Jodocus, 126
Eisenhart, George, 45
Eolicus, Paul, 118
Erasmus of Rotterdam, 152, 160,
165, 208, 268; *Annotations on the
New Testament*, 208, 275, 299-
300; *Apotheosis of that Incompara-*

ble Worthy Johannes Reuchlin, 283;
Colloquies, 321; *Copia rerum et
verborum*, 308; role in Reuchlin
affair, 282-90; views of Jews,
287-88
Erfurt, city council of, 7, 10, 11
Erfurt, Thomas of, *see* Thomas of
Erfurt
Erfurt, University of, xi, xiii, xv,
4, 81, 88, 110, 114, 170, 171,
244; administration, 11, 13, 16,
21, 22; Conrad Mutian and, 164-
67; curriculum reform (1515),
221; (1519, 1520s), 298, 304, 305;
expulsion of Hermann Buschius
and Tillmann Conradi, 236, 237;
founding, 7-9; pre-1500 humanism, 62, 63, 74, 116-18, 126-28;
role in Reuchlin affair, 248-50,
263, 264, 278, 281; scholastic
curriculum, 29, 40, 41, 45, 46;
student enrollment, 23
Eric I, Duke of Brunswick-Kalenberg, 249
Euclid, 43, 199
Euripides, 318

Fagilucus, Sigismund, 183
Fano, Cleophilus of, 225
Femel, Johannes, 238
Ferdinand, Archduke of Austria,
316-20
Ferrara, University of, 89
Ficino, Marsilio, 159, 169
Filelfo, Francesco, 75, 128, 312
Finariensis, Peter Antonius, 62,
108, 126, 127
Francis I, King of France, 208; role
in Reuchlin affair, 251, 265
Franciscan order, 4
Frankfurt-am-Main, 248
Frankfurt an der Oder, University
of, xiii, xvii, 9, 28, 211, 216,
231, 294; curriculum reform,

Library of Congress Cataloging in Publication Data

Overfield, James H., 1942-
  Humanism and scholasticism in late medieval Germany.

  Includes index.
  1. Scholasticism—Germany—History. 2. Humanism—History.
3. Germany—Intellectual life. I. Title.
B734.O96 1985   001.3'0943   84-42568
ISBN 0-691-07292-2 (alk. paper)